Jon Mills' *Psyche, Culture, World* attempts yet to synthesize philosoph̲ ̲ ̲ ̲ ̲ ̲ ̲ ̲ ̲ ̲ In parti-cular, Mills offers readers a sophisticated contemporary reactivation of the tradition of existential psychoanalysis bringing together analytic metapsychology with the insights of phenomenology and existentialism. Against those who would dismiss psychoanalysis and/or existentialist thought as passé, Mills convincingly demonstrates that a combination of these two orientations provides the best cognitive mapping available of our present set of psychical and social conundrums, of the human condition in the twenty-first century.

—**Adrian Johnston,** PhD, *Distinguished Professor of Philosophy, University of New Mexico;* author of *Prolegomena to Any Future Materialism*

Once again, Jon Mills has regaled us with yet another example of the breadth and depth of his subtle understanding of the relationship between philosophy and psychoanalysis. In this important work, Mills deftly demonstrates the philosophical underpinnings of psychoanalysis while bringing heretofore neglected aspects of phenomenology and existential philosophy to bear in illuminating the existential basis of psychoanalytic practice. His exegesis of the unconscious, myth, truth, freedom, and evil are both impressive and original. A true *tour de force* and cogent exploration of the role that existence plays in our lives.

—**M. Guy Thompson,** PhD, author of *The Death of Desire: An Existential Study in Sanity and Madness*

Jon Mills views psychoanalysis as essentially an existential enterprise about human beings as agents. He combines psychoanalysis with a rich philosophical tradition to confront key conundrums of human existence. Novel and illuminating ideas leap from the pages of this brilliant scholarly yet accessible magnum opus.

—**Douglas Kirsner,** PhD, *Emeritus Professor of Philosophy and Psychoanalytic Studies, Deakin University, Melbourne, Australia;* author of *Unfree Associations.*

Psyche, Culture, World

Across the array of topics explored in this comprehensive volume, philosopher and psychoanalyst Jon Mills argues for a fundamental return to the question and meaning of existence. Drawing on the traditions of German Idealism, existentialism, and onto-phenomenology, he offers a rich tapestry of insight and critique into the foundations of psyche, human nature, and society.

As a philosophy of mind and culture, psychoanalysis offers us a promising perspective to reengage our being in the world in meaningful ways that illuminate human existence, the mysteriousness of unconscious processes, our relation to transcendence, ethical obligations towards social collectives, and the wonder of logos for our present-day consciousness. After examining the unconscious origins of psychic reality and the contradictory nature of our internal lives, Mills examines the scope of existentialism from antiquity to postmodernism, the question of authenticity, paranoiac epistemology, the essence of evil, dysrecognition and social pathology, belief in God, myth, the ideologies of science, hermeneutics, truth, freedom and determinism, and the fate of civilization in relation to the pervasive forces that threaten our existence.

Psyche, Culture, World will be of interest to philosophers, psychoanalysts, psychologists, academics, and students in the arts and humanities, cultural studies, anthropology, myth, psychology of religion, and psychotherapy.

Jon Mills, PsyD, PhD, ABPP is a philosopher, psychoanalyst, and retired clinical psychologist. He is Honorary Professor, Department of Psychosocial & Psychoanalytic Studies, University of Essex, UK; on Faculty in the Postgraduate Programs in Psychoanalysis & Psychotherapy, Gordon F. Derner School of Psychology, Adelphi University and the New School for Existential Psychoanalysis, USA; and is Emeritus Professor of Psychology & Psychoanalysis at Adler Graduate Professional School in Toronto, Canada. Recipient of numerous awards for his scholarship, he is the author and/or editor of over 30 books in philosophy, psychoanalysis, psychology, and cultural studies.

Philosophy & Psychoanalysis Book Series

Series Editor: Jon Mills, PsyD, PhD, ABPP
Honorary Professor, Department of Psychosocial & Psychoanalytic Studies,
University of Essex, UK
Faculty, Postgraduate Programs in Psychoanalysis & Psychotherapy,
Gordon F. Derner School of Psychology, Adelphi University, USA
Faculty, New School for Existential Psychoanalysis, USA

Philosophy & Psychoanalysis is dedicated to current developments and cutting-edge research in the philosophical sciences, phenomenology, hermeneutics, existentialism, logic, semiotics, cultural studies, social criticism, and the humanities that engage and enrich psychoanalytic thought through philosophical rigor. With the philosophical turn in psychoanalysis comes a new era of theoretical research that revisits past paradigms while invigorating new approaches to theoretical, historical, contemporary, and applied psychoanalysis. No subject or discipline is immune from psychoanalytic reflection within a philosophical context including psychology, sociology, anthropology, politics, the arts, religion, science, culture, physics, and the nature of morality. Philosophical approaches to psychoanalysis may stimulate new areas of knowledge that have conceptual and applied value beyond the consulting room reflective of greater society at large. In the spirit of pluralism, *Philosophy & Psychoanalysis* is open to any theoretical school in philosophy and psychoanalysis that offers novel, scholarly, and important insights in the way we come to understand our world.

Psyche, Culture, World

Excursions in Existentialism and
Psychoanalytic Philosophy

Jon Mills

Routledge
Taylor & Francis Group

LONDON AND NEW YORK

Cover image: 'Is this art or cultural appropriation?' Copyright by
Jon Mills, 2019

First published 2023
by Routledge
4 Park Square, Milton Park, Abingdon, Oxon OX14 4RN

and by Routledge
605 Third Avenue, New York, NY 10158

*Routledge is an imprint of the Taylor & Francis Group, an informa
business*

© 2023 Jon Mills

British Library Cataloguing-in-Publication Data
A catalogue record for this book is available from the British
Library

Library of Congress Cataloguing-in-Publication Data
A catalog record has been requested for this book

ISBN: 978-1-032-30626-1 (hbk)
ISBN: 978-1-032-30625-4 (pbk)
ISBN: 978-1-003-30595-8 (ebk)

DOI: 10.4324/9781003305958

Typeset in Times New Roman
by MPS Limited, Dehradun

Contents

Prolegomenon: Towards a Psychology of Existence

Once the pillar of 20th century European philosophy, existentialism has quietly slipped off the radar as psychoanalysis gathers its fruits. With the philosophical turn in psychoanalysis comes a renewed inquiry and revitalization of key existential ideas on the nature and scope of human meaning, authenticity, and suffering in our estranged and traumatized world. The question, *What is it to exist?* has fundamentally been lost in contemporary society, where freedom and responsibility to choose and create one's life has been displaced by consumer capitalism, techno-obsessivity, hegemonic power imbalances, nihilism, scapegoating alterity, sweeping social pathology, and the fear of aloneness and death that eclipse our humanism and anguished ethical consciousness. From Heidegger's notion of "ex-sistence" as the essence of Dasein to the emergence of *Ek-sistenz* as our "standing out" through lived experience (*Lebenswelt*), Marcel's "ontological *exigence*" as the innate urge for transcendence, to Jaspers' notion of *Existenz* as the Encompassing, the modern subject largely does not know who they are, for they remain *unconscious* of the insistence of being, nor are they generally concerned with the greater questions—let alone the needs, demands, and obligations—towards existence.

With Parmenides' dictum of Being as the *is* (ἔστιν), the existent, the naked facticity of the presence of actuality, to think is to be (τὸ γὰρ αὐτὸ νοεῖν ἐστίν τε καὶ εἶναι).[1] Whatever linguistic term we employ for the expression of existence, we must confront our relation to being. Because we exist, it is incumbent upon us to live life in thoughtful ways. Anything less is to relegate us to our animal natures, of which we cannot renounce, only transform. Much of the world today does not think in thoughtful ways largely because they are enveloped in *pathos*. The wonder of being is eclipsed by the imposition of other beings eroding the very fabric of their personal existence to the degree that existence itself is a forgotten or dissociated priority.

Although psychology has traditionally been a subset or offshoot of philosophy, a relatively new discipline in the history of ideas, archaic thought has always been a psychological iteration of soul—*eros, nous, ethos*—one governed by unconscious forces *a fortiori*. We cannot divorce ourselves from psyche. In fact, we cannot help but psychologize Being for the simple matter that we are ensouled, one that, needless to say, suffers.

As we remain ensconced in anxiety, ignorance, alienation, or dislocation that defines much of our social landscape, psychoanalysis remains a powerful heuristic tool for description and explanation into human existence that is heavily indebted to the Continental philosophical tradition. Over the past two decades there has been increasing engagement in phenomenological and existential thinking imbued in psychoanalytic discourse but it has not adhered to a consistent school of thought. The purpose of this volume is to bring a philosophical focus to applied psychoanalytic concepts that have historically belonged to the discipline of philosophy.

Although philosophers are generally aware of classical psycho-analysis, they remain largely unaware of post-classical movements and the current state of psychoanalytic theory and praxis today, while most psychoanalysts remain unaware of their philosophical foundations. This book is an attempt to bring psychoanalytic discourse into conversation with Continental philosophers who may profit from dialogue around mutually engaging interests. Rather than focus on the metaphysical question of existence itself, this book analyzes the locus, breadth, and threshold of psychic existence in its multiple instantiations in society and the clinic through a psychoanalytic sensibility, what we may generically refer to as psychoanalytic philosophy.

Thematic Overview

In this array of topics, I examine the psychological dynamics informed by an unconscious ontology that generally speak to the questions and meaning of human existence and the phenomenology of culture. Drawing on the traditions of German Idealism, existentialism, and onto-phenomenology, I present a rich tapestry of reflection and critique into the foundations of psyche, human nature, and society. As a philosophy of mind and culture, psychoanalysis offers us a promising perspective to reengage our being in the world in meaningful ways that illuminate human existence, the mysteriousness of unconscious processes, our relation to transcendence, ethical obligations towards social collectives, and the wonder of logos for our present-day consciousness. After examining the unconscious origins of psychic reality and the contradictory nature of our internal lives, I explore the scope of existentialism from antiquity to postmodernism, the question of authenticity, paranoiac epistemology, the essence of evil, dysrecognition and social pathology, belief in God, myth, the ideologies of science, hermeneutics, truth, freedom and determinism, and the fate of civilization in relation to the pervasive forces that threaten our existence.

Psychic Existence

We begin with a close examination of Freud's model of the mind that fundamentally rests on an unconscious ontology beginning with his early topographical and economic writings to his mature turn with the introduction of his tripartite process theory. Spanning his seminal works on the nature of drives (*Triebe*), primary and secondary process, fantasy and ego formation, defence and compromise, and ethical self-consciousness born/e from attachment, identification, and internalization through unconscious modification into personality formation and culture, this chapter outlines the a priori nature of subjectivity that proceeds from a developmental monistic ontology based in unconscious genesis. In tracing the origins of psychic reality, we may come to appreciate the overdetermined complexities of mental life fraught with internal conflict based on the frustrated parameters of desire, the demands of the external world, and the limitations of actualizing an ethical life. After distilling Freud's key concepts throughout his *Gesammelte Werke*, we are left with a psychic system where a personal sense of self, ego, or the I is to stand in firm opposition to the It, which is purely estranged from conscious awareness. But the distinction between the I and the It is not altogether unambiguous, and as I will argue, nor theoretically resolved by Freud himself.

A persisting, endemic problem to psychoanalysis is the absence of any philosophical attempt to account for genesis, namely, the origins of psychic reality. It is not enough to say that psychic experience begins as unconsciousness and progresses to consciousness, from drive to reason, from the It to the I: we must be able to show how these primordial processes *originally* transpire and sequentially unfold into dynamic patterns of organized mental life. We have reason to believe that the I and the It are not ontologically differentiated; nor is it to be accepted at face value that the I does in fact develop from the It. What is missing in previous developmental accounts is any detailed attempt to chronicle the very processes that bring the I and the It into being in the first place. Throughout this chapter, I will be preoccupied with what I call the 'genesis problem,' namely, Beginning—the origins of unconscious life. By way of dialectical analysis, I will trace the means in which such primitive processes acquire organization, differentiation and integration, teleological progression, self-constitutive identity, and psychic cohesion. While Freud articulated the fundamental intrapsychic forces that beset human life, he did not attend to these ontological-transmutational concerns; in other words, onto-phenomenology. It is my intention to offer a dialectical account of the coming into being of the I and the It, or what I shall call the ego and the abyss, and show how psychoanalytic process psychology provides a possible solution to the question and nature of unconscious maturation.

In our next chapter we examine the inner contradictory nature of the psyche through the application of Hegel's *Logic*. Here we observe how the psyche is split. Breaming with inner divisions, we may say that the subject—we—are comprised of multiple self-states in opposition or competition with each other vying for expression, if not domination, but willing to settle for a compromise. This is largely due to the plethora of rival unconscious desires or schemata that populate mental life, but it is a universal feature of thought itself. The logic of inner division produces gaps, lacunae—holes in being that expose incongruities; but it also highlights the polarizing nature of the psyche based on an economy of splitting. Hegel shows how this binary logic is at play in the schism of thinking itself, what psychoanalysis refers to as "projective identification," namely, the negation and projection of our internal contents onto otherness, only then to come to identify with our split-off nature, and re-incorporate it back into our internal constitutions. This is the antediluvian pattern of the rotary motion of the dialectic as split-off or dissociated self-states and the manifold of object representations that transpire within unconscious process due to the vicissitudes of desire and drive, which further fuel counter-identifications that intensify in quality constellated as tensions of difference. Intensities of splitting therefore underlie the essence of psyche.

The schematic structure of mind through splitting is first initiated as a violent cleavage via negation. For Freud, it is death working silently in the unconscious in circuitous manners. For Hegel, it is pure negativity itself. Contradiction is merely one moment in relation to other psychic events—desire, wish, drive, defense, affect, fantasy—that are split-off and sequestered as independent entities with semi-autonomous organizational properties, energies, and propensities clamoring for breath and release, the multiplicities of soul. This ensures that even with the most highly cultivated and sophisticated shapes of mind—Spirit (*Geist*), there will always be contraries and psychic conflict that not only elude, but resist, reconciliation. This chapter explores the dialectic of opposites in the psyche, their resistance to unification and wholeness, and how a Hegelian and psychoanalytic conception of contradiction becomes an unconscious template that conditions mental processes and sustains internal conflict.

Simultaneously, during the rise of psychoanalysis was the explosion of phenomenology and existentialism in French and German philosophy. These movements often opposed psychoanalytic thought due to their negation of the unconscious for a privileging of consciousness. After examining the ambit of existentialism from antiquity to postmodernism in relation to psychoanalytic thought, I explore in depth how the works of Heidegger and Sartre complement a theory of psychopathology based on unconscious self-deception. Here the analysis of Dasein's struggle for authenticity will be the main focus of this chapter.

By virtue of Dasein's ontological predispositions, selfhood is subjected to inauthentic existential modalities already constitutive of its Being. In the case of the false Dasein, fallenness is exacerbated in that Dasein constricts its comportment primarily to the modes of the inauthentic, thereby abdicating its potentiality-for-Being. The false Dasein results from ontical encounters within pre-existing deficient ontological conditions of Being-in-the-world that are thrust upon selfhood as its facticity. These deficient ontological structures predispose Dasein to develop intrapsychic psychological deficits that further contribute to Dasein's false existence. Through the medium of Heidegger's existential ontology, Sartrean bad faith, and psychoanalysis, I demonstrate that the throes of selfhood encompass a dialectical course meandering through experiential modes of authenticity and falsehood, in which this very process itself is an authentic enterprise, that is, it is the necessary constitutional structure of Dasein itself as Being-toward-becoming its possibilities.

Also occurring during this time period in the human sciences was the growing interest in structuralism and semiology. Lacan's post-structural semiotics and mature tripartite theory is further explored in relation to his epistemology that hinges on the thesis of paranoiac knowledge.

For Lacan, all knowledge is imbued with paranoia. While he offers very few remarks on the matter, this claim has potential theoretical and clinical utility. Although largely unarticulated by Lacan himself, throughout this chapter I attempt to give conceptual clarity to the epistemological process of paranoiac knowledge situated in Lacan's three contexts of being. Developmentally, knowledge is paranoiac because it is acquired through our *imaginary* relation to the other as a primordial misidentification or illusory self-recognition of autonomy, control, and mastery, thus leading to persecutory anxiety and self-alienation. Secondarily, through the *symbolic* structures of language and speech, desire is foisted upon us as a foreboding demand threatening to invade and destroy our uniquely subjective inner experiences. And finally, the process of knowing itself is paranoiac because it horrifically confronts the *real*, namely, the unknown. Through our examination of a clinical case study, paranoiac knowledge manifests itself as the desire not to know.

Evil, *Pathos*, God

The question and nature of evil has been a human preoccupation since the rise of civilization, yet we can find no consensus on what constitutes its essence. Psychoanalysis generally has tended to focus upon the pathological dynamics that motivate evil actions, from primary, malignant, and traumatic narcissism to primitive defensive enactments, superego lacunae, failure in internalization and empathy, sociopathy, selfobject deficits, developmental trauma, and attachment pathology, rather than on the question of evil itself.

Are actions in-themselves sufficient to determine the essence of evil, or does psychological intent become a necessary ingredient? But what happens if these actions are unconsciously informed, even chosen, hence the product of an unconscious will towards evil? What if such intent was unconsciously harbored yet unacknowledged by the conscious subject, let alone enacted, the evil within? And what about the consequences of both action and intention as a touchstone by which to adjudicate evil? These questions tend to situate the problematic of evil within a moral realm. But what if the question and nature of evil has nothing to do with morality whatsoever?

In this next chapter, I wish to explore the essence and ethics of evil. What I will conclude is both controversial and counter-intuitive. But before we get there, I will need to prepare our discussion. After laying out various philosophical problematics, our analysis will centre around the domain and structure of violence as (a) natural phenomena, (b) subjective interiority, (c) objective instantiation, (d) systemic perpetuation, and (e) ontic universality. The degree to which our natural constitution derived from evolutionary pressures predisposes the human animal towards evil will be contrasted with developmental currents that are cultivated as a result of social interaction and the interiority of suffering. What marks the qualification of evil is the degree of ethical agency within an individual and society determined by the objective attainment of self-consciousness and voluntary choice. The evil that inhabits man in thought, intention, and deed is beyond psychological dynamics, I suggest, for violence is a metaphysical principle that saturates the natural world as a *mysterium tremendum*, at once a frightening necessity governing life yet one that signals the non-violent domain of ideality we attribute to moral idealism, paradoxically, itself a violent imposition as ethical demand.

Throughout the next chapter I offer an adumbrated critique of recognition theory through a psychoanalytic sensibility. Contemporary recognition theory relies on an overly optimistic and intellectualized view of social relations that fails to adequately consider pathological processes inherent in human motivation, particularly those that are unconsciously mediated by collective prejudice and dysrecognition. In revisiting the Hegelian struggle for recognition, much of social reality today is mired in a collective *pathos* that prevents optimal mutual recognition among social collectives. Not all people are disposed, let alone capable, of recognizing the Other. We may have to contend that, in the end, recognition means tolerance of difference and not merely acceptance of one other, which could still bring about a pragmatic co-existence even if people cannot recognize each other as equals. This is largely due, I suggest, to the ontology of prejudice, attachment deficits, and the failure to adopt empathy towards alterity.

Setting aside the illusion of theodicy, the next chapter addresses the inexistence of God. Here I argue that the God hypothesis is the invention of an idea based on a fantasy principle. Albeit a logical concept born of social convention, God is a semiotic embodiment and symbolization of ideal value. Put laconically, God is only a thought. Rather than an extant ontological subject or agency traditionally attributed to a supernatural, transcendent creator or supreme being responsible for the coming into being of the universe, God is a psychological invention signifying ultimate ideality. Here God becomes a self-relation to an internalized idealized object, the idealization of imagined value. This thesis partially rests on the psychoanalytic proposition that mental processes and contents of consciousness are grounded in an unconscious ontology that conditions the production of our conscious thoughts through fantasy formation. Although ideas have both conscious and unconscious origins, their articulation in consciousness is predicated on linguistic constructions governed by the psychodynamics of wish-fulfillment based upon our primordial desires and conflicts. The idea or notion of

God is the manifestation of our response to our being-in-relation-to-lack, and the longing to replace natural absence with divine presence. Hence God remains a deposit of one's failure to mourn natural deprivation or lack in favour of the delusional belief in an ultimate hypostatized object of idealized value.

Myth, Hermeneutics, and Science

Myth has a convoluted etymological history in terms of its origins, meanings, and functions. Throughout this chapter I offer a theoretic typology of myth by exploring the origin, signification, symbolic structure, and essence of myth in terms of its source, force, form, object, and teleology derived from archaic ontology.

Why do we need a theory of myth? Because no systematic theory exists, let alone a consensus. What I am particularly interested in addressing are not specific theories of myth, or specific myths themselves, but rather what constitutes a good theory. In particular, throughout our investigation I hope to illuminate what a proper theory of myth would be expected to offer in terms of its descriptive and explanatory power, coherency, generality, meaningfulness, and functional utility. Through my analysis of an *explanandum* and an *explanans*, I argue that both interpretation and explanation are acts of explication that signify the ontological significance, truth, and psychic reality of myth in both individuals and social collectives. I conclude that, in essence, myth is a form of inner sense.

Next, I attempt to critique some of the philosophical problematics inherent with the hermeneutic turn in psychoanalysis. The proposition that "there are only interpretations of interpretations" leads to an inescapable circularity because interpretation ultimately lacks a referent or criterion for which to anchor meaning. If we follow this proposition through to its logical end, this ultimately collapses into relativism because meaning is relative to its interpretive scheme, which further relies on other interpretative schemata for which there are no definitive definitions, conclusive consensus, or universal laws governing interpretation. How can hermeneutics escape the charge of circularity, infinite regress, disavowal of universals, its tacit relativism, and the failure to provide a consensus or criteria for interpretation? How is psychoanalysis able to philosophically justify interpretative truth claims when they potentially inhere to a recalcitrant subjectivism while claiming to be objectively valuative?

Despite burgeoning interest in psychoanalytic thought throughout many disciplines in the humanities, psychoanalysis today is facing a crisis. Confronted with methodological, discursive, epistemological, and empirical challenges to theory and practice, not to mention waning public interest in psychoanalytic treatment, psychoanalysis continues to find itself displaced from mainstream scientific and therapeutic approaches within the behavioural sciences. Not only is psychoanalysis questioned on its scientific credibility and therapeutic efficacy from other disciplines, it is even disputed within contemporary psychoanalysis itself. Criticized for its theoretical models and scientific questionability, psychoanalysis faces critique by the "new empiricists" who are at once eager to legitimize and refine the discipline, yet are radical in their dismissal of many of the cardinal elements that have historically defined the profession.

In this next chapter I challenge the ideologies of science, which are reflective of a privileged, hegemonic master discourse. The force of this discourse is built upon a fantasized objectivist epistemology and reductionist framework that is far removed from the human condition. I will attempt to argue that science lacks true explanation as it artificially reduces the human being to simplistic, naïve theories of parsimony that carry dogmatic ontological assertions about mind, human nature, and behaviour. Such reductive paradigms further ignore the role of theoretics and subjectivity that by definition saturate any empirical method, and hence color its results; not to mention import an inflated valuation of the alleged virtue of empiricism itself.

Truth, Causality, and Fate

What exactly do we mean by truth? Although the concept is nebulous across the array of theoretical perspectives in contemporary psychoanalysis, it is fundamental to all discourses. Is psychoanalysis in a position to offer a theory of truth despite the fact that at present it has no explicit, formal theory regarding the matter? A general metatheory is proposed here that allows for discrete categories and instantiations of truth as metacontextual appearance. In revisiting the ancient notion of *aletheia* as disclosedness or unconcealment, we may discover a distinct psychoanalytic contribution to truth conditioned on unconscious processes reappropriated from Heidegger's project of fundamental ontology. Construed as a dialectics of truth, this notion accords well with how psychoanalysts understand the dynamic unconscious and how it functions to both reveal and conceal. Given that clinical experience demonstrates the workings of dynamic unconscious activity, psychoanalytic theory may contribute a vocabulary relevant to philosophy by explicating the motives and mechanisms that create the appearances of contextual truth as such, phenomena whose causes have previously gone undescribed.

In addition to the quest for truth, the question, scope, and meaning of human freedom have also been a philosophical preoccupation since antiquity. The question of freedom is juxtaposed to its antithesis, namely, determinism, or more specifically, causation. One cannot sufficiently address the question of freedom without attending to the question of determinism because this antipode is dialectically constituted; hence they are mutually implicative constructs. Psychoanalysis' single contribution to this debate is that it postulates an unconscious activity that is both a problematic and a remedy, that is, both a conundrum and a plausible solution to the question of agency. It lies in the notion that internal forces operate on causality and intentionality outside of human consciousness, and particularly, self-conscious awareness; yet they derive from within the experiential subject and are predicated on a logic of internality that is self-generative, purposeful, and agentically instituted as determinate teleology, what has been traditionally called "psychic determinism."

What I wish to argue throughout this chapter is that psychic determinism is propelled by unconscious intentionality, which situates the locus of mental life within an unconscious agency responsible for determining the material expression of conscious choice and action. What we call psychic determinism is actually the expression of an underlying freedom, the freedom of unconscious expression. More specifically, freedom and determinism are bifurcations of the same ontological process that is executed by the unconscious ego in all mental productions. In other words, psychic determinism is the expression of its own freedom, and freedom is the instantiation of its determinate powers. Rather than view causation in its customary fashion as the sufficient condition(s) for the occurrence of an event devoid of freedom, future succession, or expressive value, I want to champion a conception of causality that is self-organizing and self-activating from within its own natural parameters. In this way, freedom and determinism are the same.

In the final chapter I explore the possibility of human extinction. We are facing a planetary ecological crisis due to global warming, despoliation of our natural resources, mass scale industrial pollution, desertification, deforestation, widespread collapse of ecosystems, and extreme climate change. World overpopulation is nearing a record tipping-point, where food and water scarcity will bring about more famine, drought, pestilence, and death. Global catastrophic hazards have escalated due to the environmental crisis, encroachment by man, destabilized markets, hegemonic politics, the ubiquitous dread of nuclear war, terrorism, infectious diseases, techno nihilism, and psychological self-interest driving everything from vain desire to the local economy and international relations, not to mention the anathema of evil, abuse, trauma, greed, and the psychopathology of everyday life. Our recalcitrant dependency on fossil fuel is gradually suffocating the planet. Greenhouse warming, climate catastrophes, and aberrant weather phenomena occur every day throughout the globe and yet we do very little to mitigate it, let alone reverse its course. Moreover, we have caused the Anthropocene. Despite the fact that we see the ruin with our own eyes and do practically nothing to mitigate the ecological crisis, world masses have adopted a global bystander effect, where denial and abnegation of social responsibility lie at its very core. Regardless of the degree of gravity we assign to these calculated risks imperiling our existence, we cannot ignore the ominous threat of planetary extinction unless humanity unites in moral preventative action.

We may be generally suspicious of global speculations regarding the future of humanity, but in our contemporary socio-political climate of war, social implosions, terror, violence, and hate, aggression and its derivatives continue to grip world attention, thus subjugating any hope of their abolition to the bleak forecast of pessimism. Here I address the role of negation and destruction in the process of civilization and explore the degree to which the positive significance of the negative may inform new valuation practices that in turn improve human relations and world accord. Juxtaposed to psychoanalytic anthropology, Hegel's dialectic becomes the logical model for examining the possibility of global amelioration of the pernicious forces that beset the fate of humankind. Here we must seriously question whether mankind's aggressive essentialism will eventually lead to the demise of the human race, hence the end of existence.

Note

1   *Peri Phuseōs*, Fr. 3: "For it is the same thing to think and to be" (Burnet trans.). Cf. "For it is the same thing to conceive (noein) and to be" (Gallop trans.).

About the Texts

All references to Freud's texts refer to the original German monographs compiled in his *Gesammelte Werke, Chronologisch Geordnet*, 18 vols., ed. Anna Freud, Edward Bibring, Willi Hoffer, Ernst Kris, and Otto Isakower, in collaboration with Marie Bonaparte (London: Imago Publishing Co., Ltd., 1968 [1940–1952]). Most translations are mine. Because most English-speaking psychoanalysts and philosophers neither own nor readily have access to these original texts, I have cited *The Standard Edition of the Complete Psychological Works of Sigmund Freud*, 24 vols. (1886–1940), trans. and gen. ed. James Strachey, in collaboration with Anna Freud, assisted by Alix Strachey and Alan Tyson (London: Hogarth Press, 1966–1995 [1886–1940]). References to quotations are designated by *SE* followed by the appropriate volume and page numbers.

From the *Encyclopaedia of the Philosophical Sciences*, M.J. Petry, ed., outlines Hegel's *Philosophy of Spirit* in *Hegel's Philosophy of Subjective Spirit*, vol. 1: *Introductions*; vol. 2: *Anthropology*; and vol. 3: *Phenomenology and Psychology* (Dordrecht, Holland: D. Reidel Publishing Company, 1978). Petry's edition provides a photographic reproduction of Hegel's original text published in the 1830 revision, along with the *Zusätze*, or *Additions*, supplied by Boumann when the material was republished in 1845. Petry's edition also indicates variations between the 1827 and 1830 editions of the *Encyclopaedia*. His edition has several decisive advantages over A.V. Miller's edition of the *Philosophie des Geistes*, which was translated as the *Philosophy of Mind*. In addition to having the original German text and his notations of the variations between the 1827 and 1830 editions, Petry also provides notes from the *Griesheim* and *Kehler* manuscripts.

For comparison, I have also examined Hegel's 1827–1828 lectures on the Philosophy of Spirit: *Vorlesungen über die Philosophie des Geistes* (Hamburg: Felix Meiner, 1994). I have mainly relied on Petry's translation but provide my own in places that warrant changes. References to the *Zusätze* are identified as such.

For the same reasons regarding the likely lack of familiarity with original texts, I have cited the English translations of Heidegger's *Sein und Zeit*, Sartre's *L'Être et le Néant*, Lacan's *Écrits* and *Séminaires*, and Jung's *Gesammelte Werke* (published in Switzerland) but compiled and translated in the Bollingen Series as his *Collected Works*, which were almost exclusively written in German. All references to Plato are from *The Collected Dialogues of Plato*, and to Aristotle from *The Complete Works of Aristotle*, which are generally considered by scholars to be the best English translations in circulation.

Attempts have been made to use gender-neutral referents. Most references cited in the text refer to the following abbreviations followed by their volume, section, and/or page numbers. For complete details, see References:

BN   *Being and Nothingness*
BT   *Being and Time*
CW   *The Collected Works of C.G. Jung*
E   *Ecrits: A Selection*
EG   *Philosophie des Geistes*, trans. *The Philosophy of Spirit*, part 3
     of the *Encyclopaedia of the Philosophical Sciences*
EL   *Encyclopaedia Logic*, vol. 1 of the *Encyclopaedia of the*
     Philosophical Sciences
FC   *The Four Fundamental Concepts of Psycho-Analysis*
PN   *Philosophy of Nature*, vol. 2 of the *Encyclopaedia of the*
     Philosophical Sciences
PS   *Phenomenology of Spirit*
RH   *Reason in History*, the Introduction to the *Lectures on the*
     Philosophy of History
SE   *Standard Edition of the Complete Psychological Works of*
     Sigmund Freud, 24 vols.
SL   *Science of Logic*

Chapter 1

On the Origins of Psychic Reality

Freud never actually used the words "ego" and "id" in his German texts; these are English translations into Latin taken from one of his most famous works, *Das Ich und das Es*. When Freud spoke of the *Ich*, he was referring to the personal pronoun "I"—as in "I myself"— a construct that underwent many significant theoretical transformations throughout his lifetime. By the time Freud (1923) advanced his mature model of the psyche, concluding that even a portion of the *I* was also unconscious, he needed to delimit a region of the mind that remained purely concealed from consciousness. This he designated by the impersonal pronoun *es* which he used as a noun—the *It*, a term originally appropriated from Nietzsche. The translation *ego*, displaces the deep emotional significance tied to personal identity that Freud deliberately tried to convey, while the term *id* lacks the customary sense of unfamiliarity associated with otherness, thus rendering these concepts antiseptic, clinical, and devoid of all personal associations. The *I* and the *It* expresses more precisely the type of antithesis Freud wanted to emphasize between the familiar and the strange, hence the dialectic of the life within.

When we refer to ourselves as "I," we convey a meaning that is deeply personal, subjective, and known, while references to an "It" convey distance, separateness, objectification, and abstraction. The I is familiar while the It is foreign and unknown, hence an alien presence. Because Freud wanted to preserve the individual intimacy associated with a personal sense of self, the I was to stand in firm opposition to the It which was purely estranged from conscious awareness. But the distinction between the I and the It is not

DOI: 10.4324/9781003305958-1

altogether unambiguous, and as I will argue, not theoretically re-solved by Freud himself. In fact, even psychoanalysis today in all its rich theoretical variations has not rectified this issue. While Freud (1923, *SE*, pp. 24–25, 38; 1926, *SE*, p. 97; 1933, *SE*, pp. 76–77; 1940, *SE*, p. 145) eventually conceded that the I developed out of the It, he did not explain with any detail how this activity was accomplished; he merely declared that it just happened.

It is my contention that post-classical through contemporary psychoanalytic thought still suffers from ambiguity surrounding the ill-defined nature of the development of the I from the It which has either been taken as a mere propositional assumption within psy-choanalytic theory, or has been subverted by alternative paradigms that boast to have surpassed Freud while subsuming his model within an overarching meta-historical paradigm. But a persisting, endemic problem to psychoanalysis is the absence of any *philosophical* attempt to account for genesis, namely, the origins of psychic reality. It is not enough to say that psychic experience begins as unconsciousness and progresses to consciousness, from drive to reason, from the It to the I: we must be able to show how these primordial processes *originally* transpire and sequentially unfold into dynamic patterns of organized mental life. Relational, interactionist, and intersubjective accounts focus on the interpersonally elaborated psychosocial matrix that defines, nurtures, and sustains the existence of the self (Kohut, 1984; Mitchell, 1988; Stern, 1985; Stolorow & Atwood, 1992); and we have every reason to appreciate these exciting advances in our conceptual understanding of psychic development. However, without exception, these schools of thought have not addressed the *a priori* conditions that make the emergence of the self possible to begin with, that is, the ontological ground and moments of inception of psychic reality.

We have reason to believe that the I and the It are not ontologically differentiated; nor is it to be accepted at face value that the I does in fact develop from the It. What is missing in previous developmental ac-counts is any detailed attempt to chronicle the very processes that bring the I and the It into being in the first place. Throughout this essay, I will be preoccupied with what I call the "genesis problem," namely, Beginning—the origins of unconscious life. By way of dialectical ana-lysis, I will trace the means in which such primitive processes acquire organization, differentiation and integration, teleological progression, self-constitutive identity, and psychic cohesion. While Freud articulated the fundamental intrapsychic forces that beset human life, he did not attend to these ontological-transmutational concerns. It is my intention to offer a dialectical account of the coming into being of the I and the It, or what I shall call the ego and the abyss, and show how psychoanalytic process psychology provides an adequate solution to the question and nature of unconscious maturation.

Conceptualizing the Psyche

When Freud refers to the mind, he is referring to the Greek notion *psyche*, which corresponds to the German term *Seele*. In fact, Freud does not speak of the "mental apparatus" at all, rather the "organization of the soul" which he specifically equates with the psyche. Freud adopted this usage as early as 1905 when he emphatically said: "'Psyche' is a Greek word and its German translation is 'soul.' Psychical treatment hence means 'treatment of the soul' [*Seelenbehandlung*]" (1905b, *SE*, p. 283). Furthermore, Freud (1933, 1940) equates psychoanalysis with the science of the life of the soul (*wer die Wissenschaft vom Seelenleben liebt*), which stands in stark contrast to the biological connotations associated with the English word "mind" (Bettelheim, 1982, pp. 71–75).

Well read in ancient philosophy, Plato's notion of the soul, as well as his depiction of Eros, left a lasting impression on Freud's conceptualization of the psyche. Before we proceed, however, it is important to distinguish between what we mean by psyche, self, I or ego, and the It. Historically, psychoanalysis, like other professions, has the propensity of using highly technical jargon to capture the complexities of human mental functioning. This is patently justified, but it posses a problem in conceptual discourse and mutual understanding, especially when concepts remain murky or are presumed to have universal definitions when in fact they mean many different things to different theorists and philosophic disciplines. So we may avoid equivocation of our terms, let us begin with a conceptual definition of the I.

The I or ego has a special significance for Freud associated with personal identity, self-reference, conscious thought, perception, mobility, reality testing, and the higher executive functions of reason and intelligence. *Das Ich* is not a common German expression used in everyday conversation: it is used only by professionals in a quasi-scientific context.[1] Neither are references to the self (*Selbst*) or the subject (*Subjekt*) common parlance. In fact, to refer to oneself as "*mein Ich*" or "*mein Selbst*" would be viewed as being exceedingly narcissistic. The term ego also imports negative connotations associated with inflated self-importance and self-love, such as in the words "egotistical," "egoism," and "egocentric," hence the terms I and ego have a shared meaning in both German and English. Since the word ego has become immortalized in psychoanalytic literature as well as popular culture, for customary purposes I will refer to the I and the ego interchangeably.

Freud realized that he could not adequately account for the I as being solely conscious, and therefore introduced a division between conscious and unconscious ego domains and their respective operations. What Freud was mainly concerned about in this division was to explain how certain ego properties, qualities, and tension states impacted on the nature of wish, defense, drive discharge, and self-preservation, and how the I stood in relation to an alien force and presence compartmentalized from the ego itself. The ego became a pivotal concept for Freud because it was the locus of agency, intention, and choice both consciously and unconsciously realized; however, an agency that existed alongside competing agencies in the mind. This theoretical move on Freud's part is not without conceptual drawbacks and has led many critics to question the plausibility of competing mental entities. While Freud used the terms "provinces," "domains," and "realms" to characterize such psychic activity, he in no way meant to evoke substance ontology characteristic of ancient metaphysics in vogue with some forms of materialism today. Freud explicitly abandoned his earlier neurophysiological visions of the mind represented in his *Project for a Scientific Psychology* (1895), and by the time of *The Interpretation of Dreams* (1900) adopted a corpus of the soul that admonished reductionism (see Freud, 1900, *SE*, p. 536;1916–1917, *SE*, p. 21). Characterizing Freud's theory of agency in terms of entity or substance ontology further misrepresents his views on the active processes that constitute the psyche. Freud's purported agencies are active, purposeful, malleable processes—not static, fixed, immobile structures. While Freud (1900, 1923, 1933) also prefers spatial metaphors in his description of these forces, he is quick to remind us they are only heuristic devises: the question of localization becomes a meaningless proposition when we are in actuality discussing temporal mental processes.

Freud's use of the term I imports ambiguity when we compare it to a psychoanalytic conception of the self. In some of Freud's (1914) intervening works on narcissism, his concept of the ego corresponds to the self; and in *Civilization and its Discontents* (1930), he specifically equates *das Ich* with *das Selbst* (*SE*, p. 65). This implies that the self would not contain other portions of the psyche such as the drives and the region of the repressed. This definition also situates the self in relation to otherness and is thus no different than our reference to the ego with its conscious and unconscious counterparts. In German, however, the "self" encompasses the entire human being; but on a very earthly plain, it represents the core from which the ego acts and relates mostly to the conscious aspects of personal identity. While a strong case can be made for the Self as a supraordinate (see Meissner, 2000) encompassing principle—what Freud calls the Soul (*Seele*), I believe Freud is justified here in conceptualizing the I, ego, and self as synonymous constructs. The self stands in relation to its opposite, namely—the Other, as does subject to object, and hence evokes a firm point of difference. This is precisely why Freud insisted on the dialectical presence of otherness: the I is *not* the It.

For Freud, the It is *alienus*—both alienated mind and that which is alienating. We know it as conflict and chaos under the pressure, whims, and persecutory impulses of the drives, our animal nature. They emanate from within us, but are not consciously willed nor desired. The It does not know and does not say no—*It* knows no negation (Freud, 1925b, *SE*, p. 239; 1933, *SE*, p. 74). Under the force of foreign excitations clamoring for discharge, unrest and tumult are its very nature. Yet such chaos by necessity is combated by degrees of order from the ego. Freud's introduction of the It preserves that realm of inner reality we may never directly know in itself. Here Freud insists on the Kantian *Ding an sich*, the Fichtean *Anstoss*—an impenetrable limit, obstacle, or impasse. The mind becomes demarcated by a rigid "check" that introduces irreconcilable division and contradiction; in other words, dialectic.

We may never have direct access to the It, only to the way in which it appears. We know the It through its endless derivatives—such as dreams, fantasies, slips, and symptoms, as well as that which torments us—that which we wish would remain dead and buried, forever banished to the pit—disowned, renounced, hence repressed. But things that are forgotten have a way of turning up unexpectedly. With every covering over, every concealment, there is simultaneously a de-covering, a resurfacing of the old, a return of the dead. Freud crowned the It the king of the underworld—Hades, while the I traversed the domains of its earthly surface down into the bowels of its nether-regions.

Freud's final paradigm of the mind rests on a basic logic of modification. The I differentiates itself and develops out of the It; and later, the I modifies itself again and evolves into a critical-moral agency, what Freud calls the *Über-Ich*, or that aspect of the I which stands over against itself and holds itself up to a higher authority. Here the I undergoes another doubling function, in fact, a doubling of the doubling—this time turned onto itself. What is familiarly know as the *superego* is nothing other than a split off portion of the I that stands in relation to a particular form of identification: namely, a set of values and prohibitions it internalized from familial relations and cultural experience, ideals, and principles the self strives to attain. Freud's logic of modification, however, goes unexplained, the explanatory limits of which he modestly concedes (Freud, 1933, *SE*, p. 77; 1940, *SE*, p. 145).

While Freud makes the superego (over-I, or above-I) into a critical agency that besieges the I and defiles the It, the superego is merely an extension of the ego, both the self in its exaltation as an identification and pining for its ideal form, as well as the judgement, fury, and condemnation that informs our sense of conscience, guilt, shame, and moral reproach. The ego and superego are therefore the same agency divided yet internally conjoined. Freud spoke prematurely in making the superego a third agency of the psyche, when properly speaking, it is not: it merely *appears* as an independent agent when ontologically the ego and the superego are the same. The ego is *supra* in relation to itself—what it wants to be, hence what it strives to become. And when the ego does not live up to itself—up to its own ideals—it debases itself with as much wrath and force as is brewing in the tempestuous cauldron of the It. It is no coincidence that the It and the superego share the same fist of fury—because both are fueled (with stipulations) by the drives, a point I will return to shortly. But for now it becomes important to emphasize that the psyche is a divided self with each division and modification remaining interdependent and ontologically bound.

In the end, Freud gives us a vision of the mind as composed of three ontically interrelated forces with varying qualitative degrees of organization and zest ranging from the most primitive, unmodulated evolutionary impulses to the most refined aspects of intelligence and ethical self-consciousness—all brought together under the rubric of soul. Bettelheim (1982) tells us that nowhere in his texts does Freud actually provide us with a direct definition of the soul (p. 77), although we may infer that he intended for it to stand as an overarching concept which enveloped the three agencies of mental life. We do know, however, that Freud had no intentions to imply that the soul is immortal, nor does it carry any religious connotations whatsoever. Freud (1927, 1933) was a vociferous atheist, thus his use of the term is meant to reflect our shared collective humanity.

Freud's tripartite division of the soul returns us to the Greek vision of the psyche with one exceptional difference: the soul is largely unconscious. As the seat of the passions (*eros*), reason (*nous*), and moral judgement (*ethos*), the psyche becomes a dynamic organization of competing dialectical forces. Because the notion of consciousness is a modern—not an ancient—concept, Freud is able to enrich the Platonic view by showing that irrationality and emotional forces driven by unconscious processes constantly plague the intellectual and ethical strivings of the ego. Therefore, the logocentrism that is often attributed to Freud must be viewed within the context of the pervasive tenacity of irrational pressures, although there is always a logic to the interior. Left undefined by Freud, we may nevertheless say that the psyche is the composition of competing dialectical processes that inform and sustain the division of the I from the It along with its multifarious derivatives. The psyche is pure process and experiential flow composed of a multiplicity of dialectical organizations—each with varying degrees of opposition, complexity, and strands of unification—which form a temporal continuity enduring in embodied space. While the psyche consists of unifying activity, it itself is not a static unity, rather a motional-experiential process of becoming spatio-temporally realized as mediated immediacy.

This leads us to a process account of the psyche, or for our purposes, the Self—as a supraordinate complex whole, including both conscious and unconscious parallel activities. While classical through proceeding historical and contemporary psychoanalytic models have paid great attention to the details and developmental contours of intrapsychic, interpersonal, and psychosocial life, the question of genesis—psychic Origin—and its ontological modifications, remain virtually unconsidered. In what follows, I hope to show how psychoanalytic process psychology offers a logic of the dialectic that proves useful in explaining the rudimentary development of the psyche from its most basal ontological conditions to its most robust configurations and complexifications.

The Dialectics of Unconscious Experience

Freud is a dialectician of the mind: in his final paradigm he envisioned the psyche as an active composition of multifarious, bipolar forces that stand in antithetical relation to one another and are therefore mutually implicative. The I and the It, the two classification of drives, primary versus secondary process mentation, the pleasure versus reality principle, love and hate, the individual versus society— these are but a few of the oppositional processes that inform his dialectical system. However, Freud never clarified his logic of the dialectic; instead he relied on introspection and self-analysis, clinical observation, and technical judgement based on careful consideration of the data at hand, which over time, led to radical revisions of his many core theoretical postulates. One of Freud's most modest attributes was his ability to change his mind about previous speculations when new evidence presented itself, thus showing the disciplined persistence of a refined scientific attitude he had revered as *Logos* (see Freud, 1927, 1930).

It is not altogether clear how Freud's dialectic is philosophically constituted, a topic he said nothing about, however, we may draw certain reasonable assumptions. While some dialectical forces seek unification, resolution, and synthetic integration, others do not. For example, consciousness and unconsciousness, like the I and the It, are firm oppositions, yet their distinctions become blurred in times of sleep, day-dreaming, and fantasy formation. Even when we are unconscious, the mind generates impressions and representations from the tableau of images once experienced in conscious sensation and laid down in the deep reservoir of memory within the unconscious configurations of the mind. This suggests that consciousness is on a continuum of presence and absence, disclosure and concealment, with each respective appearance being merely one side or instantiation of its dual nature, a duality highlighted and punctuated by its phenomenal valences and qualities, yet nevertheless ontologically conjoined. Consciousness and unconsciousness could not be ontologically distinct by the simple fact that each context of being overlaps and participates in the other, without which such duality could not be intelligibly conceived unless each counterpart is to be viewed as having separate essences. But if this were the case, neither could participate in the realm of the other nor could they have mutual causal influence as they are purported to possess simply because that which has a distinct ontology or being would by definition have a difference essence. Just as Aristotle's (1962) criticism of Plato's (1961) forms still stands as a cogent refutation of ontological dualism based on the incompatibility of different essences, so must we extend this assessment to the split domains of consciousness and unconsciousness. Conscious and unconscious life must have the same ontology, hence the same essence, by virtue of the fact that each informs the reality of the other: their respective differences point to their modified forms.

In order for an essence to be what it is—without which it could not exist—it must stand in relation to what it is not. Freud maintains this division of consciousness and unconsciousness from: (1) an experiential or phenomenological standpoint—that which qualitatively appears, (2) from an epistemological one—that which is known, and (3) as a conceptual, heuristic scheme—that which is conceived. However, despite his dual classification of drives, he does not maintain such duality from an ontological framework: consciousness arises *in* the ego, itself the outgrowth of an unconscious It. I will speak more to this later, but suffice it to say that Freud's dialectic permits both integration and impasse, synthesis and disunity, universality and particularity, hence contradiction and paradox. But as Freud (1933) says, the It knows nothing, above all the law of contradiction: "Contrary impulses exist side by side, without canceling each other out or diminishing each other: at most they may converge to form compromises" (*SE*, p. 73). Mental processes could only "converge" and transmute their original forms only on the condition that they participate of the same essence, hence an original ontological ground that makes the conversion of form possible.

Another example of the blurred distinctions of duality and limit in Freud's system may be witnessed in the dialectic of repression (Freud, 1915b). That which is denied conscious access, negated, and banished to the pit is not totally annulled, hence not completely opposed. Rather, it is preserved where it festers and seeks discharge through another form. Thus, opposition remains contextual, yet always has the potential of being breached.

While we may observe a boundary of firm antitheses in Freud's model, there is also a synthetic function to the ego which seeks to mediate, resolve, and channel competing desires and conflicts through intentional strategies that find their way into overt behaviour and conscious phenomenon. But there is also a regressive function to ego, and each are potentially mobilized given the particular contingencies that govern psychic economy. On the other hand, the process of sublimation has a unifying, transcending character that combats regression, despite the fact that both can be operative on parallel realms of development. This leaves Freud somewhere between what Kant (1781) referred to as the antinomies of reason or the paralogisms of the self, which correspond to irreconcilable contradictions within the mind that meet with no resolve, to the Hegel (1807, 1812, 1817a) notion of *Aufhebung*—a progressive dialectical process that cancels, surpasses, and simultaneously preserves opposition within an elevating, unifying procreative self-structure. Despite Freud's lack of clarification surrounding his dialectical logic, we can nevertheless say that his model is compatible with a process account of unconscious experience that is dialectically organized and mediated by oppositional contingent forces exerting equiprimordial pressures that are contextually realized in time.

The mind is dialectical hence relational, that is, it stands in relation—in both temporal continuity and disjunction—to that which is other-than its current form or experience. It is important to note that regardless of the form of difference we wish to theoretically or experientially highlight, all dialectical organizations of the psyche are simultaneously operative from the vantage point of their own unique constitutions and contextualized perspectives. Therefore, the perspectivism of each inhabited domain of lived (yet at times unformulated) unconscious experience is not to negate the force and presence of competing intentional faculties within the mind. It now becomes our task to more closely examine how these psychic processes are logically constituted through dialectically mediated progression, a discussion that will prepare us to engage the question of original ground.

Process Psychology

In several of my publications (Mills, 2000a, 2002, 2010), I have advocated a new theoretical approach to contemporary psychoanalytic thought called "dialectical psychoanalysis" or "process psychology." While process psychology has potential application for theoretical, clinical, and applied psychoanalysis, here I will be mainly concerned with examining its conceptual explanatory power. This approach relies largely on Hegel's (1812, 1817a) general logic of the dialectic and its reappropriation for psychoanalytic inquiry, however, without inheriting the baggage associated with Hegel's entire philosophical system. We need not adopt Hegel's overall system in order to appreciate his science of the dialectic and the logical operations in which it unfolds. Furthermore, Hegel's dialectical logic allows us to examine more precisely the nature of mental functioning and explain how unconscious modification is made possible. This has direct bearing on engaging the question of the origin of psychic reality and specifically the coming into being of the I and the It.

Process psychology assumes a fundamental axiom: mind is constituted as process. This is the essence of all psychic reality and is the indispensable ontological foundation for all forms of mental life. Every mental derivative—from unconscious to conscious, intrapsychic to relational, individual to collective—is necessarily predicated on process. Process underlies all experience as an activity of becoming. As becoming, process is pure event, unrest, or experiential flow. Essence is process. It is neither fixed nor static, inert, or predetermined, rather a spontaneous motional flux and trajectory of dynamic pattern lending increasing order, organization, and zeal to psychic development. As process, essence must appear in order for any psychic event to be made actual.

Psychic reality, with all its contours and manifestations, is dialectically constituted by competing and opposing forces that are interrelated and mutually implicative. Opposition is ubiquitous to psychic reality and operative within all subjective and intersubjective experience: that which *is* is always defined in relation to what it *is not*. Hence, there is an equiprimordality to all dichotomous relations. All polarity is mutually related and inseparable, hence one pole may only be differentiated from the other in contextual thought or by experiential perspective. Polarities of similarity and difference, identity and otherness, are phenomenal encounters in time each highlighted by their respective positionality towards the other, even though their mutual relation to opposition co-constitute their existence. Identity and difference are thus formed in relation to opposition, negation, and conflict, whereby each are ontologically interdependent and dynamically composed of fluid processes that evoke, construct, and sustain psychic organization and structure. Therefore, the subject-object contrast may only be properly appreciated as an intrinsic dynamic totality whereby each event and its internal relation is emphasized as a particular moment in the process of becoming. From the mutual standpoint of shared-difference, each individual subjects stands in relation to the multiply contoured intersubjective matrix that is generated when particular subjectivities collide and interact. This ensures that process multiplies exponentially.

The nature of psychic process is derived from an active organizing principle that is replete with conflict and destruction providing thrust, progression, and ascendence within a dynamically informed system, yet may revert or regress back to more archaic or primitive shapes of mental life under certain contingencies. Process is not simply subjective experience that is radically individualized (although it encompasses it), rather subjectivity unfolds within universal dialectical patterns—as *subjective universality*—(not as predetermined, reductive mechanisms, but as teleological, contextual operations) that lend actuality and structure to lived reality. It is important to reiterate that psychic structure is not fixed, static, or immobile, but is transforming, malleable, and mediating activity or flux that provides functional capacities and vivacity within a teleologically driven, purposeful process of becoming. Therefore, all particularities of conscious and unconscious experience (whether individually or collectively instantiated) are ontologically informed by the universal, motional principles that fuel the dialectic.

Hegel's dialectical logic has been grossly misunderstood by the humanities and social sciences largely due to historical misinterpretations dating back to Heinrich Moritz Chalybäus, an earlier Hegel expositor, and unfortunately perpetuated by current mythology surrounding Hegel's system. As a result, Hegel's dialectic is inaccurately conceived of as a threefold movement involving the generation of a proposition or "thesis" followed by an "antithesis," then resulting in a "synthesis" of the prior movements, thus giving rise to the popularized and crassly misleading phrase: thesis-antithesis-synthesis. This is not Hegel's dialectic, rather it is Fichte's (1794) depiction of the transcendental acts of consciousness, which he describes as the fundamental principles (*Grundsatz*) of thought and judgement. Yet this phrase itself is a crude and mechanical rendition of Fichte's logic and does not even properly convey his project. Fichte's dialectic is a response to Kant's (1781) *Critique of Pure Reason* where Kant outlines the nature of consciousness and addresses irreconcilable contradictions that are generated in the mind due to breakdowns in reason. For both Kant and Fichte, their respective dialectics have firm limits or boundaries that may not be bridged. Hegel (1807, 1812, 1817a,b,c), on the other hand, shows how contradiction and opposition are annulled but preserved, unified, and elevated within a progressive, evolutionary process.

While Hegel's (1812) *Science of Logic* has attracted both philosophical admiration and contempt (see Burbidge, 1993), we need not be committed to the fine distinctions of his Logic which is confined to the study of consciousness. What is important for process psychology is understanding the essential structure of the dialectic as *Aufhebung*— customarily translated as "sublation"—denoted by three simultaneous movements which at once (1) annul or cancel opposition, (2) surpass or transcend its prior moment, while (3) preserving such opposition within its new, transformed and synthesized organization. Three movements: at once they cancel or annul, transcend or surpass, retain or preserve— aspects of every transmogrification. The dialectic as process is pure activity and unrest which acquires more robust organization through its capacities to negate, oppose, and destroy otherness; yet in its negation of opposition, it surpasses difference through a transmutational process of enveloping otherness within its own internal structure, and hence elevates itself to a higher plane. Not only does the psyche destroy opposition, but it also subsumes and preserves it within its interior. Death is incorporated, remembered, and felt as it breathes new life in the mind's ascendence towards higher shapes of psychic development: it retains the old as it transmogrifies the present, aimed towards a future existence it actively (not pre-determinately) forges along the way. This ensures that that dialectical reality is always mired in the contingencies that inform its experiential immediacy. Despite the universality of the logic of the dialectic, mind is always contextually realized. Yet each movement, each shape of the dialectic, is merely one moment within its holistic teleology, differentiated only by form. The process as a whole constitutes the dialectic whereby each movement highlights a particular piece of psychic activity that is subject to its own particular contingencies. As each valence is highlighted in its immediacy or lived-experiential quality, it is merely one appearance among many appearances in the overall process of its own becoming.

Approaching the "Genesis Problem"

With the enlistment of the dialectic, process psychology offers philosophical fortification to psychoanalysis which has long been under attack for its alleged lack of scientific credibility (see Bornstein, 2001; Fisher & Greenberg, 1996; Grünbaum, 1984). Although heralding itself a science grounded in clinical observation, practice, and empirical hypothesis-testing, much of psychoanalytic theory may be philosophically supported through dialectical logic, an alternative, complementary methodology which further gains in descriptive and explanatory force when empirical accounts become tenuous or questionable. The dialectic proves especially useful when understanding the logic of modification that Freud does not adequately address, thus lending logical rigor, deductive justification, and internal coherence to procedural inquiry concerning, among other things, the nature of the genesis problem. Empirical science in general, and developmental research in particular, is in no better situation to proclaim they can determine how the ego comes into being other than by making reasonable, inductive inferences based on observable phenomenon; and this is more often accomplished through speculative inferences based on our own subjective experiences (see Frie, 1999). For example, Stern's (1985) proclamation of the "emergent self" as the earliest stage of ego development in infancy, (from birth – 2 months), does nothing to illuminate the ground from which the self emergences in the first place. There is a current tendency in psychoanalytic infant research to emphasize the relational, dyadic systems, and intersubjective domains that help constitute the ego (Beebe, Jafee, & Lachmann, 1992; Benjamin, 1992;

Lichtenberg, 1989; Mahler, Pine, & Bergman, 1975; Ogden, 1986; Stern, 1985), but this does not address the genesis question. While these developmental paradigms are insightful and informative, the ontology of the *inception* of subjectivity is ignored: psychic activity is presumed but not accounted for.

Empirical approaches (including clinical and/or phenomenological investigations) ultimately face the same strain as do purely theoretical attempts to define the origins of psychic development because we simply do not possess direct epistemological access to the primordial organizations of the subjective mind. Put laconically, we can never 'get inside' an infant's head. Biological attempts ultimately fail because they succumb to the bane of materialist reduction, thus effacing the unique quality of the lived experience that is displaced by simple location, what Whitehead (1925) calls the fallacy of misplaced concreteness. While our physical nature is a necessary condition for psychic life, it is far from a sufficient condition to account for the coming into being of psychic reality. This is not to disavow the relevance, contiguity, and importance of the biological sciences for psychoanalytic inquiry (see Gedo, 1996), only to emphasize that process thought extends far beyond psychophysicality.

While process psychology has a favorable attitude towards empirical science, it realizes that relying solely on perceived, observable (controlled) experience can be of little help when answering the question of Beginning. To approach such an issue, we must enlist the principle of sufficient reason: what is the *ground* of psychic life—the inner world? We cannot begin to answer this question without making *a priori* claims about the logic of the interior, a logic of unconscious internal modification. *Tabula rasa* approaches, typical of early modern philosophy, claim that all knowledge comes from conscious experience while *a priori* judgements tell us that certain ontological conditions of subjectivity must be unconsciously operative in order to make experience possible. While the former relies on observable experience that presuppose a psychology of cognition, the latter emphasizes the ontological and logical continuity of unconscious experience that allows for the structures and functions of consciousness to arise. *Tabula rasa* explanations are philosophically simple, myopic, and naive—long displaced by the Kantian turn in philosophy and refined by many German Idealists and postmodern thought, whereby *a priori* accounts are favored in logic, linguistics, and evolutionary epistemology. As we will see, the process of unconscious modification rests on the internal negations, divisions, projections, incorporations, and re-constitutive movements of the dialectic.

We must first start with the question of genesis, of Origin—original ground. If it becomes necessary to trace the origin and development of the mind in order to come to terms with first principles—the metaphysics of the soul, then we must attempt to conceptually isolate a ground in which all else arises. Like Freud and other empirically motivated theorists, we must situate this unfolding ground within the natural world, within the corporeal subject itself, and thus avoid appealing to a singular, first principle or category of the ultimate in which we nor the philosophers are equipped to satisfactorily answer without begging the question or steering us down into the abyss of infinite regress. Not only must we start with the natural being of the embryonic psyche—its natural immediacy, we must inevitably begin from the inside-out, progressing from unconscious internal activity to external mediated consciousness.

In what I will soon argue, as epistemologically subjective, self-attuned experiential beings, we intuit, feel, and/or know our own interiority *before* we encounter the manifold data of the sensuous outside world, although externality, biological, social, and linguistic contingencies, as well as cultural historicity are superimposed upon us *a priori* as part of our ontological thrownness (Heidegger, 1927).

From a methodological account, tracing the dialectical birth and epigenesis of the psyche from the interior to the exterior is more philosophically defendable because it does not merely presuppose the existence of the object world; instead, it constructs a means to engage external reality from its own internal psychic configurations. I do not wish to revive the irreparable schism between the failed realism/anti-realism debate, only to show how process is internally mediated and dialectically conditioned. For all practical purposes, we live and function in a world which we indubitably accept as real—things happen around us even if we don't adequately perceive them nor understand their existence or purpose; but our subjective appreciations of what is real is radically habituated by our own internal worlds and unconscious permutations thereby influencing conscious perception, judgement, and intersubjective exchange. This is why psychic reality is first-order experience.[2]

All we can know *is* psychic reality: whether inner or outer, self or other, presence or absence, perceived or imagined, hallucinated or conceived—reality is mediated by subjective mind. Although an enormous aspect of mind and personal identity involves consciousness, it is only a surface organ—the modification of unconscious life, a fraction of the activity that comprises the internal processes and pervasive throbs of unformulated unconscious experience. Our epistemological understanding of the real is ontologically conditioned on *a priori* unconscious structures governed by *intrasubjective* processes that allow the natural external world to arise in consciousness. Therefore, our encounter and understanding of psychic reality is always mediated by intrapsychic events that are first-order or first-person experiences even if such experiences operate outside of conscious awareness or are under the influence of extrinsic events.

While Freud frowned on metaphysics, his theory of mind is a metaphysical treatise replete with quandaries. Although Freud stated that the I develops out of the It and that consciousness arises in the ego, he did not proffer an adequate explanation of how this activity occurs. In fact, there are many problems with the relations between ego activity and the drives, the question of mediation by the drives, the distinctness of the I and the It, and whether they can be distinguished at all—and if so, perhaps only phenomenologically, which is not to say that they share separate essences, only different appearances. For Freud, psychic origin was proclaimed to commence in that broad category of the mind labeled *das Es*, what he earlier stipulated under the rubric of the system "*Ucs.*" Now that we have prepared the context for a process account of the mind, it is time for us to return to our original task, namely, the genesis problem, and give voice to the logic of modification Freud anticipated but left unexplained. Here we must examine the psyche's most elemental pulse from its natural immediacy, what Freud reified as the indubitable primacy of the drives.

Where *It* all Begins: The Transmogrification of the Drives

In contemporary psychoanalysis, Freud is disparaged largely due to his emphasis on the drives. This is partially the result of mistranslations of his actual German texts, however drive theory has inevitably fallen out of vogue with analysts and clinicians who value more relational approaches to theory and practice. While these mistranslations and their implications have been previously criticized (see Bettelheim, 1982; Laplanche, 1970; Lear, 1990), nowhere do we see such a gross error as in the misconception of "drive" (*Trieb*) translated as "instinct." This single mistake has misinformed five generations of English speaking psychoanalysts and clinicians whom unfortunately confuse the mind with materialist reduction. Freud never used the English term "instinct" when he spoke of humans: *Instinkt* in German always refers to animals and denotes a fixed, predetermined behavioural pattern or tropism. Freud loathed that term when speaking of the human animal. *Trieb*, on the other hand, means an inner urge, impulse, or drive which is the proper descriptor used to emphasize the notion of inner unrest, desire, and compulsion often associated with impersonal, non-intentional forces impelling the individual from within.

We may initially see why Freud's concept of drive has descriptive utility: it is an unconscious process that fuels and propels the organism. But more importantly, Freud conceives of a drive as a malleable, plastic, transformative activity—not a static, genetically imprinted or determined pressure that cannot be mediated or amended. For Freud, a drive can be altered and permutated, while an instinct is stagnant and unchangeable. Whereas the expression of a drive can be mitigated if not changed entirely, an instinct cannot undergo modification at all. "Instinct" in English, however, also typifies something that is innate. Therefore, in order to avoid duplicating confusion about the nature of drive and instinct, all references hereafter to instinctual processes should be viewed within this stipulated context of drives.

Freud's theory of the drives went through many significant transformations throughout his career, at one time focusing solely on libido (*Lust*), later to many different competing urges belonging to both unconscious and conscious processes (e.g., *die Ich-Triebe*), then finally settling on the primacy of two antithetical yet interpenetrable classifications: sex and death. Relational schools can't buy this central tenet, what Stephen Mitchell (1992) calls the "outmoded concept of drives" (p. 3); namely, that the mind is driven and influenced by multifarious, over-determined unconscious forces that are originally biologically based pressures impinging on the conscious subject and clamoring for release. But the main objection among these schools is the concentrated refutation of the role of libido over relational and intersubjective motives. Here we see the first big turn-off and subsequent resistance by the post-classical field: everything boils down to sex.

This unfortunate attitude is a deposit based on Freud's (1905a) early work on infantile sexuality; it does not take into account his mature theoretical advances (see Freud, 1933, 1940). As said earlier, Freud was not particularly impressed with having to think the same thing all the time: by the end of his life he incorporates libido or the sex drive into his conception of Eros—an encompassing life principle, similar in fashion to the Greeks' who saw the pursuit of Eros as life's supreme aim: viz. the holistic attainment of sensual, aesthetic, ethical, and intellectual fulfillment. In this sense, mind and body are contiguous. By blindly focusing on Freud's early work at the expense of his mature theory, not only is he misunderstood, but his theoretical corpus is distorted. It also leads one to presume that Freud was committed to a genetic fallacy, namely, that all psychic life can be reduced to its developmental origins—when he was not. Eros is the sublimation (*Sublimierung*) of natural desire, first materializing as drive then progressing to the cultivated activities of the ego—that is, rational self-conscious life.

For Freud (1915a), the source of a drive is unequivocally biological and somatic. This is the second big turn-off: man is viewed as a physical-instinctual machine turned on by the environment. I am of the opinion that not only do many post-classical schools of thought misunderstand the nature of drives but they ultimately misunderstand the role of biology and human embodiment. It is simply delusional to think that biology has no place in psychic economy, and those deifying relational factors through negation of the natural body are misguided. Why sex and aggression?—because they are part of our animal evolutionary past. The notion of drive underscores Freud's natural science foundation which is inextricably bound to evolutionary currents: sex and aggression are the two fundamental forces behind the inception, course, and progression of civilization, without which there would arguably be no human race.

In the historical movement of psychoanalysis, we can observe a conceptual shifting away from drive theory to ego psychology, object relations theory, self psychology, and now its current preoccupation with intersubjectivity each calling for a paradigm shift. In the early stages of psychoanalytic theory-building each post-classical movement championed a particular constituent of psychic activity (e.g., ego over object) while complementing and subsuming Freud's general psychological theory. In fact, it was Freud who launched ego psychology and the object relations movement (see Freud, 1933). Today, however, with the insistence on relational and intersubjective approaches, psychoanalysis is being plummeted into a land of false dichotomies suggesting that relation cancels drive. And even if it is conceded that the two realms co-exist, we are still asked to choose sides (see Greenberg & Mitchell, 1983, p. 390). As a result, within many contemporary analytic circles, the primacy of the drives and the unconscious itself have virtually disappeared.[3] Take Mitchell (1992) for example: "There is *no* experience that is not interpersonally mediated" (p. 2, italics added); and Stolorow: Intersubjectivity "recognizes the constitutive role of relatedness in the making of *all* experience" (in Buirski & Haglund, 2001, p. xiii, italics added). These proclamations clearly state that consciousness conditions unconsciousness, when they fail to account for what Freud had been so sensitive to investigate. While interpersonal processes are an integral and necessary aspect of psychic development, they do not by themselves negate the relevance of the drives and their mutual influence over mental life. Furthermore, Stolorow and his colleagues' (Orange, Atwood, & Stolorow, 1997; Stolorow & Atwood, 1992; Stolorow, Brandchaft, & Atwood, 1987) claim that everything is intersubjective fails to consider intrapsychic experience prior to the onset of consciousness. Unconsciousness precedes consciousness, hence subjective experience is internally mediated prior to one's encounter with the object world. In fact, drive becomes an ontological *a priori* that cannot be annulled or denied: moreover, it precedes interpersonal interaction by virtue of the fact that drive is constitutionally predicated.

We can never escape from the fact that we are embodied. Freud's insistence that the source of a drive is biologically given is simply to accept the brute facticity of our natural corporeality. The mistake many psychoanalytic theorists make is interpreting biology as reduction and that drive discharge precludes relational activity, when contrarily, Freud's conception of drive makes reduction impossible and relatedness possible. Let me explain.

Freud has to account for embodiment—our natural immediacy—in which urges and impulses arise, thus he focuses on the body as initially providing form, content, and structure to internal experience. This is why erogenous zones are corporeally emphasized. But more importantly, Freud has to show how ego activity and consciousness are also sensuous processes: attention, perception, and the greater faculties of cognition are sentient experiential actions. This is why Freud (1923) says that the ego is a body-ego, itself the projection of a surface: *It* projects itself *onto* its surface, the surface of its immediate feeling and sensuous embodiment. Therefore, drive is constituted as ego, but not at first. While Freud does not say this directly, it may nevertheless be inferred: drive becomes ego—the ego first knows itself as a feeling, craving, desirous corporeal being. But how does this occur? Freud says very little.

In "Instincts and their Vicissitudes," or more appropriately translated, "Drives and their Fate" *(Triebe und Triebschicksale)*, Freud (1915a) distinguishes between four constituents of a drive: a source, pressure, aim, and object. While the source *(Quelle)* is somatically organized, Freud is very clear that the pressure *(Drang)* or force of a drive is its very "essence" *(Wesen)*. Here he unquestionably situates the nature of *Trieb* in its activity: drive is pulsation, unrest—pure desire. The aim *(Ziel)* or motive of a drive is to satisfy itself, to achieve pleasure as tension reduction, to end the craving; and the means by which a drive is sated is through an object *(Objekt)*. Objects, especially people, are coveted for the functions they serve, and these functional objects may fulfill many competing aims as psychic life becomes more rich and variegated. In fact, drives transmogrify through many circuitous routes and take many derivative forms: what we commonly refer to as a "defense mechanism" is the teleological fate of a drive. This is an unfortunate term because "mechanism" evokes imagery of stasis, rigidity, and fixed predetermined movements, when instead defenses are fluid, mutable, and teleologically directed expressions of desire as *process systems.*

As transformed drive, a defense is a particular piece of desire, often unconsciously intended and differentiated by its function in relation to a competing urge, impulse, or counter-intention, internal danger, environmental threat, and/or potential conscious realization that must be combated. There are defenses that urge the psyche to regress while others to progress, and this is why a drive cannot be simply seen as biological reduction or devolve back to its original state. Because drives transform, they cannot return to their original form: we can never know a drive in itself, only as a psychical representative, presentation, or idea (*Vorstellung*). Furthermore, what we often experience as drive is its aim—the craving for satisfaction. Moreover, because drives modify themselves through a process of epigenesis, they make the more sophisticated forms of conscious and self-conscious life possible: from the archaic to the refined, unconscious drive manifests itself through relatedness to objects.

Freud's theory of *Trieb* is not without difficulty, and many critics proclaim that because his model of tension reduction was ultimately a hydraulic component of biological-homeostasis theory, the aim or *telos* of a drive overrides relational motivations. But this conclusion is not justified, especially when others become the objects of our satisfaction. Freud (1915a) specifically says that the object of a drive is the most variable aspect and that it may serve multiple motives simultaneously (*SE*, p. 123). Nowhere are we led to believe that relation is subordinated to biology when a drive is mediated though object relatedness. Furthermore, Freud's (1925a) later theory of Eros ultimately speaks to the desire for love and the pursuit of our most cherished ideals which he specifically equates with the Eros of Plato in the *Symposium* (*SE*, p. 218). As a result, Eros becomes a relational principle (see Reisner, 1992), a relation towards ourselves and others through the exaltation of human value. From the most primitive mind to the most civilized societies, we are *attached* to our ideals through others.

But let us return to a conceptual dilemma for Freud: how could a drive have an object? Put another way, how could a drive take an object as its aim without possessing some form of agency? As a teleological process, a drive has a purpose constituted through its aim, but how could it also be guided in its ability to *choose* objects for its satisfaction without accounting for intentionality by an unconscious agent? Here we see why Freud had to introduce the notion of unconscious agency constituted through the alien presence of the It. The It constitutes the realm of the dual classification of drives as well as the realm of the repressed. But is Freud justified in making the It into an agency? Could it be possible that unconscious actions of the ego are actually performing object choice, while the drives and repressed material merely act as a constant pressure the ego must mediate? This is particularly problematic for Freud given that he specifically tells us that the I logically and temporally proceeds from the It. Freud is very clear in his final specifications of how the psyche develops in this fashion. In *Inhibitions, Symptoms and Anxiety*, Freud (1926) states:

> We were justified, I think, in dividing the ego from the id, for there are certain considerations which necessitate that step. On the other hand *the ego is identical with the id, and is merely a specially differentiated part of it.* If we think of this part by itself in contradistinction to the whole, or if a real split has occurred between the two, the weakness of the ego becomes apparent. But if the ego remains bound up with the id and indistinguishable from it, then it displays its strength. The same is true of the relation between the ego and the super-ego. In many situations the two are merged; and as a rule we can only distinguish one from the other when there is a tension or conflict between them ... . [T]he ego is an *organization* and the id is not. *The ego is, indeed, the organized portion of the id* (*SE*, p. 97, italics added).

Freud clearly explains that the I is a modally differentiated aspect of the It which becomes the mental organization of its prior shape. Elsewhere he says: "the ego is that portion of the id that was modified ... tak[ing] on the task of representing the external world to the id" (1933, *SE*, p. 75). This corresponds to the ego of consciousness, where the material of sensuous perception and thought are mediated, stored, and retrieved from the inner world, hence underscoring the contiguous and inter-dependent levels of unconscious and conscious processes. Freud's theory of mind adheres to an architectonic process: the ego develops out of its natural immediacy, then acquires increased dynamic complexity and organization as modally differentiated shapes of earlier processes assume new forms. As previously stated, Freud's recognition that organized psychic processes develop from unorganized hence undifferentiated natural determinations insulates him from criticism that his theory of mind purports three ontologically distinct agents that participate in mutual causal relations. Because the trinity of the three provinces are modally differentiated forms or shapes of its original undifferentiated being, each participates in the same essence and thus none is an independent nominal agent. Rather they are interdependent forces that *appear* as separate entities, when they in fact together form the unification of the dynamic temporal processes that govern mental life.

Freud's model of the psyche conforms to a developmental monistic ontology: higher instantiations of mental order evolve from more primordial forces of psychic life through a process of differentiation and modification. Although the I and the It are modifications of the same ontology, it is only the I that appears, itself an unconscious derivative. The specific process of differentiation, however, goes unexplained. All we are told is that the ego becomes the higher organizing agency of the mind derived from primitive processes. In fact, Freud (1940) concedes that while drives find their first psychical expressions in the It, they are "in forms unknown to us" (*SE*, p. 145). But why did not Freud isolate the moments of differentiation and modification within the It itself? Given that drive is the basic constituent of mind which even precedes the organization of the It as a thoroughly unconscious agent, why did he not address modification at this level? Furthermore, if the ego is a secondary modification from a primary unconscious ground, then by Freud's account, drive mediation would have to take place before the ego emerges; but how could a drive possess such agency? Freud does not say.

From my account, the transmogrification of the drives gives rise to psychic agency and it is through a careful inspection into the process of modification that we can potentially resolve the genesis problem. I believe that Freud was mistaken about making the It into an agency without accounting for how the unconscious portion of the I performs the executive functions of object choice for the drives and competing unconscious material pressing for discharge. The It cannot be understood as an unconscious agency (if at all) without the implicit inclusion of the I unless the nature of a drive includes the capacity to choose objects, which is highly improbable given that only the ego is organized and synthetic in its executive tasks. In fact, Freud (1915a) tells us that the object of a drive is "*assigned* to it only in consequence of being peculiarly fitted to make satisfaction possible" (*SE*, p. 122, italics added). If the I is ontologically undifferentiated from the It, it makes the question of unconscious agency more delicate when attempting to account for teleology and intentional object choice. Rather than the I developing from the It, the ego may be properly said to develop from drive. But even more importantly, as I will soon argue, we have reason to believe that drive and ego are the same.

As it stands, there are many problems associated with Freud's contrast between the I and the It. The It is impersonal but it allegedly picks an object for the drives: how is this so? According to Freud, only the ego can do this; hence we have a problem with an executive agency, and we have a problem with the definition of a drive. Although a drive needs an object for its satisfaction, are we justified in saying that an object is a proper characteristic of a drive? This implies that an object inheres in the drive as a property of it, when this is unlikely. An object stands in relation or absence to the *telos* or aim of a drive, but it does not follow that an object is necessarily a part of a drive's constitution, only that is requires an object for its satisfaction. In order to procure an object, it requires mediation. Here enters the I. The unconscious ego mediates object choice, not drive, hence Freud introduces a contradiction in his model. He further confounds the issue by making the ego a developmental agent that does not materialize until the formative stages of early Oedipalization, a postulate corrected by Klein and many post-Kleinians, and today confirmed by developmental researchers that recognize the existence of the ego or the self at the moment of birth (e.g., see Stern, 1985).

Freud attempts to resolve his own contradiction by making the It a separate agent. But how does it have any organizing agency without the ego that lends structure and direction to it? Yet Freud (1926) equivocates the issue by saying that the I is "identical" with the It. In Freud's final tripartite model, the ego becomes the locus of mind because of its synthetic and dynamic functions that stand in mediatory relation to the other two competing agencies. Yet these other two agencies are ontologically conjoined, hence we cannot separate any one agency from the others because of their inextricability. But is it possible to save Freud from his own contradiction? Can a drive take itself as its own object? And if so, when does drive become ego? Why does it emerge to begin with? At what point does the I take on a formal unity? How does it effect its transition to executive agency? To consciousness? In order to answer these questions, we must increasingly turn our attention to a dialectical account of modification.

Arkhē

When does psychic life begin? Does the emergence of the ego properly constitute human subjectivity, or can we legitimately point towards prior ontological forces? As mentioned earlier, I do not wish to reduce this metaphysical query to a materialist enterprise, only to acknowledge that certain physiological contingencies of embodiment are a necessary condition albeit not a sufficient condition to account for psychic origin. While process psychology is sensitive to the contiguous and compatible work within the biological and neuro-sciences, this need not concern us here. If one is content with a materialist approach, let him resort to discourse on ovum and sperm. But we must proceed with a careful respect for Freud's (1900, 1933) dictum and resist the temptation of reducing the psyche to its anatomical substratum. Because empirical approaches alone cannot possibly address the epistemology of the interior or the lived quality of experiential process, we must attempt to approach the question dialectically. Put more specifically, we are concerned with isolating the experiential movements that bring about the inception of lived psychical reality. Before we can address the ego of consciousness, we must first account for original ground through a process account of the coming into being of archaic structure. Although unarticulated by Freud himself, the concept of drive allows us to engage the question of genesis.

We must now return to the question of ground. Although Freud tells us that the It conditions all other forms of psychic agency, drives and the repressed condition the It. Furthermore, since repression is a vicissitude of the drives, drives necessarily become a grounding unconscious activity. Therefore, what we can infer from Freud is that the drives become primordial. But is this enough? How do the drives constitute themselves in the first place, that is, how do they function as organized unconscious life? Moreover, how do they come into being at all?

Unconsciousness precedes consciousness, hence there is a radicalization to unconscious subjective experience. In fact, consciousness is the manifestation of unconscious structure, first expressing itself as drive. While Freud emphasized the equiprimordiality of Eros and destruction, his notion of the death drive may be arguably considered one of his most important theoretical achievements. The death drive (*Todestrieb*) is not merely the innate presence of animal aggression or externalized acts of destruction, rather it is the *impulse-toward-death*. While the drive towards death may be observed as a *will to murder*, first it speaks to the subject as a *will towards suicide*. But as Freud tells us, mainly due to antithetical, counteractive drives motivated by the desire for adaptation and self-preservation, self-destructive impulses are typically deflected and defended against through projective displacements that find fulfillment through many circuitous paths throughout our developmental histories.

Before Freud fully committed to his notion of the death drive, he gave a speculative account of the evolutionary birth and metamorphosis of animate from inanimate life. In *Beyond the Pleasure Principle*, Freud (1920) conjectures that *"the aim of all life is death"* (*SE*, p. 38), and that organic life ultimately wants to return to an inorganic state of quiescence. In considering how animate activity came into being, Freud speculated that inorganic matter would have been perfectly content with its simple unity of quiescence if not for the encroachment of neighbouring dangers that threatened its internal cohesion and integrity. As a result, libido or a life principle was erected as a defensive manoeuvre against the imminent threat of destruction from a foreign invasion. From this account, the drive towards life is a defense against a real or perceived danger that threatens to invade the organism's solipsistic world. Extending this notion to the human subject, death is paradoxically beyond the pleasure principle yet at the same time is the ultimate pleasure: death is a tensionless state. But death only becomes pleasurable to the extent that it is protracted and endured; this is why Freud says that it must be engaged through circuitous routes of self-destruction (i.e., as repetition) that bring the organism back to its original inorganic condition. In other words, violence is brought about through the subject's own hands.

Freud's bold claim has not been well received amongst psychoanalysis and has been outright rejected based on biological grounds (see Sulloway, 1979); yet death is unequivocally ontologically conditioned. Death, conflict, negation, chaos—saturates psychic structure and is the motional process behind the very evolution of the dialectic. By turning our attention to a process account of the dialectic of desire, I believe we are justified in saying that death is our original drive. Negativity is our inner being that enters into opposition with itself—its own competing, antagonistic mental processes vying for expression whether consciously or unconsciously conceived. As Hegel informs us, the mere act of confronting opposition is negative and aggressive, hence a conflictual enterprise of canceling, surpassing, and preserving such negativity within the unconscious abyss of our inner constitution. Yet the destruction inherent in all dialectical relations is merely a moment within the holistic process of elevating inner states to higher forms or modes of being. Hence, there is a *positive significance to the negative* that brings about more advanced levels of psychic progression and realization. In this way, negativity is both a grounding and transcending process of mind. Extending Freud's notion of the death drive to process dialectics allows us to show how the unconscious grounds its own ground through determinate negation. Death is teleologically directed and experienced as life turned outward, from the interior to the exterior, towards procuring the means of returning to its previous state of undifferentiated, undisturbed peace.

In considering the inception of psychic life, however, we must take Freud's thesis further. In conceiving of genesis—the birth of psychic activity, it makes more sense to me that mental life would have to experience a form of upheaval from within its own interior constitution, rather than as a response to trauma from without. Instead of a pristine, unadulterated state of quiescence, the soul, embryonic ego, or preformed unconscious agent (what Freud calls the It), would have to experience a rupture due to internal discord that would serve to punctuate its breach to life, a process of awakening from its nascent self-entombed unity. But how is this possible? Hegel (1817c) describes the process by which the unconscious soul undergoes a dialectical evolution that eventually becomes the ego of consciousness. Hegel's method is particularly relevant to the question of genesis. By taking a dialectical approach to our theoretical analysis, we may speculate how unconscious agency first materializes.

Because mind cannot emerge *ex nihilo*, we must posit the coming into being of psychic agency as a progressive unconscious, dialectical activity; in other words, as a determinate teleological drive. Given the brute facticity of our embodiment—the givenness of nature itself, mind must emerge from within its natural beginnings. In the beginning (*arkhē*), there is simple immediacy, the mere given existence or immediate *is*ness of psychical pulse, what we may loosely call *unconscious apperception*. This is unconsciousness in its immediacy, neither cohesively constituted nor developed, rather the experiential presence of its sentient being. Because that which *is*, is an unconscious, pre-reflective immediacy, we may only designate it as an implicit agent or passive activity belonging to nascent mental experience. Because it is merely implicit activity in its initial immediacy and structure, it becomes a matter of making itself explicit and mediate through laborious dialectical progression; yet this requires developmental maturation: mind has much work to do before it becomes a consciously cognizant processential being. Thus, in its pre-natal form, we may only say that mind is unconscious pulsation as lulled apperceptive experiential process.

From my account, it makes no sense to speak of nascent mind or self in the beginning as "sensori-motor aliveness" (Winnicott, 1960) or the "center of initiative" (Kohut, 1977) without explaining how selfhood and conscious life is prepared by unconscious mediatory relations. Psychoanalysts from Freud to Klein, Winnicott, and Kohut were not able to provide us with a satisfactory account of self-development from the standpoint of genesis: although the ego is a progressive developmental accomplishment present at birth only in a naive form, we must account for how prenatal maturation of the ego prepares the psyche for later self-transformations and functional tasks. This requires explicating the dialectical manoeuvres that bring consciousness into being in the first place. Because the self-development of the self simply does not pop up as the ego of consciousness, we must first examine the context and contingencies the soul first encounters in its initial immediacy. The term "soul" is used here, as with Hegel, to describe the immediacy of subjectivity as an unconscious state of undifferentiated oneness or unity with its natural corporeality. Thus, unlike Freud, who discusses the soul as the unification of unconscious and conscious life, here the soul is strictly an unconscious, affective embodiment. It does not belong to the sensuousness of consciousness, albeit sensuousness in the form of affective self-certainty is its experiential modality.

It is important at this point to reemphasize that the soul in its immediate unconscious unity, undifferentiated from its sentient nature, is a lulled or subdued experiential, apperceptive activity. The term "apperception" is used here to denote the felt sensuousness or self-apprehension of the soul's self-immediacy. In its implicitness or initial experiential form, the soul must undergo an internal evolution that arouses itself to a state of experiential *mediacy*. This is the initial dialectical instantiation of psychic life, a relation the unconscious first has with itself. And this is a process that unfolds from within itself, from within its own interior constitution. This self-relation the soul has with itself is the first transition to giving itself determinate life. Before that, soul is ontologically determined immediacy.

In its transition from implicitness to explicitness, immediacy to mediacy, it seizes upon its teleological nature as determinate being. Soul, or what I will call the incipient unconscious ego, undergoes an unrest; moreover, an intensification of its already unrestful nature as pure activity, and generates the initial movement of its own becoming. Hence unconscious being is already thrown into participation with the process of its own becoming as an unconscious trajectory of determinate mediatory relations. Thus, in the beginning stages of the soul's development, the lulled being of unconscious experience undergoes an internal tension and awakens within its natural immediacy as a sensuous, corporeal embodiment.

This is a gradual architectonic process of unfolding dialectical relations that becomes contextually realized through self-generative expression. These dialectical operations undergird psychic development and are the fundamental dynamic activities of erecting mental structures and order (as continual, interactive processes of interrelated and complementing forces) within the mind. In this lulled, rudimentary form of mind, the organism is a passive activity, asleep (as it were) in its own inwardness. We may reasonably say at this point that mind is largely a subdued flow of activity, pulsation, or calm throb of experience that is relatively simple, lacks complexity and internal cohesion, and is relatively constituted through its physiological contingencies. But unlike Freud's quiescent organism, mind undergoes a profound restlessness or inner rumble of negativity which it experiences from within its coma-like condition as an eruption to *be*. Such restlessness is due to the opposition it encounters from within its own interior—not from externality, yet perhaps it is experienced as an alien presence or presentation of tension similar to Freud's envision of drive. This drive, however, acts as an internal impetus to awaken, to move, to mobilize itself to more concrete experience: in its initial state of unconscious arousal, it takes itself as its own being which is vibrant and sentient.

Here unconscious apperception arouses itself to *be* and to project life into itself as the form of feeling self-certainty. The soul intuits its own presence as such through the affective embodied experience of its immediate self-awareness. This self-awareness, however, is not the self-reflective, directive aspects of self-consciousness belonging to the ego of conscious perception and introspection. Rather, it is a pre-reflective, non-propositional form of self-certainty as immediate subjective sentient-affective experience, what I have called, "unconscious self-consciousness." The amorphous self knows itself in its immediacy as unconscious experiential subjectivity.

But why does drive emerge to begin with? What urge or impulse awakens mind from its internal slumber? Here mind is a restless indeterminate immediacy, a simple self-enclosed unconscious unity that pulsates and exists in a state of *disquieted* quiescence. It undergoes upheaval because of certain instinctual, motivational currents pressing for expression as a primordial hunger or longing to experience, to feed, to fill itself, namely, as appetition or *desire*. Here we have something to learn from the Idealists: human subjectivity is a desirous enterprise—it yearns, it seeks, it finds. But why do we desire? In other words, what constitutes desire in the first place? Freud finds its source in somatic organizations, and we have good reason to believe that desire is a natural process emanating from the body informed by evolutionary pressures; but this does not adequately address the ontological status of desire, nor does it mean that drive devolves into biology as we have previously shown. Freud (1915a) is unmistakable in telling us that the pressure or force of a drive is its very essence (*Wesen*), hence not simply reducible to its subterranean material-efficient causal determinants. But why does unconscious desire experience such pressure to begin with? What is its *reason* to desire?

Mind desires because it stands in relation to absence or lack. Thus, drive emerges from a primal desire, the desire to fill the lack. In the most primitive phases of psychic constitution, mind is an active stream of desire exerting pressure from within itself as drive, clamoring for satisfaction, what Freud would call "pleasure." But unlike Freud who sees pleasure as tension reduction, mind may be said to always crave, to always desire. While a particular drive or its accompanying derivatives may be sated, desire itself may be said to never formally stop yearning: it is condemned to experience lack. Unlike Lacan (1977), however, who describes desire as "lack of being," here unconscious desire is *being-in-relation-to-lack*.

Within the very process of unconscious genesis, we may observe the overwhelming presence of death. The dialectic is conditioned on the premise of negation and lack, a primacy of the *not*. Nothingness or lack informs the dialectic which we experience as desire. Desire is teleological (purposeful) activity, a craving—at once an urge and an impetus—an infinite striving, a striving to fill the lack. Absence stands in primary relation to presence, including the being or presence of absence; hence this is why desire remains a fundamental being-in-relation-to-lack. While drive gradually becomes more expressive and organized into mental life, the deep reservoir of the unconscious begins to fill as psychic agency simultaneously incubates and transposes itself through its own determinate activity. In its original state, however, being and nothing, life and death, are the same.

The Ego and the Abyss

Following our dialectical analysis of the coming into being of unconscious agency, we can readily see how this developmental process proceeds from the archaic and unrefined immediacy of our sentient corporeal nature to the standpoint of ego development belonging to the higher activities of cognition: mind awakens from its initial primordial indeterminate immediacy and unfolds into a more robust, determinate progressive organization of psychic life—from the most primitive to the most exalted shapes of human consciousness. But initially mind has its form in the natural immediacy in which it finds itself as nonconscious pre-reflective, affective, embodied experience.

The self-certainty the unconscious soul has of itself in its natural immediacy may be summarized by the following dialectical phases of development: (1) mind awakens as unconscious apperception due to internal compulsions to experience and reveal itself to itself as sentient, apperceptive corporeal activity; (2) the coming into being of unconscious subjectivity undergoes a gradual internal upheaval due to the pressures of desire and drive which it (3) experiences as affectively laden, embodied sensuous self-certainty. This pre-development of the human being no doubt takes place in the prenatal fetal milieu which is essentially innately predisposed orientations of the organism belonging to and awakening as the privatization of unconscious subjective experience.

We have determined that restlessness due to desire as the experience of lack is the initial point of genesis of felt psychic expression. The psyche at this level takes itself as its initial form, which is none other than the affective self-certainty of its embodied natural immediacy. So far we have used the term "soul" to designate this intermediate process of psychic development, but are we justified in going further? When does unconscious subjectivity become an organized agency to the point that we can say there is an I and/or an It? Is it legitimate to say that as soon as there is any unconscious activity at all this constitutes agency, or must agency derive from a higher developmental state or occasion? Because there is a mediatory transition from restless desire to the urge or drive to experience *itself*, I think we are justified in saying that at this phase in the epigenesis of the unconscious mind we have the rudimentary form of ego, which has as its task to become more aware and develop even further as a subjective being in the world. Because mind mediates its immediate naturality as experiential affectivity, this constitutes a dialectical movement of determinate affirmation of self even though such determination is still profoundly primitive and elementary. This determination of the mind's self-instantiation places ego development prior to birth within its prenatal environment where it prepares for conscious awakening and thereafter. Therefore, the ego is not merely an agency constituted *at* birth, instead it is prepared in the unconscious soul long beforehand.

Schematically, we may trace the initial unfolding of the incipient unconscious ego as it progresses from (i) desire to (ii) apperception to (iii) sentience, each phase being merely a moment in the constitution of subjective agency through its own determinant dialectical mediation (See Figure 1.1). We can readily see how this process of modification continues to proliferate in a consecutive sublated dynamic fashion eventually becoming the ego of consciousness embracing and incorporating its newfound experiences and developmental acquisitions.

Up to now, I have emphasized the affective embodied experience the ego has with its own immediacy within its unconscious totality. That is, the ego only knows itself as a feeling sentient being. In fact, it has no content other than its original form of unity within its natural corporeal condition of unconscious sensuousness. This sensuousness, however, is not the sensuousness of conscious perception, instead it is

EPIGENESIS OF THE UNCONSCIOUS EGO

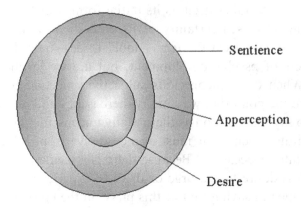

- Sentience
- Apperception
- Desire

Figure 1.1 Epigenesis of the Unconscious Ego.

the felt inwardizing of experiential immediacy. But as soon as the ego
feels itself as an experiential being, it already preforms the mediatory
action of *cognizing* its own existence. This shift from waking within
its natural immediacy to experiencing itself as a feeling agent constitutes the birth of the psyche. We may refer to this activity as a
process of *intuition* that is both a form a sensuousness as well as a
form of thought. Here, the rigid bifurcation between emotion and
thought must be suspended, for unconscious affective apperception
becomes the prototype for thinking which we attribute to conscious
subjectivity: thought—reason—is the materialization of desire. In
effect, the nascent self intuits its own being by collecting or gathering
up the sensuous data it experiences internally, from within its own
self-interior, and then posits or thinks itself *in* this state, hence this
process is both an affective and cognizing activity. This is not to
imply that the self thinks itself into existence as do contend many
modern philosophies of the will, rather thinking is initially experiential affectivity as self-certainty. While the higher operations of
conscious cognition do not concern us here, we have shown how
consciousness is dialectically prepared within unconscious subjective
experience. In this way, the unconscious ego imposes its own experiential order on the phenomenology of consciousness that arises in
the ego upon the actual physical birth of the human infant. However,

despite the intensification of the senses that accrue through cognitive development, the resonance of the ego's initial unconscious affective states become the touchstone for mind to filter and compare all subsequent experiential encounters. The life of feeling remains an essential aspect of human subjectivity.

The self experiences itself as sensuously embodied thought that eventually becomes further divided, differentiated, organized, and expressed dialectically as the higher shapes of psychic development unfold. I have referred to this generic process of psychic progression as a projective identificatory trajectory of dynamic pattern whereby the self divides itself via internal splitting, then projects its interior into externality as affirmative negation, and then identifies with its disavowed shape which it seizes upon and reabsorbs, hence reincorporating itself back into its transmuted inner constitution (Mills, 2000b). This is a progressive dynamic pattern of unconscious architectonic trajectory that moves far beyond the notion of projective identification first espoused by Klein (1946) and Bion (1962). In fact, this process itself is the ontological force of the dialectic responsible for the evolution of mind. It is from that dim interior of unconscious void where the ego must liberate and elevate itself from its solitary imprisoned existence to the experiential world of consciousness. Yet the embryonic ego first knows itself, not as a conscious subject, but as a pre-reflective, unconscious self-consciousness; in other words, as inwardizing self-intuition.

The unconscious ego comes into being as an agency that has some crude capacity for dialectical mediatory relations, and in determining the point of such transmogrifications, we can reasonably say there is determinate teleological expression. The ego's dialectical mediation of its natural immediacy and affective experience of itself as self-certainty becomes the logical model of psychic progression. It is in this way that the unconscious mind progresses from the most archaic mental configurations of unconscious impulse or urge to the refined experiences of self-consciousness. But this assessment leaves us with the difficult question of difference between ego and drive, what Freud dichotomized as the I and the It. Rather than conceive of the ego and the domain of the drives as two separate entities, I believe it becomes important to reconceptualize this duality as a monistic process of psychic differentiation and modification showing how the ego is in fact the organized embodiment and experience of drive. Because the ego is ontologically fueled by the dialectic of unconscious desire, and desire is the very force behind the appearance of drive, the division between the I and the It is essentially annulled. It is how drive *appears* as ego that we may observe such differences, while ontologically speaking, ego and drive are identical. In relation to Hegel's philosophy, I have relabeled the domain of the It as an unconscious *abyss* which I think more precisely captures the multiple processes of unconsciousness that Freud tried to systematically categorize (Mills, 2002). Yet while Freud alerts us to his view of the unconscious as consisting of three divided agencies, with the ego and superego being further split into conscious and unconscious counterparts, I envision the abyss from the standpoint of a monistic developmental unconscious ontology which gives rise to higher forms of psychic organization that interact with and interpenetrate the experiential and intersubjective contingencies which it encounters and assimilates through a cybernetic function of reciprocal dialectical relations. The abyss is that domain of unconscious mind which the ego emerges out of and yet continues to fill and engage through its relation to conscious subjective experience. In a word, the abyss is the indispensable psychic foundation of human subjectivity—the ontological *a priori* condition for all forms of consciousness to emerge, materialize, and thrive. This insures the primacy of archaic experience, unformulated affect, emotional vicissitudes, and pre-linguistic and/or extralinguistic reverberations despite the equiprimordiality of language and unconscious process.

The relation of the ego to the abyss becomes one which requires a degree of differentiation and negation performed by the ego directed towards all realms of otherness. In effect, what the ego experiences is alienation, especially its own self-alienation or alienating activity as disavowed experience, which becomes relegated to otherness and split off from its own self-identity. Such differentiation is an activity the ego performs within itself through determinate negation—I am *not* It!, but the ego is what the abyss has become from the standpoint of the ego's self-differentiation from its foreignness and its original natural immediacy. Therefore, the abyss is the materiality of nature in which the ego emerges out of but is always immersed in: it experiences itself as drive—as a desirous subjective being, which is the formative organization and expression of unconscious agency that epigenetically becomes the ego of consciousness. It is only in relation to itself that the ego forges a gap between itself and the abyss—which becomes the domain of all that the self refuses to identify as being identical to itself. We can readily see how the Freudian *Es* may be conceptually subsumed within the abyss of the ego, that element of mind *alienus* to the ego's own experiential immediacy.

We have determined that desire as being-in-relation-to-lack is the essence of mind that fuels and sustains the process of the dialectic. Desire becomes the ontological thrust behind the presence and felt experience of drive, itself the urge, pressure, or impulse towards activity; and this process gives rise to the unconscious ego awakening within its own inwardness to discover itself as a sensuous, apperceptive affective self-intuiting being that knows itself in its natural embodied immediacy. This dialectical transition from indeterminate immediacy to determinate mediacy by which the ego takes its own natural form as its initial object constitutes the coming into being of unconscious subjective agency. Despite its crude organization at this phase of its life, it nevertheless points towards the dialectical process of its own becoming as a progressive teleological expression of subjectivity eventually acquiring conscious cognition and the higher faculties of self-conscious rational thought as development sequentially unfolds. These higher planes of development are forged by the sustaining power of the dialectic, a process that takes place first and foremost within the unconscious abyss of its natural immediacy.

The ego materializes out of an abyss in which it itself remains. In this way, the unconscious ego is itself an abyss that must mediate the multiple, over-determined, and antithetical forces that populate and besiege it. In the ego's determinate activity of mediation, it sets itself in opposition to otherness which it must sublate, and this inevitably means that certain aspects of its interiority (e.g., content, images, impulses, wishes, ideation) must be combated and/or superseded. It is only on the condition that the ego intuits itself that it gives itself life felt as subjective experiential immediacy. When seen from the standpoint of the ego's mature development, the abyss becomes anything that the ego refuses to identity as belonging its own constitution.

Freud (1923) tells us that "the ego is first and foremost a bodily ego" (p. 26) by the simple fact that we are embodied. But he did not fully describe this process: the ego is first and foremost an unconscious embodiment that intuits its Self within the natural immediacy in which it finds itself. Through continual dialectical bifurcation, the ego expands its internal experiential and representational world and thus acquires additional capacities, structures, and attunement through its mediated, conscious relational contingencies and epigenetic achievements. In doing so, the ego forges an even wider and deeper abyss casting all otherness into the liar of self-externalization. Therefore the chasm between the ego and the abyss is one in which the ego creates itself. The ego of consciousness emerges from an unconscious void which it sinks back into at any given moment, thus never truly attaining ontological distinction. The ego first awakens as unconscious subjectivity within the feeling mode of its original being which it experiences as drive, the restless compulsion to experience. This is why ego and drive are not ontologically differentiated; ego is merely the appearance of drive. Drive is embodied natural desire, our original being which goes through endless transformations in the contextualization and enactment of our personal individualities and interpersonally encountered realities. Drive is transporting, and this is what governs the dialectic. The reason why the domain of drive, and more broadly, that of the abyss, seems so foreign to the ego is that from the standpoint of conscious self-differentiation, we our so much more than our mere biology. We *define* our subjective experiences, and when they come from unintended locations as extraneous temporal encroachments—from the monstrous to the sublime, they are not identified as emanating from within or by one's own determinate will.

In conclusion, I have attempted to show how dialectical psychoanalytic thought explains the coming into being of unconscious subjectivity, thus answering to Freud's adumbrated attempt to explain modification and differentiation of the I from the It. With the current focus on the primacy of emotions in organizing self-experience through intersubjective relations (Aron, 1996; Lichtenberg, 1989; Stern, 1997; Stolorow and Atwood, 1992; Orange, 1995), it is important to emphasize that process psychology explains how affective resonance becomes the locus of unconscious mediatory experience the self first has with itself. This may explain why the life of emotions yields primordial force and direction in forming psychic structure and intersubjective reality, and thus partially answers to why certain unconscious emotional experiences predate and resist articulation through linguistic mediums.

Notes

1 The noun *Ich* stands in philosophic relation to German Idealism, particularly Fichte's (1794) absolute self-positing self. Today it is almost exclusively a Freudian term.

2 This position is in stark contrast to anti-subjectivist perspectives popular among many forms of poststructuralism (Lacan, 1977), postmodernism, and linguistic analytic philosophy (Cavell, 1993). These approaches insist that the human subject is subverted by language which structures and orders all experience. I am in agreement with Roger Frie (1997) that while language is a necessary condition of human subjectivity, it is far from being a sufficient condition for capturing all aspects of lived experience. Sole linguistic accounts do not adequately explain how pre-verbal, extralinguistic, and unformulated unconscious affective experiences resonate within our intrapsychic processes. Furthermore, they assume a developmental reversal, namely, that language precedes thought and cognition rather than acknowledging pre-verbal forces, unconscious experience, and emotive processes of subjectivity that developmentally give rise to linguistic acquisition and expression. In effect, this claim boasts that meaning does not reside in the mind, rather in language itself. But words don't think, only subjective agents. Despite the historicity of language within one's existing social ontology, the way language is acquired is potentially developmentally different for each child.

3 In *Contexts of Being*, Stolorow and Atwood (1992) address three realms of the unconscious which they call (i) prereflective—largely culled from Brentano, Sartre, and early phenomenologists, but ultimately dating back to Fichte, (ii), dynamic—a recapitulation of Freud, and (iii) the unvalidated—from my account, extrapolated from Binswanger and Sullivan (pp. 29–36). But the theory and practice of the intersubjective approach is unquestionably focused on the nature of lived *conscious* experience and affective attunement to emotional resonances within the patient through an empathic-introspective stance (a method, attitude, and/or sensibility derived from Kohut, 1971). For example, Stolorow claims, "In place of the Freudian unconscious ... we envision a multiply contextualized experimental world, an organized totality of lived personal experience, more or less conscious" (Foreword to Buirski & Haglund, 2001, p. xii). But regardless of current analytic propensities that focus on the understanding and response to conscious rather than unconscious processes, it does not negate the dynamic presence of subjective unconscious activity. Most recently, Timothy Zeddies (2000) revisits the notion of the unconscious within relational perspectives emphasizing the intersubjective and dialogically constituted processes that comprise the relational matrix particularly in reference to the patient-analyst relationship.

References

Aristotle (1962). *Nichomachean Ethics*. Martin Ostwald (Trans.). Englewood Cliffs, NJ: Prentice Hall.

Aron, L. (1996). *A Meeting of Minds*. Hillsdale, NJ: Analytic Press.

Beebe, B., Jafee, J., & Lachmann, F. (1992). A Dyadic Systems View of Communication. In N. Skolnick & S. Warchaw (Eds), *Relational Perspectives in Psychoanalysis*. Hillsdale, NJ: Analytic Press.

Benjamin, J. (1992). Recognition and Destruction: An Outline of Intersubjectivity. In N. Skolnick & S. Warchaw (Eds.), *Relational Perspectives in Psychoanalysis*. Hillsdale, NJ: Analytic Press.

Bettelheim, B. (1982). *Freud and Man's Soul*. New York: Vintage Books.

Bion, W.R. (1962). A Theory of Thinking. In E.B. Spillius (ed.), *Melanie Klein Today: Developments in Theory and Practice. Vol. 1: Mainly Theory*. London: Routledge, 1988.

Bornstein, R.F. (2001). The Impending Death of Psychoanalysis. *Psychoanalytic Psychology*, 18(1): 3–20.

Buirski, P., & Haglund, P. (2001). *Making Sense Together: The Intersubjective Approach to Psychotherapy*. Northvale, NJ: Jason Aronson.

Burbidge, J. (1993). Hegel's Conception of Logic. In F.C. Beiser (Ed.), *The Cambridge Companion to Hegel*. Cambridge: Cambridge University Press.

Cavell, M. (1993). *The Psychoanalytic Mind: From Freud to Philosophy*. Cambridge, MA: Harvard University Press.

Fichte, J.G. (1794). *The Science of Knowledge*. P. Heath & J. Lachs (Trans. & Eds.). Cambridge: Cambridge University Press, 1993.

Fisher, S. & Greenberg, R.P. (1996). *Freud Scientifically Reappraised*. New York: Wiley.

Freud, S. (1968). *Gesammelte Werke, Chronologisch Geordnet*, 18 Vols. A. Freud, E. Bibring, W. Hoffer, E. Kris, & O. Isakower, in colloboration with M. Bonaparte (Eds.). London: Frankfurt am Main, 1940–1952.

Freud, S. *The Standard Edition of the Complete Psychological Works of Sigmund Freud*, 24 Vols. (1886–1940), J. Strachey (Trans. & Gen. Ed.) in collaboration with A. Freud, assisted by A. Strachey and A. Tyson. London: Hogarth Press, 1966–1995.

Freud, S. (1895). *Project for a Scientific Psychology. Standard Edition*, Vol. 1.

Freud, S. (1900). *The Interpretation of Dreams. Standard Edition*, Vols. 4–5.

Freud, S. (1905a). *Three Essays on the Theory of Sexuality. Standard Edition*, Vol. 7.

Freud, S. (1905b). Psychical (or Mental) Treatment. *Standard Edition*, Vol. 7.

Freud, S. (1914). *On the History of the Psycho-Analytic Movement. Standard Edition*, Vol. 14.

Freud, S. (1914). On Narcissism: An Introduction. *Standard Edition*, Vol. 14.

Freud, S. (1915a). Instincts and Their Vicissitudes. *Standard Edition*, Vol. 14.

Freud, S. (1915b). Repression. *Standard Edition*, Vol. 14.

Freud, S. (1916–1917). *Introductory Lectures on Psycho-Analysis. Standard Edition*, Vols. 15–16, [1915–1917].

Freud, S. (1920). *Beyond the Pleasure Principle. Standard Edition*, Vol. 18.

Freud, S. (1921). *Group Psychology and the Analysis of the Ego. Standard Edition*, Vol. 18.

Freud, S. (1923). *The Ego and the Id. Standard Edition*, Vol. 19.

Freud, S. (1925a). The Resistances to Psycho-Analysis. *Standard Edition*, Vol. 19. [1924].

Freud, S. (1925b). Negation. *Standard Edition*, Vol. 19.

Freud, S. (1926). *Inhibitions, Symptoms and Anxiety. Standard Edition*, Vol. 20.

Freud, S. (1927). *Future of an Illusion. Standard Edition*, Vol. 21.

Freud, S. (1930). *Civilization and its Discontents. Standard Edition*, Vol. 21.

Freud, S. (1933). *New Introductory Lectures on Psycho-Analysis. Standard Edition*, Vol. 22, [1932].

Freud, S. (1940). *An Outline of Psycho-Analysis. Standard Edition*, Vol. 23, [1938].

Frie, R. (1997). *Subjectivity and Intersubjectivity in Modern Philosophy and Psychoanalysis*. Lanham, Maryland: Rowman & Littlefield.

Frie, R. (1999). Psychoanalysis and the Linguistic Turn. *Contemporary Psychoanalysis*, 35: 673–697.

Gedo, J. (1996). *The Languages of Psychoanalysis*. Hillsdale, NJ: Analytic Press.

Greenberg, J. & Mitchell, S. (1983). *Theories of Object Relations*. Cambridge: Harvard University Press.

Grünbaum, A. (1984). *The Foundations of Psychoanalysis*. Berkeley: University of California Press.

Hanly, C. (1992). *The Problem of Truth in Applied Psychoanalysis*. New York: Guilford Press.

Hegel, G.F.W. (1807). *Phenomenology of Spirit*. A.V. Miller (Trans.). Oxford: Oxford University Press, 1977.

Hegel, G.F.W. (1812). *Science of Logic*. A.V. Miller (Trans.). London: George Allen & Unwin LTD., 1812/1831/1969.

Hegel, G.F.W. (1817a). *The Encyclopaedia Logic*, Vol.1 of the *Encyclopaedia of the Philosophical Sciences*, T.F. Geraets, W.A. Suchting, & H.S. Harris (Trans.). Indianapolis: Hackett Publishing Company, Inc., 1817a/1827/1830/1991.

Hegel, G.F.W. (1817b). *Philosophy of Nature*. Vol.2 of the *Encyclopaedia of the Philosophical Sciences*, A.V. Miller (Trans.). Oxford: Clarendon Press, 1817b/1827/1830/1970.

Hegel, G.F.W. (1817c). *Hegels Philosophie des subjektiven Geistes / Hegel's Philosophy of Subjective Spirit*, Vol.1: Introductions, Vol.2: Anthropology,

Vol.3: Phenomenology and Psychology, M.J. Petry (Trans. & Ed.). Dordrecht, Holland: D. Reidel Publishing Company, 1817c/1827/1830/1978.

Heidegger, M. (1927). *Being and Time.* San Francisco: Harper Collins.

Kant, I. (1781). *Critique of Pure Reason.* N.K. Smith (Trans). New York: St. Martin's Press, 1965.

Klein, Melanie (1946). Notes on some Schizoid Mechanisms. *International Journal of Psycho-analysis,* 27: 99–110.

Kohut, H. (1971). *The Analysis of the Self.* New York: International Universities Press.

Kohut, H. (1977). *The Restoration of the Self.* New York: International Universities Press.

Kohut, H. (1984). *How Does Analysis Cure?* A. Goldberg & P. Stepansky (Eds.). Chicago: University of Chicago Press.

Lacan, J. (1977). *Écrits: A Selection.* A. Sheridan (Trans). New York: Norton.

Laplanche, J. (1970). *Life and Death in Psychoanalysis.* Baltimore: Johns Hopkins University Press.

Lear, J. (1990). *Love and Its Place in Nature: A Philosophical Interpretation of Freudian Psychoanalysis.* New York: Noonday Press.

Lichtenberg, J. (1989). *Psychoanalysis and Motivation.* Hillsdale, NJ: Analytic Press.

Mahler, M.S., Pine, F., and Bergman, A. (1975). *The Psychological Birth of the Human Infant.* New York: Basic Books.

Meissner, W.W. (2000). The Self as Structural. *Psychoanalysis and Contemporary Thought,* 23(3): 373–416.

Mills, J. (2000a). Dialectical Psychoanalysis: Toward Process Psychology. *Psychoanalysis and Contemporary Thought,* 23(3), 20–54.

Mills, J. (2000b). Hegel on Projective Identification: Implications for Klein, Bion, and Beyond. *The Psychoanalytic Review,* 87(6), 841–874.

Mills, J. (2002). *The Unconscious Abyss: Hegel's Anticipation of Psychoanalysis.* Albany: State University of New York Press.

Mills, J. (2010). *Origins: On the Genesis of Psychic Reality.* Montreal: McGill-Queens University Press.

Mitchell, S.A. (1988). *Relational Concepts in Psychoanalysis: An Integration.* Cambridge, MA: Harvard University Press.

Mitchell, S. (1992). True Selves, False Serves, and the Ambiguity of Authenticity. In N. J. Skolnick & S. C. Warshaw (Eds), Relational Perspectives in Psychoanalysis, pp. 1–20. Hillsdale, NJ: Analytic Press.

Ogden, T.H. (1986). *The Matrix of the Mind.* Northvale, NJ: Aronson.

Orange, D.M. (1995). *Emotional Understanding.* New York: Guilford Press.

Orange, D.M., Atwood, G., & Stolorow, R.D. (1997). *Working Intersubjectively: Contextualism in Psychoanalytic Practice.* Hillsdale, NJ: Analytic Press.

Plato (1961). *The Collected Dialogues of Plato.* E. Hamilton & H. Cairns (Eds). Princeton: Princeton University Press.

Reisner, S. (1992). Eros Reclaimed: Recovering Freud's Relational Theory. In N.J. Skolnick & S.C. Warshaw (Eds), *Relational Perspectives in Psychoanalysis*, pp. 281–312. Hillsdale, NJ: Analytic Press.

Stern, D. (1985). *The Interpersonal World of the Infant.* New York: Basic Books.

Stern, D. (1997). *Unformulated Experience: From Dissociation to Imagination in Psychoanalysis.* Hillsdale, NJ: Analytic Press.

Stolorow, R. & Atwood, G. (1992). *Contexts of Being: The Intersubjective Foundations of Psychological Life.* Hillsdale, NJ: Analytic Press.

Stolorow, R., Brandchaft, B., & Atwood, G. (1987). *Psychoanalytic Treatment: An Intersubjective Approach.* Hillsdale, NJ: The Analytic Press.

Sulloway, F. (1979). *Freud: Biologist of the Mind.* Cambridge, MA: Harvard University Press.

Whitehead, A.N. (1925). *Science and the Modern World.* New York: Free Press.

Winnicott, W.D. (1960). Ego Distortion in Terms of the True and False Self. In D.W. Winnicott (ed.), *Collected Papers.* London: Tavistock, 1958.

Zeddies, T.J. (2000). Within, Outside, and In Between: The Relational Unconscious. *Psychoanalytic Psychology*, 17(3): 467–487.

Chapter 2

Psyche as Inner Contradiction

Our Divided Nature Within

The psyche is split. Brimming with inner divisions, we may say that
the subject—we—are comprised of multiple self-states in opposition
or competition with each other vying for expression, if not domination, but willing to settle for a compromise. This is largely due to the
plethora of rival unconscious desires or schemata that populate
mental life,[1] but it is a universal feature of thought itself. The logic of
inner division produces gaps, lacunae—holes in being that expose
incongruities, but it also highlights the polarizing nature of the
psyche based on an economy of splitting. Hegel shows how this
binary logic is at play in the schism of thinking itself, what psychoanalysis refers to as "projective identification," namely, the negation
and projection of our internal contents onto otherness, only then to
come to identify with our split-off nature, and re-incorporate it back
into our internal constitutions.[2] This is the antediluvian pattern of the
rotary motion of the dialectic as split-off or dissociated self-states and
the manifold of object representations that transpire within unconscious process due to the vicissitudes of desire and drive, which
further fuel counter-identifications that intensify in quality constellated as tensions of difference. Intensities of splitting underlie the
essence of psyche.

The schematic structure of mind through splitting is first initiated
as a violent cleavage via negation. For Freud, it is death working
silently in the unconscious in circuitous manners.[3] For Hegel, it is
pure negativity itself.[4] Contradiction is merely one moment in

DOI: 10.4324/9781003305958-2

relation to other psychic events—desire, wish, drive, defense, affect, fantasy—that are split-off and sequestered as independent entities with semi-autonomous organizational properties, energies, and propensities clamoring for breath and release, the multiplicities of soul. This ensures that even with the most highly cultivated and sophisticated shapes of mind—Spirit (*Geist*), there will always be contraries and psychic conflict that not only elude, but resist, reconciliation.

On the Non-Contradiction of Contradiction

In his lectures on metaphysics, Heidegger tells us that "the principle of contradiction has 'ontological' significance because it is a basic law of the logos, a 'logical proposition.' Accordingly, the suspension of the principle of contradiction in Hegel's dialectic is not an end to the domination of the logos but only it's extreme intensification. Hegel should have given the name 'logic' to what is actually metaphysics."[5] For Derrida, "Hegelianism represents the fulfillment of metaphysics, its end and accomplishment."[6] And for Žižek, Hegel's logic is "simply a systematic deployment of all the ways available to us of making claims about what there is, and the inherent inconsistencies of these ways."[7] Among good company, Todd McGowan has recently offered his own interpretation of the mercurial philosopher's ontology of contradiction.

Since the contemporary renaissance in Hegelian studies, there is no dearth of commentators and expositors offering their own interpretation of Hegel's philosophy. A profound and prolific writer, Hegel offers a majestic metaphysical system based on the logic of the dialectic. One has to metabolize Hegel over years to distill the essence of his project. For McGowan, this distillation lies in the pithy crack of contradiction. There is no escape from contradiction, no pristine flight into the Absolute as a foreclosure of contradiction, and no freedom from it, as it is an ontological necessity that gives us a radical freedom, the emancipation of reason.

Hegel's Logic is not the kind that schoolmasters teach, not the formal predicate or deductive logic of mathematical equations, syllogistic forms, and conditional proofs with established rubrics of inference, quantifiers, and identity rules that obey the laws of non-contradiction. Instead, for Hegel there is no self-identity, no pure unification of opposites, no supersession of thought into a grand synthesis of everything, at least not according to McGowan. Rather, contradiction may never be eliminated nor reasoned away, as it is the ground of Being and thinking itself.

McGowan's reading and compelling analysis of Hegel's key texts is original and perspicacious, if not controversial for reducing Hegel's entire oeuvre into a single category. From a psychological perspective, this is self-evident: no human being thinks, feels, or acts in perfectly non-contradictory ways. From a psychoanalytic point of view in particular, this is impossible, for the psyche is divided and consists of a cacophony of innumerable competing wishes, conflicts, and compromises as a way to cope with the multiplicity of desire and defense besieged by anxiety and its external social conditions, and hence McGowan seizes on the *principle of the non-contradiction of contradiction* that lies dormant in every philosophy whether one likes it or not. Name me a subject, let alone a life, that is not contradictory! There is none, because we constantly contradict ourselves in desire, emotion, thought, and deed. This is the internal ontic condition of every human being, our relation to a fleeting interior in the process of becoming Other to itself, another that is not self-identical or stable. This flux or instability in being is the defining characteristic of subjectivity. As McGowan puts it, "The point is not just accepting contradiction but seeing how it drives our thinking and our actions. We don't retreat from contradiction but seek it out."[8] Why would we seek out conflict? Because we are internally divided and allow different self-states to express themselves uninhibitedly even to our own detriment. We want because we lack. When we satisfy a particular desire we are not fully sated, so we want something else beyond satisfaction. The fantasy of satisfaction beyond the present is what drives us, but it never delivers a full meal. Objects are pursued, used, and disposed of, yet we continue to want. The illusion of satisfaction drives us, but unconsciously we know it is neither sustainable nor permanent. This is also the processual thrust behind the Hegelian dialectic: desire has no bounds, no limitations, no endings. It simply gobbles up and regurgitates, in ascendance and decay.

Why contradiction? We seek out diversity and novelty, hence strangeness, which can complicate relations with others rather than merely complementing one another. But McGowan can be accused of missing the Hegelian big picture: he stays focused on contradiction and misses the inherent holistic propulsion of the dialectic. In fact, he is fixating on only one *function* of the dialectic, the negative moment, when the negative is also progressive in the greater process of trying to seek resolution. I say *trying*, because every logical mediation passes into another movement as a constant pining for unification; but there is no guarantee, because there is no preestablished endpoint. Contradiction is one moment of mediation even when contradictions do not resolve, although they can become more complex and robust through dialectical evolution. Although I agree with McGowan that contradiction is central to psyche because we are all at odds with ourselves, I wonder why he generalizes this one element to signify and epitomize the totality of the dialectic when in Hegel's system this is merely a continuation of gradual, sequential, ongoing sublated movements in the process of *Geist* coming to express and understand itself as a self-articulated complex whole—the coming into being of pure self-consciousness, despite remaining incomplete as an in- determinate openness. As Hegel says, the logical unfolding of Spirit is a "*circle* returning upon itself" through mediation and self-reflection, "*a circle of circles*," the return of archaic ontology—of origins, "en- souled by the method reflected into itself."[9]

Indeterminacy is a state of undifferentiated immediacy (or the simple unity of being or presence). It is only when thought ingresses into this state that it becomes differentiated mediacy. Every media- tion forms a new immediate and then must be differentiated into further contents, forms, patterns, etc., and this is what constitutes a dialectical progression. The minute something is identified or given an identity, it is already mediated as standing in opposition to what it is not, hence difference, but this opposition is inherent to identity, so you cannot have a sense of self without difference that stands in re- lation to opposition, even if you identify yourself as a certain thing or belonging to a class of social objects (despite being a subject).

Indeterminacy could be whatever you fail to identify as designating a particular being, thing, or process. This indeterminate spacing symbolizes the unconscious, what we don't know or experience di- rectly. It could be an intermediary state, a meso-domain, an ambig- uous classification, a non-determined entity, an open possibility, a paradox, aporia, or anything that lacks a determinate signifier that linguistically or socially determines its identity, significance, and meaning. It simply lacks designation, and by this accord, it lacks. Anything that is not determined or determinate ontologically lacks, hence contradiction becomes the absence of presence that presently lacks being. And because lack is pure negativity, it is not identified or reified. Given that contradiction implies non-determination, it is ultimately about freedom and the heterogeneity of desire.

On the Dialectic

McGowan's thesis is that Hegel's entire philosophy is based on a structure and logic of contradiction. We may rightly anticipate his critics' response: he has overstated his case. What about the generative, progressive, and complex organization of the dialectic in general, not merely the reiterative clash of contradiction? McGowan's Hegel is reduced to impasse rather than outlining a procreant, overdetermined dynamic self-articulation of mind that progresses towards increased complexification, which emerges in higher shapes of consciousness and social collectives through the laws of sublation (*Aufhebung*). Rather than opposition remaining fixed in a stalemate or mutually repetitive fight, he appears to downplay the teleological sequence of Hegel's system as determinate freedom.

McGowan tells us: "At each step of the dialectic, the image of the possible end to contradiction seems to drive the dialectic forward toward another articulation."[10] This conclusion assumes a predetermined fixed teleology oriented towards its destined path and terminus, like Aristotle's acorn, rather than a fully open non-determined teleology that forges its own destiny and route towards its own freely realized self-completion, but one that is never fully complete, only more stout, and open to unannounced contexts, contingencies, and future possibilities, not causally predetermined outcomes. After all, Spirit only comes to understand itself by looking back at the process of its own becoming.

Rather than an end to all contradiction, mind contemplates and elaborates on contraries as an organic, self-reflective cognizing emersion into its interiority. Following the logic of a developmental monistic ontology, world or universal spirit seeks greater forms of awareness through acquired complexity, and not simply a reiteration of contradictions. It is about mediating oppositions in a more so-phisticated evolving pattern of self-instantiation, the reinstitution of archaic ground coming to know itself and its operations as world collectivity, the coextensive and mutually implicative interrelation-ship of subjectivity, objectivity, and intersubjectivity.

When McGowan makes statements such as contraction is "the driving force of all movement of being,"[11] "the animating principle of the entire system,"[12] and "the driving force of the concept,"[13] he is displacing the dialectic and giving contradiction *agency* rather than seeing how this agency is the vitality of psyche itself. While it is true that contradiction sustains the subject as a desiring entity, which cannot be eradicated, just as the Absolute is the *fantasy* of pure reason itself—like this could ever be attained, this does not mean there is no progression to sublation. McGowan denies this: the movement of "thought is not ... a progressive one."[14] Although McGowan provides a compelling argument that thought never eliminates contradiction, but can merely only reconcile it (if it is lucky), he does askew the traditional reading of Hegel's texts where Hegel specifically refers to the sublation of spirit as an historical, progressive unfolding process, or in other words, a negating-subsuming-transcending matrix in its quest for truth, ethical enlightenment, and the unity of knowledge actualized through its objective social achievements.

Spirit or the self is pure activity, unrest, and flux.[15] Mind is in a constant state of psychic turbulence as pure process, a purposeful activity of becoming. The unrest of *Aufhebung* is a progressive un-folding of cancelling, preserving, transmuting, and elevating oppo-sition within its internal structure. Here opposition is raised to a higher unity. As I have argued elsewhere,[16] sublation has a threefold meaning: (1) to suspend or cancel, (2) to surpass or transcend, and (3) to preserve. In the *Encylopaedia Logic*, Hegel makes this clear: "On the one hand, we understand it to mean 'clear away' or 'cancel,' and in that sense we say that a law or regulation is canceled (*aufge-hoben*). But the word also means 'to preserve.'"[17] This is prepared in Hegel's *Science of Logic*:

> "*To sublate*" has a twofold meaning in the language: on the one hand it means to preserve, to maintain, and equally it also means

to cause to cease, to put an end to. Even "to preserve" includes a negative element, namely, that something is removed from its immediacy and so from an existence which is open to external influences, in order to preserve it. Thus what is sublated is at the same time preserved; it has only lost its immediacy but is not on that account annihilated.[18]

Hegel's designation builds on this "twofold meaning" and introduces a threefold activity by which mental operations at once cancel or annul opposition, preserve or retain it, and surpass or elevate its previous shape to a higher structure. This process of the dialectic underlies all operations of mind and is seen as the thrust behind world history and culture. The dialectic is the *essence* of psychic life, for if it were to be removed, consciousness and unconscious processes would disappear.

Aufhebung is itself a contradiction; the word contradicts itself. Thought as a contradiction is constituted in and through bifurcation, a rigid opposition as antithesis. Thus, as a process, reason cancels the rigid opposition, surpasses the opposition by transcending or moving beyond it in a higher unity, and simultaneously preserving the opposition in the higher unification rather than simply dissolving it. The preservation is a validating function under which opposition is subsumed within a new shape of consciousness. Reason does not merely set up over and against these antitheses; it does not only set up a higher unison but also reasons a union precisely through these opposites. Thus, the dialectic has a negative and a positive pole. McGowan's Hegel appears to omit the exalted character of Spirit, its tendency to elevate itself as it passes through its various robust shapes on its ascent towards the Absolute. Although contradiction is never eliminated, as everything is incorporated, retained, and superseded, Hegel's dialectic also allows for regression and withdrawal back to earlier developmental phases emanating from the feeling soul, what we may equate with basic desires, affects, sentiments, and internal conflicts, not to mention the neurotic and pathological manifestations of mind. McGowan's reading of Hegel could lead to an infinite repetition of contradictions and conflict that meet with no resolve. The positive significance to the negative is underplayed as he does not concentrate on the whole dialectical process, just on the moment-to-moment vacillation between oppositions as absolute difference mired in parallax rather than on their complementarities that are mutually implicative and ontologically interdependent.

Contradiction as Repetition Compulsion

The locus of contradiction is merely the repetition of difference and opposition within temporally mediated events through the return of the archaic rotary motion of the dialectic. Contradiction is only one moment of dialectical process in the movement of engaging in exceedingly more complicated mediations of oppositions in the coming into being of collective agency. McGowan perseverates on this one element as the essence of Hegel's system when it is not necessary to overplay this uncontested point that contradiction underlies psychic process. He could have stayed attentive to this one facet of internality and social repetition without detracting from his thesis rather than insist it is the fulcrum of Hegel's overall philosophical project.

While it is true that every assertion contains its negation as opposition, through opposition mutation and developmental maturations ensue. Everything is process: nothing remains a static thing or entity. Difference, opposition, and negation ensure a perennial deflection of contradictions. Difference and opposition are ontic constructs that stand in relation to previous moments or movements of the dialectic or to entities in the world. All objects are mediated categories through human subjectivity. They may or may not directly contradict, which is determined by their values, as everything is valuational to consciousness. The ontology of contradiction underscores our divided nature, namely, the upheaval of subjectivity within society, which is in fact based in a philosophy of trauma. The traumatic act of opposition, difference, contradiction—is the ontological presence of negativity saturating every aspect of our being in the world. The ubiquity of contradictions signals the multiplicity of particularity, the negating universality of an endless sea of instances, that is, of experiences and their heterogeneity, or perhaps, to appropriate Deleuze's term, "heterogenesis,"[19] the diffraction of pure thought spreading out like a rhizome.

Hegel's logic of the dialectic can be viewed in psychoanalytical terms as a repetition compulsion of defense, as a return of the archaic expressed through antipodal contents and relations due to their multifarious instantiations. Oscillating between contradictions is an unconscious operation of the compulsion to repeat, what spurs compromise or symptom formations—voices from the unconscious tendency to self-destruct, the eclipse of reason for the irrationality of infantile wish. Mind seeks higher transcendental plains but it also succumbs to regression, masochistic withdrawal, and devolvement into its more primitive (original) conditions. This is clear from Hegel's corpus.[20] He does not offer a Pollyannaish philosophy of completion through the dissolution of opposition. Every assertion contains its negation as opposition and through opposition. Defense is a compromise formation, the attempt to quell the decent of opposition in the subjective mind and in social realities. This necessarily means that contradictions have their own internal dramas within all facets of subjectivity that must tarry with the negativity inherent in all opposing differences that are mutually implicated in all human relations. This is what we may call the tension of opposites.

On the Tension of Opposites

We are ontologically dependent upon the Other, the State, the Law. Emancipation from contradiction is impossible, but it does not mean that unitive processes are not at work. Shifting theoretical contexts, the psychology of C.G. Jung on the question, being, and truth of opposites bears a comparison to Hegel's philosophy and McGowan's thesis in particular.

The term "transcendence" has a convoluted semiotic history, particularly in philosophy and religion. Jung applies the notion in a psychological sense rather than a logical or metaphysical one. His 1916 paper "The Transcendent Function," written after his break with Freud and during his so-called "confrontation" period, laid dormant for decades, buried in his files until students discovered the manuscript and distributed it for publication in 1957. In his 1958 revision and Prefatory Note published in the *Collected Works*, Jung believes it was the foundational precursor to his method of active imagination whose trajectory is oriented towards an integration of the personality as a whole. This is a seminal early work that is closely related to the question and process of individuation and the psychological quest of holism, which focuses on the dialectical tension of opposites, one-sidedness, compensation, and balance within his conceptualization of the self as a developmental pursuit of the numinous within a trajectory towards achieving a unifying, totalizing, or refined personality, namely, the synthesis of soul. We may immediately question whether this form of unification and holism is possible, but the notion of a psychic "function" that leads to the experiential lived reality of a phenomenal felt transcendence within the subject harbors qualitative psychological-spiritual value. For Jung, the transcendent function was posited as arising from the "union of conscious and unconscious contents,"[21] and as an attempt to wrestle with the abyss of contradictions that lie within the psyche, specifically the "autonomous" nature of the unconscious that fuels and sustains these contradictions.

This early essay highlights Jung's insights that "the unconscious behaves in a compensatory or complementary manner towards the conscious"[22] and vise-versa. What consciousness experiences is reflexively encountered in the unconscious where competing forces and fantasies are at play, and when denials, defenses, and restrictions are imposed by thought, including practical or moral reason, this intensifies contradictory elements in both domains that seek a natural discharge. If a balance cannot be achieved, then this can lead to "one-sidedness," which is an over-compensation, but one that Jung says is "an unavoidable and necessary characteristic of the directed process"[23] mediating contradictions. Jung believed that a synthetic method could be applied in thought (whether in self-analysis or clinical treatment), which facilitates the unconscious becoming more conscious of its internal contraries and overdetermined dynamics, and hence brings about a new inner "attitude." Because Jung saw the psyche as a "self-regulating system,"[24] mutual compensatory functions serve to balance the complementarity and collaboration between conscious and unconscious factors. This tendency towards compensation acts as a regulating principle of the two psychic domains directed towards each other. By bringing together opposites and their mutual contradictions, this leads to a *third* function that may be comparable to a rudimentary dialectic: unification leads to a higher movement in thought, understanding, and judgement.

Contradictions in the psyche lead to dialectical tensions that can potentially be brought into dialogue with one another through self-conscious reflection or therapy, which can "modify the conflicting standpoints" through comparison, exchange, and "to distinguish them clearly from one another."[25] The point for Jung is that no one can deny contradictions in the psyche, in the stratified levels and parallel processes of both conscious and unconscious life, nor deny the Other within us the right to exist. Sometimes opposites are simply held in tension with each other, or in suspension or abeyance, hence allowed a co-existence, or they are transformed through confrontation with each other that allows for a creative movement out of their suspension that leads to a new inner process or situation where opposites are conjoined and integrated, what Jung equates with "wholeness and freedom."[26] Here we may observe a simpatico with Hegel.

This early essay foretells Jung's more mature work on the conundrum and resolution of opposition exemplified in his preoccupation with the coincidence of opposites (*coincidentia oppositorum*) and their complexity (*complexio oppositorum*), hence giving rise to complementarity, tensions, conflicts, compensation, and their conjunction (*coniunctio oppositorum*), therefore leading towards their union as balancing activities of the psyche teleologically oriented towards achieving a cultivated and integrated personality. Although we may question the possibility of a synthesis of internal opposition that leads to a greater principle of unity through the sublation of soul, Jung always maintained that the individuation process was a singular journey that was oriented towards greater self-awareness and actualization peculiar to each person, an idiosyncratic process of inner liberation and meaning, never a preordained destination. The only thing that is unavoidable, fated, or inescapable is our encounter with contradiction.

Coda

That which it is *not* establishes what it *is*. Being in the mode of being what I am not is the circular return of the rotary institution of contradiction. The conclusion is unequivocal: we are never complete. Desire has no bounds, no restraints, no final realization. Desire is life; it animates existence. Our divided nature within, our contradictory dispositions (in thought, feeling, pulsions, and action) is inevitable due to the teeming instantiations of desire that can never be psychologically unified in a concrete holism, but perhaps only as a conceptual (abstract) scheme Hegelianism affords. This reflects our being in relation to lack that not only can never be quenched, its fulfillment would represent and signal its end: the death of desire would mean the terminus of the dialectic, its demise. If this were the case, Psyche, Spirit, Mind—*We* would no longer exist. The main point is that we have a multitude—if not infinity—of contradictory realities that populate our psychic lives. These copious realities constitute the heterogeneity of psyche. Being able to tolerate ambiguities and mediate, sustain, and incorporate tensions between antipodes in the mind (and in society) is a cardinal goal of individuation, one's own self-defining process of becoming as the courage to be oneself.

Notes

1 See Mills (2010) for a thorough discussion.
2 Mills (2000), Hegel on Projective Identification: Implications for Klein, Bion, and Beyond.
3 Freud (1925), *An Autobiographical Study. SE*, Vol. 20, p. 57.
4 See Hegel, *Phenomenology of Spirit*, § 32; *Science of Logic*, pp. 55, 443, 449, 479.
5 Heidegger (1959), The Limitation of Being, pp. 187–188.
6 Derrida (1968), The Pit and the Pyramid, p. 73.
7 Žižek, (2006), *The Parallax View*, p. 28.
8 McGowan (2019), p. 7.
9 *Science of Logic*, p. 842.
10 McGowan (2019), p. 54.
11 Ibid, p. 14.
12 Ibid, p. 32.
13 Ibid, p. 40.
14 Ibid, p. 17.
15 *Phenomenology*, § 22.
16 See Mills (2002), pp. 11–13; 194–196.
17 *EL* § 96, *Zusatz*.
18 *SL*, p. 107.
19 Deleuze (2007), p. 365.
20 See Mills (2002) for a detailed review of Hegel's philosophical psychology.
21 Jung, The Transcendent Function. *CW*, Vol. 8, p. 69
22 Ibid.

23 Ibid, p. 71.
24 Ibid, p. 79.
25 Ibid, p. 89.
26 Ibid, p. 90.

References

Deleuze, G. (2007). *Two Regimes of Madness: Texts and Interviews 1975–1995.* Ed. D. Lapoujade, Trans. A. Hodhges & M. Taormina. New York: Semiotext(e).

Derrida, J. (1968). The Pit and the Pyramid. In A. Bass Trans., *Margins of Philosophy*, pp. 69–108. Chicago: University of Chicago Press, 1982.

Freud, S. (1925). An Autobiographical Study. In J. Strachey Trans., *The Standard Edition of the Complete Psychological Works of Sigmund Freud*, Vol. 20, pp. 7–74. London: Hogarth Press.

Hegel, G.W.F. (1807). *Phenomenology of Spirit.* Trans. A.V. Miller. Oxford: Oxford University Press, 1977.

Hegel, G.W.F. (1812/1831). *Science of Logic.* Trans. A.V. Miller. London: George Allen and Unwin Ltd., 1969.

Hegel, G.W.F. (1817/1827/1830). *The Encyclopaedia Logic.* Vol. 1 of *Encyclopaedia of the Philosophical Sciences.* Trans. T.F. Geraets, W.A. Suchting, & H.S. Harris. Indianapolis: Hackett Publishing Company, Inc, 1991.

Heidegger, M. (1959). The Limitation of Being. In *An Introduction to Metaphysics*, Trans. R. Manheim, pp. 93–206. New Haven: Yale University Press.

Jung, C.G. (1916/1958). The Transcendent Function. In *The Structure and Dynamics of the Psyche. Collected Works*, Vol. 8, pp. 67–91.

McGowan, T. (2019). *Emancipation After Hegel: Achieving a Contradictory Revolution.* New York: Columbia University Press.

Mills, J. (2010). *Origins: On the Genesis of Psychic Reality.* Montreal: McGill-Queens University Press.

Mills, J. (2002). *The Unconscious Abyss: Hegel's Anticipation of Psychoanalysis.* Albany, NY: State University of New York Press.

Mills, J. (2000). Hegel on Projective Identification: Implications for Klein, Bion, and Beyond. *The Psychoanalytic Review*, 87(6), 841–874.

Žižek, S. (2006). *The Parallax View.* Cambridge, MA: MIT Press.

Chapter 3

Existentialism and Psychoanalysis: From Antiquity to Postmodernism

The term "existentialism" is so ambiguous that it has essentially become a meaningless word: it is associated with a number of disparate
philosophical doctrines, social-political movements, and artistic sensibilities, that it becomes slippery to pin down its core philosophical
tenets to such a degree that an undertaking of this kind would be no
less rendered moot. We may nevertheless say that existentialism is a
form of phenomenological philosophy that relies on certain reflective
methods of studying human consciousness instantiated in the individual, society, and culture, which emerged as a popular general
movement characteristic of 20th century European thought represented across many disciplines including literature, the humanities, and the social sciences.

Sartre is often heralded as the father of existentialism, but surely
philosophical preoccupation with the question and meaning of
human existence dates back to antiquity. In philosophy there is often
a distinction made between the nature of "being," a broad ontological category, and that of "existence," what we generally confine to
the study of human subjectivity. From the Platonic notion of the soul
to mediaeval Aristotelian theology, to modern materialism, and
transcendental idealism, there has always been a primary fascination
with the longings and mysteries of human experience.

Sartre (1943) formally inaugurated the existential movement with
its first principle in his magnum opus *Being and Nothingness* when he
stated that "existence precedes essence." What he meant was that
existence is prior to essence, and that essence is what man makes of
his life through his lived subjective concrete acts. But this dictum goes

DOI: 10.4324/9781003305958-3

back to Descartes (1641) three centuries earlier in his *Meditations* where he avows that "I am, I exist" (p. 17). The cogito knows itself to be necessarily and indubitably true whenever it puts itself forward or is conceived in the mind. Hence Descartes showed that we know that we exist long before we know who or what we are in our essence. Even the mediaevalists believed in the necessity of starting with the experiential givens of the sensuous world and then proceeding by induction, abduction, and abstraction to the ultimate intuitive awareness of unchanging essences and internal truths—thus if anyone was an existentialist, it was surely St. Thomas (Greene, 1948). And here enters modernism. All modern philosophers from Descartes to Kant were preoccupied with the reconciliation between nature and mind, science and religion, self and society, and causality and freedom, thus giving rise to the late modern philosophies of the will and our continued preoccupation with the transcendence of the ego. For Fichte (1794), the father of German Idealism, the absolute self-positing self was a pure assertion—*I*! Schopenhauer (1818) was so enamored with the I that he believed it was the foundation for that which is both determined and that which is determining, thus *The World as Will and Representation*—the fundamental realty is will, a will that suffers. And Hegel (1807, 1817) meticulously argues that *Geist* is a self-articulated process of becoming: essence must appear in order for anything to exist, hence to be made actual (see *PS*, p. 89; *EL*, p. 199).

What does this all have to do with psychoanalysis? Everything! Anxiety and death, alienation and responsibility, meaning and possibility—the very ontological conditions that inform human subjectivity as both normative and pathological. For Kierkegaard, we live in extreme anxiety and trembling over death and dread, and despair over who we are, the very thing that defines our being, the very thing that orients us towards our future, hence our possibilities; and for Kierkegaard, that meant the ethical and spiritual life of man. Nietzsche also could not tolerate the herd mentality, where truth was far from being found in "the crowd;" but unlike Kierkegaard, he saw life as meaningless and in need of nihilistic revolt, of the transvaluation of values—to create oneself afresh—though a will to power. But the single most unremitting question for our existential man is the nature of freedom.

Sartre was an extremist: human subjectivity was radical freedom, the unabated obligation to choose how one is to be. For Sartre (1943), we are condemned to freedom—we cannot not choose, or else we plummet into self-deception or bad faith (*mauvaise foi*). The human being is not a thing, but a process of transcendence that must seize upon its freedom in order to become and define itself via its authentic choices. Psychopathology is a failure to seize upon one's freedom. Sartre's magnus opus is a treatise on existential analysis, and in many ways shares affinities with psychoanalysis, but he had one beef: Sartre could not accept nor tolerate the idea of an unconscious mind because it fractured his very thesis that we are all unconditionally self-determining. How could we be free if choice was governed by alien forces from within? Despite enjoying wide popularity, perhaps for this single attack on Freud, Sartre was not destined to find many followers among psychoanalysts of his day.

It was with Heidegger (1927) that existential analysis began to find a broader voice, and this was largely due to the dissemination of his thought by Swiss psychiatrists, Ludwig Binswanger and Medard Boss. Heidegger's influential work, *Being and Time*, one of the most celebrated texts of the 20th century, is essentially about the throws of human existence, what he refers to as *Dasein*—the concretely existing human being who is there in the world. Dasein has a relationship with itself, others, and its environment, which is constitutive of its facticity—as a being thrown into a preexisting social ontology. Like Sartre, Heidegger was preoccupied with explicating the essential elements of human existence as being in relation to its own struggles with anxiety and death, freedom and inauthenticity, and transcendence as a temporal phenomenon of seizing one's possibilities. Like Sartre's notion of bad faith, Heidegger showed that human beings have a propensity for being neurotic and living in self-deception as the fallen *Das Man*, those who gravitate towards the herd and fail to live their lives genuinely. But as with Sartre, Heidegger could neither accept the primacy of the unconscious nor the governing causality it implicitly brings forth in our conscious lives. And here, in my opinion, is a cardinal reason why existentialism remains foreclosed and underappreciated by the psychoanalytic community. While psychoanalysis underscores the primacy and ubiquity of unconscious mentation, existentialism cannot bear to have its freedom curtailed.

But this did not stop existential analysis from flourishing in Europe, and to some extent in the United States, at least for a time. The novelists, poets, journalists, and playwrights, from Dostoevsky to Rilke, Kafka, Ortega, and Camus, many of which were contemporaries of Sartre and Heidegger, swept-over the masses, also drawn to the philosophical-religious aspirations of Martin Buber, Gabriel Marcel, Paul Tillich, Frieda Fromm-Reichmann, and Erich Fromm; and in the field of mental health, Jaspers, Binswanger, Boss, Bally, Laing, Saasz, Van den Berg, Frankl, Minkowski, Ellenberger, Rollo May, and Yalom, just to name a few, did much to pave the way towards appreciating existential analysis and phenomenological psychopathology. In fact, Boss and Bally were classically trained analysts, while Binswanger, although in Switzerland, became a member of the Vienna Psychoanalytic Society at Freud's recommendation when the Zurich group split off from the International (May, 1983); although many existential therapists were under Jungian influence.

In the States, there was much more interest in existential analysis during the 1950s, perhaps in part due to burgeoning interest in humanism, social political thought, critical theory and neo-Marxism, the marginalized anti-psychiatry movement, the backlash against positivism, the seduction of Eastern spirituality, and the dehumanization of industrialized, materialistic culture. In the end, existentialism remains a multitudinous set of precepts, some systematized, but mainly recalcitrant to systematic reduction. But one irrefutable premise is that we as subjective agents are never static or inert creatures, rather we are a process of becoming, an observation made by the ancients from Heraclitus to Laotzu.

One could argue that psychoanalysis has always been an existential enterprise, and nowhere do we see this more poignantly realized than in Freud. Freud's entire metapsychology could be said to be an existential treatise on the scope, breadth, and limits to human freedom. Freud was profoundly engaged with the questions of life and death, determinism and choice, self and other, alienation and causality, so much so that his mature model of the mind is none other than a return to the Greek concept of the soul. But what Freud is capable of showing that the existentialists and phenomenologists refuse to accept, is that the unconscious is also self-determining, hence the coming to presence and actualization of freedom.

Now we seem to live in a postmodern time of skepticism concerning the existence of the self (see Frie, 2003). While postmodernism has no unified body of theory, one unanimous claim is the demise of the subject. Although postmodern thought has propitiously criticized the pervasive historical, gendered, and ethnocentric character of our understanding of the world, it has done so at the expense of displacing several key modern philosophical tenets that celebrate the nature of subjectivity, consciousness, and the teleology of the will. Consequently, the transcendental notions of freedom, autonomy, and authentic choice that comprise the fundamental activities of personal agency are altogether dismantled (Mills, 2003).

In the empirically driven world of contemporary scientific psychology, postmodernism may appear as an interesting yet marginalized phenomenon. In this sense it shares the eccentricity historically associated with existential, phenomenological, and psychoanalytic accounts that have fought for recognition from traditional psychological paradigms. However, within the larger intellectual community that comprises the humanities and behavioural sciences, we may observe a divide between science on the one side, and postmodernism on the other, each with its purported critics and adherents. Yet strangely enough, scientific and postmodern approaches yield similar implications for the fate of the self. Because scientific psychology is largely entrenched in empirically and biologically based materialistic frameworks, the dynamic activities of mind—including consciousness, cognition, and subjectivity—are imperiled by reductionist strategies. While postmodernism boasts to have subverted the subject, materialists have reduced it to a brain state. Either way, subjectivity, selfhood, and personal agency are displaced.

Eclipsed by postmodernism, psychoanalysis is even beset from within its own discipline. Hell bent on displacing classical psychoanalysis, the relational schools, or what has been called the American Middle Group, is content with chucking Freud altogether, while in my view, this movement is mainly a re-invention of the analytic wheel. While Freud has been largely discarded in the States, albeit subsumed by the rest of the world, relational and intersubjective schools are at least turning to philosophy to find a fresh breath of ideas, despite it merely being a return of old paradigms under a new guise. Contemporary psychoanalysis may become a friend to existential thought, for it is much more open to developing an appreciation for philosophy in general. With the recent translation of Heidegger's *Zollikon Seminars*, given at Boss's invitation to the psychiatrists of Zurich over a ten-year period between 1959 and 1969, we may anticipate renewed interest in reiterating the question of *Dasein* in the consulting room. But how is Heidegger as a professor of psychiatry? Let us look at a brief passage from his *Seminars*.

Heidegger: How does Dr. R. relate to the table before him?

Listener A: He is sitting behind it and looking at it.

Heidegger: At one with this, the "nature" of Dr. R.'s Dasein also reveals itself—but as what?

[Five minutes of silence]

Heidegger: I remain silent because it is senseless to want to lecture you about Dr. R's existing. Everything depends on your learning to *see* the matter for yourselves, that you are patiently attentive to the matter, so that it may reveal itself to you in the totality of its own proper meaningfulness.

Listener C: Dr. R is separated from the table by an interval of space.

Heidegger: What, then, is space?

Listener D: The distance between Dr. R. and the table.

Heidegger: What is distance?

Listener E: A definition of space.

Heidegger: What, then, is space as such?

[Ten long minutes of silence ...] (cited in Boss, 1978–79, pp. 10–11).

Well, from this example, perhaps I am a little overly optimistic that Daseinsanalysis will make a comeback; but I am still rather hopeful. Nevertheless, existential, phenomenological, and continental perspectives in philosophy complement psychoanalytic discourse, thus providing a fecundity of overlap in conceptual thought and practice that the relational schools have been increasingly acknowledging over the past few decades.

It can be said that psychoanalysis is fundamentally a theory and method geared towards insight, truth, and the amelioration of human suffering, while philosophy is the pursuit of wisdom, truth, human excellence, and rational meaning, what Freud (1927, 1930) himself identifies as *Logos*. I see these two disciples as embracing similar convictions that human existence is ultimately about developing our potential, fulfilling our possibilities, and living an authentic life through the liberation of ignorance and the malicious forces that threaten our happiness. This takes courage and fortitude, but it first and foremost takes awareness. In this way, therapy is a *liberation struggle*—Know thyself! This Delphic decree is the psychoanalytic motto. Insight or self-knowledge takes a commitment to educating oneself to what truly lies within—the complexity and competing flux of the inner world, and this is never an easy endeavour. It takes another to nurture and draw this out, to validate and reinforce, to encourage and to guide, to hold and reassure. This begins with the most primary of all relations, the relation of the embryonic self to that of its mother (or surrogate), then to its family and community at large, and finally to the social institutions that foster and beget the cultivation of self-consciousness. This is why a relational approach to treatment mirrors the natural process of self-development, for the self is equiprimordially given over to the other, and the other to the self: the subject-object split is foreclosed. Each is dynamically informed by a dialectical system of mutual implication, interaction, exchange, negotiation, and force.

Despite the vogue postmodern trend that displaces personal agency and the self, I have attempted to emphasize that human subjectivity is an indispensable and emergent experiential process of becoming. Heidegger is very clear that "Dasein exists," not as an epipheno-menon of larger cultural and linguistic forces, but as a subject who emerges within them equiprimordially. Dasein is the subjective human being who lives in a world composed of multiple dynamic organizations that are psychologically, socially, and temporally rea-lized in relation to the past, the present, and future possibilities. And just as Sartre emphasizes our subjectivity as radical freedom, and psychoanalysis as the pursuit of bringing to light that which lies hidden from our immediate conscious awareness, we exist in relation to what we can become. Ultimately in both the existential and psy-choanalytic traditions, we can only become freer through knowledge.

References

Boss, M. (1978–1979). Martin Heidegger's Zollikon Seminars. B. Kenny Trans., *Review of Existential Psychiatry and Psychology*, 16: 1–21.

Descartes, R. (1641). Meditations on First Philosophy, In J. Cottingham, R. Stoothoff, & D. Murdoch Trans., *The Philosophical Writings of Descartes: Vol. II.*, Cambridge: Cambridge University Press, 1984.

Fichte, J.G. (1794). *The Science of Knowledge*. Tans. & Eds. P. Heath & J. Lachs. Cambridge: Cambridge University Press, 1993.

Freud, S. (1905). Psychical (or Mental) Treatment. *Standard Edition*, Vol. 7. London: Hogarth Press.

Freud, S. (1923). *The Ego and the Id*. *Standard Edition*, Vol. 19. London: Hogarth Press.

Freud, S. (1926). *Inhibitions, Symptoms and Anxiety*. *Standard Edition*, Vol. 20. London: Hogarth Press.

Freud, S. (1927). *Future of an Illusion*. *Standard Edition*, Vol. 21. London: Hogarth Press.

Freud, S. (1930). *Civilization and its Discontents*. *Standard Edition*, Vol. 21. London: Hogarth Press.

Freud, S. (1933). *New Introductory Lectures on Psycho-Analysis*. *Standard Edition*, Vol. 22. London: Hogarth Press [1932].

Frie, R. (Ed.) (2003). *Understanding Experience: Psychotherapy and Postmodernism*. London: Routledge.

Greene, M. (1948). *Introduction to Existentialism*. Chicago: University of Chicago Press.

Hegel, G.F.W. (1807). *Phenomenology of Spirit*, Trans. by A.V. Miller. Oxford: Oxford University Press, 1977.

Hegel, G.F.W. (1817). *The Encyclopaedia Logic*, Trans. T.F. Geraets, W.A. Suchting, & H.S. Harris. Indianapolis: Hackett Publishing Co, 1991.

Heidegger, M. (1927). *Being and Time*. Trans. by J. Macquarrie & E. Robinson. San Francisco: Harper Collins, 1962.

May, R. (1983). *The Discovery of Being*. New York: Norton.

Mills, Jon (2003). A Phenomenology of Becoming: Reflections on Authenticity. In R. Frie (Ed.), *Understanding Experience: Psychotherapy and Postmodernism*. London: Routledge, pp. 116–136.

Sartre, J.P. (1943). *Being and Nothingness*. Trans. by H.E. Barnes. New York: Washington Square Press.

Schopenhauer, A. (1818). *The World as Will and Representation: Vol. 1–2*. Trans. by E.F.J. Payne. New York: Dover, 1969.

Chapter 4

The False Dasein: From Heidegger to Sartre and Psychoanalysis

What does it mean to be authentic? Perhaps this is a question one can never adequately answer. As elusive as the meaning of being, the question of authenticity existentially moans for a response. Although Heidegger was primarily concerned with the question of Being (*Sein*) rather than the nature of beings (*Seiende*), he was deeply interested in the interface between philosophy and psychology (Boss, 1978–1979; Guignon, 1993; Richardson, 1993).[1] Despite Heidegger's apathy toward Freudian psychoanalysis (see Craig, 1988; Richardson, 1993), his conceptualization of Dasein has direct and significant contributions for psychoanalytic thought. While there are potential conceptual quandaries between the technical, "ontological" discourse of Heideggerian theory and the applied, "ontical" discourse of psychodynamic approaches,[2] Heidegger's existential ontology has profound implications for understanding the role of the unconscious and the questions of authenticity, truth, and agency.

For Heidegger, authenticity is a uniquely temporal structure and a process of unfolding possibility. It is a state of being that is active, teleological, contemplative, and congruent—an agency burgeoning with quiescent potentiality. As such, authenticity is the process of becoming one's possibilities: by nature it is idiosyncratic and uniquely subjective. Thus, the pursuit of authenticity becomes a key therapeutic endeavor. Generally we might say that selfhood vacillates between authentic and inauthentic modes; that it tarries with genuine inauthenticity only to find itself genuinely authentic. Selfhood therefore participates in many forms on its acclivity toward apprehending its possibilities. Perhaps selfhood is beyond this antithetical

DOI: 10.4324/9781003305958-4

distinction; it merely is what it is. Perhaps authenticity is beyond the individual; it ultimately belongs to the very ontology that constitutes Being itself. This becomes particularly relevant to how Being is actualized within the process of therapy as the personal attainment of one's possibilities.

Heidegger tells us that humankind has the recalcitrant need to divulge itself as inauthenticity. Not only does Dasein unveil itself in the everyday mundane modes of existence, but it does so in a false manner. But what does it mean for Dasein to be false, that is, what are the conditions that influence the development of inauthenticity? Within this context, truth and falsity are regarded not in terms of their epistemic verity, but in reference to Dasein's states of authentic and inauthentic disclosedness. From this standpoint, is it possible that the very ontological structures of Dasein itself are false? Can the human being be thrown into a deficit world, a world tainted by fallenness and inauthenticity, so much so that it predetermines Dasein's Being-in-the-world as a falsehood? To what degree is our social environment structurally differentiated into various existential modalities that are themselves pathological, thereby affecting the very ways in which the self is disclosed? I will demonstrate that selfhood encompasses a dialectical course undulating through experiential modes of authenticity and inauthenticity, in which this very process itself is an authentic one; this is the necessary *a priori* condition of Dasein itself as Being-toward-possibility.

Dasein and Fallenness

In his philosophical treatise *Being and Time* (1927), Heidegger offers an existential ontology of selfhood as *Dasein* (to be there, presence, existing), the actual human subject who is there, as part of a world. I will retain Heidegger's terminology, as is customary, but for all practical purposes we are referring to the human being. In Dasein's original disclosedness as Being-in-the-world, one is thrust into the ontological contingency of "Being-in" an environment (*Umwelt*) and "Being-with" others (*Mitwelt*) and with-oneself (*Eigenwelt*), which underlies all participation, engagement, and concrete involvement with the world that is *given* in one's immediate preoccupations and concerns. Thus, the world itself is constitutive of Dasein's Being for

"Being-in-the-world is a state of Dasein which is necessary *a priori*, but it is far from sufficient for completely determining Dasein's Being" (*BT* § 54). As Heidegger explicates, Dasein's Being takes on a particular character *a priori*, and exists within the modes of authentic and inauthentic disclosedness.

> Dasein exists. Furthermore, Dasein is an entity which in each case I myself am. Mineness belongs to any existent Dasein, and belongs to it as the condition which makes authenticity and inauthenticity possible (*BT* § 53).

The modes of Dasein's disclosedness are already structurally constituted in Dasein's Being-in-the-world. However, they are only the existentiale conditions that make authenticity and inauthenticity possible. As Heidegger points out, these two modes of disclosedness must have ownership, that is, they necessarily belong to the subjective, singular person. For our purposes, Dasein is to be understood within the context of being a self.

As the self, Heidegger delineates the factuality of Dasein characterized by humankind's naked "thereness," one's abandonment as thrown into the publicness of "the they." As human beings disclose themselves in the everydayness of Being-in-the-world, they discover that they have been thrust into an environment without consultation or choice in the matter whatsoever, and by definition have been abandoned to chance factors which already constitute their Being. Therefore, there is a fundamental propensity of Dasein, one which belongs to everydayness and manifests itself as *das Man*. Das Man, one among "the they," is Dasein's ontological destiny. The world is a world in which one shares with others in communal proximity. Thus, Dasein's communal structure lends itself to a participation that cannot be annulled, namely, that of *they*ness. By virtue of Dasein's communal character, one cannot *not* participate in a world determined by the pragmatics of society and the everyday concerns that structure Dasein's activities.

For Heidegger, the question of authenticity becomes intimately associated with the existential character of Dasein as concern and solicitude. He states:

> If Dasein-with remains existentially constitutive for Being-in-the-world, then ... it must be Interpreted in terms of the phenomenon of *care*; for as "care" the Being of Dasein in general is to be defined. (*BT* § 121)

Just as Dasein's relation to the environment is that of practical concern, Dasein's relation to the communal world is that of personal concern. As Heidegger explains, this form of concern belonging to everydayness by necessity will ultimately lead to modes of inauthenticity. As the "anonymous one," the uniqueness of selfhood is diffused and lost in depersonalization and "averageness."

> Being for, against, or without one another, passing one another by, not "mattering" to one another—these are possible ways of solicitude. And it is precisely these last-named deficient and Indifferent modes that characterize everyday, average Being-with-one-another. (*BT* § 121)

Heidegger expounds upon another structural element in the ontological constitution of Dasein, that of "fallenness." This is the universal tendency of human beings to lose themselves in the everydayness of present concerns and preoccupations to such a degree that it does nothing but alienate them from their personal and unique future possibilities, thus reducing the fallen *das Man* to a mere "presence-at-hand." He posits:

> This "absorption in ... " [*Aufgehen bei*] has mostly the character of Being-lost in the publicness of the "they". Dasein has, in the first instance, fallen away [*abgefallen*] from itself as an authentic potentiality for Being its Self, and has fallen into the 'world'. (*BT* § 176)

Everydayness and fallenness are ontological and natural predispositions of Dasein, therefore devoid of any value judgements attached to them; nevertheless, they are modes of inauthenticity that cannot be avoided nor refused. The degree to which one participates in these inauthentic modes has a direct bearing on the existential status of falsehood.

As a perpetual mode of inauthenticity, the falseness of Dasein becomes manifested as a "'levelling down' [*Einebnung*] of all possibilities of Being" (*BT* § 127). The fallenness of Dasein is expressed most ostensively through idle talk, curiosity, and ambiguity. Gossip is an inauthentic use of discourse which simply repeats what is heard and accepted by the public without critically examining the grounds or validity of the subject matter under question. Idle talk is merely a repetition of the conventional, an unscrutinized acceptance of the interpretations of the public. The fallen *das Man* is not concerned with understanding the ontological priorities of what is blindly accepted as truth or fact, only in reiterating the public clichés of the "anonymous one." Curiosity, which parallels gossip, underscores Dasein's hunger to explore one's environment merely for the sake of discovering novelty that provides excitement, a pleasurable distraction, and knowledge simply in order to have known. Curiosity, therefore, is not motivated out of the need for authentic understanding; it is merely an inauthentic form of solicitude. Ambiguity, on the other hand, is the dubious nature of information which is disseminated by "the they," which makes it impossible to determine what was disclosed in genuine understanding and what was not. This ambiguity is not only about the public gossip, but also in reference to Being-with-one-another, and Dasein's Being-toward-itself, hence, an inauthentic relatedness.

At this point, we must further clarify what we mean by Dasein's falsehood. In Section 44 of *Being and Time*, Heidegger (1927) discusses the relationship between Dasein, disclosedness, and truth. This was the beginning of his later preoccupation with the preSocratic notion of ἀλήθεια, which he translates as *Unverborgenheit* or "unconcealedness." Truth or *aletheia* is a form of disclosure, unconcealment, or uncoveredness that reveals itself through that which appears. Heidegger continues his analysis in "On the Essence of Truth" (1930), where he offers a more comprehensive engagement of this subject. Truth may only be disclosed from its hiddenness in a clearing that opens a space for unconcealment. Equally, as each space reveals the potentiality for truth to be made known, there is also conversely a closing, in that truth may only be revealed in the wake of concealment. Such movement of uncovering in the presence of covering underlies the dialectical participation of the nature of truth.

Given Heidegger's very careful analysis of *aletheia*, how can Dasein be false? From this standpoint, truth and falsity are in reference to unconcealed states of Dasein's disclosedness, not in terms of their epistemological status. Therefore, the anonymous one, the fallen *das Man*, the identification with "the they" of everydayness as averageness is a direct allusion to a constricted Dasein. This inauthentic mode of Being is a retreat from the ontological obligations that Dasein demands. In these extreme modes, Dasein is a reduced self, a stifled existence, a false Being. In addition, the false Dasein as Being-in and Being-with "the they," starts to take on an existential character which is more negative, similar to Kierkegaard's notion of "the crowd," or even more pejoratively, the Nietzschean "herd." The Dasein who has fallen into falsehood closes itself off from authentically Being-in-the-world, and even more significantly of Being-with and Being-toward itself. In psychoanalysis, this might be chalked up to the defense mechanism of denial, that is, people need to deny the ontological obligations of Dasein in the service of more primordial psychological needs or conflicts, such as psychodynamic motivations surrounding security, attachment, and, as Heidegger points out, "tranquility." But as he continues to point out, this tranquility leads to an "aggravation" and alienation of Dasein from itself. Heidegger states:

> When Dasein, tranquilized, and 'understanding' everything, thus compares itself with everything, it drifts along towards an alienation [*Entfremdung*] in which its ownmost potentiality-for-Being is hidden from it. (*BT* § 178)

Fallenness leads to the "downward plunge" into the inauthentic Being of "the they" in which authentic possibility is lost in obscurity and under the guise of "ascending" and "living concretely." Is it possible, however, that this downhill plunge is a necessary one which provides the dialectical movement towards the fulfillment of Dasein's possibilities? Perhaps this turbulent necessity is the very authentic movement of Dasein towards itself as *becoming*. Rather than falling away from itself, Dasein is falling into itself. But this is only possible if Dasein becomes aware of its possibilities that it hides from itself. At this point we must ask, Why does Dasein close off its possibilities in the tranquility of fallenness rather than seize them authentically? In other words, why do we hide ourselves from our own potentiality-for-Being? Perhaps Dasein is afraid, afraid of its freedom.

Dasein in Bad Faith

In offering an existential analysis of authenticity, we have determined that Dasein's fundamental structure is ontologically oriented towards fallenness. In the case of the false Dasein, fallenness is exacerbated in that the subject constricts its comportment primarily to the modes of the inauthentic, thereby abdicating its potentiality-for-Being. Why would Dasein abnegate its potentiality? While theoretically distinct from Heidegger's existential ontology, Sartre's conception of in-authenticity further contributes to our understanding of the psychological-ontical processes immersed in Dasein's falsehood.[3]

In his magnum opus, *Being and Nothingness* (1943), Sartre introduced the notion of *mauvaise foi*, or bad faith. For Sartre, consciousness is Being, "a being, the nature of which is to question its own being, that being implying a being other than itself"; that is, "to be conscious of the nothingness of its being" (*BN*, p.86). In other words, authentic Being is literally *no-thing*. Conversely, self-negation is the pinnacle of inauthenticity. The failure to define oneself as *other-than* what one is, is to reify oneself as a thing and thus deny the possibility of a future transcendence. Sartre asserts that "consciousness instead of directing its negation outward turns it toward itself. This attitude, it seems to me, is *bad faith* (*mauvaise foi*)" (*BN*, p. 87).

Broadly stated, bad faith is characterized by self-deception, a lie to oneself. But how can one lie to oneself? Only if one is not consciously aware of such intentions to lie or to deceive. For the individual in bad faith, the nature of such a lie "is not recognized by the liar as *his* intention" (*BN*, p. 88, original emphasis). While a genuine lie is a "behaviour of transcendence," the bad faith lie is a denial of such possibility. Such is the case that liars find themselves as the victim of their own self-deception and live in falsehood.

> By the lie consciousness affirms that it exists by nature as *hidden from the Other*; it utilizes for its own profit the ontological duality of myself and myself in the eyes of the Other. The situation can

not be the same for bad faith if this, as we have said, is indeed a lie to oneself. To be sure, the one who practices bad faith is hiding a displeasing truth or presenting as truth a pleasing untruth. Bad faith then has in appearance the structure of falsehood. Only what changes everything is the fact than in bad faith it is from myself that I am hiding the truth (*BN*, pp. 88–89, original emphasis).

Sartre's notion of bad faith is intimately linked to his model of consciousness. He recognized two levels of consciousness: (1) consciousness as intentionality and self-reflection, and (2) prereflective consciousness. The former is consciousness as such and encompasses awareness of the self as a human subject. Prereflective consciousness, on the other hand, is the form of consciousness prior to being aware (of) an object for reflection. This is similar to Freud's notion of pre-consciousness, that is, one is not immediately aware of an internal event or object but could be if one's attention were drawn to that particular object for reflection. But we could say that self-deception is always informed by unconscious defense. Sartre vociferously repudiated the notion of the Freudian unconscious; instead, his model espouses Brentano's concept of intentionality. Consciousness is always conscious *of* or *about* something—conscious of some object we posit or place before us for reflection. Therefore, there is no inertia to consciousness; consciousness is not an object nor does it exist in itself. For Sartre, consciousness can be positional or non-positional. Consciousness that posits places an object before it for immediate reflection. Non-positional consciousness is consciousness by itself. Consciousness is experienced as a "lack," a *hole* in being. In Sartre's view, consciousness is nothingness, a freedom compelled to fill its own lack through future projects. Therefore, consciousness is what it is not and is not what it is. For Sartre, we are more than what we can be if we are reduced to what we are. What we are is freedom, and as freedom we are transcendence.[4]

Bad faith can manifest in various existential modalities, from singular situational choices to patterns of self-deception, such as in disavowal or Pollyannish denial, or as one could argue, character structure. Nevertheless, there is a double face to bad faith, namely: (1) *facticity* and (2) *transcendence*. In the first case, bad faith is the failure to accept one's facticity. In the second, it is a failure of transcendence. For example, Sartre portrays a woman who consents to go out with a man for the first time and in her bad faith she denies his intentions behind the seductions of his conduct. "She does not want to realize the urgency" of the moment and "refuses to apprehend the desire for what it is" (*BN*, pp. 96–97). Throughout the flirtations, her companion places her in such a position as to require an immediate decision, only to be protracted and disguised by the various procedures she uses to maintain herself in this self-deception. Her "aim is to postpone the moment of decision as long as possible" (*BN*, p. 97). In Sartre's example, the woman has failed to project a future, and has allowed herself not to take notice of the reality of the situation. Her decision rests in the locus of prereflective consciousness: she chose not to posit a future with her suitor, thus deceiving herself of such possibility.

> She has disarmed the actions of her companion by reducing them to being only what they are; that is, to existing in the mode of the in-itself. But she permits herself to enjoy his desire, to the extent that she will apprehend it as not being what it is, will recognize its transcendence (*BN*, pp. 97–98).

According to Sartre, the woman has reduced herself to a thing, a passive object in which events happen to her that she can neither provoke nor avoid. In bad faith, the person is in possession of the truth, but fails to acknowledge it as such, thereby avoiding the responsibility it requires.

For Sartre, authenticity or good faith is when you represent yourself to yourself in the mode of being what you are not. The bad faith attitude is one in which the individual seeks to flee from their freedom and the obligations it demands by construing oneself as a thing, a Being-in-itself, rather than a Being-for-itself. Instead of, "I am in the mode of being what I am *not*," the bad faith attitude is "I am in the mode of being what I am," thus, a thing-in-itself. In short, as human agents we *must* choose. As long as one consciously chooses in freedom and accepts full responsibility for one's actions, one is in good faith. Human beings define and redefine themselves via their choices. Decisions are made in the interest of a value or one is in bad faith. This is the case when one fails to choose, or more appropriately, when one *chooses not to choose* authentically.

Sartre's portrayal of bad faith elucidates the psychological nuances of self-deception that are structurally instantiated in Dasein's ontical practices. For Heidegger, bad faith would be a deficient mode of Dasein's Being-in-the-world; more specifically, Being-with-oneself and Being-toward one's future authentic possibilities. Within this general context, Dasein's fallenness is bad faith, a falsehood, a retreat into the everydayness of theyness, cloaked by self-deception. Furthermore, to deny our human reality as freedom by defining ourselves as a thing is Dasein's propensity to reduce itself to a mere "presence-at-hand."

If Sartre's depiction of bad faith is accurate, then every human being is in self-deception at one time or another. In fact, this is a necessary ontical condition of Dasein itself. Due to our penchant to fall into inauthentic modes of Being-in-the-world, Dasein will inevitably engage in such deceptive practices. For Sartre, we are condemned to freedom, which necessitates radical responsibility for our Being-for-itself. However, choices are made in the context of our ontological facticity and thus are affected by a milieu which, by definition, is deficient or inauthentic. Sartre's position ultimately demands for Being to transcend its ontological structures via choice. To what degree is this possible? Furthermore, he ostensibly denies the primordial motivations attributed to a dynamic unconscious. While Sartre rejected the psychoanalytic project, his delineation of inauthenticity contributes to the psychodynamic conceptualization of the primacy of ego organization in personality development. Again, we might say that bad faith is a defensive form of denial, a disavowal in the service of unconscious motivations, conflicts, and wishes. Sartre assumes that *every* Being has the *same* developmental capacities and intrapsychic structures to choose authentically as free agents. But what if one's freedom to recognize authentic choices has been truncated due to structural deficits in psychological development? Here, is it possible that Being itself is robbed of its full potential for authenticity?

The False Self

While the predisposition towards inauthenticity is an elemental condition of Dasein's facticity, the specific psychological dimensions of Dasein's falseness require further exploration. Dasein's psychological structures become more lucid with the assistance of a psychoanalytic explication of the self.

What would it be like to not know who you are, to be alienated from your true sense of self? What would it be like to have to construct an identity that is ingenuine and artificially manufactured? What would it be like to not feel real? Within psychoanalysis, there has been a burgeoning interest in the clinical literature on the concept of the false self (Cassimatis, 1984; Chescheir, 1985; Khan, 1971; Lerner, 1985; Naso, 2010; Schacht, 1988). The inauthentic self, or the "as if" personality, further deepens our understanding of the false Dasein.

Winnicott (1960) formally introduced the notion of the false self. While some parallels exist between Heidegger's exposition of the fallen Dasein and Sartre's depiction of bad faith, Winnicott's contributions to understanding the question of authenticity deserve special merit. For Winnicott, a false self is the result of developmental conflict encountered in the child-maternal relationship or its equivalent. As a result, a false self is constructed as a defensive system which remains unconsciously maintained. Winnicott's theoretical framework falls within a defense model that is ultimately tied to drive theory within the interpersonal context of the mother-child dyad but it may be readily interpreted through an attachment paradigm. While having a ground in Freudian metapsychology, Winnicott's conceptualization of the false self is essentially a relational theory centring on ego defensive manoeuvres that arise in response to environmental demands. More specifically, within the infant-mother milieu, the child struggles to manage libidinal/creative impulses that are solely intrapsychic; however, this takes place within the context of the relational matrix or intersubjective field. Therefore, within the stage of the first object relationships, various defenses are constructed in response to external demands, and particularly that of the maternal object. Ego organization is in the service of adaptation to the environment and procurement of object attachment. Repeated compliance to such demands, concomitant with a withdrawal from self-generated spontaneity, leads to an increased stifling of impulses constitutive of the natural drive for spontaneous expression, thereby culminating in a false self development.

For Winnicott (1960), the idea of a true self originates in the capacity of the infant to recognize and enact spontaneous needs for self-expression. "Only the True Self can be creative and only the True Self can feel real" (p.148). The notion of the self as the centre of spontaneity that has the "experience of aliveness" constitutes the core or heart of authenticity. However, this ability to enact such spontaneous gestures is contingent upon the responsiveness of the "good-enough mother" within an appropriate "holding environment." Thus, the etiology of the true and false self is contingent upon the quality of maternal responsiveness. Winnicott postulates:

> The good-enough mother meets the omnipotence of the infant and to some extent makes sense of it. She does this repeatedly. A True Self begins to have life, through the strength given to the infant's weak ego by the mother's implementation of the infant's omnipotent expressions (p. 145).

The true self flourishes only in response to the repeated success of the mother's optimal responsiveness to the infant's spontaneous expressions. If the mother is "not good-enough," she does not facilitate the infant's omnipotence and repeatedly fails to meet the child's spontaneous gestures with appropriate responsiveness. Instead she substitutes her own gestures with which the infant complies. This repeated compliance becomes the ground for the earliest modes of a false self existence due to the mother's inability to sense and respond optimally to her baby's needs.

Like Heidegger's hermeneutical treatment of Dasein's ontology, Winnicott obviates the subject-object dichotomy with regards to the ontical structures of the self. The maternal holding environment is part of the very ontic structure of Dasein: it is constitutive of Dasein's Being. Failure in empathic attunement, mirroring, and optimal responsiveness is a deficient mode of Being-with, a precondition of the false Dasein's inauthenticity. Within this context, freedom becomes abridged and affects the true self development *as it would have unfolded* if Dasein's ontological constitution of Being-with had been different. Authenticity is curtailed by the demands of others. In this sense, there is no authentic self distinct from Being-with others. Winnicott supports this claim: "This compliance on the part of the infant is the earliest stage of the False Self, and belongs to the mother's inability to sense her infant's needs" (p. 145). Under these circumstances, perhaps a false self is not false at all. The false structures are authentic ones, that is, they are superimposed and constitutive of a true self, albeit a deficient one. Due to the historicity of various ontological contingencies that are themselves deficient modes of Being-in-the-world, Dasein is subjected to differential power relations by the very ontological positioning of worldhood itself. The same could be said of growing up in a traumatized society where every structural relation to being in the world is negatively affected. Dasein's Being-with others and toward-oneself will be greatly affected by other's deficiencies. Winnicott (1960) explains that:

> the infant gets seduced into compliance, and a compliant False Self reacts to environmental demands and the infant seems to accept them. Through this False Self the infant builds up a false set of relationships, and by means of introjections even attains a show of being real, so that the child may grow up to be just like mother, nurse, aunt, brother, or whoever at the time dominates the scene (p. 146).

The defensive functions of the false self are constructed for one cardinal purpose, namely, "to hide and protect the True Self" (p. 142). "The False Self defends the True Self; the True Self is, however, acknowledged as a potential and is allowed a secret life" (p. 143). But what is the nature of this true or authentic self which is allowed a secret life? Winnicott does not offer an adequate explanation, he only points to the ability to enact spontaneous gestures of self-expression: "The True Self appears as soon as there is any mental organization of the individual at all, and it means little more than the summation of sensori-motor aliveness" (p. 149). But is this a sufficient understanding of authenticity? Doesn't the notion of authenticity carry with it, if not demand of it, that Dasein *can* to some degree transcend its mere thrownness; that is, choose actively to seize upon its subjective agency despite its environment?

Clearly Dasein is more than its physiological and material contingencies. On one level, to be authentic or true is to act in accord with one's genuine and congruent, innate strivings and yearnings. Within the various psychoanalytic domains, authenticity may conform to the influence of unconscious drive determinants, ego mastery of the self and the environment, object relatedness and the pining for relational attachments, and the psychic need for mirroring and idealizing selfobject experiences that form the rudimentary basis of a vital and cohesive self. Whatever the nature or *being* of these authentic strivings are, Winnicott assumes they exist, are hidden, and are preserved unconsciously due to the character structure of defense.

Winnicott concludes that the false self takes on a role which appears to be "real," when in fact it is artificial. Indeed, this pseudo-real appearance takes on a "personal living through imitation" in which the child may "act a special role, that of the True Self *as it would be if it had had existence*" (p. 147, original emphasis). However, for Winnicott, the true self always exists behind the mask of the false persona, lying dormant, concealed, and protected. The false self, as defense, is "a defence against that which is unthinkable, the exploitation of the True Self, which would result in its annihilation" (p. 147). Thus, the etiology of the false self may be said to arise out of the deficient modes of other Daseins, which were foisted upon the child with various ontological and psychological exigencies to comply with or perish under. It may be said that a false personality constellation, such as a histrionic persona, is constructed in reaction to the fear of death of the self. Such fear of annihilation is the most archaic form of existential anxiety, a primordial denial of Dasein's Being-toward-death.

The unconscious displacement of the emerging annihilation anxiety is organized within the interpersonal matrix of the infant's earliest attachments or object relations. Within this context, Masterson (1981) defines the false self as "a collection of behaviors, thoughts and feelings that are motivated by the need to cling to the object," and thus suppress the longings for separateness and individuation (p. 101). Within contemporary object relations theory, the false self functions defensively as a means to ward off separation anxiety and abandonment fears that ultimately represent the inability to integrate whole self and object representations, which in turn become the formative basis of a cohesive self. As a result, the capacity for spontaneity, autonomous self-assertion, and the expression of creativity is stymied and lost in falsehood.

Winnicott's developmental model anticipates Kohut's (1971, 1977, 1984) psychoanalytic self psychology. For Kohut, the self is a bipolar structure composed of two dimensions: (1) the pole of ambitions and strivings, and (2) the pole of values and ideals. The former constitutes mirroring selfobject experiences in which the authentic core self is the centre of initiative, self-assertion, autonomy, and vitality. The second pole is attained via the identification process and merger with omnipotent, calming, infallible selfobjects that are in turn internalized and become the intrapsychic structural foundation of the self. As Kohut (1978) theoretically moved away from the metapsychology of classical theory, the primacy of the self replaced the vicissitudes of the drives as "the center of our being from which all initiative springs and where all experience ends" (p. 95). The self, as the centre of initiative and psychic motivation, depends upon the quality of selfobject experiences for its structural integrity and cohesion. Within this context, a false self would develop out of repeated failure in empathic attunement and optimal responsiveness in the early selfobject milieu. If the self becomes defined in the context of others' narcissistic needs, capacities for self-soothing and self-esteem regulation are thwarted due to a depleted or fragmented self structure.

The false self can manifest in various modalities and in degrees of its falseness. The more psychologically adjusted false self organization may be represented by the overly compliant, obsequious, acquiescent, interpersonally polite attitudes that accompany the expectations of social convention. This may be similar to Heidegger's description of Dasein's everydayness as fallenness in the modes of idle talk, curiosity, and ambiguity. In terms of Sartrean bad faith, one makes inauthentic choices which are situational, repetitive, or characterological in the service of avoiding one's responsibility to accept freedom. In other words, by choosing not to choose authentically, we reside in the everyday inauthentic mode of "theyness" as fallen *das Man*.

For contemporary psychoanalysis, Dasein's tendency towards fallenness serves primary motivations for relational attachment, emotional-interpersonal involvement, and validation of the self. In the case of the false Dasein, such wishes are inordinately intensified due to intrapsychic structural vulnerabilities of the self. Alice Miller (1981) discusses a particular form of false development, that of individuals who are raised by narcissistic parents and are cajoled into being responsive and attuned to everyone else's needs at the expense of their own. Children who are treated as objects to meet the narcissistic fulfillments of their parents may develop a virtuous yet tragic gift, the gift of empathy. Gifted children in this sense may develop skills of empathic attunement to anticipate, respond to, and meet the wishes of others in order to gain love and attention of their own; but only at the steep price of sacrificing their true self.

Still more towards maladjustment, one could say the false self is the "actor" who puts on a theatrical facade but is unable to remove such persona; the actor becomes over-identified in the role and loses one's authenticity in one-sidedness.[5] Under the rubric of such one-sidedness, individuals seek to make themselves into a "thing," a Being-in-itself rather than a Being-for-Self. Winnicott (1960) asserts, "Whereas a True Self feels real, the existence of a False Self results in a feeling unreal or a sense of futility" (p. 148). He continues: "The best example I can give is that of a middle-aged woman who had a very successful False Self but who had the feeling all her life that she had not started to exist" (p. 142). In the severe forms of the psychiatrically impaired, a false self system consists of an organization of various part-selves, none of which are so fully developed as to have a comprehensive personality of their own. This clinical phenomenon is what R.D. Laing (1959) spoke of as the *divided self*. In a divided self, there is no single false self, rather only partially elaborated fragments which might constitute a personality. In the Daseinsanalytic tradition (see Kockelmans, 1978), for Laing, as well as for Ludwig Binswanger, Medard Boss, Karl Jaspers, and more contemporarily Rollo May, a false self develops out of ontological insecurity, thereby leading to an overall constricted Dasein. To the extreme, the false or divided self may experience a dissociation of personality or a radical splitting of its embodied and disembodied aspects.

The Call of Conscience

Up until now, we have delineated the ontological and psychological structures of the false Dasein as inauthenticity maintains itself in the throes of selfhood. By virtue of Dasein's ontological predisposition as Being-in-the world, selfhood is subjected to inauthentic existential modalities already constitutive of its Being. Such disclosedness to worldhood is formatively installed in Dasein's constitution. Dasein's propensity towards fallenness is therefore necessary and unavoidable. However, if environmental conditions are such that Dasein's ordinary ontological structure is subject to more extreme forms of inauthenticity, the false development of the subject may not be eluded. The false Dasein results from interactions with pre-existing deficient modes of Being-in-the-world that are thrust upon selfhood as its facticity. These pathogenic ontological structures lead to further vulnerabilities that predispose Dasein to develop psychological deficiencies as well. Such intrapsychic conflicts and structural limitations of the self further contribute to Dasein's *pathos* as deficient modes of Being-in-the-world and Being-toward-Self.

Given these assumptions, worldhood itself may be said to be a falsehood, plagued by bad faith and copious forms of psychopathology. Can Dasein transcend its predicament, or is it destined to live inauthentically? As Heidegger and Sartre would contend (albeit conceptualized differently), ultimately the self is free. However, freedom exists within the context of Dasein's ontological constitution. For Ricoeur (1965, 1966), Dasein primarily exists as fallenness in the sense that the will is enslaved by its actual conditions. In the case of the false self, Dasein is constricted by virtue of its ontological relation to a deficient environment that contributes to deficits in one's psychological development. Assuming this is the case, does this imperfect condition lead to another proclivity of Dasein to fall even further into inauthenticity? That is, if the environment into which one was hurled was ontologically inadequate to begin with, is not this bound to affect one's future overall Being-in-the-world? Is not the subject's Being-in and Being-with others and with-oneself greatly precluded from genuine authenticity, or at least the full possibility of such? And where do freedom and responsibility fit in for Dasein's future possibilities?

We as human beings have no control whatsoever over our thrownness (as authenticity in the toils of inauthenticity). However, as Heidegger and Sartre would insist, Dasein has the capacity and responsibility to choose authentically, thereby, actualizing its freedom to become and fulfill its possibilities. However, is this a correct assumption? Winnicott and Kohut underscore the point that one's true self or authentic Dasein may be structurally deficient, hence false. This structural deficiency is due not merely to Dasein's historicity, which may bring about self-deception, but also to developmental interactions that form the psychological basis of a cohesive self. That is, the very intrapsychic foundation of the self is deficit and replete with tumultuous unconscious conflict, thereby influencing choices and the modes Dasein assumes in the pursuit of authenticity. Perhaps the false Dasein does not have these capacities that are more authentically developed in other people, thereby encumbering the ability to form genuine good faith comportments characteristic of an authentic posture. Is it possible that the individual's intrapsychic structures are so deficit that the emergence of a false character organization is not false at all, only deficient in comparison to others' whose ontological and developmental constitutions are proportionally less false? Is the false Dasein destined to make choices that are dynamically informed by such limitations under the influence of psychic determinism? Are these processes set firmly in place as unwavering constitutional vulnerabilities, or is there an inner motivation, so that underdeveloped structures would resume their appropriate developmental trajectory if given the opportunity? And what would constitute this opportunity—a modification of Dasein's introspective capacities as recognizing and then actualizing its freedom within the context of its thrownness? Would this also require a modification from the social environment as well? Does the hidden true self strive for authentic expression despite its false structure, or is this false structure its very true or authentic mode to begin with?

If selfhood is abandoned to falsehood that is already constitutive *a priori* of its Being, then the false Dasein will structurally exist (both ontologically and developmentally) in authenticity, but in deficient modes. In other words, false self structure is authentic given Dasein's ontological contingencies that inform these deficient modes of Being. However, these constitutional deficiencies may lead the false Dasein to develop even further deficient modes of Being-in-the-world, including, at the very least, the psychoanalytic observation that we are all neurotic, it is simply a matter of degree. But these ontological deficiencies may further lead to states of psychopathology. The false

Dasein is a real system; it is primary and true although it is stifled in its development. Due to these partially underdeveloped psychic structures, it is unformed in its potential, whereby its internal states directly perpetuate inauthentic modes of Being. Although the false Dasein is real, it is deficient and impedes more healthy aspects of the self from flourishing. Therefore, the *lie* or the falsehood is experienced as psychically real albeit in the modes of the inauthentic.

At this point we must ask: To what degree does the false Dasein have responsibility to its authentic possibilities? Can the false subject overcome its fallenness and its psychological vulnerabilities as well? Can it alter its ontological and developmental status? Heidegger differentiates: "The Self of everyday Dasein is the *they-self*, which we distinguish from the *authentic Self*—that is, from the Self which has been taken hold of in its own way [*eigens ergriffenen*]" (*BT* § 129). Can the false Dasein take hold of its true nature as transcendental possibility? Like Sartre's position on self-deception, Winnicott would maintain that the false self hides the inner realities of the true self. In this interpretation, unlike Sartre's, the unconscious cannot be denied. These authentic strivings, wishes, and yearnings will always be allowed to have a secret life in the night-like abyss of the unconscious mind, and their disillusionments will be endured. But what resonates within the nocturnal pit of Dasein's core Being? Perhaps it is Dasein's transcendental authenticity as the "potentiality-for-Being which must be made free in one's *ownmost* Dasein alone" (*BT* § 178).

For Heidegger, authenticity is ultimately self-relatedness (within world-relatedness) marked by the embracing of Dasein's responsibility towards genuine care. This care, in other words, is an ownership of Dasein's freedom that, in turn, opens a space for sublimated authenticity, which perennially exalts itself in its self-world relation. For Heidegger, this necessitates the "call of conscience," the voice of Dasein within Dasein that summons us to respond to an authentic appeal to transcend the corrupted public everydayness of Being and to call Dasein to a new possibility of Being. It is the voice of authentic Dasein's Being-toward authentic possibility. It summons *me*, it commands me towards myself. Such authentic relationship to our true possibilities of Being-toward-possibility must be born/e out of our own experience, clamoring for a higher unity of Being. Authentic Being-one's-Self requires an existentiell modification of the "they" in

which "Dasein specifically brings itself back to itself from its lostness" (*BT* § 268). Authentic Dasein must "make up" for not living
and choosing genuinely and must first make possible its authentic
potentiality-for-Being. Dasein comes to find itself through the disclosure of conscience as an inner voice. The receptivity of the voice
calls Dasein to a "giving-to-understand" the authentic self, in which
the call "passes over" the they-self and finds its true home in its enlightened understanding of its authentic actuality. Heidegger articu-
lates:

> One must keep in mind that when we designate the conscience as
> a "call," this call is an appeal to the they-self in its Self; as such an
> appeal, it summons the Self to its potentiality-for-Being-its-Self,
> and thus calls Dasein forth to its possibilities (*BT* § 274).

As conscience, Dasein calls itself; it is both the caller and the one
being called. The voice of conscience has the character of an appeal
"*summoning* to its ownmost Being-guilty" (*BT* § 269). Such guilt,
however, is not a moral or psychological guilt, rather an indebted,
beholden obligation Dasein has towards its responsibility to become
and fulfill itself as Being-in-the-world. Dasein must seize upon such
guilt in that it "owes" something to itself and to others. It is the call
of care, in which its lostness is recovered in its apprehension of its
obligation to be *other-than* what it is in its everydayness.

But what does the voice say? It says nothing. The content or
substance of such call is empty; it is the inner voice without words, an
appeal without authority, a summons without a notice, merely the
"call of care." The call is the inner guidance of truth, an enlightenment that "points *forward* to Dasein's potentiality-for-Being" (*BT*
§ 280). This call comes from the uncanniness it experiences in its guilt,
which makes Dasein inextricably responsible for its own authentic
becoming. Such uncanniness arouses a ubiquitous anxiety, directed
towards its truth as "resoluteness." As a distinctive mode of Dasein's
disclosedness, resoluteness is the truth of Dasein's authenticity as
Being-one's-Self, as concern for Being-alongside what is ready-to-
hand and the solicitous care of Being-with-others. As positive solicitude in Dasein's Being-with, authenticity is a special form of concern, that which is a "leap ahead" of the Other, a genuine care that

helps the Other "become transparent to himself *in* his care and to become *free for* it" (*BT* § 122). Equiprimordially, such transparency must apply to Dasein's Being-toward-itself as care.

On one level, the truly authentic Dasein is idiosyncratic, it is uniquely subjective and personal, much like Jung's individuation process. Heidegger supports this position:

> When the call gives us a potentiality-for-Being to understand, it does not give us one which is ideal and universal; it discloses it as that which has been currently individualized and which belongs to that particular Dasein. (*BT* § 280)

Within this context, authenticity is a Being who contemplates itself, a Being who transforms itself. As authenticity, Dasein is care. Authenticity is Dasein's possibility *as such*; a fundamental relatedness of possibility-toward-becoming as an indeterminate openness to oneself. Authenticity is then, simply, *to be*, to be in selfhood that is a fundamental openness, rather than a self-enclosed, self-enslaved participation in everydayness. It is the relatedness of Being-toward-transcendence in its purist form.

But what are we to make of Heidegger's final determination of authenticity? One is left with a sense of generic ambiguity. Authenticity is opaque and equivocal. It follows a voice that does not speak, it points to a direction that is not visible, it summons us to respond to a calling we cannot identify; yet it appeals to an obligation that cannot be disowned. Perhaps authenticity is *beyond* what words can define, only Dasein knows its truth. Yet this conclusion always runs the risk of collapsing into relativism or radical subjectivism. Despite Heidegger's insistence that the authentic call is "individualized," we may nevertheless say it is in the *form* of care, which becomes a *subjective universality* belonging to a phenomenology of becoming.

Is there such a clear-cut demarcation between authenticity and inauthenticity? I think not. Instead of these antipodes, we need to understand selfhood as an epigenetic development on a continuum of authenticity, in a state of becoming as emerging freedom. How are we really to determine the criteria of what constitutes an authentic from an inauthentic Dasein when these ontic-existentiell conditions are indissolubly determined in Dasein's own Being? This would mean authenticity transcends normative standards, as only *you* can fashion your own life. If Dasein is its disclosedness, in that we disclose ourselves and then discover ourselves in our disclosing or unconcealment, then the false Dasein is only one mode of Being-in-the-world capable of finding itself in its lostness and recovering its authenticity in its freedom. Therefore, the false Dasein is capable of hearing the call, understanding the message, responding to the subpoena by following the path of possibility, and transcending its thrownness in its Being-toward-becoming. The horizon of possibility is Dasein.

Concluding Reflections

Throughout our quest for authenticity, we have seen how inauthenticity is maintained within an authentic falsehood ontologically constituted in Dasein's existential disclosedness. Despite the false Dasein's inauthentic comportment as Being-in-the-world, we have determined that it *is* indeed possible for Dasein to transcend its inauthenticity, even in the case of the false self, by apprehending its authentic Being-toward-possibility in its potentiality-for-Self. In other words, despite intrapsychic deficits characteristic of the psychoanalytic description of the false self, Dasein *can* ennoble itself in actualizing its freedom. Perhaps the interface between Heideggerian philosophy and psychoanalysis provides us with a clearer window into the possibilities for selfhood and gives us a more profound grasp on what it is to be.

In conclusion, I believe there is, for Dasein, a *double edge of centredness*: namely, the authentic centre of selfhood is one in the same, inseparable and ontologically undifferentiated in that authenticity and inauthenticity exist in symbiosis as the core dialectical function of Dasein's Being. Dasein is beyond the authentic and the impure; a disclosure of such unification is its wholeness. In the phenomenon of falsehood, everydayness is a deficient mode, yet a necessary complement to the dialectical organization of selfhood. In this sense, existence is neutral: it discloses the conditions not only for fallenness, but also for transcendence as Dasein's emphatic destiny. The choice can only be Dasein's. As a temporal trajectory, authentic Dasein is a *movement*, an incessant opening and closing of itself to itself, entering into the mode of the inauthentic only to discover its authenticity in such violent process. Indeed, this process is an authentic one, a continual movement on the continuum, sublimating and elevating itself in awareness, understanding, and action. Authenticity is therefore merely a moment, the indeterminate immediate. Bound within its temporal unfolding, authenticity is *Being-in-becoming* one's possibilities. As the possibility-for-Self, authenticity is only one appearance among many appearances. It emerges from itself and passes away back into itself, coming to be what it already is, the process of its own becoming. As an existentiell, the discovery or realization of one's inauthentic modes of Being necessitates, if not commands, a dialectical progression towards the fulfillment of one's authentic possibilities in the endless search of the true self. This double edge is Dasein.

Notes

1 Heidegger's close friendship with the Swiss psychiatrist Medard Boss is well known. After Heidegger's mental breakdown and institutionalization at Haus Baden Sanatorium, and after he had been stripped of his ability to teach in public university, at Boss' invitation, Heidegger gave seminars to psychiatrists in Zurich for over ten years on his existential-ontological treatment of Dasein and its theoretical applications to psychological practice. As the founder of Daseinsanalysis, Boss was instrumental in introducing Heideggerian philosophy to the mental health professions in Europe, which eventually made its way into the American existential psychology movement in the 1950s and 1960s. From the published Heidegger seminars, Boss (1978–1979) informs us that Heidegger expressed the hope that his thinking could break away from purely philosophical inquiry to benefit those in human suffering including psychiatric populations. An interesting historical note is that Heidegger was hospitalized in Boss' clinic after a purported suicide attempt following interrogations by the denazification commission surrounding his involvement in the National Socialist Party prior to WW II, where he received treatment by psychoanalyst Dr. Viktor von Gebsattel (see Askay & Farquhar, 2011).

2 Some may argue that psychology is not ontology and the conceptual link between the two is illegitimate. Although Husserl (1950) entertained ontological psychology despite claiming his method of phenomenology was not psychologism (see *Cartesian Meditations*, § 59), this was not a problem for Hegel, so I am proceeding with the assumption that our understanding of the human condition is grounded in a structural ontology. However, I do not wish to equivocate the ontological-ontical terminology or treat them as though they are interchangeable. My aim is to proceed with a clear respect for the line between ontological/ontical and existential/existentiell. For Heidegger, "*Understanding of Being is itself a definite characteristic of Dasein's Being*. Dasein is ontically distinctive in that it *is* ontological" (*BT* § 12, italics in

original). The ontic, that which concerns beings, and the ontological, that which concerns ways of being, are differentiated by virtue of their apophantical and hermeneutical referents. Existential understanding, on the other hand, is an understanding of the ontological structures of existence, that is, what it is to be Dasein, while existentiell understanding is a person's self-understanding, that is, an understanding of his or her own way to be or what he or she is. Although Heidegger does differentiate the ontological from the ontical, the ontical can only be possible vis-á-vis the ontological, thus, our social and individual practices embody an ontology. Also see Dreyfus (1991) for a general commentary.

3   Although Heidegger's and Sartre's phenomenological ontologies are conceptually distinct with variegated subtleties, the question of authenticity is central to both of their philosophies. Albeit conceived differently from Heidegger's inauthentic Dasein, Sartre's notion of bad faith, as the renunciation of human freedom in the service of self-deception, contributes to our understanding of selfhood enthralled in the toils of inauthenticity and further anticipates the psychodynamic exploration of underlying defensive processes characteristic of the dynamic unconscious. While Heidegger offers a comprehensive hermeneutical treatment of Dasein in its relation to selfhood, Sartre depicts more acutely the psychological processes involved in the formation and maintenance of inauthenticity. While respecting the distinctions and divergences between Heidegger's and Sartre's ontological discourses, it becomes important to illuminate Dasein's falsehood in terms of its inauthentic ontical relations, which is the primary task of psychoanalysis. The equivocation of these different terminologies are therefore intended to facilitate the conceptual bridge between the existential-ontological structures of Dasein and their relation to the existentiell-ontical manifestations of inauthenticity that will be further addressed within a psychoanalytic account of the self.

4   Sartre's (1963) later notion of freedom stressed the "practico-inert," demarcating the scope of freedom as always being situated (as determined) within concrete historical, social, cultural, and economic limits. This parallels Heidegger's notion of thrownness.

5   In Jung's analytical psychology, one-sidedness is generally used to denote a mental construction of the self that is false. Within a Jungian context, one-sidedness with one's persona would be an over-identification with the archetypal nature of the collective unconscious that is constricted. Following Jung's notion of the Principles of Equivalence and Entropy, one-sidedness would be an over-emphasis and incompensatory discharge of mental energy, hence unequally distributed within the psyche.

References

Boss, M. (1978–1979). *Martin Heidegger's Zollikon Seminars*. B. Kenny (Trans.). *Review of Existential Psychiatry and Psychology*, 16.

Cassimatis, E.G. (1984). The "False Self." *International Review of Psycho-Analysis*, 11(1): 69–77.

Chescheir, M.W. (1985). Some implications of Winnicott's concept for clinical practice. *Clinical Social Work Journal*, 13(3): 218–233.

Craig, E. (1988). An encounter with Medard Boss. *The Humanistic Psychologist*, 16:34–47.

Dreyfus, H.L. (1991). *Being-in-the-World*. Cambridge, MA: MIT Press.

Freud, S. (1923/1989). *The Ego and the Id. Standard Edition*. New York: Norton.

Guignon, C. (1984). Heidegger's "Authenticity" Revisited. *Review of Metaphysics*, 38: 321–339.

Guignon, C. (1993). Authenticity, Moral Values, and Psychotherapy. In C. Guignon (Ed.), *Cambridge Companion to Heidegger*. Cambridge: Cambridge University Press.

Hegel, G.W.F. (1812). *Science of Logic*. A.V. Miller (Trans.). London: George Allen & Unwin, 1969.

Heidegger, M. (1927). *Being and Time*. J. Macquarrie & E. Robinson (Trans.). San Francisco: Harper Collins, 1962.

Heidegger, M. (1949). On the Essence of Truth. In *Martin Heidegger, Basic Writings*. D.F. Krell (Ed.) San Francisco: Harper Collins, 1977.

Husserl, E. (1950). *Cartesian Meditations*. Dordrecht, Netherlands: Kluwer Academic Publishers, 1993.

Khan, M.M. (1971). Infantile Neurosis as a False Self Organization. *Psychoanalytic Quarterly*, 40(2): 245–263.

Kockelmans, J.J. (1978). Daseinsanalysis and Freud's Unconscious. *Review of Existential Psychology and Psychiatry*, 16: 21–42.

Kohut, H. (1971). *The Analysis of the Self*. New York: International Universities Press.

Kohut, H. (1977). *The Restoration of the Self*. New York: International Universities Press.

Kohut, H. (1978). *The Search for the Self: Selected Writings of Heinz Kohut, 1950-1978*. Two Volumes. P. Ornstein (Ed.), New York: International Universities Press.

Kohut, H. (1984). *How Does Analysis Cure?* Chicago: University of Chicago Press.

Laing, R.D. (1959). *The Divided Self*. London: Penguin Books.

Lerner, P.M. (1985). The False Self Concept and its Measurement. *The Ontario Psychologist*, 17(6): 3–6.

Masterson, J.F. (1981). *The Narcissistic and Borderline Disorders*. New York: Brunner/Mazel Publishers.

Miller, A. (1981). *The Drama of the Gifted Child*. New York: Basic Books.

Naso, R.C. (2010). *Hypocrisy Unmasked: Dissociation, Shame, and the Ethics of Inauthenticity*. Lanham, MD: Aronson.

Richardson, W.J. (1993). Heidegger Among the Doctors. In John Sallis (Ed.), *Reading Heidegger*. Bloomington, IN: Indiana University Press.

Ricoeur, P. (1965). *Fallible Man*. C. Kelbley (Trans.). Chicago: Henry Regnery Company.

Ricoeur, P. (1966). *Freedom and Nature: The Voluntary and Involuntary*. E. Kohak (Trans.). Evanston, IL: Northwestern University Press.

Sartre, J.P. (1956). *Being and Nothingness*. H.E. Barnes (Trans.). New York: Washington Square Press.

Sartre, J.P. (1963). *Search for a Method*. New York: Vintage/Random House.

Schacht, L. (1988). Winnicott's Position in Regard to the Self with Special Reference to Childhood. *International Review of Psycho-Analysis*, 15 (4): 515–529.

Winnicott, D.W. (1960). Ego Distortions in Terms of True and False Self. In *The Maturational Processes and the Facilitating Environment*. New York: International Universities Press, 1965.

Chapter 5

Lacan on Paranoiac Knowledge

If you were to randomly open any text of Lacan's and begin to read, you might immediately think that the man is mad. In a word, his writing is psychotic: it is fragmentary, chaotic, and at times incoherent. First of all, his style of spoken discourse, given in lecture format before appearing in print, is infamously troublesome. Secondly, his fragmented texts obstinately oppose conforming to formal articulate systematization. As a result, Lacan is not very accessible, either as a stylist or a theoretician. For these reasons he invites controversy and is often misinterpreted.[1]

Because Lacan was a fearsome polemicist, radical eccentric, and unorthodox practitioner bordering on the scandalous, despite recent receptivity, within mainstream psychoanalysis, his name has become a dirty word. Although he was hailed as the "master" by his adherents, vociferous criticism of the "French Freud" mounted vast condemnation for his exploitation of psychoanalytic technique labeled as manipulative, abusive, unethical, and perverted. It comes as no surprise that he would be inevitably blamed (perhaps unfairly) for the suicide of some of his analysands,[2] thus leading to his eventual expulsion from the psychoanalytic community (Haddad, 1981; Lacan, 1964a). Although the recognized genius that often accompanies his legend has by no means vanished from academic circles, due to the arcane and inconsistent nature of his writings, Lacan's theoretical *oeuvre* has been dismissed by some as a "delusion" (Roustang, 1990).

It is rather ironic that Lacan's theoretical innovations are sometimes characterized by the language of the psychoses, for his theory

DOI: 10.4324/9781003305958-5

of knowledge is tinged with a psychotic hermeneutics. "Paranoia" is derived from the Greek, *para*—outside of or beside—as in "*beside oneself*"—and mind (*nous*, νόος), thus beyond intelligible thought (*noēsis*), hence madness. It can also be said that Lacan's splintered, disparate, and often implicit theoretical structure personifies his very notion of desire: desire is beyond structure, beyond words—it is merely the unutterable, ineffable. That which remains nameless, indescribable—unknown—is surely that which haunts us; and it is ominous precisely because it is alien.

For Lacan, all knowledge is imbued with paranoia. Like Lacan's conception of the *Real*, which has no formal text, his comments on paranoiac knowledge are limited to only a few fragments in his *Écrits* and his *Seminars*, thus lacking clarification and systematic rigor. Because his scant remarks on the subject have genuine theoretical and clinical value, it is my intention in this chapter to provide a conceptual model explicating the scope, breadth, and process of paranoiac knowledge, thus showing how Lacan's insights have clinical utility. By way of illustration, I will examine a case of paranoia.

Developmentally, knowledge is paranoiac because it is acquired through our *imaginary* relation to the other as a primordial misidentification or illusory self-recognition of autonomy, control, and mastery, thus leading to persecutory anxiety and self-alienation. Secondarily, through the *symbolic* structures of language and speech, desire is foisted upon us as a foreboding demand threatening to invade and destroy our uniquely subjective inner experiences. And finally, the process of knowing itself is paranoiac because it horrifically confronts the *real*, namely, the unknown. Through our examination of a clinical case study, paranoiac knowledge manifests itself as the desire not to know.

Prolegomena to Lacan's System: The Relation between Knowledge and Paranoia

Lacan is very difficult to understand, especially for Anglo audiences, hence non-French speaking culture, which makes the interpreter's task ever so daunting. Such difficulty is in no doubt why, in part, most psychoanalytic clinicians in North America and Britain remain confused about—if not oblivious to—his theoretical visions. Even worse, there is no unified agreement among Lacanians on how we should interpret Lacan. His invented jargon is highly esoteric, drawing on and re-appropriating concepts from many different fields of study including philosophy, anthropology, semiotics, and mathematics, and thus can evoke both admiration and dismissal. Here I am reminded of Freud's comment on a decorative centrepiece: it's nice to look at, but no one dares to touch it. The confusional aspects of Lacan's discourse becomes particularly vexing when Lacan himself declares that he is intentionally trying to confound the very audience who seeks to understand him (Lacan, 1955–1956c, p. 164). For these reasons, Lacan's technical jargon cannot be easily converted into a user-friendly guide. Moreover, many of his concepts have multiple meanings that even oppose each other when viewed from different contexts within his system. Although I attempt to mitigate some of the confusion surrounding his discourse, it will be necessary for me, throughout this chapter, to retain much of his technical language, without which many of his theoretical distinctions would go unrecognized. I hope classical Lacanians will forgive me if I simplify his theoretical corpus or fail to represent him with more nuanced precision.

It is not necessary to adopt Lacan's entire system, which is neither essential nor desirable, in order to appreciate what he has to offer to our topic at hand. In fact, many of Lacan's positions—such as the decentring of subjectivity for the reification of language—radically oppose contemporary psychoanalytic thought to the degree that Lacan becomes essentially incompatible. Notwithstanding, with the ever-increasing linguistic turn in psychoanalysis, Lacan becomes an important figure to engage. Because language is a necessary condition (albeit not a sufficient one) for conceptual thought, comprehension, and meaning to manifest (see Frie, 1997; Mills, 1999), human knowledge is linguistically mediated. But the epistemological question—that is, the origin of knowledge—requires us to consider prelinguistic development, intrapsychic and interpersonal experience, and the extra- or nonlinguistic processes that permeate psychic reality, such as the constitutional pressures of the drives (*Triebe*) and affective states (from the monstrous to the sublime) that remain linguistically foreclosed as unformulated unconscious experience. In other words, although signs and signifiers are an indispensable part of psychic life, other mental processes transpire independently of internalized conscious language or semiotics. When these aspects of human life are broadly considered, it becomes easier to see how our linguistic-epistemological dependency has paranoiac a priori conditions. From Hegel to Freud, Heidegger, and Lacan, knowledge is a dialectical enterprise that stands in relation to fear—to the horror of possibility—the possibility of the *not*: negation, conflict, and suffering saturate our very beings, beings whose self-identities are linguistically constructed.

The relation between knowledge and paranoia is a fundamental one, and perhaps no where do we see this dynamic so poignantly realized than in childhood. From the "psychotic-like" universe of the newborn infant (e.g., see Klein, 1946); to the relational deficiencies and selfobject failures that impede the process of human attachment; to the primal scene and/or subsequent anxieties that characterize the Oedipal period, leading to the inherent rivalry, competition, and overt aggression of even our most sublimated object relations—fear, trepidation, and dread hover over the very process of knowing itself.

What is paranoid is that which stands in relation to opposition, hence that which is alien to the self. Paranoia is not simply that which is beyond the rational mind, but it is a generic process of *noēsis*—" I take thought, I perceive, I intellectually grasp, I apprehend," and hence have *apprehension* for what I encounter in consciousness. With qualitative degrees of difference, we are all paranoid simply because others hurt us, a lesson we learn in early childhood. Others hurt us with their knowledge, with what they say, as do we. And we hurt knowing. "What will the Other do next?" We are both pacified yet cower in extreme trembling over what we may and may not know— what we may and may not find out; and this is why our relation to knowledge is fundamentally paranoiac.

For Aristotle, "All men by nature desire to know" (*Metaphysics*, I(A):980a22). This philosophic attitude is kindled by our educational systems perhaps informing the popular trite adage, "knowledge is power." But whose? There is no doubt that the acquisition of knowledge involves a power differential, but what if knowledge itself is seen as too powerful because it threatens our psychic integrity? In the gathering of knowledge there is simultaneously a covering-over, a blinding to what one is exposed to; moreover, an erasure. I ~~know~~ (No)! Unequivocally, there are things we desire to know nothing about at all; hence the psychoanalytic attitude places unconscious defense—negation/denial (*Verneinung*) and repression—in the foreground of human knowledge, the desire not to know.

When we engage epistemology—the question and meaning of knowledge—we are intimately confronted with paranoia. For example, there is nothing more disturbing when after a lifetime of successful inquiry into a particular field of study it may be entirely debunked by the simple, arrogant question: "How do you know?" Uncertainty, doubt, ambiguity, hesitation, insecurity—anxiety!: the process of knowing exposes us all to immense discomfort. And any epistemological claim is equally a metaphysical one. Metaphysics deals with first principles, the fundamental, ultimate questions that preoccupy our collective humanity: "What is real? Why do I exist? Will I *really* die?" Metaphysics is paranoia—and we are all terrified by its questions: "Is there God, freedom, agency, immortality?" *Is? Why? Why not? Yes, but why?!* When the potential meaning and quality of one's personal existence hinge on the response to these questions, it is no wonder why most theists say only God is omniscient. And although Freud (1927) tells us that the very concept of God is an illusory derivative of the Oedipal situation—a wish to be rescued and comforted from the anxieties of childhood helplessness, He—our exalted Father in the sky—is *always* watching, judging. Knowing this, the true believer has every reason to be petrified. For those in prayer or in the madhouse, I can think of no greater paranoia (see Mills, 2017).

Three Realms of Being

Human knowledge is paranoiac—it torments, persecutes, *cuts*. This is essentially what Lacan (1953–1954) means when he says "my knowledge started off from paranoiac knowledge" (p. 163), because there are "paranoid affinities between all knowledge of objects as such" (1955–1956b, p. 39). In order to understand what Lacan means, it is necessary to provide a preliminary overview of his ontological treatment of the human condition, which he situates in three realms or contexts of being, namely, the Imaginary, Symbolic, and Real. By closely examining a few of Lacan's key works, it will become increasingly clear that aggressivity suffuses the very fabric of human knowledge, a paranoiac residue of the dialectic of desire.

It may be useful to think of three main periods that characterize Lacan's work. Although his early period (1932–1948) focused on the role of the imago, his middle period (1948–1960) concentrated on the nature of language that subordinated the world of images to linguistic structures and practices. During his late period (1960–1980), Lacan was preoccupied with a formal systematization of psychoanalysis via logic and mathematics that sought to provide a coherent explanatory framework involving the three realms or registers of mental life. As a cursory definition, we might say that the Imaginary (*imaginaire*) is the realm of illusion, of fantasy, belonging to the sensuous world of perception. In contrast, the Symbolic (*symbolique*) is the formal organization of psychic life that is structured through language and linguistic internalizations implemented as semiotic functions, thus becoming the ground of the subject; while the Real (*réel*) remains foreclosed from epistemic awareness within the abyss of unconscious desire. The real is delimited—the *Ding an sich*: it remains the mysterious beyond, the heart of desire. For Lacan, desire is persecutory by virtue of belonging to the Other, first originating in a specular imago, then constituted through the domain of language and speech as superimposed demand.

These three domains of mental functioning constitute psychical reality and compose the fundamental basis or ground of the human being, which may be metaphorically viewed as a Borromean knot: each realm may operate autonomously on parallel planes but they are entirely interdependent and intersect at any given moment. The three registers are held together in tension by a negative dialectic that fundamentally oppose each other, yet at times may coalesce; but there is no Hegelian *Aufhebung* or ultimate synthetic progression. Instead we can envision a pressure-cooker held together by conflict. Together as a whole these opposing domains form a dynamic structure or process system that accounts for all human experience through their interrelatedness.

Imaginary forms of relating to the world fundamentally comprise what Lacan (1936–1949) refers to as the "mirror stage" in the early formative development of the I or ego (*moi*). The infant sees itself in the mirror, face, or actions of the other but mistakes the other for itself as an imaginary relation. In other words, following Hegel (1807), the nascent mind comes to recognize itself through the other, which produces a crude semblance of self-definition. The visual (mirroring) imago lends a degree of coherence and organic wholeness to the infant's hitherto internal state of undifferentiated experience or primary narcissism, and hence introduces for the first time the notion of a separate sense of self from others, which provides definitional form and structure to ego development. The imaginary therefore belongs to the realm of spurious identifications and idealizations based on the interplay between images and fantasies that are necessary (albeit insufficient) for the construction of the self, which is the initial unfolding of self-identity.

In essence, for Lacan, there is no real self or ego because the infant's internal world is determined by external images it internalizes through identificatory mergers; and this early form of ego development conditions all subsequent organizations of the self. This process largely consists of identifications with (idealized) images that ingress (from the outside as alien activities) into the infant's incipient sense of self, which result in failures of recognition of self and subject. Rather than view ego development from a Freudian lens, which situates intrapsychic activity as the locus of mental life, Lacan instrumentally endows externality with determinate powers of psychic causation. In effect, the ego is a fantasy of self-relation defined by the Other. What this means is that all forms of epistemology are derived from external sources and are caused from without or outside the psyche. An imaginary mode of relating to the world is fundamental to psychosis, but it is also a general basis of self-knowledge, which Lacan (1936–1949) states always has an alienated and paranoid quality.

The symbolic plays a central role in Lacan's system, which in my assessment, although debatable, is ultimately the *cause* of the subject's being. Lacan believes that the unconscious is "structured like a language" and, indeed, he equates the unconscious with language itself (see Lacan 1955–56a, p. 11; 1955–56b, p. 119; 1955–56c, pp. 166–167), which is predicated on consciousness and cultural determinism. For Lacan, because the symbolic temporally exists prior to the contingent birth of the subject, this, in turn, determines the essence of the subject. Therefore, the subject is constituted by the symbolic function. For Lacan, the subject is conditioned upon its "entrance into language" under the symbolic Law (*E* 1957, p. 148), which ultimately makes the unconscious a cultural category captured by his formula: "the unconscious is *discours de l' Autre*' (discourse of the Other)" (*E* 1960, p. 312).

Because the symbolic order, namely, the Other (as familial and communal interaction, language, culture, and so forth) is causally superimposed, this corresponds to the creation or constitution of the human subject. Here Lacan precariously subverts the notion of freedom within psychic agency as if everything is conditioned on language. This commits him to a particular brand of external determinism, rather than the internal (psychic) determinism of classical theory. Furthermore, for Lacan, the ego is an "illusion of autonomy" based on its *méconnaissances* and imaginary relations to others (*E* 1936–1949, p. 6); and, unlike Freud, who places natural desire within an internal burgeoning process of unconscious expression, for Lacan, even "man's desire is the *désir de l' Autre* (the desire of the Other)" (*E* 1960, p. 312). In Lacan, we may call into question whether human agency even exists, for he sees agency as belonging to the authority of the Letter or signifier. Although we may attempt to salvage a notion of agency in Lacan by the way we choose to (re)interpret his text, or by redirecting shifts in emphasis that recast his positions within a framework compatible with the ontology of freedom, if we follow Lacan to the letter, the human subject is determined by the structures and parameters of speech. Here there is no intrapsychic mediation that confers meaning, rather signification is conferred through the act of speech itself. As Vanheule (2011) describes, "the process of generating meaning also has the effect of producing subjectivity" for "subjectivity is generated via the signifying chain" (p. 44). In other words, we don't simply employ language, we *are* language. Language creates being, hence the signifier and the act of speech determines the subject.[3]

Instead of viewing speech and the laws of grammar, syntax, sign and signification, and so forth as an invention and production of human subjectivity, Lacan turns the table. Rather than the human being who has agency and creates linguistic expression and meaning, language is granted the exalted status of supreme Order or Law that determines the contours of intrapsychic life. How can the structural mechanisms of speech, such as metonymy, cause the subject when we are accustomed to conceptualizing the experiential ego as the agent responsible for speaking? Here, like Fichte's Absolute Self as pure self-posit, language institutes itself; in other words, it brings about its own being. But language does not think itself into existence or institute itself *ex nihilo*; rather, it is the anthropological product of human creation. If language is fundamentally a human activity born of psychic creativity and cultural expression, then how can it cause anything independent of the linguist or user of language? If language is the invention of human thought and ideation mediated through mind, then how could it exist outside of human consciousness? Words don't think. This would require a special ontological status, as if it were some cosmic macroanthropos. For Lacan, human subjectivity is always composed by something outside of itself. What this means is that Lacan's entire metaphysics is conditioned on an environmental determinism that is the functional basis of the human being despite later introducing the notion of the real as the placeholder for the materiality of natural desire and its ineffability.[4]

The real surfaces as the third order, standing in juxtaposition to the imaginary and the symbolic, intimately intertwined yet beyond the previous domains. The real has no formal text, it is deliberately undecided. It is neither symbolic nor imaginary, rather it remains foreclosed from the analytic experience which relies on speech. The real is the domain of the unconscious, that realm of psychic territory we can never know as such in itself; it remains beyond the epistemic limitations of the symbolic, yet is disclosed in every utterance. We may say that the real is the seat of desire whereas the imaginary and symbolic orders devolve into it. The real is the presupposed psychical reality, the raw substrate of the subject awaiting structure through linguistic acquisitions. Lacan's notion of the real should not be confused with "reality," which is in some ways knowable (at least theoretically), yet the subject of desire may only suppose the real—the *thing in itself*—as reality for the subject is merely phantasmatic. For Lacan, the real is the "impossible," it is the realm of the unthinkable, the unimaginable; and this is precisely why the real cannot be penetrated by imagination or the senses. The real is that which is missing in the symbolic order, that which is untouchable, indescribable by language, yet "the ineliminable residue of all articulation." (*E*, 1977, p. x).

According to Malcolm Bowie (1991), the imaginary, symbolic, and the real are not mental entities, rather they are *orders* that serve to position the individual within a field that traverses and intersects it. The word "order" suggests a number of important connotations for Lacan. Analogous to botanical or zoological taxonomy, (a) there is a hierarchical arrangement of classes whereby (b) internal principles of similarity and congruence govern membership in each class. Furthermore, (c) higher levels of classification have superior cognitive status, suggesting that (d) a series of commands or orders are being issued from some undetected source—presumably the real—the night of the mind. No limitations are placed on the Lacanian orders; they may be used to explain any form of human condition from the most banal mental mechanism to the most severe forms of psychopathology. Within the three Lacanian orders, each perspective is realized from its own unique vantage point, revealing an insight into psychic organization that forecloses the others, yet envelopes them. However, by themselves, each fails to fully represent and articulate the greater dynamic complexity that characterizes the parallel processes and temporal unification of the three orders.

As multiple processes, the Lacanian three orders are not stable, fixed processes; rather they are under the constant pressure of evolution, vacillating between antithetical movements of progression and regression, construction and decay. The three orders pressurize each other constantly, having short-term moratoriums. In other words, the three orders are in conflict with each other and, when operative, attempt to exert their own unique influence over the other orders. This in turn creates overdetermined and multiple, dynamic levels of psychic reality. In their dialectical transitions, each order encroaches on the other—the symbolic defining and organizing the imaginary, the imaginary hallucinating the real. Furthermore, the real always wedges its way through the gaps of conscious intentionality, giving desire a voice through the medium of perception and speech. At any given moment we live in all three realms of being, each operative and dynamic within their own orders parallel to each other, yet they are integrative, structured, and complex. Although the real is the most obscure concept for Lacan, it reintroduces a vibrant theoretical life to psychoanalytic inquiry that underscores the primacy of an unconscious ontology which Freud was so instrumental to advance. Despite its mysterious appeal shrouded in inconceivability, the real is the reverberation of its own truth disclosed on its own terms and understood through its own language, the idiom of desire.

Through the Looking Glass

Lacan's inaugural theory of the self was formally introduced in 1936 to the 14th International Psychoanalytic Congress and published the following year under the title "The Looking-Glass Phase." This single contribution launched a radical new portrait of ego formation in psychoanalytic thought. One reason why his theory is so radical and controversial is that, for Lacan, the ego, with qualifications, does not exist—at least not in the ordinary sense psychoanalysis has come to view the notion. The ego is a mistake (*méconnaissance*), thus it is merely an illusory projection of autonomy and control. In other words, the ego (*moi, Ich*) or "I" is merely a *wish*—itself the product of social construction.

At this point, it may be useful to distinguish between what Lacan means by the self, the ego, and the subject. The "self," "ego," or "I," which is used synonymously throughout much of Lacan's writings, is typically equated with our conscious perceptions and definitions of ourselves. Therefore, when Lacan (1955–1956b) says that "meaning is imaginary" (p. 65), he is saying that our ego is conceptually bound to our conscious self-*image* or self-representations. The term "subject" (*Sujet*), on the other hand, typically refers to the unconscious—that which is alien and lies outside of conscious self-awareness; although we conventionally refer to the whole person when we use the term subject, as Lacan did throughout his writings. Lacan, as does Freud and Jung, privileges the unconscious over the conscious ego, and hence emphasizes that all foreign desires, thoughts, parapraxes, and so on, which slip out during acts of speech are tantamount to revealed It (*Es*) processes (Fink, 1997). However, Lacan does not make the distinction between the conscious and unconscious portions of the ego as Freud (1923) does, nor is he inclined to attribute "agency" to the unconscious, even though he concedes we have a tendency to attribute subjectivity to it. While Freud (1933, p. 6) spoke of the trichotomy of the psyche or "Soul" (*Seele*)—not the "mental apparatus," which is a mistranslation—as the temporal unification of the dynamic processes that constitute psychic life, Lacan makes the unconscious subject completely non-personal. For our purposes here, however, it may be less confusing if we think of the subject as the whole human being composed of both conscious and unconscious organizations.

The mirror stage is the initial point of self-discovery, hence the dawn of the nascent ego insofar as the "I" is discovered in the eyes of the other. From the recognition of the self through the looking glass, or through another as its metaphorical representation, the emergence of self-consciousness is constituted in and through alienation. Taken over from Hegel's (1807) theory of desire and recognition, Lacan (1953–1954) states that "the original, specular foundation of the relation to the other, in so far as it is rooted in the imaginary, [is] the first alienation of desire" (p. 176). In the realm of the imaginary, the budding ego first recognizes itself in an object outside of itself, in the mirror image of the other. This illusory order is the initial constitution of the self, as the first matrix of the ego, which is the psychically formative period that occurs between the ages of six to eighteen months of infancy.

Through Kojève, Lacan was deeply influenced by Hegel, especially by his lordship and bondage chapter outlined in the *Phenomenology of Spirit*. For Hegel, one's sense of self is contingent on the recognition of the other, and this contingency itself fosters a paranoid dynamic. We all seek recognition, this is a basic human need. The ego is affirmed by the other, but not at first. There is originally the experience of inequality, whether this be the child's relation to the parent or the servant's relation to the master. Ultimately the desire for recognition becomes a fundamental battle for dominance and validation in which each subject struggles to overcome the objectification of the other. From this standpoint, the sense of one's fundamental contingency on recognition is basically paranoiac and may regress to that paranoid state whenever one becomes acutely aware of that contingency.

Drawing on the ethological research of Tinbergen and Lorenz regarding the perceptual functions of animal behaviour, and on Freud's thesis of identification, Lacan emphasizes the organizing function of the imago as the perceptual *Gestalten* that forms the most elemental contours of psychical structure. For Lacan, as for Hegel, the initial recognition of the "I" does not entail the subject's self-awareness of itself as a fully self-conscious agent. This is a developmental achievement mediated by its burgeoning modes of identification. For Lacan, however, this primordial form of identification "situates the agency of the ego ... in a fictional direction" (1936–1949, p. 2), namely, in the gaze of the other which gives the illusory semblance of self. In other words, images symbolize, reflect the 'I,' and thus resemble a constituted self that are the initial stimuli for ego-boundaries and body differentiation to be forged. The mirror phase is therefore the world of perception, forever cast under the penumbra of the imaginary.

As early as his essay on "The Mirror Stage," Lacan's mature theory of desire is already implicit, it is already prepared. The mirror experience functions as the coming into being of identity, the initial formation of the self—a self that is dialectically and intersubjectively constructed through desire, as the relation of being to *lack* (*manque*). Lacan emphasizes the "internal thrust" of desire within the pre-supposed subject, yet desire is always *caused* or given over, through internalization, by the Other. As a result, desire is always characterized by absence and incompleteness. Such void, such hole in being clamors in "anticipation" for presence, for fulfillment of its lack, facilitated by the parental imagos that the premature ego identifies with, thus giving an illusory sense of totality and completeness. We may say that such illusory completeness is fantasized, hallucinated *as* reality, thus the fulfillment of a wish. However, the dislocated images mirrored in the other subjected to the illusion of cohesiveness of identity are in fact *defensive* processes enacted to ward off fragmentation anxiety: the genesis of ego development is the life of desire.

The Other as Persecutory

Lost in its alienation, the Lacanian subject discovers itself in the imaginary, recovered through the mediation of the other, giving itself meaning through the symbolic, struggling on the threshold of the real. But for Lacan, there can never be an absolute self, no autonomous "I" or transcendental ego that exists apart from the Other; the "I" is always linked "to socially elaborated situations" (1936–1949, p. 5) mediated by linguistic structures ontologically constituted a priori within its social facticity. Thus, in many respects, the *I* is the *Other*.

It is through the image of the other that the infant comes to grasp awareness of its own corporeal integrity and seize the first measure of control over its body movements. The imago serves as an "alter-ego," an organizing, stabilizing function which coordinates cohesiveness out of internal chaos and provides homogeneity out of primal discord. Through the imaginary, the ego is no more than a return of an image to itself.[5] The paradoxical structure of the imaginary is therefore the polarity between alienation and recognition. Lacan sees recognition as the recovery of the alienated image facilitated through the mirroring of the other. As the subject finds or recognizes itself through an image (insofar as recognition is the misrecognition of its autonomous ego as an illusory mastery), it is concurrently confronted with its own alienated and alienating image; hence this process becomes an aggressive relation.

Lacan describes the degree of "aggressive disintegration" that torments the inchoate ego in "the form of disjointed limbs, or of those organs represented in exoscopy, growing wings and taking up arms for intestinal persecutions" (1936–1949, p. 4).[6] The persecutory fantasies that accompany early ego development may indeed take the form of "images of castration, mutilation, dismemberment, dislocation, evisceration, devouring, bursting open of the body, in short, the ... *imagos of the fragmented body*" (1948, p. 11). Feldstein (1996) notes that the imago allows the infant to elide a fundamental rupture in which "anxiety-producing images of the fragmented body are disavowed because such untotalizable self-differences could give rise to paranoid perceptions; ... [thus] paranoia is related to the mirror-stage attempt to manufacture a future-perfect mastery" (p. 135). It becomes essential for the ego to split, compartmentalize, and/or project its negative introjects from its internal experiences and internalize soothing ministrations in order to defend against such hostile intrusions. Therefore, the stabilizing and "fixating" quality of the positive imago serves a cohesive function. As the imago (accompanied by maternal ministrations and validating presentations) helps constitute the burgeoning I, the salutary power of the specular image becomes a unifying and integrating activity.

The organizing and synthesizing functions internalized over maturation become unifying yet mobile fixtures of the child's inner representational world. Such internalizations are fortified through ongoing identifications that provide the illusion of self-cohesion, which further serve to ward off primordial anxiety associated with fragmentation, decomposition, and loss of undifferentiated bliss with the imago. This is also a prevalent theme for Klein (1946) and post-Kleinians (Bion, 1959; Segal, 1957): ego organization is besieged by the horrors of persecutory-annihilation anxiety. Unlike Klein, however, the self is the introjection of the other, not the projection of the self discovered in the other. For Lacan, the self is causally given over by the other; thus the self is the Other internalized in all its variegated forms.

Given the plethora of images and fantasies that populate the early stages of the imaginary, it becomes increasingly clearer to see how the other becomes a persecutory object. The other, and particularly the other's desire, is always a potential threat to the subject because it is an alien force that stands in firm opposition to the subject, an antithesis that evokes rivalry and competition. This is why Lacan (1955–1956b) says that "all human knowledge stems from the dialectic of jealousy, which is a primordial manifestation of communication" (p. 39). The subject first encounters the other as *opposition*—an opposition that *desires*. As such, the other is in possession of something the subject lacks. We are jealous of what the other has, which naturally evokes feelings of rivalry, competition, and envy. This naturally leads Lacan to conclude that "the object of human interest is the object of the other's desire" (p. 39). What the subject desires in otherness is the other's desire, thus bringing about a primordial confrontation with death: in opposition there is always the possibility of being annulled. "The dialectic of the unconscious always implies struggle, the impossibility of coexistence with the other [is] one of its possibilities" (p. 40). This could be Hegel speaking. Whether the other is the object of desire that enjoys a degree of liberty which the subject lacks, or whether the Other is the symbolic order imposing an austere reality on the subject's inner world through the violation and demands of speech, the acquisition of knowledge becomes a paranoiac enterprise.

Aggressivity and Identification

Within the initial phases of the imaginary, aggressivity becomes paramount for Lacan. The image as an alienating presence may be an ominous, rivalrous threat that the subject fears as dangerous. Although the imago may be a validating-soothing-sustaining introject that provides the self with illusory stability, it may also become colored by the projection of one's own innate destructive impulses organized in one's paranoiac relation to the imago. The doubling function of the imaginary, as the medium for both self-recognition and self-alienation, serves as the initial developmental impetus behind the dialectical unfolding of desire.

The interface between identification, aggression, and the captivation of the specular imago in the imaginary register serves paradoxical functions. For Lacan, the "captation" of the mirror image is both entrancing and intrusive; it fascinates yet it captures. As the image of oneself is given over by the other, there is a new psychical action, that of identification, which for Lacan is the moment of the inception of the ego. While Freud (1921, 1933) envisions identification as the development of an emotional bond with a significant figure, Lacan focuses on the dialectical capacity to form judgments of identity and difference. Through identification, the baby finds the image a captivating albeit imprisoning force chained to the pull of the imaginary. For Lacan, this incarcerating point of attraction implies that the ego momentarily becomes fixed and static. Unconscious fantasy systems largely serve a defensive function in the preoedipal child, fueling illusory misrecognitions as a way of fending off the aggressive violation of the imago's encroachment.[7]

There is an a priori manifestation of destruction within the imaginary order: aggressivity is ontologically constituted within any dyadic relation. The imaginary capture of the mirror is mired in destruction, for as Lacan emphasizes, any imaginary relation generates rivalry and conflict. Recall that what we identify in opposition is the other's desire which we long to possess. Identification therefore generates an ambivalent tension between possession and lack. Identification with a rival evokes the dialectic of presence and absence, mastery and servitude; thus the initial point of confrontation entails the recognition of what one has not yet procured or mastered. For example, we may say that the mother's image is castrating because it is more powerful. Fear, dread, or shame may be evoked by a simple look: the other's desire is exposed through a gaze. Thus, the boundary of the imaginary becomes difference. For Lacan, this dual relation between the infant-mother dyad encases desire within an interminable narcissistic battlefield.

It is important to note that aggressivity and aggression are not the same. Aggression is a derivative of the death drive (*Todestrieb*) while aggressivity is the acting out of aggression through the symbolic and imaginary orders. Following Freud (1920), aggressivity is both the deflection of self-destruction and a defensive, protective reaction to an external threat. Lacan (1948) shows that aggressivity is immured within the structures of subjectivity "by its very constitution" (p. 9), and avouches that "aggressivity in experience is given to us as intended aggression and as an image of corporeal dislocation" (p. 10). As we have said, imagoes can be noxious and disfiguring, thus leading to fragmentation and a fracturing of the body. The ego attempts to fantasize the illusion of mastery and unity in the face of these dislocated and contrary experiences characteristic of the child's fragmented bodily states, which are displaced as aggressivity directed towards others. Richard Boothby (1991) argues that "aggressivity is a drive toward violation of the imaginary form of the body that models the ego. It is because aggressivity represents a will to rebellion against the imago that aggressivity is specifically linked in fantasy to violations of the bodily integrity" (p. 39). Thus, for Lacan (1966), "the notion of aggressivity corresponds ... to the splitting of the subject against himself" (p. 344). Such "dehiscence" in the nascent ego gives rise to persecutory anxiety, hence the origins of knowledge are paranoiac in their "most general structure."

> What I have called paranoiac knowledge is shown, therefore, to correspond in its more or less archaic forms to certain critical moments that mark the history of man's mental genesis, each representing a stage in objectifying identification.
>
> (Lacan, 1948, p. 17)

Knowledge—the other's knowledge—is always lurking with pernicious intent to get in and *kill* the ego. The objects of identification are inherently baneful: they eviscerate desire simply because they are the other's desire. As the child's identificatory powers increase, so does the capacity for aggressivity. When the burgeoning ego identifies with the other's desire, it models the other and hence enters into an aggressive rivalry over the object of the other's desire. Following Hegel (1807), Lacan (1953–1954) sees this process as a competition for recognition:

> The subject's desire can only be confirmed in this relation through a competition, through an absolute rivalry with the other, in view of the object towards which it is directed. And each time we get close, in a given subject, to this primitive alienation, the most radical aggression arises — the desire for the disappearance of the other (p. 170).

Lee (1990) aptly tells us that "aggression directed toward others is found at the very center of the *moi's* structure, as it comes into being through the dialectic of the child's narcissistic identifications with various visual images" (p. 27). Such identification, says Lacan (1948), is also an "erotic relation, in which the human individual fixes upon himself an image that alienates him from himself, that are to be found the energy and the form on which this organization of the passions that he will call his ego is based" (p. 19).

For Lacan, the aggressivity injected into the very process of ego identification itself "determines the awakening of his desire for the object of the other's desire" (1948, p. 19). Lacan essentializes aggression as an ontologically indispensable psychic process that infuses narcissistic ego development. Aggressivity breaches the margin of libidinal self-investment as it falls on the fringe of self-destruction. Such "narcissistic suicidal aggression" operative with the formation of the ego is due to the alienated and lethal assault of the imago, which unleashes a violence on the subject to the point of self-extinction. As the other, *objet a* (sometimes referred to as *objet-petit-a*) is the signifier of desire; thus the subject is an-*other* plundered by the object's desire. Bowie (1991) explains that "the original act of identification is the original narcissistic declaration too; into the very constitution of the ego its destruction is already woven; the only escape from alienation is an aggravation of the alienated state" (p. 34).

For Freud, narcissistic object-choice is the process of conversion (*Umwandlung*) of aggressivity into love, a process that hinges on the repression of the drive toward aggression in the face of socialization and object attachment. For Lacan, this two-phase process is compressed into one: narcissism and aggressivity are correlatives. Julien (1994) expatiates on this claim:

> Narcissism, in which the image of one's own body is sustained by the image of the other, in fact introduces a *tension*: the other in his image both attracts and rejects me. I am indeed nothing but the other, yet at the same time, he remains *alienus*, a stranger. This other who is myself is other than myself. (p. 34)

As the ego is formally laid down in the imaginary relations of the mirror stage, aggressivity is embedded in love by virtue of this dual relationship. Duality implies difference, exclusion, antithesis. My desire is *their* desire!—it is already tainted with ugliness. A fundamental dichotomy is already constituted by this a priori relation, a rigid *either/or* leading to what Lacan calls the "fraternal complex:" *either* I kill the other *or* the other will kill me. As the immature ego is imperiled by perceived hostile and persecutory advances by the other's desire, the child is immersed in a destructive reality, which it must endeavor to deflect, project, and keep at bay. At the same time aggressivity contaminates the inner I, the ego is subjected to its own libidinal and relational strivings to attach to an ideal love object. From a Kleinian perspective, the oscillation between ideal and persecutory object relations is further enhanced during the depressive position. As paranoid anxiety gradually devolves into (yet remains subsumed within) depressive anxiety, the ego is besmirched by fears of destruction and loss of love. This is very much in keeping with Lacan's position: the ego's ambitendent, aggressive-erotic structure is the narcissistic foundation for *jouissance*—the realm of excess—desire's pleasures in death.[8]

For Lacan, death plays a pivotal role in the organization of the psyche: "aggressivity gnaws away, undermines, disintegrates; it castrates; it leads to death" (1948, p. 10). Schneiderman (1983) suggests that desire itself is the desire for death, one that is "cultivated to the extent that death is kept at a distance" (p. 74). The pleasure of death is not to be experienced as a real death, rather as the euphoria of *jouissance*, the pleasure of its sublimation. This sublimation, however, is not bound to the homeostatic (economic) laws that govern the

pleasure-principle, rather it exceeds it. We might say that death satisfies desire, but only if it is sustained, prolonged. Death is only
satisfying if it is protracted. The pleasure of death, hence the process
of death, makes the experience of satisfaction satisfying.

Boothby (1991) cogently shows that Lacan's treatment of the death
drive is pivotal in his theoretical innovations that intimately link
death with the functions of speech, language, and desire. As Lacan
(1954–1955b) states, "the death instinct is only the mask of the
symbolic order" (p. 326). Thus, the death drive hides behind the veil
of speech. Language castrates *jouissance*, it alienates desire from
satisfaction and thus introduces a division within the subject leaving a
palpable void (Ragland, 1995). Lacan's repositioning of death provides us with a hermeneutics of unconscious desire. With reference
to Freud, Lacan (1958) suggests that "life ... has only one meaning,
that in which desire is borne by death" (p. 277). Desire is the spawn
of intrusion, violation, and laceration from the Other—speech and
language are by nature aggressive; they *cut*.

The *De*-Structure of Language

As we have seen, Lacan's developmental picture of the ego is clearly
imbued with a negative dialectic: imagoes are alien and threatening,
identification is formed in relation to lack, object relations are primarily aggressive and rivalrous, and desire is always imposed. From
this account, the ego is vigilant and suspicious; hence it takes a
paranoid relation towards the world at large which becomes unconsciously fortified. But when the ego acquires language, paranoia
takes a symbolic turn signified through the demands of speech. The
notion of the symbolic order of mental functioning came to the fore
during the Rome Report.[9] Developed by Saussure and Jakobson, and
taken over by Lévi-Strauss' formalization of the elementary structure
of kinship with its reliance on Jakobson's binarism, Lacan's emphasis
on symbols refers not to icons or stylized figurations, but rather to
signifiers that he extends into a general definition with differential
elements; in themselves without meaning, signifiers acquire value only
in their mutual relations, which form a closed order (*E* 1977, p. ix).
Language lends structure to the psyche, thus it is the symbolic that
gives order to the subject. In fact, for Lacan, the subject is primarily

determined by the symbolic function of signifiers, speech, and language. The relationship between the imaginary and the symbolic is contrasted by the experiences of the ego and its images on the one hand, and the fortification of linguistic attributions on the other. We are thrown into the realm of the symbolic: language is already constituted a priori within a pre-existing social ontology, predefined, predetermined. Lacan (1957) tells us: "language and its structure exist prior to the moment at which each subject at a certain point in his mental development makes his entry into it" (p. 148). Symbolization attempts to give desire structure and order. Submitted to its systemic facticity, desire is molded by linguistic ontological pressures.

The introduction of the symbolic category marks a radical departure from Freud's metapsychology, indeed a re-writing of the structure of the psyche. Borne out in "The Agency of the Letter in the Unconscious or Reason since Freud," Lacan (1957) deliberately refigures Saussurian linguistics, insinuating the radical claim that not only is the unconscious structured like a language, but the unconscious *is* language (also see, 1955–1956, p. 11, 119, 166). For Lacan, the unconscious is not just conceived metaphorically as language, it is literally the Letter, thus the signifier. He states: "But how are we to take this 'letter' here? Quite simply, literally … the unconscious is the whole structure of language" (1957, p. 147). More specifically, letters (words) function as an infinite deferral within the signifying chain. This infinity in the link of signifiers shares affinities with Freud's concept of primary process thinking: signifiers break through obstacles, they know no limits, there is merely a constant flow. The agency (*instance, Instanz*) of the letter suggests that there is an authority to language, indeed an "insistence." Furthermore, Lacan's reference to "reason since Freud" refers to what reason has become since Freud due to his insistence on the agency of the unconscious; hence the unconscious is our reason why the illusory is our consciousness.

The symbolic order was important to Lacan precisely because it was inclusive and versatile, capable of referring to an entire range of signifying practices (Bowie, 1991; Fink, 1995; Marcelle, 1992). Due to its coherence and malleability, the symbolic category links the world of the unconscious to the structures of speech, and thus even more broadly to a social linguistic ontology. While repression is the prototype of the unconscious for Freud (1923, p. 15), language is the *sine qua non* of Lacan's new symbolic science.

Lacan's admiration of the symbolic is clearly contrasted to his derisive view of the imaginary.[10] The symbolic is the seat of motion and heterogeneity, thus transcending the field of illusory similarity: opposition and difference are firmly retained. The symbolic gives rise to the subject distinct from the imaginary ego, as an order of being that is always intermittent and disjoined (Bowie, 1991). Thus the symbolic is characterized by the ontology of absence, negativity, and nothingness. The relation between absence and presence, vacuity and abundance accents the power of signification. Lack has as much signifying potency as excess and none may operate alone without evoking antithesis. For Lacan (1953, 1957, 1960), the signification of lack parallels castration, as the "Name-of-the-Father" is the symbol for an authority that is both punitive and legislative. As the "paternal metaphor" that inheres in symbolization, lack is given significance in relation to otherness structured in symbolic opposition to the subject. Without such dialectical positionality, desire would succumb to a psychotic universe imprisoned within an absence of signification.

The imaginary is mediated by signifiers, thus language is crucial in the construction of identity (Sarup, 1992). For Lacan, words are interpreted and given meaning retroactively; the behaviour and verbal communication of another is always in need of interpretation, refracted through language. Lacan (1960) emphasizes the inter-personal demand for recognition that operates within the dialectic of desire. Within contemporary psychoanalysis, Kohut (1971, 1977, 1984) has made the need for validation and recognition the pinnacle motive force of desire: the subject craves attunement and mirroring from its selfobject milieu. While Lacan's (1953, 1958) mature period deifies the symbolic at the expense of decentring the subject, his approach nevertheless underscores the "lack of being" that characterizes desire, the "want-to-be" (*manque-à-être*) that characterizes the dialectic of recognition (p. 259, 274).

While Lacan (1964c,d) says that "the unconscious is structured like a language" (p. 149, 203), language itself can be dialectically destructive: the symbolic has the capacity to *de-structure* as it imposes order and meaning. The symbolic is an imposition, it places a demand on the subject. Language by its very nature is assaultive:

through distinctions, disjunctives, and classifications it makes exclusions and omissions, thus dividing particulars from universals as it discriminates, separates, and categorizes. The order and structure of the letter as an insistence is only possible in the wake of disorder and destruction that is determined by its dialectical relation. The metonymy of what *is*, is defined by what it is *not*. Language breaks up meaning and fractures it through negation, an act of de-structuring based on engagement with opposition. While the symbolic order frames, composes, and constructs, it can conversely displace one meaning for another.

The very structure and imposition of the symbolic can geld and dismember. Words take on signifying functions that activate cognitive, affective, and fantasy systems, which rip through the very core of our being. Speech—the spoken word—is the medium of caustic oral aggression that can be so acerbic and devaluing that it may scar one's self-concept and inner representational world. Negation— "No!"—by its very definition and execution introduces lack, absence, and deprivation. This is why so often we see conflicted individuals fixate on what was said or unsaid by others, thus assuming obsessional forms and repetitions. The perseveration of thought affixed to lack can be a living hell. Speech creates psychic pain through the affliction of desire and lack, as does silence—a poignant withholding. This may be why we all have "paranoid affinities" in relation to how the other uses language and speech: we fear evaluation and judgement—the other's desire, hence the unknown.

The Desire Not to Know

We have shown that the paranoiac process of acquiring knowledge has its genesis in the imaginary, first as the subject's misidentification with its alienated image in the reflection of the other, and second as the fundamental distortion and misrecognition of external objects (also see Muller & Richardson, 1982). Human knowledge is paranoiac because the subject projects its imaginary ego-properties into objects, which become distorted and perceived as fixed entities that terrorize the subject with persecutory anxiety in the form of the other's desire. While the terrifying part-object experiences of the dislocated body arise in the imaginary, the symbolic register introduces another form of fragmentation. Desire and speech by their very nature impose a command. Knowledge is saturated with paranoia because it threatens to invade the subject, and it is precisely this knowledge that must be defended against as the desire not to know.

Interpreting Lacan, Bruce Fink (1997) tells us that just as patients do not possess a genuine desire for change, they further lack a genuine desire for self-knowledge. While people may show interest in knowing why their lives and interpersonal relationships are unsatisfactory, and specifically what keeps interfering with their adjustment and happiness, Lacan (1955–1956a) suggests that there is a more fundamental unconscious wish not to know any of those things. "The subject's entire subsequent development shows that he wants to know nothing about it" (p. 12). In *Encore*, Lacan (1972–1973) further adds that "the unconscious is the fact that being, by speaking, enjoys, and … wants to know nothing more about it"—that is, "know nothing about it at all" (pp. 104–105). This is why patients often resist therapy and avoid the process of self-examination and change. They have no desire to know the root of their symptoms or neurotic mechanisms, what functions their defenses serve, and why they are instituted in the first place. This is why Lacan says that patients do not want to give up their symptoms because they provide familiarity and meaning: we enjoy our symptoms too much! (Žižek, 1992). This is the insidious structure of *jouissance*, namely, pleasure in pain, or the satisfaction individuals find in dissatisfaction to the point that they wish not to give it up. As Ragland (1995) asserts, "the inertia of *jouissance* … makes a person's love of his or her symptoms greater than any desire to change them" (p. 85). From this standpoint, the unconscious is first and foremost sadomasochistic: it inflicts a perverse pleasure through suffering at its own hands.

There is a self-destructive element to the enjoyment of symptoms, a revelry in the realm of excess to the point that truth or knowledge must be suspended, disavowed, or denied. This is why Lacan thinks that all knowledge of objects as such become tainted with paranoia: they threaten the subject's *jouissance*, and thus must be defended against as the desire not to know. So we may see how Lacan's theoretical insights have clinical applicability, let us now turn our attention to a case of paranoia.

The Case of Mrs. Z

The patient is a 48 year old white female with a presenting clinical picture of paranoid agitation, domestic violence, and suicidal gestures in response to her suspicion that her husband was having an extra-marital affair. She was voluntarily admitted to an inpatient psychiatry unit of a general hospital after she was found intoxicated standing in the rain nude for approximately two hours. Upon confronting her husband about the alleged affair, Mrs. Z had reportedly slapped and hit him and then set a blanket on fire in the upstairs bedroom of their house before running outside in the cold with no clothes on, refusing to come back inside saying she would rather die. She deliberately tried to hide from a small neighbourhood search party but was eventually located and brought to Emergency by the police. This was the patient's first hospitalization and she had no previous psychiatric history.

Mrs. Z has been married to her husband for 23 years and has a 20 year old daughter whom recently got married and moved out of the home. Following her daughter's marriage, the patient was removing something from her husband's car when she noticed that there was a crack in the upholstery of the driver's seat. Apparently the seat was splitting at the seam in the upper right-hand corner, yet she paid it little attention. A week had passed when she noticed that the rip in the seam had widened and with panic she immediately fantasized that her husband was having vigorous sexual relations with another woman in the car, thus causing damage to the seat. Upon having this fantasy, Mrs. Z reported that she recalled an event that took place approximately four months prior to her daughter's wedding when she thought she smelled perfume on her husband's shirt while doing the laundry, something she dismissed at the time. This recollection further revived a painful 20 year old memory of when her husband blurted out another woman's name during intercourse, leaving an unabated narcissistic injury; yet he assured her at the time his slip was only a fantasy and that he had never been unfaithful, an explanation which she believed.

After discovering the torn seat for the second time, Mrs. Z's suspicions started to assume more paranoid qualities, thereby producing obsessional preoccupations that her husband was cheating on her each day as he went to work. She started checking and cleaning the car every night as he returned home hoping *not* to find evidence to corroborate her intuitions. One evening, however, she found a small piece of wire fencing underneath the passenger's front seat and concluded that someone had been in the car. When she asked her husband to explain how it got there, he could not, only suggesting that she must have overlooked the object when she previously vacuumed the car.

The patient now started to record the gas mileage each day as her husband drove to and from work. She had already driven the same route he normally takes and recorded the mileage so she could have a baseline for comparison. When the mileage on the odometer proved to be significantly higher than expected on his next return from work, she confronted her husband on the discrepancy and accused him of having an affair. He vociferously denied any such thing and told the patient that she was paranoid. Mrs. Z admitted that while she had little proof at the time, she thought her husband was lying because he could not look her directly in the eye.

Convinced of her husband's infidelity, Mrs. Z purchased a voice-activated tape recorder and secretly concealed it in her husband's car. Upon returning from work that evening, the patient retrieved the tape recorder from the car and listened to the tape in its entirety. Initially the tape played back familiar sounds of a moving car on the road, conveying common traffic noises and music from the radio. After approximately 20 minutes of listening to the tape, Mrs. Z reported that she began to feel foolish that she had mistrusted her husband. But just as she was ready to turn off the tape, she reportedly began to hear her husband converse with another woman. The conversation soon led to passion as she heard the couple engage in the act of sexual relations.

Mrs. Z immediately confronted her husband on the affair to which he point-blankly denied. When she then produced the tape recorder and explained how she had hidden it in the car recording his entire drive to work, he supposedly became frantic and disoriented. But when she played the section of the tape of the man conversing with the woman, he emphatically stated, "That's not my voice!" Steadfastly denying that he was the one on the tape, the husband conjectured that someone from work must be stealing his car during the day, driving to some undisclosed location to have sex with some woman, and then returning the car before he gets off from work. At first Mrs. Z could not believe his story, but he assured her that he was not the man on the tape. Because the sound of the recording was crude, she had reason to doubt her previous assessment. Furthermore, he informed the patient that someone could have had access to his car unbeknownst to him because he routinely leaves his keys on a hook at the office so not to lose them before he takes the company truck to the construction site each morning. However, he could not explain why two strangers would do such a thing or what possible motives they could have. He could think of no one at work with whom he had conflict or who would be inclined to take his car.

Wanting to believe her husband, Mrs. Z accepted his story and tried to convince herself that someone was playing a prank on them. It is during this time that she began abusing alcohol on a daily basis in order to cope. A few days had passed before she secretly resumed planting the tape recorder in the car. When she listened to the tape the second time, however, she suspected that the tape had been tampered with or changed. Over the days that followed, the patient was convinced that someone was removing the tape recorder, changing the tape from side A to side B, and re-placing it in its original position with an altered recording. In desperation, she confided in her daughter and other family members that her husband was having an affair, but he had convinced them that she was mistaken. Mrs. Z had continued to hide the tape recorder in the car for sometime and reportedly recorded another discussion between a man and a woman. Maintaining his innocence, the husband speculated that the strangers must have made a duplicate set of keys to the car since he no longer left his keys hanging publicly on a hook in the office for people to take at their leisure.

The couple maintained this charade for a few more weeks, first getting an anti-theft device—"The Club"—and securing it to the wheel when away from his car at work, and then installing an elaborate car-alarm system. These protective devices were to no avail, because the alleged "strangers" were still apparently taking the car. When Mrs. Z heard once more what she perceived to be her husband's voice on the tape conversing with another woman, she became increasing more accusatory, volatile, and inebriated on a regular basis. The patient began to secretly follow her husband to work to spy, watching to see if he would deviate from his route or if she could catch the culprits. After a few days of observing nothing unusual, she began to suspect that her husband knew that he was being followed and the car observed. Around this time, the patient reported that she started noticing objects in the house missing, and that dish towels were being removed from the kitchen drawer but returned days later folded incorrectly. Her family was convinced that she was "crazy." Her paranoia was either due to an overly active imagination or alcohol, and her drunkenness was simply a means of "getting attention."

Although the complexities of this case are by no means exhausted in this short description, we may nevertheless see how the patient's discovery of her husband's transgressions was tinged with paranoia. Even during her hospitalization, the patient was struggling with accepting the realization of his infidelity which persecuted her as paranoiac knowledge. She did not wish to know, and the desire not to know marked by a disavowal of the evidence at hand was experienced as a persecutory assault on her psychic integrity. Lurking in the shadows, this knowledge stalked her, prowling in the recesses of her mind in the form of fixed repetitions and fantasies thus leading to obsessional cycles of fear, dread, anxiety, and rage—violating her self-cohesion.

In discussing a case of hysteria, Freud (1893–1895) referred to the "blindness of the seeing eye" as not wanting to know (p. 117, fn. 1). But Mrs. Z's desire not to know was not merely a desire to remain ignorant of her husband's deeds, it was a desire not to know *his* desire. As Lacan (1959–1960a) puts it, "the moving force of paranoia is essentially the rejection of a certain support in the symbolic order" (p. 54)—she could not accept his desire, hence his demand. The need to mobilize specific defensive manoeuvres designed to deny the possibility of the truth in the service of self-deception was exacerbated by the acute nature of her paranoiac intrusions: she was painfully exposed to the other's desire. In his lecture, "The See-Saw of Desire," Lacan (1953–1954) writes:

> What is ignorance? Certainly it is a dialectical notion, since it is within the perspective of truth that it is constituted as such. If the

subject does not refer himself to the truth, there is no ignorance. If the subject doesn't begin to ask himself the question what is and what is not, there is no reason for there to be a true and a false, nor even, beyond that, reality and appearance. (p. 167)

The structure of human knowledge is paranoid for the simple reason that it is constituted in dialectical relation to truth: To know or not to know?—that is the question. In either instance, there is an apprehension to knowing because of the possibility of being subjected to a painful realization: in this case, the other's desire. She *sees*, she *saw*—hence "See-Saw," and this must be negated. Having knowledge or not is in relation to presence and lack. Paranoia is a reaction to anxiety generated in response to desire as demand and/or in relation to absence.

Mrs. Z knew the truth but it had to be disavowed; she so desperately wanted to remain ignorant of the affair that she inverted and displaced the truth through the mechanism of misrecognition. In the most general sense, she became lost in the imaginary and could not see the real for what it was. Lacan (1953–1954) asserts:

Misrecognition represents a certain organization of affirmations and negations, to which the subject is attached. Hence it cannot not be conceived without correlative knowledge. If the subject is capable of misrecognizing something, he surely must know what this function has operated upon. There must be, behind his misrecognition, a kind of knowledge of what there is to misrecognize. (p. 167)

The patient's misrecognition is a function of her desire not to know what she knows. She is "attached" to her own wish. What she wishes to know is a symptom of her misrecognition, namely that her husband could not be guilty of desiring another woman. In fact, her self-deception was so entrenched that she had reportedly taken the tapes to a private investigator for a voice-analysis, the results of which were still pending during her hospitalization. Because her husband denied that the voice on the tape was his, yet had no explanation to account for the alleged incidents, the patient felt this was the only way to reconcile the situation. Lacan (1953–1954) adds, "[s]he misrecognizes, or refuses to recognize ... but everything in the way [s]he behaves indicates that [s]he knows that there is something that [s]he doesn't want to recognize" (p. 167). What Mrs. Z refused to recognize was her husband's desire. "The delusional intuition is a full phenomenon that has an overflowing, inundating character for the subject" (Lacan, 1955–1956b, p. 33). She so badly wanted to believe the untruth that she set out to prove him innocent: "The voice-analysis will exonerate him!" she exclaimed. During her hospitalization she had still hoped that the voice match would come back negative, which would prove in her mind that unidentified strangers were the offenders, yet as Lacan informs us, deep down she had already recognized the truth which she so despairingly wanted not to believe. But as Lacan (1959–1960b) says elsewhere: "nothing is more ambiguous than belief" (p. 171). He further states: "At the basis of paranoia itself, which nevertheless seems to be animated by belief, there reigns the phenomenon of the *Unglauben* (disbelief)" (1964e, p. 238). If the voice-analysis exonerated her husband, her paranoia would be confirmed only on the condition that it was not him, a wishful expression of her desire not to know. But if the results were inconclusive, she would continue to be plagued by suspicion, mistrust, and doubt.

Mrs. Z's misrecognition was maintained through periods of "transitivism," what Lacan refers to as moments of "see-sawing" in which the subject takes the other's actions (or thoughts) to be equivalent with her own. The patient's husband did not want her to know and he deliberately and calculatingly lied to cover up his deed and desire. Through projective identification, she identified with his desire, which she introjected and made her own. "He would not do such a thing because he loves only me. He would not hurt me!" Wanting to accept his story—his lie, she misrecognized his original desire for his counter-intention, namely his reparatory, secondary-wish for her not to know the truth. But all his reassurances and pleading could not stave off what she had already affirmed yet negated. She recognized his desire for what it was — "this other negates [me], literally kills [me]" (1955–1956c, p. 209): it gnawed on her as a slow emotional torture. Forced on her as a savage assault, violence and self-abuse was her only recourse—the destructive affliction of the other's desire.

The Subject of the Other

Whether paranoiac acquisitions arise in the fragmented images and dissociated impulses that characterize the experience of the incipient ego, in the imaginary relations governing fantasy, wish, conflict, and defense, or in our confrontation with the Other, the epistemic-phenomenological process of knowing is dynamically informed by unconscious paranoiac pressures. This is most evident when we confront the other's desire. As Hegel articulated over 200 years ago, the desire for recognition produces a primordial confrontation leading to "the desire for the disappearance of the other" (Lacan, 1953–1954, p. 170). When we encounter impasse from the affliction of others, we simply wish for them to vanish. Desire is a demand to which we yield or oppose. Language imposes itself on us as demand to which we are enslaved, thus explaining in part why we fear knowing anything beyond our immediate control. Whether constructed or discovered, the process of examining what *is* and what is *not*—being and nothingness—is driven by paranoia—itself the dialectic of being in relation to lack.

But paranoiac knowledge is not merely a fear of the unknown, it is a trepidation of knowing a particular truth that the subject may find horrific. Whether knowing elicits revulsion, shame, envy, or hate, it is the other's desire that is revealed in relation to our own. The juxtaposition of what is known to what is concealed always evokes the affirmation-negation contrast. As Lacan (1955–1956b) says, "paranoid knowledge is knowledge founded on the rivalry of jealousy" (p. 39) due to the subject's realization of lack in relation to the object of the other's desire. "This defines, within the speech relationship, something that originates somewhere else — this is exactly the distinction between the imaginary and the real" (p. 39). The object of otherness is a primitive alienation that we wish to possess, and is therefore the object of a primary identification. For Lacan, desire originates from the outside—*it* speaks. This is why he says that when the other talks about himself, he speaks to us about something that has spoken to him.

But we may ask: What part of the subject speaks from within? Analysis tells us the unconscious—the realm beyond conceptualization, namely, the real. In the imaginary and symbolic domains, we are bombarded by alienation, opposition, and demand, but *the un-conscious is the house of being* (see Mills, 2010), and our relation to the real is a self-relation we know very little about. "The unconscious is something that speaks within the subject, beyond the subject, and even when the subject doesn't know it, and that says more about him than he believes" (Lacan, 1955–1956b, p. 41). Here we may say that the unconscious is even more alienating than the imaginary, because we are ultimately estranged from ourselves—from our own inner world. Lacan's underworld is a disembodied subject constituted by the Other yet shrouded in an ineffable residue of persecution that can never be known in itself as such. Elsewhere Lacan (1964b) says: "In the unconscious there is a corpus of knowledge (*un savoir*), which must in no way be conceived as knowledge to be completed, to be closed" (p. 134). Therefore, the goal of psychoanalysis may be said to be the creative discovery of *aletheia* (ἀλήθεια). Truth is a process of disclosedness or unconcealment, a process which may never be completely actualized (Mills, 2014).

We have an ambivalent relation to the unconscious—the desire to know is opposed by the desire to remain oblivious. For Lacan, the real is that place of limit—that which is lacking in the symbolic order: it is truly most horrific by the mere fact that it can never be known in itself. There is ultimately no safety in the unknown, and that is why the phenomenology of the lived experience carries with it the para-noiac residue of the uncertainty of the life within. The imaginary and symbolic orders interpenetrate the real, which in turn inform how the unconscious interpellates consciousness. Consciousness becomes an appearance, an illusory articulation of what cannot be rightfully articulated. This is why consciousness can only reveal through images and symbolization the differentiated and modified forms of un-conscious reality. For Lacan (1954–1955a), objects that terrify us, such as

> the anxiety-provoking apparition of an image ... summarize what we can call the revelation of that which is least penetrable in the real, of the real lacking any possible mediation, of the ultimate real, of the essential object which isn't an object any longer, but this something faced with which all words cease and all categories fail, the object of anxiety *par excellence*. (p. 164)

The real resists articulation because it is simply "the impossible," thus subjecting consciousness to the paranoid abyss of the ineffable. Freud (1900) was the first to insist on the primacy of the underworld: "The unconscious is the true psychical reality; *in its innermost nature it is as much unknown to us as the reality of the external world*" (p. 613). And just as the nature of symptoms have a sense (Freud, 1916–1917), Lacan emphasizes the primal communication of the real as that indescribable language, that which is *paranoos*, thus beyond mind (νόος). It is not *I* who speaks; rather, *It* speaks in me.

Notes

1 From his *Seminar* on the psychoses, Lacan (1955–1956c) says, "I'm not surprised that my discourse may have created a certain margin of misunderstanding ... . I would say that it is with a deliberate, if not entirely deliberated, intention that I pursue this discourse in such a way as to offer you the opportunity to not quite understand" (p. 164).

2 It is important to keep in mind that Lacan saw many disturbed patients, and those who suicide are typically already quite ill.

3 This particular facet of Lacan's theory may be the single most philosophical conundrum in his metaphysical system. If speech produces the subject, then, I suggest, he hypostatizes the signifying chain (language) as a being or creator entity (which implies agency through causal imposition). Through the reification of language, he specifically gives semiotics—the laws of language, signification, and speech production—the ontological status of Being caused by the qualitative particularity of the signifying chain. Here the chain (i.e., the structure of speech and its infinite deferral of signifiers) is attributed agency as some overarching causal (although not fixed) law(s) that presides over the subject superimposed from an omnipotent external force, which creates the subject at any given moment. The subject is therefore the epiphenomenon of an inscripted linguistic act that is fleeting and ephemeral, but paradoxically contains no ontological status of its own. Here speech—not the subject—has the determinate power to create, yet it possesses no real agency. Words don't think. Despite these concerns, it does not negate the fact that his theory has clinical utility.

4 The implication of this position carries with it certain philosophical problematics. Lacan assumes that just because externality temporally predates the birth of the human subject, that the human being is strictly determined by environmental forces. Contra Hegel and Freud, who believe that a certain internally derived intrapsychic activity apprehends the external world of givens and modifies its self-structure through its own self-determinations; or Heidegger and Sartre, who believe that Dasein can transcend its thrownness, Lacan commits

himself to a hard determinism that leaves little wiggle-room for the notions of human agency, freedom, choice, and self-determinate action.

5 Lacan never studied Hegel with precision and would have likely been unaware of his writings on the anthropology of the soul and his treatise on psychology (theoretical spirit) outlined in the *Encyclopaedia of the Philosophical Sciences*. As I have argued elsewhere (Mills, 2002), Hegel actually shows that "the very condition for the possibility of self-conscious reflection and recognition is that the self must already be familiar with its own self" (p. 137) as a form of pre-reflectivity or unconscious self-consciousness with its own internal experiences and self-relations, or it would not be capable of recognizing itself in the mirror reflection of the other.

6 Here we may see Klein's influence on Lacan's thinking, where at one point he referred to her in a lecture as an "inspired gut butcher" (Kristeva, 2001, p. 229).

7 This view must be contrasted to the pleasant, soothing presence of the imago, and particularly the maternal imago, that is gradually internalized by the child, thus becoming a stabilizing and cohesive function informing psychic structure (Cf. the various developmental models of Bowlby, 1980; Klein, 1946, 1957; Kohut, 1978; Mahler, Pine, & Bergman, 1975; Stern, 1985).

8 Eros has many faces, even in death. There is a perverse pleasure in death; for Freud, the fusion of libido within self-destruction, for Lacan, the experience of *jouissance*. Unfortunately, there is no adequate translation of this word in English. 'Enjoyment' is suffused in its meaning but does not convey the sexual connotations retained in French. In one sense, *jouissance* denotes the intense pleasure of orgasm; *Jouir* is slang for 'to come.' However, pleasure does not quite capture its precise meaning for the residues of death are encrusted in its essence. Therefore, we may say that *jouissance* is pleasure in the realm of excess: "[it] is the essence or quality that gives one's life its value" (Ragland, 1995, p. 87).

9 "The Function and Field of Speech and Language in Psychoanalysis" was delivered to the Rome Congress held at the Istituto di Psicologia della Università di Roma, 1953.

10 For Lacan, the implications of the imaginary are often pejorative, suggesting that the subject seeks to remove itself from the flux of becoming by reducing itself to the stagnant aura of illusion. Although Lacan introduced some positive valence to the imaginary in later theoretical postulations, it largely remains a negative construct. It may be argued, however, that we can never escape the captivating presence of the imaginary. After all, it is the world of perception and fantasy, of wish and defense. We can never transcend the illusory.

References

Aristotle. (1958). *Metaphysics*, Book 1, In W.D. Ross trans., *The Pocket Aristotle*. New York: Washington Square Books.

Bion, W.R. (1959). Attacks on Linking. In Spillius, E.B. (ed.), *Melanie Klein Today: Developments in Theory and Practice. Volume 1: Mainly Theory.* London: Routledge, 1988: 87–101.

Boothby, R. (1991). *Death and Desire: Psychoanalytic Theory in Lacan's Return to Freud.* New York: Routledge.

Bowie, M. (1991). *Lacan.* Cambridge, MA: Harvard University Press.

Bowlby, J. (1980). *Attachment and Loss.* London: Hogarth Press.

Feldstein, R. (1996). The Mirror of Manufactured Cultural Relations. In R. Feldstein, B. Fink, & M. Jaanus (eds.), *Reading Seminars I and II: Lacan's Return to Freud,* Albany, NY: SUNY Press.

Fink, B. (1995). *The Lacanian Subject: Bewtween Language and Jouissance.* Princeton, NJ: Princeton University Press.

Fink, B. (1997). *A Clinical Introduction to Lacanian Psychoanalysis.* Cambridge, MA: Harvard University Press.

Freud, S., & Breuer, J. (1893–1895). *Studies on Hysteria.* Standard Edition: Vol.2. London: Hogarth Press.

Freud, S. (1900). *The Interpretation of Dreams.* Standard Edition: Vols.4–5. London: Hogarth Press.

Freud, S. (1916–1917). *Introductory Lectures on Psycho-Analysis.* Standard Edition: Vols.15–16. London: Hogarth Press.

Freud, S. (1920). *Beyond the Pleasure Principle.* Standard Edition: Vol.18. London: Hogarth Press.

Freud, S. (1921). *Group Psychology and the Analysis of the Ego.* Standard Edition: Vol.18. London: Hogarth Press.

Freud, S. (1923). *The Ego and the Id.* Standard Edition: Vol.19. London: Hogarth Press.

Freud, S. (1927). *The Future of an Illusion.* Standard Edition: Vol.21. London: Hogarth Press.

Freud, S. (1933). *New Introductory Lectures on Psycho-Analysis.* Standard Edition: Vol.22. London: Hogarth Press.

Frie, R. (1997). *Subjectivity and Intersubjectivity in Modern Philosophy and Psychoanalysis: A Study of Sartre, Binswanger, Lacan, and Habermas.* Lanham: Rowman & Littlefield Publishers.

Haddad, G. (1981). "Une pratique" (A Practice). *L'Ane,* 3; September 20.

Hegel, G.W.F. (1807). *Phenomenology of Spirit,* trans. A.V. Miller. Oxford: Oxford University Press, 1977.

Julien, P. (1994). *Jacque Lacan's Return to Freud: The Real, the Symbolic, and the Imaginary.* New York: New York University Press.

Klein, M. (1946). Notes on some schizoid mechanisms. In *Developments in Psycho-Analysis.* London: Hogarth Press.

Klein, M. (1957). *Envy and Gratitude*. In *Envy and Gratitude and other Works, 1946-1963*. London: Hogarth Press, 1975.

Kohut, H. (1971). *The Analysis of the Self*. New York: International Universities Press.

Kohut, H. (1977). *The Restoration of the Self*. New York: International Universities Press.

Kohut, H. (1978). *The search for the self: Selected writings of Heinz Kohut: 1950–1978*. 2 Vols., ed. P. Ornstein. New York: International Universities Press.

Kohut, H. (1984). *How Does Analysis Cure?*, eds. A. Goldberg and P. Stepansky. Chicago: University of Chicago Press.

Kristeva, J. (2001). *Melanie Klein*. trans. R. Guberman. New York: Columbia University Press.

Lacan, J. (1936). The Mirror Stage as Formative of the Function of the I. In A. Sheridan trans., *Écrits: A Selection*. New York: Norton, 1977.

Lacan, J. (1948). Aggressivity in Psychoanalysis. In A. Sheridan trans., *Écrits: A Selection*. New York: Norton, 1977.

Lacan, J. (1953). The Function and Field of Speech and Language in Psychoanalysis. In A. Sheridan trans., *Écrits: A Selection*. New York: Norton, 1977.

Lacan, J. (1953-1954). The See-Saw of Desire. In J.A. Miller (ed.), *The Seminar of Jacques Lacan, Book I: Freud's Papers on Technique, 1953–1954*, trans. J. Forrester. Cambridge: Cambridge University Press, 1988.

Lacan, J. (1954-1955a). The Dream of Irma's Injection (Conclusion). In trans. S. Tomaselli, ed. J.A. Miller, *The Seminar of Jacques Lacan, Book II: The Ego in Freud's Theory and the Technique of Psychoanalysis, 1954–1955*. Cambridge: Cambridge University Press, 1988.

Lacan, J. (1954-1955b). *A, m, a, S*. In S. Tomaselli, ed. J.A. Miller (trans.), *The Seminar of Jacques Lacan, Book II: The Ego in Freud's Theory and the Technique of Psychoanalysis, 1954-1955*. Cambridge: Cambridge University Press, 1988.

Lacan, J. (1955-1956a). Introduction to the Question of Psychoses. In trans. R. Grigg, ed. J.A. Miller, *The Seminar of Jacques Lacan, Book III: The Psychoses, 1955-1956*. New York: Norton, 1993.

Lacan, J. (1955-1956b). The Other and Psychoses. In trans. R. Grigg, ed., J.A. Miller, *The Seminar of Jacques Lacan, Book III: The Psychoses, 1955–1956*. New York: Norton, 1993.

Lacan, J. (1955–1956c). The Hysteric's Question. In trans. R. Grigg, ed. J.-A. Miller, *The Seminar of Jacques Lacan, Book III: The Psychoses, 1955–1956*. New York: Norton, 1993.

Lacan, J. (1957). The Agency of the Letter in the Unconscious or Reason Since Freud. In *Écrits: A Selection*, trans. A. Sheridan. New York: Norton, 1977.

Lacan, J. (1957-1958). On a Question Preliminary to Any Possible Treatment of Psychosis. In A. Sheridan trans., *Écrits: A Selection*. New York: Norton, 1977.

Lacan, J. (1958). The Direction of the Treatment and the Principles of its Power. In trans. A. Sheridan, *Écrits: A Selection*. New York: Norton, 1977.

Lacan, J. (1959-1960a). *Das Ding*. In trans. D. Porter, ed.J.A. Miller, *The Seminar of Jacques Lacan, Book VII: The Ethics of Psychoanalysis, 1959–1960*. New York: Norton, 1992.

Lacan, J. (1959-1960b). The Death of God. In trans. D. Porter, ed. J.A. Miller, *The Seminar of Jacques Lacan, Book VII: The Ethics of Psychoanalysis, 1959–1960*. New York: Norton, 1992.

Lacan, J. (1960). The Subversion of the Subject and the Dialectic of Desire in the Freudian Unconscious. In A. Sheridan trans., *Écrits: A Selection*. New York: Norton, 1977.

Lacan, J. (1964a). Excommunication. In trans. A. Sheridan, ed.J.A. Miller, *The Four Fundamental Concepts of Psycho-Analysis*. New York: Norton, 1981.

Lacan, J. (1964b). Presence of the Analyst. In trans. A. Sheridan, ed. J.A. Miller. *The Four Fundamental Concepts of Psycho- Analysis*. New York: Norton, 1981.

Lacan, J. (1964c). Sexuality in the Defiles of the Signifier. In trans. A. Sheridan, ed. J.A. Miller, *The Four Fundamental Concepts of Psycho-Analysis*. New York: Norton, 1981.

Lacan, J. (1964d). The Subject and the Other: Alienation. In trans. A. Sheridan, ed. J.A. Miller, *The Four Fundamental Concepts of Psycho-Analysis*. New York: Norton, 1981.

Lacan, J. (1964e). Of the Subject Who is Supposed to Know, Of the First Dyad, and Of the Good. In trans. A. Sheridan, ed. J.A. Miller, *The Four Fundamental Concepts of Psycho-Analysis*. New York: Norton, 1981.

Lacan, J. (1966). *Écrits*. Paris: Éditions du Seuil.

Lacan, J. (1972-1973). On the Baroque. In trans. B. Fink, ed. J.A. Miller, *The Seminar of Jacques Lacan, Book XX: Encore, 1972–1973*. New York: Norton, 1998.

Lacan, J. (1977). *Écrits: A Selection*, trans. A. Sheridan. New York: Norton.

Lee, J.S. (1990). *Jacques Lacan*. Boston: Twayne Publishers.

Mahler, M.S., Pine, F., & Bergman, A. (1975). *The Psychological Birth of the Human Infant*. New York: Basic Books.

Marcelle, M. (1992). *Jacques Lacan: The French Context*, trans. A. Tomiche. New Brunswick, NJ: Rutgers University Press.

Mills, J. (1999). Unconscious Subjectivity. *Contemporary Psychoanalysis*, 35(2), 342–347.

Mills, J. (2002). *The Unconscious Abyss: Hegel's Anticipation of Psychoanalysis*. Albany, NY: SUNY Press.

Mills, J. (2010). *Origins: On the Genesis of Psychic Reality*. Montreal: McGill-Queens University Press.

Mills, J. (2014). Truth. *Journal of the American Psychoanalytic Association*, 62(2), 267–293.

Mills, J. (2017). *Inventing God: Psychology of Belief and the Rise of Secular Spirituality*. London: Routledge.

Mitchell, S.A. (1988). *Relational Concepts in Psychoanalysis: An Integration*. Cambridge, MA: Harvard University Press.

Muller, J.P., & Richardson, W.J. (1982). *Lacan and Language*. New York: International Universities Press.

Ragland, E. (1995). *Essays on the Pleasures of Death: From Freud to Lacan*. New York: Routledge.

Roustang, F. (1990). *The Lacanian Delusion*. New York: Oxford University Press.

Sarup, M. (1992). *Jacques Lacan*. Toronto: University of Toronto Press.

Schneiderman, S. (1983). *Jacques Lacan: The Death of an Intellectual Hero*. Cambridge, MA: Harvard University Press.

Segal, H. (1957). Notes on Symbol Formation. *International Journal of Psycho-Analysis*, 38, 391–397.

Stern, D. (1985). *The interpersonal world of the infant*. New York: Basic Books.

Vanheule, S. (2011). *The subject of psychosis: A Lacanian perspective*. London: Palgrave MacMillan.

Žižek, S. (1992). *Enjoy Your Symptoms! Jacques Lacan in Hollywood and Out*. New York: Routledge.

Chapter 6

The Essence of Evil

Does evil exist, or is it a social invention? Is evil an action, a disposition, a property, a consequence, and/or a characteristic that necessarily makes it what it is, essentially? Does it hinge on creating pain for others—from relatively benign modes of discomfort to harm and gratuitous suffering? Does malicious intent have to be involved; or simply just intent, even if not malicious? Surely pain can result without intent, so what is the relationship between harm and human motivation? What if an event that brings about harm and suffering was not due to a direct action, but rather a failure to act, such as in a weakness of will, the bystander effect, or a miscarriage of moral courage? Here we may describe evil as the abnegation of responsibility, the failure to choose, the denial of freedom. But what happens if these failures are unconsciously informed, even chosen, the product of an unconscious will towards evil? Or are these queries contingent upon value judgements we ascribe to events and their causal attributions?

The question and nature of evil has been a human preoccupation since the rise of civilization, yet we can find no consensus on what constitutes its essence. The instantiation of evil unequivocally contributes to the necessary social manufacturing of law and order, religion, morality, justice, and systemic mechanisms of restraint, as well as punishment, that govern individual and collective relations within all societies. Psychoanalysis generally has tended to focus upon the pathological dynamics that motivate evil actions, from primary, malignant, and traumatic narcissism to primitive defensive enactments, superego lacunae, failure in internalization and empathy, sociopathy,

DOI: 10.4324/9781003305958-6

selfobject deficits, developmental trauma, and attachment pathology, rather than on the question of evil itself. For example, is evil a human phenomenon, or does it have a metaphysical structure? What makes evil (by necessity) what it is, or is it merely a relative enterprise fashioned by our subjectivities? Any determination of evil stands in relation to the meaning of value and the value of meaning, for what differentiates a natural act (such as animals killing prey, extreme weather phenomenon resulting in environmental disasters with loss of life, and so forth) from a human act is the construction of meaning and value inquiry within ethical agency. Furthermore, are actions in-themselves sufficient to determine the essence of evil, or does psychological intent become a necessary ingredient? What if such intent was unconsciously harbored yet unacknowledged by the conscious subject, let alone enacted, the evil within? And what about the consequences of both action and intention as a touchstone by which to adjudicate evil? These questions tend to situate the problematic of evil within a moral realm. But what if the question and nature of evil has nothing to do with morality whatsoever?

In this chapter, I wish to explore the essence and ethics of evil. What I will conclude is both controversial and counter-intuitive. But before we get there, I will need to prepare our discussion. After laying out various philosophical problematics, our analysis will centre around the domain and structure of violence as (a) natural phenomena, (b) subjective interiority, (c) objective instantiation, (d) systemic perpetuation, and (e) ontic universality. The degree to which our natural constitution derived from evolutionary pressures predisposes the human animal towards evil will be contrasted with developmental currents that are cultivated as a result of social interaction and the interiority of suffering. What marks the qualification of evil is the degree of ethical agency within an individual and society determined by the objective attainment of self-consciousness and voluntary choice. The evil that inhabits man in thought, intention, and deed is beyond psychological dynamics, I suggest, for violence is a metaphysical principle that saturates the natural world as a *mysterium tremendum*, at once a frightening necessity governing life yet one that signals the non-violent domain of ideality we attribute to moral idealism, paradoxically, itself a violent imposition as ethical demand.

What is Evil?

Let us first begin with basics. In classical Greek, κăκός historically signifies that which is intrinsically "bad," whereby the term "evil" is a transliteration. Etymologically the origin of the word is unknown, but many philologists believe it is derived from the proto-Indo-European root *kakka*, taken from κακκάω—to defecate. In other words, evil is shitty. The term is taken up in numerous contexts in classical antiquity and has generally informed our modern conception of all valuative discourses today. κăκός refers to (a) persons and their character: *bad, lowly, wretched* (see Herodas, *Mimographus*, 3.42); (b) of appearance: *ugly*; (c) of birth: *ill-born, mean*; (d) of courage: *craven, cowardly*; (e) of kind: *worthless, sorry, unskilled*; (f) of things: *pernicious* (see Homer, *Odyssey*, 10.64); (g) of omens: *unlucky*; (h) of words: *abusive, foul*; (i) of actions: *to do harm or ill to another* (*Illiad*, 2.195); and (j) in the moral sense: *base, evil*. Interestingly, κăκός is a cognate of καλός, its opposite, namely, the good, the beautiful.[1] Here we may see how good and evil are dialectically related and mutually implicative. In other words, we cannot have any discussion of either concept without invoking the other. This makes evil, by definition, contingent on a notion of good, which is itself equally presupposed, debatable, and problematic.

There is a natural simplicity to splitting based upon a perfunctory economy. This is an elementary aspect to mental functioning and observed endlessly as a normative process, whether in society or in the clinic. This natural (hence normal, inborn, instinctual, or organic) tendency to think in terms of binaries—same/different, good/bad—is a rudimentary mechanism of thinking that is superimposed on all experience. It is only with cognitive development and the acquisition of self-consciousness or a reflective function (often referred to as mentalization) that the binary proclivity is breached through attempts at entertaining complexity, holism, integration of opposite perspectives, and synthetic attempts at unification or reconciliation of opposition and difference. But this synthetic function, I argue, is a developmental or ideological ideal that is never fully achieved as a hierarchical reality when it comes to certain matters, especially those involving the human emotions, including the notions of right and wrong. In fact, an ideology of right can intensify this bifurcation and fortify a rigid antithesis that blinds us to the opposing perspective, which further introduces a danger of imposing an absolutism on phenomena, phenomena that by definition are open, transient, fluid, and pluralistic, thus radically resisting unification. Here there is no transvaluation of values, no *Aufhebung*, no discernable space beyond good and evil; rather we have an impasse, a gap, lacunae, or parallax where there is no synthesis among the two polarities. We cannot make each opposition—the fork between good and evil—a unified position based on fanciful logic alone. It defies all social realities. It betrays what we know about the human psyche as an unconsciously desirous and conflicted animal. There will always be a firm obstacle, limit, or check between these opposing forces in the mind. Yet it all depends upon what perspective you take.

Evil is typically construed on the negative pole of the dialectic, a construct defined in relation to absolute difference. Evil as contrast to its opposite highlights its one-sided polarity, one based on pure negation, yet this duality forms an ontological unit. Since antiquity, evil has been signified by its privative function and formally instantiated as innate badness, namely, that which deracinates and generates social disharmony by lacerating all semblances of moral order. It is none other than the introduction of radical negativity, to the degree that existential preoccupations with its recalcitrant presence has generated the psychological need for elaborate systems of theodocy to explain its occurrence. Here reconciling the appearance of evil with the good and with the question and meaning of God has elevated the notion of evil to a metaphysical factor. Historically, God has been extricated from evil while being attributed instead to fallen angels or man, yet this fantasy is hardly intellectually worthy of support. In today's secular world, the reification of evil to a supernatural hypostatization (i.e., the Devil) is an untenable explanation for the atrocities committed by human beings. In the absence of divine presence or intervention, evil is exclusively a human phenomenon.

What would a secular theory of evil look like? First we must explore whether we can pinpoint its essence, namely, that which necessarily circumscribes and defines what it is, without which it would not nor could not exist. Here I am chasing after the question of universality: Can evil be shown to have an essence, and if so, does it apply universally across modes of human phenomena that are adjudicated to be or deemed as evil? This would imply, all things being equal, that any universal attribution of evil would carry epistemological and hermeneutic agreement to warrant such generalizations, even if only confined to theory. But is this possible? This would mean, hypothetically, that no one instance or particularity would elude the label of evil if it was deemed a universal attribution. This surely would challenge the notion of context, contingency, accident, and chance. Perhaps we should not assume that universality and context are mutually exclusive, especially when they ontically inform each other. Perhaps evil may be viewed as a certain positionality as fixation on one side of its dialectical polarity, what may also be said of the good, whereby both positions form a tension arc between their oppositions. Here we may posit that both good and evil involve a radical splitting of the other, one that is obstreperous to mediation or synthesis.

Because evil is historically by definition the absence or privation of good, it requires opposition in order to lend it structure and meaning. Here evil is value laden, hence it stands in relation to the question and nature of morality. This presupposes that evil cannot be amoral as it signifies a judgement about value and agency. But what if evil is in itself a relative construct, that there are no absolutes? What if it has no value? Then this would imply that there is neither good nor evil, for valuation itself is either held in abeyance, neutralized, suspended, non-existent, or devolves into a meaningless construct. But how can a material act or embodied event lack valuation;how can it escape human judgement? Perhaps we may conclude there are no absolutes due to the relativity of conferring value judgements while still observing appearances of evil that are universal. Conversely, can the notion of pure negativity carry with it a metaphysical value even if it lies outside of human valuation? In other words, can evil exist without agency? These are difficult questions to sustain.

Evil is often defined as an act of transgressing, which in many cultures corresponds to something that is wrong, yet we immediately encounter the thorny issues of determining what constitutes wrongness, the non-good, and what it means to transgress, as these determinations stand in relation to a contextual and collective attribution of meaning as valuation. Here evil is not merely an intellectual concept, or the religionization of human desire and action, for it stands in relation to an absolute value that has been contravened, devalued, or occluded. But because value judgements are determinative and transpire within a given material culture and linguistic social structure replete with local customs and prejudices of meaning, the question of absolute value may succumb to relativity. Regardless of the questionable antipodes and extremity of either absolutism or relativism, the essence of evil is found in its contextual valuation whether absolute, universal, or relative in its instantiation and scope. This necessarily places valuation at the heart of any determination of evil, and since valuation stands in juxtaposition to greater collective meaning structures within any given society, evil becomes a social artifact.

The term "evil" is burdened by its history. In the Judeo-Christian tradition that has dominated Western thought, evil is considered to be that which violates God's will. We may already see an ideology at play by presupposing a Supreme Being to begin with, one that dominates world discourse and preys on the fears, emotional vulnerability, ignorance, and religious prejudices of contemporary cultures. Promulgating such a way of thinking further reinforces the unconscious social fantasy that such a reified Ideal exists by which all humans will be compared to and judged by divine authority. In ancient times, the God posit served many pragmatic and psychological purposes, but it hardly serves as a touchstone let alone justification for an operational definition of evil. I see no valid rational argument for perpetuating this psychomythology that evil is deviation from God's way, when God is merely a social construction born of a fantasy principle and instituted as a cultural symbolic (Freud, 1927; Mills, 2017).

But we must take seriously the notion that evil is the privation or absence of good. This was set out by Aquinas in his *Summa Theologiae* (see Part I: Treatise on The Distinction of Good And Evil [Q 48–49]), which was earlier echoed by Augustine (*Confessions*, Bk 3, vii [12]), what Plotinus believed was a psychic or subjective event, hence belonging to the soul (*Enneads*, I, 2.1–3; 8.8), not a godhead, yet at the same time an ontological condition based upon the fact that we are embodied. But the privation (*steresis*) theory of evil (*kakon*), although debatable, may be said to have its genesis in Aristotle who discussed the notion of lack, such as when something is deprived of an attribute belonging to its nature, for "a thing comes to be from [it's] privation" (see *Physics*, bk 1: 191b15). With stipulations, this may be (loosely) interpreted to mean, that which is evil comes into being from what it is lacking. Perhaps this is merely an inverse tautology: evil is the lack of goodness. Of course this sentiment is inherited from Plato: evil is the destroyer and corrupter of all things (*Republic*, 10.608e), which can never be done away with (*Theaetetus*, 176a). That which is deemed objectively beneficial is good, and that which is deemed evil is not. As for the nature of evil, it is derived from the natural "desire of food of drink of sex," but not for the momentary pleasure it produces, but rather from its "consequences" (*Protagoras*, 353c-e). Here we may see a kernel of neoPlatonism influencing the Christian perversion of pathologizing human nature as sinful. Despite the fact that discourse on the nature of evil was inspired by the pre-Socratics, and can be historically found in virtually all records of early civilization, good and evil have become the positive and negative exemplifications of moral absolutes.

Radical Evil

Kant's treatise on evil does not attribute evil to original sin, nor to a turning away from God, nor does it conform to the Augustinian denial of evil since it is nothing but the privation of good (*privatio boni*), not even to human want or desire, but rather is due to free choice (*Willkür*). Evil is the product of our determinate powers of choice because, for Kant, we are radically free to determine the grounds for the sake of which to behave. This places the onus of responsibility squarely on the existential agent making such choices, and not on natural inclination, impulse, or desire, for as Kant (1793) tells us, "the source of evil ... can lie only in a rule made by the will for the use of its freedom, that is, in a maxim" (p. 17). So even though we are born with innate needs, desires, leanings, dispositions, and impulses, man is the author of his nature due to acts of freewill as choice that either conform to or neglect the moral realm. This so-called freedom of the moral will that generates maxims upon which all human beings supposedly construct for themselves, is a purely determining, autonomous spontaneity of choice and is therefore influenced by many "incentives." And for Kant, "the moral law, in the judgment of reason, is on itself an incentive, and whoever makes it his maxim is *morally* good" (pp. 19–20), whereas deviation from the moral injunction makes one an "evil man."

Kant believes that such a disposition towards choosing good or evil is a matter of free choice, and as such, natural a priori predeterminations are contradictory to the principles of choice as one cannot freely choose what is given or thrown. But are dispositions always freely chosen? Are not urges, impulses, inclinations, and wants also mediated by other forces outside of one's immediate agentic will, awareness, and intent? Propensities, he argues, are acquired, and therefore not necessarily innate, although they are naturally predisposed by virtue of the fact that we crave and have penchants and susceptibilities; but how can he justify the claim that we are predisposed to be inclined to freely choose any course of action unless we are subjected to particularized experiences? Moreover, if we are predisposed to be free agents, are we not necessarily conditioned on naturalized tendencies? Our corporeality is a necessary condition for actualizing free choice, although it is far from a sufficient one.

If we are naturally predisposed to freely choose, then are we not naturally predisposed to choose evil, necessarily so? Left to our own natural devises, would we not likely choose what feels good in the moment regardless of any moral maxims, much like a child in the candy store? Moral laws are not naturally given, for they are acquired: morality is the education and imposition of culture.

We can no more presuppose the moral law as a transcendental good than we can of evil, for every human activity is based in naturalized psychology. Kant behaves as though the so-called moral imperative is a metaphysical given in the universe much like the physical laws governing our world and the cosmos, when it may be forcefully argued that morality is a human phenomenon. When Kant repeats his ethical mantra that "there is no propensity to moral evil, for such a propensity must spring from freedom ... in the moral capacity of the will" (p. 26), he is presupposing a moral capacity to begin with adapted as a rational decision to live one's life according to moral maxims. On the one hand Kant wants to champion a radical freedom by virtue of our capacity to choose evil, while on the other denying an *inherent necessity* to such a choice that is by nature a "natural predisposition" (p. 27). In the end, for Kant, all choices derive from maxims of the will.

What is "radical" for Kant is the deliberate act of choosing evil in light of our conscious awareness of the moral law, which is tantamount to the free choice of violating our moral duty, hence a corruption of the will in selecting evil maxims; although we are naturally inclined to do so, we are nonetheless responsible and accountable for it, which is brought on by ourselves (p. 28). Evil is radical in the sense that it "corrupts the ground of all maxims" (p. 32), which is subjectively chosen through perversity of the heart, human frailty, impurity, and vulnerability to wickedness and vice (see p. 24), for it ultimately "puts out of tune the moral capacity to judge" (p. 34). Yet, for Kant, the moral law is transcendentally given, hence presupposed, as is the notion that human beings freely choose their actions through rational means. Here Kant's theory of radical evil suffers from a theoretical prejudice to begin with, namely, the belief in sober rationalism, as though people conduct their lives in deliberate fashions that embrace ethical principles and rules of behaviour conforming to logical axioms in choice and action. This could not be farther from the truth of our primordial natures, for moral deliberation is a developmental triumph of the will mediated by many psychological dynamics that ultimately inform any rational comprehension of choice.

Kant ultimately makes evil a rational enterprise of choosing to follow a maxim in discord with duty and allegiance to the moral law, or what duty demands, as if morality is a purely rational decision. Furthermore, ethical attunement is either aligned or misaligned with some realm of moral metaphysical realism, once again freely chosen or ignored, rather than attributed to a moral idealism invented by humanity. Kant fails to reconcile the tension arc between the faculty of desire and freewill and begs the question of ethical duty by presupposing a transcendental moral law, as though it is preordained; not to mention that we choose maxims to follow in rational ways rather than as emotionally expedient, mediated events under the press of a whole host of extraneous factors and cultural environs. For example, when he says that "the predisposition to *personality* is the capacity for respect for the moral law as *in itself a sufficient incentive of the will*" (pp. 22–23), he fails to understand human nature as driven by other competing dynamic processes and conflicts that condition this will, especially those imposed by unconscious currents and environmental determinants. Here evil impositions can come from a multitude of directions having very little to do with freewill. Evil begets evil whether chosen or not.

Is not the moral law an achievement of culture, at once an invention and imposition of civilization? Kant's view of good and evil as rational choice succumbs to the prejudices of his day concerned with upholding a Christian explanation of man's aberrant behaviour while salvaging a theodicy that insulates God from allowing evil. In the end it is hardly a satisfactory account of the irrational, emotional, libidinal, and aggressive predilections that fester within our human natures clamoring for release in various forms, under various guises and valences, and in various circumstances that stimulate their appearance. Contra Kant, moral law is not the provenance of *"divine command"* (p. 37), but rather a human calling.

The Relativity of Evil

I have a country home on a modest fishing lake surrounded by many acres of forest and bush in the lush Canadian wilderness. My closest friend was visiting from the States when my wife, while taking a walk with our daughter on the property, called me on her cell phone alerting me to her discovery. There were several large fish pooling together in a shallow area of the lake near a water drain that connects to a stream. She had no clue what kind of fish they were, but she found the discovery of concern. I immediately feared they were Asian carp attempting to migrate upstream to spawn in the spring. Asian carp are an invasive species that kills practically everything in its ecosystem and have received much attention from anglers and ecologists in Ontario, hence stimulating governmental campaigns designed to combat their contamination of indigenous waters. The invasion of Asian carp have been so damaging in the United States that it is estimated that approximately ninety percent of the ecosystem in the Mississippi River has been decimated. I am a catch-n'-release bass fisherman, forester, and conservationist, and the last thing I want is my precious fishing paradise destroyed by unwelcome intruders. Upon this news, I immediately grabbed a large fishing net and walked briskly with my friend to the scene of the crime.

As I feared, these were not largemouth bass but 1–2 foot carp waiting for the right moment to swim upstream. I instinctively started to scoop them out one by one with my net in a frenzied manner and threw them onto the shore to die. Only a few escaped back into the lake. When the deed was done, I looked at my friend's face and could immediately see his visible discomfort with my murderous act. Was this evil? From my perspective, I was protecting my lake. From his, this was morally reprehensible. Here witnessing the killing of living creatures was disturbing, and I must admit I did not enjoy it one bit, but I felt compelled to safeguard my habitat. One could even say this basic instinct, as biologists will tell you, is evolutionarily programed despite the elevation or sublimation of self-consciousness we typically confer onto reason and moral conscience. But herein lies a clash of values that provoke basic ethical questions. Despite the fact that we are hardwired towards predation, adaptation, and survival, should human consciousness be obliged to rise above its naturalized tendencies? Should one kill another living thing? Is it evil to set a mousetrap or swat a fly? Moreover, is it innately base? Necessarily so? Or do we value some entities more than others to justify our acts of killing? World societies face these dilemmas every day. In other words, is killing intrinsically evil?

Of course we may differentiate the act of killing from murder, as the world masses must eat, and have no malicious intent when harvesting grain, plants and vegetables, or slaughtering animals to put food on the table in order to be healthy and thrive. The cold brute fact of nature is that we must necessarily kill in order to live. Despite the well-intentioned, ethically conscientious objector who demands that we as humanity transcend our primitive natures as desirous, self-enhancing agents, most of the world pays very little attention to this moral question when a hungry stomach cries out to be fed. Here we value our own sustenance over an axiological category or lower form of life that we determine is secondary to human need. But here I had no intention of eating these fish. They were an atrocious enemy that needed to be eradicated in order to preserve what I have and value. This basic splitting in my consciousness at the time may be compared to a simple economy that justifies hurting others, including murder and warfare, based on the notion of relativized experiential value.

On Universality

On January 10, 2015, Nigeria's militant Jihadist group Boko Haram (which literally means "Western education is forbidden"), after going on a mass killing spree in Baga on Lake Chad, strapped explosives to a 10 year old little girl and sent her off into a market in Maiduguri as a human detonator (Nadeau, 2015). This atrocity comes after the April 14th, 2014 kidnapping of nearly 300 school girls from the Chibok Government Secondary School by the terrorist group, of which the girl is believed to be one of the abductees. Although reported accounts vary, as many as 276 were snatched, many of which are still missing, all of which are believed to be used as sex objects and domestic servants.

On December 16, 2014, seven members of a Pakistani Taliban extremist group entered the back door of an army public school in the dustbowl border city of Peshawar and indiscriminately opened fire with machine guns and explosives strapped to their vests, killing 132 schoolchildren. The Taliban proclaimed the attack was a vendetta for an army offensive in North Waziristan in June that beset militant insurgents. Pakistan's Taliban spokesman Mohammed Umar Khorasanin plainly stated their motive: "We targeted the school because the army targets our families ... We want them to feel our pain" (Inayat, Qazi, & Bacon, 2014). Among the copious voices of world outcry, Canadian Prime Minster Stephen Harper said in a news conference:

> I think it's hard for any of us as rational and compassionate people to understand terrorism, to understand why people would want, in the name of some political cause, to simply terrorize, hurt, kill innocent people, whole sections of society, but I think it is just beyond, it is beyond our comprehension why somebody would target children.

(Canadian Press, 2014)

These words read alone do not convey the felt emotionality of his speech. This psychological perplexity of disbelief nicely encapsulates the unfathomability of bearing witness to a universal horror. What is beyond comprehension is that innocent helpless children would be brutally murdered by deliberate, malicious, and calculated actions of men. It is as if the response of the collective psyche were to say: "How could human beings do this? Only animals prey, for they are instinctual evolutionary organisms that have no self-reflective function or moral conscience by natural design. Humans are supposed to be different." But whether we accept the inherent animality to humanity or not, the line has been crossed.

It is only on the condition that slaughtering innocent children in cold blood would be permissible in any possible world that one would even question its moral significance. In other words, it would never occur to most civilized people to ask whether it is moral or immoral to kill innocent children who have done nothing to others, for the Kantian categorical imperative already speaks a universal language of prohibition. In such instances, where the masses identify with the purity and holiness of childhood, whether as a cultural symbolic or through the direct empathic identification with their own families and personal lives—namely, their own relatives and the child within, the immediate dissociation of understanding any rational means behind such atrocities is emotionally unfathomable for the simple fact that it disrupts our psychic need for a moral order in the universe. Such an imposed confrontation with universal horror forces us to question the presupposed universality of a moral universe to begin with, for it eclipses all value as we know it. Here our rational "unfathomability" that is "beyond comprehension" is none other than our own emotive dissociation to the realization (that must be disavowed) of the *dissociation of ethics*—hence the renunciation of "right"—perpetrated by the Other. In other words, we would have to suspend or abandon a universal concept of what is right and wrong, not to mention entertain a mentalized stance that others would not share our own sense of values. Here lies the pathological breach, an incipient a priori knowledge, that human nature is at base a primitive, feral process that fractures all illusory notions of a civilized, just, and loving world, for it only takes one act of barbarism to remind us that evil is no illusion.

On the Question of Essence

Let us begin to try to sketch out a more refined definition of evil. First of all, as stated earlier, I categorically reject the notion of the personification of evil as a supernatural force or being derived from theosophic perspectives, theodicy, or onto-theology.[2] Having said this, there are certain metaphysical principles that are operative in any account of evil, such as the institution and/or experience of pure or radical negativity, disorder, disharmony, or disintegration as a structural process endemic to the instantiation of destruction and decay, but these factors may also be viewed as a necessary complementarity to life, for without such events, there can be no change or growth, only stasis. I cannot conceive of the universe without process, therefore without privation, variation, difference, conflict, and negation, there would be no motion, evolution, or creativity; hence negativity in itself cannot be condemned as evil, and in fact may be deemed a metaphysical good because it leads to variation, heterogeneity, and plurality. But this discourse on metaphysical evil hardly satisfies our quest for an answer to essence.

Natural disasters and tragedies happen every moment, from the Lisbon earthquake that sparked the theodicy movement to overcome the aporia of how such systemic destruction could even be allowed by a benevolent godhead, especially now when the problem of evil and gratuitous suffering remains the most severe challenge to justified theology (Francis, 2013)—to the banality of death, from the butcher's block to political warfare and military science; but we do not impart a malevolent intent to the impersonal hands of cosmic forces. They merely happen through the blind random mutation of organic nature, as well as influenced or expedited by human intervention, as we may readily observe as global populations slowly destroy our planet through climate change, global warming, pollution, exploitation of natural resources, desertification, and the despoliation of our ecosystems. But when people burn coal to warm their homes or cook food, there is no malignant intent to cause harm, only to survive. Despite the fact that these continued practices, if allowed to go unrestrained or unchecked, may bring about the demise of our planet, to call them intrinsically evil would mean that we must abort our natural inclinations towards self-sustenance dependent upon a social infrastructure that promulgates and provides the necessities of life. This is not to say that societies should not improve upon such cultural institutions through collective education and social consciousness, but to call them inherently evil, I suggest, is misguided. After all, most people value their own immediate concrete lives over an abstract principle or a fish in the sea, even if such suspension of reason or ethical myopia leads to slow global suicide.

We must first attempt to isolate a key ingredient before formulating an answer to the question of the essence of evil. In paraphrasing Aristotle, for something to be, it must necessarily contain certain essential qualities, elements, or forms that make it what it is, without which, it could not be or exist. In other words, if something does not possess certain features, it would not be fundamental to its nature, hence it would not be a vital aspect to its ontological structure. The essence of anything must be indispensable, critical, requisite or basic, hence the lifeblood of its being. Does evil have an essential form? Does it have essential properties? And what would they be?

If evil necessarily encompasses pure negativity, and negativity is an indispensable property to its constitution and appearance, then its instantiation must issue forth or bring about a modicum of violence. Violence may have many appearances, from the pulsating threat of passion or power to the intensity of fear, intimidation, felt aggression, overt hostility, brute force, abuse, ferocity, fury, viciousness, cruelty, savagery, death, and so on. Violence may also be lulled, implicit, or expectant, an immanent looming presence that suffuses our world, even if conspicuously absent, an invisibility that is felt. In this regard, violence is hidden but is always there. We may say this is metaphysical violence, as origin, as *arkhē*, the violence of Being. Mind is an original form of violence, a violent coming into being, an awakening as internal rupture, as upheaval, as the self-violent manifestation of interruption.

Slavoj Žižek (2008) identifies *subjective* violence as the phenomena of subjective experience, which is the most salient among the masses perpetrated by an identifiable agent or entity. By contrast, *objective* violence[3] is both symbolic, that which is constituted through language and semiotic orders of understanding, as well as the myriad forms it may sociologically appear. In fact, language itself is violent: it places a proverbial demand on the other whether solicited or not through aggressive encroachments and superimposed universals of meaning; while *systemic* violence is instantiated through our economic and political institutions that are operating as concretely inscribed mechanisms within our cultural infrastructures and social ideologies. Here we must differentiate the ontological structural elements of evil from their subjective phenomenological-hermeneutical counterparts.

A defining characteristic that differentiates subjective from objective evil is that subjective experience or its qualitative, hermeneutic equivalent may elude a universal appraisal of its definition. This may be due to a lack of shared personal experience or history, linguistic meaning, social convention, consensus, or objective standards of measurement and their interpretation that separates the individual from the collective. We have already encountered this with the problem of relativity. Here empathy may play a key ingredient in sympathizing with how another may interpret a particular personal experience as evil or not, but the form of the experience and its adjudication is nevertheless a solipsistic enterprise. The question becomes whether or not it is universalizable. Here is where a potential objective dimension materializes, namely, does it resonate with other subjects and their subjectivities that can form some basis of consensus that is adopted as social convention. Whether this makes something objective is still another matter, for one can envision a community of others that hold onto propositional attitudes, false beliefs, emotional prejudices, distortions of truth and realty, and socialized delusions based on intersubjective fantasies peculiar to a group, mass, or culture. The God posit is a good example.

Let us propose a distinction between (a) an evil *act* and (b) an evil *intention*. An act always leads to some form of a consequence, while an intention may be passive, active, conscious, unconscious, and either linked to a motive or action, suspended, disavowed, or even held in check, hence non-enacted. For example, an act that brings about death may be accidental, such as a motor vehicle accident, but there was no intent to kill. The same applies to forces of nature, such as a tornado or tsunami: weather has no personal intention to destroy, it is merely a series of random or teleonomic physical events. In these cases death and destruction result from acts without intent; despite being tragic, dreadful, and disastrous, I would not classify these as examples of evil. Hence for something to be evil, this requires *agency*. This implies that a certain modicum of intentionality is at play in operationalizing evil. Here an intention always possesses an *aim*. And when it comes to the human psyche, this would necessarily require consciousness (even if consciousness lies on a continuum) that aims at a particular act as an intentional meant object. This means that an act that brings about a certain negative consequence we deem evil must stem from an intentional stance, hence it is deliberate although not necessarily deliberated, as acts may be spontaneously enacted and not particularly well thought-out; albeit it would have to stem from an intention all the same, for no action is devoid of a motive or purpose driving an act, even if it is unconscious.

This brings us to speculate that a certain state of mind must be operative in acts of evil, whether this be (a) *dispositional* or (b) *intentional*, as well as bearing a particular (c) *qualia* or (d) *psychic form* (e.g., emotion) attached to the intentional act. And here is where we may consider a state of mind that is ontically or dispositionally aggressive, which is the manifestation of the purely negative split of the dialectic. Here violence becomes an ontological feature structurally infused in the very essence of evil. This commits us to accepting a universalizing principle to evil, for every form of evil must participate of a rudimentary violence. We may further say that in its pure (abstract) form, dispositional violence is the inscription of radical negativity, while evil is the manifestation (hence the appearance or enactment) of dispositional violence. Not only is this subjectively constituted in each person (namely, dispositional evil), it materializes in empirical reality when externalized in society. In other words, it takes on objective properties and consequences, is institutionally organized, signified, and represented in the concrete universals that comprise our social, economic, and political suprastructures, and as Žižek points out, is systemically politicized through reinforced ideologies operative within hegemonic, socio-symbolic, and cultural unconscious processes. Not only is there a phenomenal appearance to evil, it is ontologically encrypted in the very fabric of worldhood itself.

From the side of phenomenology, the qualitative appearance of intentionality manifests as a certain mode of dispositional violence that takes on a malevolent form: namely, there is a certain malignancy, spitefulness, and maliciousness directed towards an object of aggression. Therefore, there must be a certain desire to hurt or cause pain to another person or thing, even if this is a prereflective act. Here the *agent*, the *intent*, and the *act* must display its dispositional violence, while the consequence may or may not bring about an evil outcome based upon the success or failure of the intentional act to achieve its goal. For example, the intent to inflict pain, suffering, or death on another may be thwarted, but the intentional act itself is nevertheless evil. Here we may say it is predisposed. The corollary is that dispositional violence ontically informs intentionality and action, including the act of thinking itself. This means that people are evil, and not merely their behaviour. Here we may conclude that the disposition towards evil is structurally constituted, because human nature is predisposed towards violence in thought and deed. This means that the customary, hackneyed definition of evil as deliberate malicious intent falls short because it fails to account for its innate, deep structural psychic precursors.

Evil exists without malicious intent; it merely becomes a question of disclosedness or concealment. Hence the ontology of evil may or may not be enacted based on impulse and restraint, therefore relegating the domain of evil to a bifurcation between desire, emotionality and thought on the one hand, and the behavioural instantiation of intentional action on the other. In other words, we are inherently evil (as that which is onto-structurally innate), but not all people engage in evil endeavours. Here a principle of restraint supersedes our base primitive constitutions, if not for the beacon of reason attuned to the reality principle, due to identification and empathy for others, the development of conscience, and the pursuit of the good or virtue as an ethical comportment. But this involves a process of socialization and domestication based on self-renunciation and a taming of the inner shrew, as Freud (1930) famously points out, the sublimation and foil to our primitive propensities.

Thus far we have deconstructed evil as having an ontological (hence a necessary and universal) edifice based upon our primordial psychic constitution that interpellates the individual and society by natural proclivity and desire, as well as through the objective institutionalization of social, semiotic, and symbolic practices that condition our being in the world. Therefore, the psychic dimension of evil is *structural* as both (a) innate disposition due to our organic embodiment fueled by drive and desire, as well as (b) socially superimposed by concrete (hence environmental) materiality via our thrownness into culture. Here structuralization accounts for the universality of our corporeal and cultural embodiment as an objective fact suffused with metaphysical violence. But the *phenomenal* dimension of evil is concerned with lived subjectivity or *psychic qualia*. This may be radically relative or germane to personal experience under hermeneutic variants even if shared by a collective ethos.

We have already determined that a degree of intentionality must be operative (even if prereflexive) in conditioning the phenomenology of evil, but the qualitative forms of such appearances must emerge from dispositional violence that ingress in the intentional act. The subjective state of mind is pertinent, as there is an affective qualitative manifestation of maleficence that is mobilized in evil intentionality through a negative emotional intensity of the will. However, we cannot restrict our definition to conscious intentionality, nor recapitulate the narrow, pedestrian view that evil is born from malicious intent, or in the words of Heidegger (1978) that "the essence of evil is in the malice of fury, not in the mere baseness of human action" (p. 355). Evil is not merely about intention and action, or destruction of the moral law, or institution of the signifier, but rather is unconsciously structuralized as primordial, ontological violence in the very masonry of the human psyche itself, hence the humanization of evil; yet one we can't help but moralize.

The Normativity of Evil

If evil is structurally constituted in all human beings, then evil is normative. It exists in all cultures, conditions our social relations with others, and is carried out in a variety of ways by people just like you and me. No one is immune from its signature or affliction. This is part and parcel of our fermenting *pathos* (πάθος). It is the new psychopathology of everyday life. Psychoanalysis has cogently shown, like the Zimbardo and Milgram experiments, that human nature is oriented towards hurting others, including ourselves. All human beings have sadistic wishes, impulses, and aggressive tendencies—from jealousy, envy, rivalry, hate, the diabolic, death wishes, punishment fantasies, and the need to humiliate and destroy—this is part of our unconscious animal nature morphed by experiencing the world; while personal and social defenses keep us from consciously embracing our unconscious destructive principles vying for pleasure, greediness, decadence, excess, and egoistic hedonism. These empirical facts speak towards our unconscious motivations that condition our waking conscious choices. Of course there are different instantiations of evil as qualitative classifications of the wrong offering gradations in concrete appearance, but my point is that evil is ontologically prepared as a primordial violence permeating Being itself. Asteroids collide, cosmic dust flickers, and every astronomical event is a physical-energetic negotiation: there is no ontic difference in this basic proposition governing the universe *or* human relations, for each is merely a modification of the metaphysics of experience.

In most discourse on evil, no one talks about unconscious intentionality, the evil within. And it is only by accident, on the occasion and condition of a non-conscious choice through the proverbial slip or faulty achievement (*Fehlleistung*), that evil is allowed expression. Despite the fact that we are dominated by reflective choice via the puissance of consciousness, this does not eradicate the force and reverberation of unconscious teleology. In psychoanalysis, which has discovered the fact that universally, we not only have the *capacity* to kill, we all have the *wish* to commit murder. In those who have developed sufficient superego defenses of conscience and moral values, this wish is bulwarked against a strong desire for denial, repression, renunciation, and undoing—even reaction formation, such as those going into helping professions to reverse or annul this unconscious artifact by making reparation for our lingering guilt. The violentization of human proclivity is historically proven and biologically conditioned, the backbone of civilization, one that is far more civil today than in its *arkhē*. But the way we come to apprehend our "nature" is humanized, as mentioned earlier, by our freedom to choose certain paths of thought and action, even under the strain of a lack of mentalization or affect regulation that colors our penumbra of ethical choices.

In what Adam Morton (2004) refers to as the "barrier theory of evil," he emphasizes that "the essence of evil motivation is the failure to block actions that ought not even to have been considered" (pp. 55–56). Here, he insists, most people filter out harmful actions to others when considering the right course of action, however, this does not displace motivation itself. Furthermore, it does not consider the fact that many actions are motived and executed by unconscious telic forces that scarcely recognize the foreseeable results or outcomes they may have on others, especially when such prereflective enactments are carried out unconsciously. This framework which to adjudicate evil also presumes a Kantian bias that moral motivation and behaviour are rationally contemplated with self-conscious foresight to consider the penalties of our actions. The notion of instituting barriers and refraining from the wrongful breach of barriers once put into place are important factors in understanding patterns of motivation, yet motivation and action are not always amenable to following a learned strategy or habitual procedure as rational deliberation of choice; rather people simply act and deal with the consequences later. Here we may observe that consciousness is often foreshadowed by overdetermined, psychodynamic events that affect the conscious motivation and action of the agent, even if under disinhibition or self-deceptive currents. This may explain, in part, why the far majority of evil acts are committed by normal or average people rather that criminals and violent sociopaths. The failure to construct barriers affecting our conscious choice of actions is only one such component of evil, regardless if it is unconsciously conceived or organized. Therefore, the barrier theory of evil conforms to a deeper structuralization process we may refer to as the "defense theory of evil," which is subject to the free reigns of imagination mediated by unconscious fantasy and compromise formation.

As a semiotic, the word "evil" has become too readily equated with moral outrage, which always stands in relation to a value judgement. And since a value judgement is a human phenomenon, the criteria of determining a proper interpretation of a *concept* of evil remains our task. We have already determined that evil may be ensconced in the realm of thought and not merely action, and that violence is interred in thought. Thoughts can do violence to those who think and harbor them, who suffer, let's say due to unremitting hate, and they manifest in the most normative of situations, such as through symptoms, somatization, affect dysregulation, sleep dysfunction, memory disturbance, and so forth. Here thought may be a form of self-evil, even if it is self-instituting and involuntary, hence the product of one's own self-victimization, even if such original victimization was due to the encroachment and internalization of the Other.

Evil as Appearance

Rather than focus on the myriad forms of evil that appear throughout humanity, and they are innumerable, let us address evil as appearance as such. It was Hegel (1830) who famously argued that "essence must *appear*" (*EL* § 131), for appearance is the requisite for anything to be made actual. This simple yet sophisticated observation is logically prepared: the coming into being of any phenomenon is ontologically conditioned on its essential a priori fulcrum. Here we may summon the principle of sufficient reason: every mental event must stand in relation to its original form from which it is derived. In other words, there must be an original ground for every mental event that stands in relation to every mental object. For Hegel (1807), "appearance is essence" (*PS* § 147), for nothing can exist unless it is real, hence has being or presence. Here evil appears as essence revealed through its marbled modes of manifestation.

Hegel's doctrine of essence is conditioned on the notion that whatever comes into being is always mediated by its previous appearances. Evil is mediated by prior shapes, the conduit that allows psychic reality to appear as concrete reality. This includes human history, as well as any contextualization of our thrownness, what I have referred to as "archaic primacy" (Mills, 2010). This further means that evil has a prehistory and a metaphysical structure: appearance emerges from a primordial ontic ground. In the *Phenomenology*, Hegel (1807) tells us:

> The inner world, or supersensible beyond, has, however, *come into being*: it *comes from* the world of appearance which has mediated it; in other words, appearance is its essence and, in fact, its filling. The supersensible is the sensuous and the perceived posited as it is *in truth*; but the *truth* of the sensuous and the perceived is to be *appearance*. The supersensible is therefore *appearance qua appearance*. (*PS* § 147)

This "inner world" is none other than a psychic one, an unconscious presencing that has been made objectively real—the instantiation of the evil within. Essence appears and appearance fills *its* essence; more specifically, appearance fills *with* essence. The "truth" is "posited" in itself as a supersensible beyond, but it may never be beyond appearance, for truth is equated with appearance as such. In Hegel's (1830) words, "Essence therefore is not *behind* or *beyond* appearance, but since the essence is what exists, existence is appearance" (*EL* § 131). In other words, by extrapolation, evil is "really actual," or it would not appear. This makes evil an ontological presence within humanity. But the ontology of evil is not a static or hypostasized thing; rather it is a process of emergence that is always transforming, leaving debris in its path. In fact, Hegel warns us that evil is not fixed nor simply contained in an absolute unity with the good, but rather it "*wants* to be on its own account" as "semblance of inward negativity" (*EL* § 35, *Zusatz*), one that is exteriorized. The negativity within must manifest, it must materialize in order for evil to be actual. Its reality is to be found in its appearances, but it lies deeply hidden within its interior, an interior that conditions all appearance, evil or otherwise.

Hegel (1830) argues that evil is to be equated with "cognition" itself due to a "schism," split, or "universal separation" from the "immediate knowledge" or unity with the good, a cleavage introduced through the act of thinking and self-reflection, a turning away from the simple unity of "innocence in the moral sphere" (*EL* § 24, *Zusatz* 3). Here he evokes the Mosaic myth of the Fall. Man is sinful by nature, and here we need no sophisticated theory to argue that humankind transgresses on itself and within itself, that it surpasses limit and restraint, and by definition, this is the same function ascribed to thinking itself. Thinking violates innocence; it breaches simplicity and breaks up unities through instituting negation, difference, and self-reflection as internal relation. As Hegel puts it, "It is thinking that both inflicts the wound and heals it again" (*EL* § 24, *Zusatz* 3). In the Garden lies the tree of life and the tree of knowledge, the cognition of good and evil; and herein stands our "entry into the antithesis," the forbidden, the realm of the *not*. Cognition wants to surpass itself, to explore new territory, to enact its desire, the desire to know, and to transgress its curtailment of knowledge. This is the saga of the human spirit (*Geist*) as mind discontent with its immediacy, the fate of desire enslaved as self-relation wanting to satiate the lack.

What Hegel concludes is nothing other than profound: mankind by nature is evil, not because we are born of original sin, but because we think. It is only on the condition that we are autonomous subjects that make us evil, for this is the price of freedom, one that "wills in his particularity without reference to the universal," that is, without considering others. This is why Hegel concludes that "evil" is individual "subjectivity." In other words, our subjective experiences and actions are the locus of ignobility, which stand in opposition to an objective corollary holding itself up to be a universal ideal, namely, humanity's symbolic godhead.

The Greeks defined truth through a privative expression —ἀ-λήθεια, through the *via negativa*, a negation or reversal of the closed, the unseen. Evil is disclosed through its openings, or more precisely, through its openness into the light of being. Evil as appearance is everywhere, even if hidden, concealed, or non-manifest, dwelling below in the cellar of non-appearance, waiting to be born, unveiled, released. Evil's disclosedness or unconcealment reveals a particular truth about the inherent nature of our *pathos*, one that feels compelled to no longer remain hidden. This holding fuels a festering that cannot be contained, as it is destined to make itself known, to show itself, to shine. The shining of evil is the face of man, the image of a fallen ideal, the petty iteration of subjectivity, the human mirror of self-negativity.

The Ethics of Evil

We live in a sick society, one chosen yet unconsciously determined. Here evil is the natural consequence of the cost of freedom. We kill people for this cost, for the privilege, politics, and principle of freedom, itself a lamentable and ethically dubious dilemma. Military intelligence has studied and strategized about the best way to kill people, to deracinate, to dismember their spirits, to rob them of soul, to crush entire peoples of their dignity to the degree that warfare and state murder have become both a technological and mechanized industry. A weapon is an instrument designed to kill—from the steel and bronze age to a drone. The atomic bomb was invented for one thing: human extermination.

The technology of evil is witnessed everyday on our television sets, from Wall Street to mass scale corporate corruption, to internet fraud, and cyber bullying, all abetted by advances in computer science. The use of global information exchange, digital communication, social media, robotics, nanotechnology, and the engineering of terror has become its own science. From WikiLeaks, Edward Snowden, to the Arab Spring and *Charlie Hebdo*, no nation is immune from its own homegrown transgressions. Sometimes the craft or art of *techne* enlists a certain psychological intelligence condoned through state torture, such as inducing learned helplessness through waterboarding and "rectal rehydration" at Guantanamo, to rape warfare used in the ethnic cleaning campaigns perpetrated in Bosnia, Croatia, Kosovo, and Rwanda.

The ethics of evil is the distortion of an inverse relation, namely, the justification of self-righteousness while perpetrating evil under the guise of moral superiority. When ethical arguments are employed to justify evil acts, we reason in a hegemonic circle of self-interest that betrays a philosophy of right, even if such actions are deemed necessary in order to combat an identifiable threat. Ethical rationale can be exercised by any individual, group, or nation state to legitimate its activities and foreign policies affecting other lives regardless of the legitimacy of one's belief system, veracity of events, or the flimsiness of moral reasoning employed. Under the rubric of national security and the crusade against terror, people simply "disappeared" into CIA custody, were detained against their wills without criminal charges laid, and systemically subjected to the use of "enhanced interrogation techniques," a euphemism for torture, in the hopes that reliable intelligence could be procured despite the legal and ethical prohibitions against torture instituted since the Geneva Conventions' forbiddance of it even during times of war. Not only is this a good example of moral hypocrisy under the justification of state ethics, as are drone attacks, military commissions, and mass electronic surveillance by a superpower that bases its global political platform on democracy, freedom, and human rights, it furthermore underscores the universality of national self-interest at the expense of democracy itself.

When nation is against nation, narcissistic national identity forms a firm antithesis against the other that becomes legalized within state foreign policy or totalitarian rule, even if duped or deluded. Under the Bush Administration following 9/11, the United States manufactured a war on terror because it needed to have enemies to pillory as revenge for its castrated ego. Here the Other becomes alien, a xenophobic object prone to hurt us. And after they found Saddam Hussein tucked away down a spider hole, there were no weapons of mass destruction to be found. But he served a utilitarian public purpose: he was the symbolic Bad Man who was put to death under state execution, itself a practice deemed evil despite enjoying a cathartic welcome by the West.

We may readily observe the paranoid position at work on a global scale: otherness is the enemy. This primal fear is even further spread within our own nations and communities, where private lives are under state surveillance, neighbours spy upon neighbours, race riots are on the rise, and home invasions are the norm. Under Big Brother, anyone could disappear. And with global economic unrest due to the fuel crisis, Russia's infringement on the Ukraine to seemingly attempt to recover its lost Soviet Union has generated a new paranoia where citizens can't speak freely due to fear of police arrest or public assassination. Paradoxically, after the country had lost almost half of its value and people couldn't afford a mortgage payment, the nation's approval ratings for Vladimir Putin skyrocketed. Whereas in the United States, the disgruntled public craves a swing of the pendulum towards any politician selling hope for a recovering economy, Russia can't get enough of its leader while blaming the greedy West for its own financial malaise.

When the class genocide in Rwanda occurred, initiated by rival ethnic tensions between the Hutus and Tutsis, where mass mayhem organized by Hutu paramilitary personnel and locals having much to gain from the systematic extermination of the Tutsis, the world remained curiously passive and silent. Even after reports of entire villages and individual family members killing their own kind with machetes and the crudest of utensils were known to be factual, the West looked on as a detached spectator unwilling to do anything until it was too late. Lethargic in its enthusiasm to intervene, after nearly a million dead, world superpowers finally felt motivated to lift a finger to stop the genocide at the U.N.'s beckoning. The Dark Continent, I suggest, held little value to democratic and developed countries who had little to gain and many economic costs to bear for intervening in a country that is (symbolically) associated with poverty, famine, AIDS, overpopulation, and disease, hence the alien Other. But when SARS, Swine-Flu (H1N1), Ebola, and now covid can conjure up the paranoid position and threaten a global pandemic, the world has become more gracious and attuned to social realities that affect us all. The cold hard facts are that some peoples and countries are valued over others based upon their discernable worth; others on their discernable threat. Even humanitarian aid is never devoid of political self-interest, especially if it means thwarting global anxiety.

Is it evil not to think of other peoples, cultures, and continents, to not consider their needs and social challenges? This would not only imply an admonition as failure to acquire self-consciousness and empathic attunement for the other, but rather incites an intransigent condemnation for not caring to do so in the first place. Yet Levinasean ethics barely occur to the masses engrossed in their everyday lives, let alone being handed down a moral sentence for not thinking about the plight of the disenfranchised abstract sufferer residing somewhere in an arbitrary land. It is too much for the individual psyche to bear, that's why it is turned over to the collective social psyche to contemplate and do something about. Even in the most well-intentioned and conscientious soul who envisions a better humanity and wishes to serve altruistic causes, in the end we do what we can, because that's all we can do. Is it evil that we don't do more, that we cease to try because we value our own needs over others? Or do we merely accept our humanism that we cannot live up to the demands of our own ideals we place on ourselves? Here I am reminded of Hegel's beautiful soul: when we become aware of our imperfections we bear an unhappy consciousness. Here the self is divided: we can posit the Ideal but simply can't actualize it. Here moral lassitude becomes another banality.

Institutionalization

When we think about the institutionalization of evil in recent times, from colonial imperialism, totalitarianism, and fascism, we often think of large scale suprastructures that superimpose an oppressive bureaucratic machinery on its citizenry; but we may observe how these unconscious cultural fantasies operate as entrenched ideologies unquestioned by the masses. The caste system in India may be said to foster a form of institutional racism where social class is determined by blood, history, custom, and skin color. The upper class or Brahmans hold wealth, power, status, and education, while the Untouchables are held in contempt and allocated the most unpleasant and revulsive of all vocations in the most horrid of conditions such as sanitation, domestic servitude, and back-breaking manual labor. Aryan descendants with lighter-skinned pigments are more aesthetically valued while the more darker-skinned Indians are viewed as ugly, an attitudinal phenomenon we may also witness in Africa. There is an air of superiority by birth and provenance and an aura of disdain, condemnation, and vilification of the underclass, even though the advantaged groups rely on their sweat and subservience for their privileged lifestyles. Hugh discrepancies between rich and poor determine the social infrastructure, where the elite govern the masses, political and social institutions are rife with corruption and abuse of power, and the citizenry have neither tangible access to housing, education, or work. The subcontinent is suffocating in pollution and every major city is a conglomeration of slums. Poverty, death, disease, crime, infestation, filth, lack of sewage, vagrants, panhandlers, homelessness, frantic desperation, and abject hopelessness abound, where the majority of its billion people are illiterate, disenfranchised, and penniless. In fact, India has one of the highest illiteracy rates in the world (United Nations, 2014), followed by China and Sub-Saharan Africa. Abandoned children, the deformed and handicapped, and destitute mothers roam the streets begging for food with emaciated babies in their arms. An endless swarm of hovering hands pounce on tourists and locals alike hoping to get a rupee or American dollar for free.

Fairy tale romances are non-existent for marriages are arranged by patriarchy based on caste, birth, and class as a union of families, not love, where relationships are determined, not freely chosen, lest one betrays the family, established social order, and the entrenched cultural tradition that sustains this institutional practice. It is no wonder why Buddhism branched off from Hinduism and that Islam was successful in converting much of the underclass, each under the teachings that all men are equal regardless of race, caste, or custom.

In other developing countries, such as in the Middle East, where despots, dictators, and autocrats rule their totalitarian regimes, women and children are systematically oppressed, often under the edicts of Islam. Here we may observe a widespread institutional practice in most Arab countries that grant men both legislative and property rights over their wives and children, where strict observance to Muslim law is harshly imposed, including denying women access and rights to education, individual autonomy, and independent finances in order to keep them enslaved, including controlling their dress, physical mobility, and behavioural practices, and granting them virtually no criminal protection or civil liberty rights under the law. Women and children may be beaten or raped against their will by men with practical immunity from prosecution, and transgressions by females may be subject to penalty by death. Public stoning, immolations, and honor killings (from Pakistan to Canada), where women turn on other accused women, including mothers and family members who are willing participants, are salient phenomena fueled by culturally engrained misogyny.

In vast parts of China and India, female (sex-selected) infanticide is ubiquitous due to the cultural devaluation of women. Concentrated in northeast Africa, Yemen, Iraqi Kurdistan, the Middle East, and portions of Asia, female genital mutilation (circumcision) is legally imposed against their will (usually in childhood), often under horrendous unsanitary conditions that permanently disfigure and endanger the survival of its victims due to lack of sterilization and post-medical complications, all condoned under the dominion of male patriarchy. These primitive practices are designed to fortify a man's power and authority by turning women into functional objects of domestication, obedience, and sexuation where only a man has the right to pleasure. Furthermore, in many of these countries, as throughout South and East Asia, children are sold into slavery by parents to pay for family debt or for profit, as are human organs offered on the black market to help pay for passage to another land. Human trafficking and the child sex trade industry have become an international pandemic, often abetted by institutional corruption and systemic pathology thriving on high profit margins with no signs of a conscience.

Israeli legislative policy is designed to promote and privilege an exclusive Jewish state, actively recruits immigration from European Jewry, hence lending asylum and giving economic and material benefits (including housing, transportation, and tax-shelters) to Jews over non-Jewish Israeli's, imposes higher costs of living and excise taxes on domestic Palestinians and other Israeli Arabs who refuse to live and work in the West Bank, although entire generations had previously owned property and ran family businesses throughout the country before the declaration of Israel. A democratic state that maintains class privilege and financially rewards one ethnic group over others who live and work in the same country, own property, and are equally part of the same society would be an unfathomable occurrence in North America.

Israel is concerned with occupying rather than compromising over disputed land, and retaliates with military bombardments that deliberately target civilian neighbourhoods where innocent lives are lost. And with Palestinian resistance compelled to fight and galvanize subversive insurgencies and initiate clandestine missile fire, keeping hate and resentment alive, Israeli citizens break out the lawn chairs, crack a beer, and watch the military pick off houses in Gaza. Here each side points the finger while calling the other "terrorist." This is a good example of the paranoid-schizoid position at play where radical splitting and projective identification leads to reiterations of violence as proportional exchange, like a Ping-Pong ball traversing each side of the net until one opponent slams a victory in the current round. But this is followed by endless rounds of repetitions in fixed perpetuation of retaliatory aggression to the point that systemic acrimony towards the Other justifies state institutional racism and military barrages. It is understandable how Israel suffers from dread due to centuries of European and Russian anti-Semitism while living in the shadow of the Holocaust, but with the messianic clash of religions and fundamentalist supporters of Islamic State (e.g., ISIS/ISIL) recently killing Jews in Paris and Copenhagen, the tinderbox could explode without warning, especially if Iran continues with its nuclear development program, a spark that could ignite a Third World War.

The Evil Within

When my daughter was not quite 4 years old, my wife gave birth to our second child. Upon bringing our daughter to see her mother and newborn baby sister for the first time in the hospital with roses in hand, we visited them both at bedside, our new baby swathed in a blanket. After giving our eldest a flower to give to her mother, she took the stem and starting poking her baby sister in the belly like it was a knife. To my daughter, this wasn't her baby sister, but rather a *thing*, an intruding object that commanded special attention and displaced her importance in a fraction of a second. There was nothing playful about her action: she wanted to hurt or kill it, for she wanted it to die, or simply vanish. It came to steal away her mother. It had taken her place. We may joke about Oedpalization, sibling rivalry over parents' affections, or the feelings of abandonment and hatred for the replacement object, but there was an air of innocence to this event, an evil normalcy, so to speak, conveyed in this automatic behaviour.

Everyone is intrinsically evil: it is a structural invariant of the human psyche as normativity. Why is this so? Because everyone is predisposed to aggressivity and violence, to mistreating others, to intentionally inflicting verbal, emotional, relational, and/or physical pain, even abuse of various forms and vicious maliciousness no matter how unsavoury the thought, or how one vociferously objects to or disavows such characteristics, or how saintly a person may appear. Show me one person who has committed no evil! Who has not demonstrated some form of violence? In Derrida's (1978) words, "A Being without violence would be a Being which would occur outside of the existent: nothing; nonhistory; non-occurrence; non-phenomenality" (p. 147). To uphold such a proposition would be a ludicrous denial of our humanity.

Psychoanalysis has illuminated this psychological fact to the point that it bears no further justification or empirical demonstration, for all one has to do is observe a child in daycare or turn on the evening news. Our world is a festering cesspool of pathology. But we cannot say the same about the good. Goodness or virtue is not structurally intrinsic like evil; rather it is a developmental achievement acquired through socialization and education, unless one prefers to define goodness as a purely biological-ethological category belonging to our animal bodies, such as nurturing and protecting one's young. But this also requires aggression to meet its aim. Animals kill in order to eat, nurture, protect, and defend. Just as this innate inclination belongs to our natural constitutions, so does our dispositional urge towards violence. It is as natural as breathing to have aggressive fantasies and to kill—for food, self-preservation, out of fear, protection of others, and so forth, hence falling under the rubric of natural law theory. The naïve notion that we are born good and become bad is as infantile as the most guileless fantasy that we have fallen from God's grace into sin by natural desire, corruption, and choice. Not only is this illogical, for it would mean denying our embodied facticity, it also negates all empirical facts that we are libidinal and aggressive creatures by virtue of our evolutionary phylogenetic pressures. Many psychoanalysts today do not take seriously the notion of drive theory or phylogeny, when it is a biological fact that human psychology is conditioned on and derived from our naturalized material embodiment. It is beyond dispute. We are capable of anything, from killing to loving, to giving into instinct and impulse, to ethical sociality, to self-sacrifice for an ideal, to transcending our basic animality for the greater Other.

It seems superfluous to even have to argue for the obvious, but I shall briefly recapitulate why evil is structurally inherent as part of our unconscious ontology. Roughly, the argument goes, because we (the human race) are biologically conditioned towards aggression through dispositional violence, it is a natural predisposition that can be both activated and inhibited. Potentiality (<Lat. *potentia*) is enough to warrant the ontological label of dispositional evil, for if there was neither a potential for evil, its inhibition, or its actualization, then we would not be human. The potentiality is inherent within everyone, and a variety of circumstances can kindle or defuse its possible occurrence. These sociological factors do not concern us here, but suffice it to say that drives are stimulated by external factors.

The inner a priori ontological preconditions towards evil, however, do not mean that all human beings will enact their evil tendencies. This is subject to many factors including inhibition, defense, compromise, and transformation, as well as their failures, which always stand in relation to social systems, institutionalization, and inter-subjective relations. But the point here is to emphasize that to be human is to always stand in relation to the evil within. In fact, our humanization requires us to confront our evilization. We would not be human without such a confrontation, for this demands that we examine our interior and social environs, and analyze what is pre-ferably good from what is characteristically bad. Although this conundrum is a contentious enterprise that is inscrutable and open to many estimations, it is also a social requirement that influences the parameters of institutional law and order. Without such dialogue, we would merely be slaves to self-interest and biological instinct at our own peril.

It is rather elementary to remind the reader of the primacy of the drives (*Triebe*), nor do I find it necessary to regurgitate a dissertation of their defense (cf. Mills, 2010). The basis of Freudian theory from its inception allowed for the polymorphous perversity of the drives if not for the simple fact that desire has no bounds. Desire is free-floating and can attach to any object. While desire is unbounded in itself, only a drive can appear bound, whereby its aim is to achieve satisfaction. Although drives may be temporarily sated by infusing or incorporating an object in reality or fantasy (which is completely variable and arbitrary), desire is always an incessant craving that is never satiated. Because the fantasized object of a wish is always transient and never permanent, unconscious fantasy and its potential foci are fodder for the imagination ripe for the enactment of evil. This means that our libidinal investments will always entail aggressive complementarities in the strife and gratification of any wish fraught with controversy, competition, compromise formation, and defensive countermeasures that define psychic process. This structural tension produces antithetical dialectical relations that influence the intern-ality and manifestation of our *pathos*.

Whether derived from instinct or simple learning theory, the pleasure-pain principle that is operative in all psychological motiva-tion driving human action is an ontological given. The human or-ganism is hardwired or preprogramed to process mental events in concord with basic biological parameters that inform our disposition to think and act. But these parameters are nevertheless subject to modification, realignment, and redistribution of psychic energies that give shape and content to their contextual expressions. Our ontological thrownness presupposes the logic of the interior based on a simple economy of splitting objects of experience into counterparts, each with a positive and negative vector. This dialectical division must be instituted in thought, as Kant, Fichte, and Hegel demonstrate at the most fundamental level, and hence a determination of difference through negation is unconsciously interjected into every mental act while mediating any experiential object. What follows is that early fantasy life is dominated by evil impulses, sadistic urges, primitive affects, and paranoiac anxieties we project onto objects and re-introject or re-gather back into our internal constitutions. Here we may say that inborn aggression as instinct is a *primary evil*, for it is structurally constituted in nature as dispositional violence and not merely chosen. What is chosen is how it shall be autonomously processed by mind. That which is not equiprimordially given a priori is retroactively mediated by consciousness. Since the disposition-towards-violence is ontologically given phylogenetically, it is no surprise that we see it everywhere.

The human psyche has a peculiar tendency to use and abuse objects of functional immediacy, namely, for disposable means of gratification. But this is often hidden and unacknowledged because it takes place behind the back of consciousness. The phylogenetic or tribal evolutionary origin of aggression as dispositional emotional violence is part of our thrownness into the human race. The theoretic speculation of an inherent death drive (*Todestrieb*), although controversial, does not preclude the reality of dispositional violence oriented towards human aggression, but rather accounts for it as a destructive ontological principle channeling negation and conflict within a psychobiological framework. The human psyche is born/e of negativity and radical splitting, which initiates a procreative or generative process that is simultaneously life enhancing yet paradoxically self-destructive. The logic of the interior that suffuses unconscious organization fuels this antithetical impulse as a will towards life and death, hence creating antinomies and impasses in their ability to meet resolve or find a synthetic node of unification. But as Freud (1920) reminds us, before the will towards murder as an externalized aggressive fantasy belying our true primitive natures, there is also a primal impulse as suicidal self-negation that may be equally enacted through volitional eruptions in psychic space. The analyzed mind cannot deny these human predilections, because they materialize every day in the clinic and the social world, which tells us something irrefutably profound about human nature. The human animal fights the evil within on a daily basis as an inherent self-renunciation we are obliged to accept on the one hand, and as the refusal to take ownership of our desire on the other, that which is part of our clashing dialectical symmetries, hence the formal dynamics underlying the structural tensions bolstering our unconscious *pathos*. Here self-repudiation is only possible on the condition that we secure a psychic space for the fulfillment of our pathologies, where we may unconsciously enjoy our evil fantasies mired in the kingdom of *jouissance*, that realm of excess so satisfying yet so repugnant that it *cuts*.

The dispositional wickedness of urge, affect, fantasy, behavioural impulse, and thought is scarcely capable of being eradicated, only mitigated. What ultimately matters is control over its enactment. This is the functional introduction of an ethical social introject as a prohibitive law or ideal that facilitates human sublimation over brute instinct often initiated by empathic identification with others based in human attachment. But the fantasy life of world masses carry on in a sordid underworld where satisfaction is achieved through the contemplation of the nefarious as a fantasized internal drama that brings about both horror and relief, but only on the condition that it is consigned to fantasy with our self-reflective awareness of such. Those who are not able to maintain an internal reflective ego or mentalized stance of self-consciousness may beckon the dark call of the shadow, the demonic, or whatever term we may wish to employ to signify the destructive forces of evil. Thinking evil thoughts and wishing evil deeds or events is not the same as doing them. This defensive containment of self-restraint makes all the difference in the world between a civilized human being and a criminal. And this frames our problematic: it is in the locus of decision, of concreteness, where we find evil. Despite the fact that we are all dispositionally evil, it may never come to light.

So here we have a crucial difference in the value parameters we assign to our definition of evil. Although we may be constitutionally predisposed towards evil, it does not always appear. That is, evil dispositions and intentions may be relegated to thought rather than actions, hence inhibited and transformed. What this means is that evil remains hidden in some while disclosed, unconcealed, or enacted by others. This makes the qualia and empirical quantification of evil contingent upon its modes of manifestation, or how it appears. But our pithy unsavoury conclusion is anything but trite: everyone by nature is evil; it's just a matter of degree.

Notes

1 Initiated in the 19th Century, and now in its 9th revised edition, Liddell and Scott's *Greek-English Lexicon* is generally considered among classicists to be the finest compilation to date of the classical works of antiquity where the etymological sources of ancient words derive and correspond to contemporary linguistics and modes of discourse. See pages 870 and 863 respectively of Volume 1 for καλός and κᾰκός (good and evil).
2 It is for this reason that I have deliberately omitted any discussion or critique of Boehme and Schelling, whose projects were to reconcile evil with human freedom and God.
3 Here Žižek annexes the notions of subjective and objective forms of violence from the Jains, where *ahimsa*, or the principle of non-violence, is central to Jainism as a religious valuation practice.

References

Aquinas, St. T. (ca. 1256–1272). *Summa Theologiae*. Translated by The Fathers of the English Dominican Province [1947]. http://www.sacred-texts.com/chr/aquinas/summa/

Aristotle (1984). *Physics*. In J. Barnes (Ed.), *The Complete Works of Aristotle. 2 Vols.* (The revised Oxford trans.). Princeton, NJ: Princeton University Press, pp. 315–446.

Augustine (2008). *Confessions*. H. Chadwick (Trans.). Oxford: Oxford University Press.

Canadian Press Video (2014, Dec. 16). Stephen Harper calls Pakistan attack heartbreaking. *Globe and Mail*. http://www.theglobeandmail.com/news/news-video/video-stephen-harper-calls-pakistan-attack-heartbreaking/article22106356/ Retrieved December 28, 2104.

Derrida, J. (1978). *Writing and Difference*. A. Bass (Trans.). London: Routledge & Kegan Paul.

Freud, S. (1920). *Beyond the Pleasure Principle*. In Freud 1966–95 [1886–1940]. *The Standard Edition of the Complete Psychological Works of Sigmund Freud*, Vol. 18, pp. 1–64.

Freud, S. (1927). *The Future of an Illusion*. In Freud 1966–95 [1886–1940]. *The Standard Edition of the Complete Psychological Works of Sigmund Freud*, Vol. 21, pp. 1–56.

Freud, S. (1930). *Civilization and its Discontents*. In Freud 1966–95 [1886–1940]. *The Standard Edition of the Complete Psychological Works of Sigmund Freud*, Vol. 21, pp. 57–145.

Francis, B. (2013). *Gratuitous Suffering and the Problem of Evil*. New York: Routledge.

Hegel, G.W.F. (1807). *Phenomenology of Spirit*. A.V. Miller (Trans.). Oxford: Oxford University Press, 1977.

Hegel, G.W.F. (1830). *The Encyclopaedia Logic*. Vol. 1 of *Encyclopaedia of the Philosophical Sciences*. T.F. Geraets, W.A. Suchting, & H.S. Harris (Trans.). Indianapolis: Hackett Publishing Company, Inc., 1817/1827/1830/1991.

Heidegger, M. (1978). *Wegmarken*, 2nd Ed. Frankfurt am Main: Klostermann.

Herodas (1922). *Mimographus*. W. Headlam (Ed.). Bristol: Bristol Classical Press.

Homer (800 B.C.E.). *The Odyssey*. S. Butler (Trans.). http://classics.mit.edu/Homer/odyssey.html

Homer (800 B.C.E.). *The Iliad*. S. Butler (Trans.). http://classics.mit.edu/Homer/iliad.html

Inayat, N., Qazi, S., & Bacon, J. (2014, Dec. 17). Death Toll Reaches 141 in Massacre at Pakistan School. *USA Today*. http://www.usatoday.com/story/news/world/2014/12/16/taliban-storms-military-school/20469711/ Retrieved December 28, 2014.

Kant, I. (1793/94). *Religion within the Limits of Reason Alone*. 2nd Ed. T.M. Greene & H.H. Hudson (Trans.). New York: Harper Torchbooks, 1934.

Liddell, H.G., & Scott, R. (1843). *A Greek-English Lexicon*. 2 Vols. Oxford: Clarendon Press.

Mills, J. (2017). *Inventing God: Psychology of Belief and the Rise of Secular Spirituality*. London: Routledge.

Mills, J. (2010). *Origins: On the Genesis of Psychic Reality*. Montreal: McGill-Queens University Press.

Morton, A. (2004). *On Evil*. New York: Routledge.

Nadeau, B.L. (2015). Nigeria Is Letting Boko Haram Get Away With Murder. January 13, 2015. *The Daily Beast*. http://www.thedailybeast.com/articles/2015/01/13/nigeria-is-letting-boko-haram-get-away-with-murder.html. Retrieved January 13, 2015.

Plato. (1961). *Protagoras*. In E. Hamilton & H. Cairns (eds.), *The Collected Dialogues of Plato*, Princeton: Princeton University Press, pp. 308–352.

Plato. (1961). *Republic*. In E. Hamilton & H. Cairns (eds.), *The Collected Dialogues of Plato*. Princeton: Princeton University Press, pp. 575–844.

Plato. (1961). *Theaetetus*. In E. Hamilton & H. Cairns (eds.), *The Collected Dialogues of Plato*. Princeton: Princeton University Press, pp. 845–891.

Plotinus (1992). *The Enneads*. S. MacKenna (Trans.) Burdett, NY: Larson Publications.

United Nations (2014). India Tops in Adult Illiteracy: U.N. Report. January 29, 2014. *The Hindu*. http://www.thehindu.com/features/education/issues/india-tops-in-adult-illiteracy-un-report/article5629981.ece. Retrieved February 23, 2015.

Žižek, S. (2008). *Violence*. New York: Picador.

Chapter 7

Recognition and *Pathos*

Axel Honneth (1995, 2012; Fraser & Honneth, 2003) has advanced Hegelian thought in many noteworthy ways, especially in engaging psychoanalysis; however, considerations from psychoanalytic thought and practice suggest that his recognition theory depends on a patently optimistic, if not idealistic, view of human nature. This is especially clear in the case of social collectives (not to mention governments) who regularly fail to interact through reciprocal recognition even when they become aware of their mutual dependency on each other. For instance, people often acquiesce to others for defensive reasons, especially when they are afraid, rather than because they recognize them as being morally equal. Submission to another's will typically thwarts the probability of the other's aggression being directed towards them, hence protecting the self. This observation equally applies to Habermas' theories of moral consciousness, communicative action, and discourse ethics, which presupposes that human beings by nature are rational animals, and that through linguistic dialogue societies can reinvigorate Enlightenment paradigms of social justice free of domination from otherness based on cooperative speech exchange. In particular, Habermas' (1990, 1993) theory of communicative rationality (*kommunikative Rationalität*) assumes that norms, rules, and procedures for communication and argumentation can be established in the moral-practical realm and have a rational outcome by necessity, when this seems to ignore the non-rational, desirous, emotional, prejudicial, political, and unconscious motivations that govern human discourse and action. From a psychoanalytic point of view, this is unrealistic, if not a wishful fantasy, since it is evident that collectives are largely possessed

DOI: 10.4324/9781003305958-7

by unconscious complexes, emotional seizures, attitudinal prejudices, and irrationality, to the degree that unadulterated reason is not even remotely possible, let alone valid. Such highly rationalized accounts of human relations seem to ignore basic psychological dynamics of human motivation based in neurotic propensities, affective dysregulation, dispositions towards aggression, the effects of trauma, and internal conflict that militates against any pure cognitivist paragon.

Critical theorists have not fully appreciated the insights of psychoanalytic perspectives that deviate from overtly sanguine views valorizing anthropological conditions leading to optimally cohesive social arrangements. To explore the limits of Honneth's position that world societies can achieve reciprocal recognition, I wish to examine the dark side of recognition, namely, its asymmetrical pathological dynamics. Throughout this essay I will explore how these dynamics are informed by early developmental contingencies in attachment, self-formation, social relations, and the negation of difference, addressing the psychodynamics of how dysrecognition and refutation of the Other lead to insidious pathologies within society and the clinic.

Critical theory has traditionally been concerned with the broader social fabric of institutionalized cultural practices that inform a collective ethos with a keen eye on analysing dysfunction and advocating for real changes in society. This includes critiquing authoritarian politics, safeguarding against totalitarianism, democratizing social justice, and extending an ethical hand in our post-Holocaust world. This shift in social self-consciousness stresses the importance of validating alterity rather than sustaining rival differences between individuals, societies, and nations that fail to acknowledge the need for mutual recognition of the Other. But in today's climate, the Hegelian master-slave dialectic seems to be very much alive: most developing and non-industrial countries live in servitude to powerful others or the state, and in democratic nations, citizens are largely dependent upon capitalistic enterprises, for which they serve and enrich. In fact, subjugation and domination of otherness is flourishing throughout the globe. Entire peoples are vanquished, refuted, nullified, and denounced simply because they proclaim to have different needs and worldviews. When difference and protest persist, they are often overpowered and persecuted under the guise of resistance to conformity to the prevailing forces that enslave them in their actual conditions of oppression.

Our attachments to others, people relations, and intersubjective communal matrices form the psychological edifice of our dependency on others and social institutions organized around just and unjust modes of recognition that are structurally, systemically, and semiotically constituted. When this basic bedrock of relationality is disrupted or vitiated, society experiences anxiety, emotional pain, and retrograde backlash. Individuals, social groups, and civilizations that are victimized by repeated dysrecognition and base negation of their values and collective identities are subjected to a cultural *pathos* against their will.[1] As a result, they/we suffer.

Hegel and Jung

While Freud knew very little of Hegel's philosophy,[2] Jung read his works. He was not a fan. Not only did Jung think Hegel was grandiose when talking about Spirit, he equated Hegel's language with that of a psychotic.[3] I wonder if this was because Jung felt threatened, namely, that Hegel had tread too close to home, hence endangering Jung's originality when he postulated a collective unconscious? After all, *Geist* emerges from an unconscious abyss only to find itself as the culmination of pure self-consciousness, the coming into being of psychic presence.

As I have stated elsewhere (Mills, 2002; 2013, pp. 40-41, n6), Hegel is not only concerned about articulating personal subjective psychology, but also tracing the coming to presence of a universal collective unconscious that anthropologically conditions all of humankind. For Hegel (1807), individual psychology is subsumed within higher social orders objectively constituted within the ethical life (*Sittlichkeit*) of a collective community having its origins within the family and society. The collective communal spirit draws its source and energy from "the power of the nether world" (*PS* § 462), what Jung calls the collective unconscious. For Hegel (1807), collective spirit "binds all into one, solely in the mute unconscious substance of all" (*PS* § 474). This "unconscious universality" contains the ethical and divine as well as the abnormal, hence the "pathos" of humanity, the "darkness" of the "underworld" (*PS* § 474). Hegel states:

[H]uman law proceeds in its living process from the divine, the law valid on earth from that of the nether world, the conscious from the unconscious, mediation from immediacy—and equally returns whence it came. The power of the nether world, on the other hand, has its actual existence on earth; through consciousness, it becomes existence and activity. (*PS* § 460)

Almost a full century before the emergence of depth psychology, Hegel's psychological insights are profound. In this passage, he clearly recognizes that the personal and collective unconscious developmentally and logically precedes consciousness and further sees that each domain maintains its dialectical relation with the other. Universal self-conscious Spirit "becomes, through the individuality of man, united with its other extreme, its force and element, *unconscious* Spirit" (*PS* § 463).

The universalization or actualization of the unconscious becomes important for Hegel in the depiction of spirit as a dynamically informed, self-articulated totality or complex whole. Thus, he not only focuses on human psychology and collective unconscious forces that determine individual and social relations, but also points to the generic structural operations of the mind that have their origins in the unconscious, which make human consciousness and thought possible. Here Hegel anticipates psychoanalysis, and particularly Jung's notion of the collective psyche.

Many compatible philosophical positions are operative in both Hegel's and Jung's projects, including the value placed on individuation within the pursuit of wholeness (Kelly, 1993). Both Hegel and Jung emphasize that psyche is a teleological process of becoming as a progressive unfolding of its interior into outward appearances and robust instantiations of spirit or soul. From Hegel's Absolute Spirit to Jung's Self, the psyche looks to complete itself, to manifest in higher modes of consciousness, to fill the lack, to unify opposites and elevate itself on its quest for truth and fulfillment as an organic developmental process, all emanating from an original unconscious ground.

The Need to be Acknowledged

Arguably one of the most widely cited sections of the *Phenomenology of Spirit* is Hegel's (1807) discussion of lordship and bondage.[4] In pithy form, spirit or mind (*Geist*) ultimately achieves ethical self-consciousness only by recognizing the other as an equal being. But this is a developmental achievement. In our intersubjective engagement with others, there is a battle for recognition that takes place between subjects. Yet at first, parties in this struggle are unaware that they are looking for recognition, which is unconsciously mediated, hence the meaning of which is initially unclear to those involved. It is only through the process of confronting otherness that we become cognizant of what we truly want. We may observe how this is ontically infused in all spheres of life and plays a key role in our psychological health and social progress, for every human being wants to be recognized by others as an instantiation of human desire. This naturally extends to society. Before society raises itself to the status of improving its cultural practices for the sake of its peoples, including institutionalized ethics, law and order, and distributive justice, it must start with this basic psychic fact. Those who are deprived of recognition suffer and are condemned to harbor grave feelings of invalidation of their personhood in virtual aloneness.

In days of serfdom and feudalism that existed in the High Middle Ages, people were ruled by autocracy and the aristocracy, of which recognition was merely a one-way relation. The governing Lord was recognized and the serf did the recognizing. In fact, this was a matter of life or death—fear and despair kept one alive by obedience and subservience to a potentially cruel Master. Hegel believes this struggle over being acknowledged is a necessary one in order to be truly independent and free, as the odyssey of pure self-consciousness (viz., social awareness) is a progressive unfolding of recognizing its own ethical nature unified in self-knowledge as a higher truth and culmination of civilized social life. In other words, true recognition by society requires collective reason and action where all people are seen (theoretically and pragmatically) as equal, hence comprising and participating in and of a society (or the state) harmonized in egalitarian principles, and as such constitutes the will of the people. But this is not the case for all societies. As we may plainly see in our world governed by violence, chaos, proto-fascism, dictatorship, despotism, and oppression of the masses, absolute self-consciousness (namely, enlightened society) remains merely an abstract ideal, especially for non-democratic nations.

Regardless of the limits of human societies within today's climate of globalization failing to unite individuals, ethnic groups, and disparate cultures in a collective ethos, Hegel's theory of recognition has tangible, applied concrete merits. In fact, the problem of recognition may constitute the majority of our world ills today. From the cradle to the grave, a child wants the love, emotional attunement, validation, and acceptance that only a parent can afford, just as a parent wants reciprocal acknowledgement for their role in raising their child, as well as forgiveness for their imperfections, even in the final moments while lying in their death bed. This speaks to a universal theory of human nature. So why does most of the world live in negation of this collective need where radical splitting is instituted and alterity signals the proclivity to deny, withhold, aggress upon, and deracinate the other? Although this phenomenon is complex and overdetermined, let us return to basics using Hegel as our guide.

People are unreflectively seen as being mere objects—as *things* that exist "out there" in the world, because they are divorced from our emotional and personal lives in order for us to psychologically function—or we'd all be basket cases! It is only when we contemplate the nature of this otherness that we are confronted with our own normativity: others are and have a self that exists independently from "me." "What is this other? What does the other have that I don't have? What do I want? What do I lack that the other has?" These questions lie on the sunrise of self-consciousness, because we are instantly made aware of the external reality of other human beings who are just like us in essence although we have separate identities, personalities, and longings. We become aware of our desires through reflection upon (and as projected onto) the other, on the subject that stands before us even though we see this other as an independent (impersonal) object. When we recognize the other as a desirous and intentional being, we are immediately made aware of the subjectivity of the other, one we have an obligation to address. "What does this other want?" This leads us to one of Hegel's most important insights: when we confront otherness, we are entangled in desire and lack, which initiates a skirmish for recognition.[5] Who will be acknowledged in this mutual otherness? Here subjectivities stand fundamentally opposed to one another.

Hegel (1807) pushes the issue further and forces us to face a most grave predicament: when mutual opposition confronts each other, "each seeks the death of the other" (*PS* § 187). This understandably creates a crisis situation. Who will be defeated? In our contemporary world of cutthroat competition, economic exploitation and rivalry, political dominion, legal intervention, military strategizing, and transgovernmental manoeuvering of hegemonic policies, which ideology will win out over others? One side must acknowledge that they are weaker and the other stronger, so when posturing and rhetoric fail, a natural deference ensues, much like what we see in the animal kingdom governed by evolutionary currents. One must bow down and accept their inferiority and servitude, while the other maintains the status of victor. What used to be a literal fight to the death is now largely a symbolic one depending upon where you live or come from. Genocide in Rwanda, Sierra Leone, Myanmar, and the Democratic Republic of the Congo are cordial reminders in recent decades of what can happen when power differentials implode. But this happens on a more pedestrian plain everyday everywhere in the world. People want respect: when they are dismissed or insulted, they emotively react with counter-contempt and rancor, if not narcissistic rage and the need to devalue or shame the other in the heat of the moment. This can even precipitate violence and the need for revenge due to wounded pride. From Trump to fake news, denial over the pandemic, and a gullible inane public, we are living in precarious times of transition and outright stupidity.

What is often recognized is not the equality of the other, but rather a scornful inequality, namely, the narcissistic fact that people often do not care about alterity over their own lives and self-interests, to the point that the Other becomes a dangerous threat to one's safety. Although we may acknowledge that others are independent persons, it does not mean that we "respect others as persons" (Hegel, 1821, § 36). On the contrary, respect is earned. Avoidance, withdrawal, and submissiveness, on the other hand, are defensive modes of self-survival, especially in the face of a powerful opponent. Do our world societies (i.e., Hegel's Objective Spirit or Jung's collective psyche instantiated in a state) think about the common universal good for all, or merely their own self-regard and political pressures invested in their own nation and communities? Despite there may be checks and balances designed to help treat citizens fairly, this does not generalize to a universal society of cosmopolitans (namely, citizens of the cosmos) who value all human life equally. Of course such hypostatization of a so-called collective mind only makes sense as an abstract conception that embodies the spirit of democracy, as imperfect as this may be. But when it comes down to actualizing a universal good, humanity becomes a multiple personality split in its desires, needs, conflicts, demands, and dissatisfactions.

There is always a tension arc between the individual and the collective that stands in relation to pure freedom versus ideality as a good for all. We should never presuppose that we all have the same values and opportunities to pursue and obtain life goals equally, for we all have different historicities and restrictions that condition the developmental, ontic, cultural, material, and economic substrates that in turn curtail our opportunities, liberties, worldviews, and outcomes. So when Honneth (2012) says that a distributional schema of justice "would have to be replaced by the involvement of all subjects in a given relationship of recognition" (p. 45), this seems to violate human nature. Not all people are disposed, let alone capable, of recognizing the other. We may have to contend that, in the end, recognition means tolerance of difference and not merely acceptance of the other, which could still bring about a pragmatic co-existence even if people cannot recognize each other as equals.

In today's society we live in fear of death for looking at someone the wrong way, of seeing *their* desire for what *you* are imagined to possess, or what they lack and want, to the point that you could be mugged for the change in your pockets, raped at whim, or shot in the face just because somebody didn't like the way you looked at them. The gaze, the look—the *stare* is an invitation to aggression. We are instinctively obsequious and show assent or acquiesce when we are afraid. We avoid the face of the other—hence look away, dodge confrontation, and yield; conversely, just as we look for conflict, seek out a fight, hate the other (just for being other), and retaliate in perceived defeat simply because we have the need to find foes. Some object *must* become a designated whipping post as a form of displacement. Eye aversion is the best way to evade engaging with the other—simply a faceless entity that is deemed a threat worth avoiding yet one already identified as a powerful object for inducing fear in the first place. We can sniff out their aggression, their malice, their negativity and so-called (intuited) evil propensities. Disavowal and disassociation become common defenses. The other is as alien to us as we are to them, and we hope that they will just leave us alone, if not disappear. In the face of conflict, we simply want the other to vanish.

But what happens when the Other wants something from us, or demands our recognition, let alone restitution, as if it were a right? Our proverbial backs go up. Yet the Truth and Reconciliation Commissions in response to Apartheid, the scandal over the US federal Chinese Exclusion Act and interning Japanese Americans in WWII, as well as First Nations children in Christian residential schools in Canada, and the process of family members publically addressing (and sometimes forgiving) murderer's openly in courts of law (such as with the organization Murder Victims' Families for Reconciliation) show how recognition has healing properties. But it does not undo injustice. Inequality and disparities are everywhere. We all have to get in line before we are acknowledged let alone recognized, some as subjects in their own right, but mostly as objects wanting something from others equally viewed as things in mutual opposition. Here the notion of equality by some may be seen as entitlement by others, which challenges the status quo at the same time the establishment offers its own political offensives. We develop our defenses, some cynical, caustic, stoic and/or emotionless, others manic and counter-aggressive, in order to deal with the Other's demands and in facing our own lack. Envy, jealousy, and passive-aggressiveness are common dispositions. Protest and violence are eruptions of frustration sometimes fueled by paranoiac relations. Facing alterity always involves an interpersonal negotiation between mutual conflict, competing values, emotional prejudices, and privileged self-serving agendas. This takes place in all facets of society as it does in the consulting room.

From the Psychological to the Social

As with Freud's (1921) qualification that individual psychic processes can never stand apart from social psychology and the cultural environs that impact on both personal subjectivity and the objective conditions that interpolate society, so too many critical theorists had turned to psychoanalytic paradigms to bolster social philosophy. For Marcuse (1955), psychological categories are political categories and are inseparable from the broader sociological forces that shape civilization. As he tells us, "psychological problems turn into political problems: private disorder reflects more directly than before the disorder of the whole, and the cure of the personal disorder depends more directly than before on the cure of the general disorder" (p. 21), namely, sick society. Marcuse is very clear in his insistence that the individual is determined by "the societal forces which define the psyche" (*Ibid*). Here Jung is lurking in Marcuse's closet. Yet at the same time, psychology becomes the foundation of sociology and the cultural dynamics and institutional organizations that in turn inform the psychological.

If you begin with the premise that all human beings are psychological creatures and that all inner experience is psychologically mediated, then by natural extension this would apply to the notion of the social, and specifically the politics of desire instantiated within any community. And if you start with the premise that the psychological is shaped by the social, then the same argument applies. Groups are psychologically informed and inform others right down to a single subject, whether this applies to our families, cohorts, communities, the provincial or nation state, and so forth. From Jung to Heidegger and Lacan, we are thrown into a collective psychic matrix and socio-symbolic order that informs our being in the world. Here the individual develops within the social, and the social within the individual.

One does not have to bifurcate the arrangements of society from naturalized psychology to see how their dynamic processes and co-occurrence pressurize and inform one another within a systemic unit. We can surely observe how certain structures and political policies within societies lead to more problems in living and suffering in individuals, and how natural psychological processes such as desire, envy, greed, rage, entitlement, aggression, and so on are intensified and play out through pathological enactments when societies undergo material deprivation, economic austerity, tragedy, trauma, war, political oppression, etc. When social institutions, capitalistic enterprise, and the populace do not acknowledge or recognize disenfranchised subgroups and the extreme hardships they face due to race, socioeconomic, and educational disparities that privileged classes do not face, social fabrics begin to fray in tatters.

The struggle for recognition, as psychoanalysis shows, is present from birth onward—from daycare to death, as each of us are mired in familial, societal, and cultural conflict that saturates our being in the world. The failure to recognize the other, and more insidiously, chronic invalidation and repudiation of different peoples, produces and sustains intersubjective and interethnic aggression to the point of murder and war. Here the Hegelian struggle for life and death is a lived reality that affects our conception of social justice and institutionalized forms of recognition. But the point I wish to make here is that dysrecognition may in fact trigger and sustain violence based on an emotional revolt in reaction to political injustice. Let's call this the "Fuck You!" attitude. Indeed, aggression is not only instinctual, for lack of a better word, hence emanating from biological forces, it is also triggered by relational or interpersonal failures at validation and empathy that are sociologically instituted. When such dysrecognition is performed and sustained by the state, here we may say that a certain unconscious politics is operative on both the individual and collective level of a given society, which can lead to a vicious cycle of perpetration, victimization, and social malaise that always psychologically penetrates those who are marginalized. And this may be intensified as a posttraumatic act that resurrects earlier psychic pain experienced in childhood, especially when invalidation, abuse, and insecure attachments inform the next generation of social pathologies.

Unconscious Politics

Much of psychoanalysis is in simpatico with critical theory in its tacit hopes of bettering society; but psychoanalytic observations can be quite pathologizing as well, and for good reason. Here the two disciplines are critical of the way collectives think and behave. We may speculate that this has to do with, on some level, the way people are raised and taught to think and act in a given cultural milieu, yet we must begin with rudiments. What do people require psychologically in order to thrive? Beyond recognition, I suggest, and I am in good company, lies psychic needs for love, validation, and empathy. These are essential for healthy development. When they are lacking, with-held, truncated, or absent, a person, and even whole societies, may develop a traumatic reaction to life. This notion is quite simple in fact, a basic ingredient of the human aspect.

All people as individuals have basic psychic needs, which feed and sustain a society. If those needs are thwarted or disabused, then this creates a fundamental retrograde backlash that has detrimental repercussions on people's health and wellbeing, as well as the pro-ductive social functioning of the collective. It is not rocket science. If you are deprived of the essential psychological nutrients of life, let alone if you are abused, oppressed, disenfranchised, or suffer developmental traumas, then this impacts on us all. People are unhappy, suffer, and develop psychological disorders that do not allow them to function adequately, let alone meet higher-level ex-pectations for psychosocial adaptation to common stress. The quality of subjective life is tarnished and society is affected in every tangible way, from economics to healthcare to lost productivity and creativity, to the qualitative erosion of living a good existence. People act out, become aggressive, anxious and depressed, fall into crisis or despair, or become dysfunctional in every conceivable manner, which creates an ambiance for internal implosion, whether this is projected outwardly or interiorized into self-destructive modes of being and behavioural patterns. The bottom line is that all individuals require that certain psychological needs be met or there will be subjective suffering that spews forth on any communal collective regardless of their content or context, typically beginning with one's immediate family, which only perpetuates a transge-nerational transmission of *pathos* that infects any given society and the broader cultural identifications and organizations at large. When this happens, whether conspicuously or cryptically, what is empirically predictable is a future world full of more suffering and pathology.

One of the major roadblocks that derail a discernable intellectual picture of the need for mutual or collective recognition is in deci-phering the anathema of unconscious politics that underlie beha-vioural acts of every person in the world. People, societies, and governments do not act rationally, nor should we expect them to. We do not live in a purely adjudicated intellect or logical universe, but rather one derived from the prisms of our base urges, impulses, emotions, and internal conflicts that must undergo a developmental and educational process of exercising self-constraint, affect regulation, behavioural modification, and instructional training in order to achieve psychological and social maturity. The gleanings of reason, truth, virtue, and wisdom are higher order accomplishments.[6] But this is hardly achieved by everyone. In fact, this level of psychic cultivation is more of an outlier than an actualization for most people. At most we are all striving for the attainment of certain values and ideals. What is more commonplace is that we succumb to our own immediate shortcomings and conflicts, ethical limitations of character, and attitudinal prejudices that condition how we relate to self, others, and the world.

We develop internal resistances, oppositions, and counter-struggles to internalized and interiorized conflict from birth onward. This is simply an economic (if not evolutionary) reaction to protecting the self against real or perceived threat and emotional pain. This naturalized tendency is partially derived from (if not determined by) unconscious desire and its reactionary defenses and resultant disharmonies fueled by affective currents that merely seek their own resolutions and satisfactions over others, which are projected upon society at large. Here we may observe a basic splitting mechanism in the psyche: identity and division become irreconcilable, where there is no discernable point of synthesis or sublation. People see their own esoteric or group microcosm as the hallmark of truth and reality that takes objective priority over others, when such myopic identifications are in dialectical competition with alterity. In other words, the Other is negated in principle based on one's own reinforced preferences that take precedence and are more personally important, the underside of narcissistic hubris. This attitude is the foundation of every country and nationalist (or populist) movement who values its own citizens over other countries as a pragmatic necessity governing political identificatory self-interest ranging from every partisan preference and local whim to domestic and foreign decree.

We must seriously question the prejudicial unconscious forces that drive political states of affairs, from individual and communal choices to international policy, for collective humanity is neither unified in its aims nor prioritizes matters outside of its immediate scope of parochial concerns or regional inclinations. Is the political unconscious a universal phenomenon, namely, is it structurally inscribed in the very ontological fabric of the psyche? This would suggest that, with qualifications, notwithstanding divergent groups and individualities that comprise a community of followers identified with attaining certain material gains, enjoyment, or reinforcing a self-serving perspective or worldview, all people are predisposed a priori to favour certain unconscious attitudes even if they are irrational and ultimately self-destructive. And it is unequivocally taking place on a mass scale across all civilized parts of the world.

What we are witnessing in concrete forms is how the collective psyche is divided based on unconscious politics identified with certain ideologies fortified by cultural relativity and animus towards alterity. Here we should question the capacity of collectives to make rationally informed judgements when wish, self-interest, and insular governmental hegemonies make decisions that affect us all. Yet government is elected by the people in democratic countries, which brings us to question why in recent political times the majority of citizens would vote for leaders—say, in the United Kingdom and America, who are anti-environment, anti-immigration, xenophobic, racist, bigoted, religiously intolerant, misogynistic, anti-gay, and pro-war, just to name a few indecencies. From *Brexit* to the election of U.S. Republican President Donald Trump, humanity should beckon a call to reason. It is no surprise to psychoanalysis that we are witnessing the disintegration of culture, for illogical decisions are unconsciously chosen based on emotional prejudices, which speaks to the greater manifestation of collective social life immersed in its own *pathos*.

The Ontology of Prejudice

Prejudice forms a basic constituency in our psychic constitutions, for we all pass judgements on others based on our preferential appraisal of what we value and are accustomed to find familiar and/or pleasing. The dialectical tension between difference and similarity carries a certain psychological hold over people, for our earliest familial identifications are based in shared experiences and values, and we gravitate towards those who we feel attracted to due to communal affiliation and shared meaning. But the double edge of the dialectic (as negativity resulting in higher unity) exposes us to a dilemma, for the dialectic is the ontological dynamic underlying prejudice itself. Here we may be reminded of Adorno (1966): the dark side of the negative is always emphasized in any act of judgement. In fact, it is the structural edifice for judgement to exist. Most societies *need* to have enemies, that is, they need to have an emotional whipping boy or designated scapegoat to beat and project all of their inner conflicts, frustrations, rage, hate, homicidal fantasies, and so forth onto, or else we would have never invented poetics, theatre, drama, the arts, music, religion, politics, and so on, for the human psyche requires forms of displacement and sublimation in order to transform internal discord, affect, and ambivalent experience into palatable outlets so we may psychologically function and adapt to real, perceived, or felt adversity.

The reality of racism, ethnic discrimination, inter-ethnic rivalries and hostilities, micro-competitions and devaluations within sub-cultures and fringe subgroups, and emotional prejudices cast onto objects of alterity are all too human universal propensities: to deny them would be an incredulous attempt at posturing political correctness in favour of truth. The mass contempt in many nations for immigrants, refugees, migrant workers, and asylum seekers of different ethnic and national persuasions, even if only a minority view, speaks to the underground psychic reality of human prejudice worried that the Other will steal their chickens, jobs, sexual partners, and enjoyment. A recent example of this was a mob of over 1000 South Africans that raided a Somali neighbourhood in Pretoria killing foreign African settlers based on a hate campaign against foreigners, immigrants, and refugees who are accused of creating unemployment and increasing crime.[7] Here the "foreigner" is transferentially constructed as the elected evil Other who will mooch, pillage, and soak up the citizenry's pleasures and deprive them of their national birthrights and liberties, and who are moreover left flipping the bill for the outsider to enjoy a free lunch. "Keep that piece of shit out of my country!" This is a common visceral opinion among many American, British, and European communities, to such a degree that the immigrant, migrant worker, or refugee should be deprived of subsidy, welfare, food stamps, unemployment insurance, access to healthcare, education, daycare, and other privileges just because of their foreign status or so-called lack of entitlement to "free" services on the government's dime.[8]

This exclusionary phenomenon speaks to both the individual and collective rupture of feelings of security and safety that are perceived to be imperiled when political changes occur in social strata and potential emergent threats manifest, a paranoid and/or hysterical process that lies at the very heart of human psychological motivations, as it would be illogical not to fear what is unknown and unfamiliar for what is domestic, customary, and familiar. Here the Other is categorically, oppositionally constituted even if there is no discernable threat at all. Difference signifies its own meaning based on dissimilarity, fear, and potential personal loss and sacrifice of a country's members or their own kind. Here the personal idiosyncrasy of selective identification with a certain element of one's culture, language, nationalism, or social complex can wreak political consequences. And even when altruistic and humanistic movements prevail, there is always a spoiler introduced based on human frailty, desperation, and the inevitability of pathological enactments. When German citizens took to protest over the Syrian and North African migrants who allegedly robbed, looted, and sexually assaulted their women after being graciously accepted into their country during the 2015 refugee crisis (which of course happens every day everywhere regardless of where you come from), not to mention several United States Governors refusing to allow refugees to settle in their home states once it was discovered that ISIS connections were part of the Paris attacks based on refugee involvement, it is no surprise why panic would set in and the floodgates would be closed based on mass protest. These events even sparked President Donald Trump to ban Muslims (as everyone knows) from entering the US, and to build a wall on the border of Mexico to keep out the "illegal freeloaders." Here it becomes obvious that the foreign unknown Other as "alien archetype" (Mills, 2018, p. 19), who has their own needs, desires, adversity, and trauma, will likely have their own "psychological baggage" and material losses that other nation states will have to pay for, and this is likely how a large percentage of the populace thinks. Why else would people get so emotionally bent out of shape by an influx of new people into their country? The fear of so-called "hard working" citizens supporting and taking care of foreigners on their sweat and taxes, where food, shelter, transport, economic subsidies, and entertainment (such as access to TVs, cell phones, computers, and the Internet) are given away without merit (even in the spirit of humanitarian aid), spur bad feelings among the working class and rich alike. Who wants a dependent child when you never wanted to get pregnant to begin with?

Part of the problem facing us is that prejudice is ontologically constituted in the most rudimentary aspects of human consciousness as psychological disposition. Like the nature of the dialectic, prejudice has both negative and positive valences. While violence and destruction are the instruments of prejudice, so too is caring and love. Prejudice is not merely a negative construct; prejudice defines our valuation practices, which are the Mecca of individual and communal life. Rather than conceive of prejudice as simply a pathological anomaly, prejudice is also responsible for our most revered ideals. As I have said elsewhere (Mills & Polanowski, 1997, pp. 11–13), prejudice in its essence is the preferential self-expression of valuation, as corrupt as that may be.

A World without Recognition

Although it is problematic to make mass generalizations, it may not be entirely illegitimate to say that we largely live in a world where there is no proper recognition of the Other as the equiprimordial complementarity of the Self. In other words, it's too cognitively overwhelming to uphold the radical Levinasean responsibility to the Other over the immediacy of one's life and duties to family and those who we value, as if we could become Jesus and minister to a world collective. This ethical ideal defies logic, real human limitations, and the psychological disposition of the masses. But speaking metaphysically, the dialectical onto-interconnectedness of identity and difference ensures that self-in-relation to alterity is a mutually implicit dynamic. When we attempt to analyse the human condition extraspectively or scientifically, and look into the psyche or soul through an introspective analysis of our interiority, we can discern the universal experiences that all people engage in psychologically, only to recursively fall back into bifurcation that maintains rigid antitheses.

The self is experienced and thought *not* to be the other. The *Them* is eclipsed for the *I*, while the *We* becomes occluded.

We may argue that, strictly speaking, humanity is not an identity at all, but rather a collection of identities or subjects who largely exist and relate to one another in opposition to mutual difference. Despite the fact that we all maintain shared identifications and values with others throughout our globalized world, not everyone is recognized, nor is this remotely possible given that people are divided based on their desires, conflicts, beliefs, values, identities, and moral principles. Here we should maintain no pretense of a pristine Hegelian sublation (*Aufhebung*) of the subjective individual within objective social consciousness, where the pinnacle of ethics and justice reach their logical zenith in the concrete universals of culture, for this is merely a theoretical abstraction. In fact, much of social reality resists sublation, and can indeed regress or withdrawal back to early primitive instantiations governed by *pathos*.[9] The Absolute unity of the individual within the social as the logical culmination of pure self-consciousness is simply an illusion, although one that may spur along our continual pining for refining social systems of democracy, law, ethics, and justice. Here reformation and advance are culture's teleological endeavour. Whatever values and ideals societies adopt, they are always mediated through unconscious psychic processes[10] that condition (and taint) the collective, even when there are good intentions involved. Although the fantasy of wholeness conceived through Hegel's philosophy of mind as a self-articulated, dynamic complex holism arriving at pure unification of the individual within the collective is a noble ideal, a sentiment similar to Jung's notion of individuation, such a grand logical synthesis belies the empirical confounds that reflect social reality today marked by division, fracturing, and splitting of peoples, groups, and nations that radically resist unity. The projection of our aggression, hatred, and destructive envy onto a hating Other only ensures mutual conflict and dysrecognition, where some compromises conceivably occur. Despite these limitations and inevitable frictions between individuals and societies, collective identifications among people about ideals and social values do facilitate advances in ethical self-consciousness, which have a concrete impact on social policy and legislative reform that in turn restructure social institutions and the domestic practices of citizens.

Perhaps the most we can expect is a Fichtean (1794) infinite striving for perfection, although we will likely have to settle for only achieving a quantum and quality of improvement. Here the idea of cultivating social betterment as participating in the ethical leads us to value the notion of mutual recognition as an ideal value. If what we crave and want for ourselves—namely, to be acknowledged, validated, and understood—is to be denounced in another as a reciprocal human being mirroring the inverse of who we are and experience, then this form of negation and hypocrisy not only casts a shadow on the other, but also sullies ourselves as an offense to virtue. Yet this idealist language does not inspire mass psychology, which typically devolves into the particular lives, longings, sufferings, and priorities of singular personalities who live among a sea of rivals all competing for recognition and personal gain.

One of the reasons for our impasse in achieving collective recognition of all people is a failure to possess, nurture, and demonstrate empathy for others. This failure is intimately tied to a subset of the problem, that is, our inability to foster global identifications with others. Empathy is based on an intersubjective identification with the other as an experiential self just like we are. Each of us stands united in spirit as an egalitarian subject that feels and needs. This basic shared identification with our fellow human beings is what gives empathy its value. But this is never easy to universally expect, let alone institute or institutionalize on a grand scale. It is an awareness that needs fostered, the seeds of which begin in early childhood facilitated by a healthy, emotional holding environment grounded in secure attachments to parents, caregivers, and family members or their surrogates. Through personal experiences of being recognized, validated, shown care and psychological warmth, as well as feeling loved and understood, empathy for others develops as self-realization of the good and the need to embrace it, as does our emotional intelligence in socialization practices. Feeling felt, seeing the pain in others' eyes, and recognizing the experience of the other as a reciprocal self-relation to one's own interior helps to open up an ethical stance we are obliged to extend to the other as a fellow *Thou*, or more appropriately, *You*—a recognition of personhood. This is a form of ethical self-consciousness as felt-compassion that not all people are psychologically capable of harboring or showing based upon their own personal plight or tragedies, family upbringing, cultural displacement or disenfranchisement, developmental traumas, and so forth. But this does not mean that empathy cannot be awakened or taught. If global societies were to promote empathy as an educational imperative and intrinsic valued commodity as an end in-itself institutionalized within a given community or culture—as well as promoting the value of fostering loving emotional attachments to others, which begins in the home, the world would be a better place.

Suffering and Society

Jung (1917b) suggests that neurosis is the failed attempt to heal a universal split in the collective psyche. Here he may be said to mirror the concerns that preoccupy critical theorists.

> We always find in the patient a conflict which at a certain point is connected with the great problems of society ... [T]he apparently individual conflict of the patient is revealed as a universal conflict of his environment and epoch. Neurosis is thus nothing less than an individual attempt, however unsuccessful, to solve a universal problem.
>
> (Jung, *CW*, 7 § 438, p. 265)

Jung attributes this collective neurotic manifestation to the "shadow-side of the psyche" that has attained the character of "*autonomous complexes*" in their own right on a mass scale (p. 266, italics in original). Here it is easy to appreciate where Jung is coming from. When social reality is burdened with *pathos*, it leads to a sick soul. Neurosis is an attempt to repair social pathology through compromise formation.

During the same year, in *On the Psychology of the Unconscious*, Jung (1917a) also wrote that: "Neurosis is intimately bound up with the problem of our time and really represents an unsuccessful attempt on the part of the individual to solve the general problem in his own person" (*CW*, 7 § 18, p. 20). This seems to suggest that by curing the individual one cures society.[11] The more individuals who are less encumbered by unconscious conflicts are more likely to influence societies that will be less split or conflicted given that healthy people make societies healthier. If neurosis is a failed attempt to remedy social problems, then psychological symptoms are the manifestation of social malaise. But this does not mean that individual healing will cure a sick society. Self-correction or restoration cannot be simultaneously superimposed onto the greater masses as an isomorphic correlate that transmogrifies material society in its concrete structures and communal reality. At most we can say is that if neurosis is indeed an unsuccessful attempt to unconsciously resolve a collective problem, social amelioration may only be achieved through collective actions. Self-healing cannot be generalized to the collective unless the collective takes measures to generalize to the healing of individuals. Individual cure may have very little to do with healing on a grand scale, especially when social collectives are bombarded by mass disparities and individual suffering within the collective. Here social dysrecognition only perpetuates collective suffering.

When one is treated like a thing and not recognized as a proper human being, the subject begins to relate to others as things in an ocean of objects where the kernel of the value of reciprocal recognition devolves into negation, intransigent antagonism, strife, fear of alterity, paranoia, sustained aggressivity, and repetition compulsion. When cultural trauma saturates attachment and socialization patterns, we can assuredly predict a future full of human suffering, where psychic and sociological impairment leaves many existential stains. Here we must recognize that the many faces of pathology transfigure our internal natures and scars the social landscape, even when a given individual or society recognizes the collective good in recognizing others.

Notes

1 For the ancient Greeks, *pathos* defined the human condition: to be human is to suffer.
2 By Jean Hyppolite's (1971) account, "Seemingly, Freud had not read Hegel" (p. 57); but we do know that he was at least acquainted with his philosophy. In a paper titled, "The Importance of Philosophy for the Further Development of Psychoanalysis," delivered at the International Congress for Psychoanalysis at Weimar in 1911, James Putnum advocated the need for philosophical integration within psychoanalytic investigation. From Ernest Jones' (1955) biography on Freud, he states:

[Putnum's] burning plea for the introduction of philosophy—but only his own Hegelian brand—into psychoanalysis did not meet with much success. Most of us did not see the necessity of adopting any particular system. Freud was of course very polite in the matter, but remarked to me afterwards: "Putnum's philosophy reminds me of a decorative centerpiece; everyone admires it but no one touches it." (pp. 85–86)

3 Jung (1947) disparagingly writes:

A philosophy like Hegel's is a self-revelation of the psychic background and, philosophically, a presumption. Psychologically, it amounts to an invasion by the unconscious. The peculiar high-flown language Hegel uses bears out this view: it is reminiscent of the megalomanic languages of schizophrenics, who use terrible spellbinding words to reduce the transcendent to subjective form, to give banalities the charm of novelty, or pass off commonplaces as searching wisdom. (*CW*, 8, p. 170)

4 It is important to note that Hegel's treatment of self-consciousness and the struggle for recognition in the *Phenomenology* (1807) is presented differently in the *Encyclodaedia* (1971, 1978) and the *Berlin Phenomenology* (1981). The most noticeable distinction is the brevity of the latter works. Hegel's master-slave discussion, or what we may refer to as lord and servant, and more generally the "*relationship* of *mastery* [*Herrschaft*] and *servitude* [*Knechtschaft*]" (Hegel, 1978, *EG* § 433), is given the briefest summation in the *Encyclopaedia* where the discussion from recognition to universal self-consciousness is contained in only six paragraphs and one remark, excluding the additions, and little additional elaboration is offered in the Berlin manuscript. This is undoubtedly why almost all interpretations of desire and recognition rely exclusively on the Jena *Phenomenology*. Furthermore, all references to stoicism, skepticism, and unhappy consciousness are eliminated. This terse account suggests that perhaps Hegel wanted to distance himself from his earlier commitments outlined in the *Phenomenology*, or else that he thought he had treated the subjects adequately beforehand. When we examine his later works, Hegel emphasizes the subjection of the other to the domination of desire as a "thoroughly selfish *destructiveness*" (Hegel, 1978, *EG* § 428, *Zusatz*) that is only concerned with its immediate satisfaction in conquering opposition. Recognitive self-consciousness is the immediate confrontation of two egos, each extending its self into the other. During this moment, the self has an "immediate intuition" of itself as well as the recognition of an "absolutely opposed and independently distinct object" (Hegel, 1978, *EG* § 430). When the other is seen merely as an object and not a subject, this ensures there will be no mutual recognition. See Mills (2002, pp. 143-149) for an extended discussion.

5 While discourse on desire and lack is thought to have derived from Sartre and Lacan—who essentially purloined Hegel's theory when he was exposed to Kojève's (1929) lectures on Hegel's *Phenomenology*, which Lacan (1991) borrows from liberally, these notions originate from Hegel. Desire immediately apprehends what it is not from what it would like to be, hence the self starts from a place of inequality, deficiency, and lack. Hegel (1978) explains:

> The self-conscious subject knows itself to be *implicitly identical* with the general object external to it. It knows that since this general object contains the *possibility* of satisfying desire, it is *adequate* to the desire, and that this is precisely why the desire is stimulated by it. The relation with the object is therefore necessary to the subject. The subject intuits its *own deficiency*, its own onesidedness, in the object; it sees there something which although it belongs to its own essence, it lacks (*EG* § 427, *Zusatz*).

6 This is why, according to Hegel (1807), we all must be subjected to a master (e.g., a parent, teacher, clergy, the law) in order to achieve maturation in thought, intellect, restraint, moral disposition, aesthetic sensibility, and spiritual realization. In his words, "In order to be free, in order to be capable of self-control, all peoples have therefore had first to undergo the strict discipline of subjection to a master" (1978, *EG* § 435, *Zusatz*). Although we tend to think of masters as problematic and oppressive, in this context I wish to emphasize that the notion of achieving discipline, success, and mastery is facilitated by adult upbringing, instruction, education (*Bildung*), and self-refinement.

7 There have been many anti-foreigner attacks in recent years in South Africa targeting migrants and refugees, including mobs killing foreign African immigrants in 2008 and 2015. Violence has largely been directed towards Nigerians, Zimbabweans, and Congolese, which has escalated tensions between South Africa and other African countries (see York, 2017).

8 Just as a side note, we would not want to live in a world where everyone has a PhD. We need people to work, to do certain jobs that others are not willing to do, able to, or could not do in order to keep the economy functioning and healthy, and to buy real estate and take care of a nation's aging population. Here is a perfect example of our mutual dependency on each other.

9 In *Origins: On the Genesis of Psychic Reality*, I provide my own revisionist amendments to Hegel's dialectical method that takes into account the nature of dialectical regression, temporal mediacy, and the ubiquitous nature of contingency that challenges universal pronouncements of an Absolute unity of mind (see Mills, 2010, pp. 51–58).

10 Although the different schools of psychoanalytic thought offer their own nuanced theoretical frameworks, one universal belief is that there are unconscious processes operating within the psyche that stand in relation to social

organizations that reinforce them. See Mills (2014) for comprehensive overview of the philosophies of the unconscious in Hegel, Freud, Jung, Lacan, Heidegger, Sartre, Winnicott, and Whitehead.

11 Giovanni Colacicchi (2018), personal communication.

References

Adorno, T.W. (1966). *Negative Dialectics*. New York: Bloomsbury, 1973/2007.

Fichtean, J.G. (1794). *The Science of Knowledge*, trans. and eds.P. Heath & J. Lachs. Cambridge: Cambridge University Press, 1993.

Fraser, N., & Honneth, A. (2003). *Redistribution or Recognition? A Political - Philosophical Exchange*, trans. J. Golb, J. Ingram, & C. Wilke. London: Verso.

Freud, S. (1921). *Group Psychology and the Analysis of the Ego. Standard Edition*, Vol. 18. London: Hogarth Press.

Habermas, J. (1990). *Moral Consciousness and Communicative Action*. Cambridge, MA: MIT Press.

Habermas, J. (1993). *Justification and Application: Remarks on Discourse Ethics*. Cambridge, MA: MIT Press.

Hegel, G.W.F. (1981). *The Berlin Phenomenology*, ed. and trans. M.J. Petry. Dordrecht, Holland: D. Reidel Publishing Co.

Hegel, G.W.F. (1978). *Hegels Philosophie des subjektiven Geistes / Hegel's Philosophy of Subjective Spirit*, Vol.1: Introductions, Vol.2: Anthropology, Vol.3: Phenomenology and Psychology, ed.M.J. Petry. Dordrecht, Holland: D. Reidel Publishing Company.

Hegel, G.W.F. (1807). *Phenomenology of Spirit*, trans. A.V. Miller. Oxford: Oxford University Press, 1977.

Hegel, G.W.F. (1817/1827/1830). *Philosophy of Mind*. Vol.3 of the *Encyclopaedia of the Philosophical Sciences*, trans. W. Wallace & A.V. Miller. Oxford: Clarendon Press, 1971.

Hegel, G.W.F. (1821). *Philosophy of Right*, trans. T.M. Knox. Oxford: Oxford University Press, 1967.

Honneth, A. (1995). *The Struggle for Recognition*, trans. J. Anderson. London: Polity Press.

Honneth, A. (2012). *The I in We: Studies in the Theory of Recognition*. Cambridge, UK: Polity Press.

Hyppolite, J. (1971). Hegel's Phenomenology and Psychoanalysis. In W.E. Steinkraus (Ed), *New Studies in Hegel's Philosophy*. New York: Holt, Rinehart and Winston.

Jones, E. (1955). *The Life and Work of Sigmund Freud*, Vol 2. New York: Basic Books.

Jung, C.G. (1917a). On the Psychology of the Unconscious. *CW*, 7, 1–122.

Jung, C.G. (1917b). New Paths in Psychology, *CW*, 7, 245–268.

Jung, C.G. (1947). On the Nature of the Psyche. *CW*, 8: pp. 159–234.

Kelly, S. (1993). *Individuation and the Absolute: Hegel, Jung, and the Path Toward Wholeness*. New York: Paulist Press.

Kojève, A. (1929). *Introduction to the Reading of Hegel: Lectures on the Phenomenology of Spirit*. Assembled by R. Queneau, & A. Bloom (Ed), & J.H. Nichols, Jr. (Trans). Ithaca: Cornell University Press, 1969/1980.

Lacan, J. (1991). *The Other Side of Psychoanalysis: The Seminar of Jacques Lacan, Book XVII*, trans. R. Grigg. New York: Norton, 2007.

Marcuse, H. (1955). *Eros and Civilization.* London: Penguin Press, 1970.

Mills, J. (2002). *The Unconscious Abyss: Hegel's Anticipation of Psychoanalysis.* Albany, NY: SUNY Press.

Mills, J. (2010). *Origins: On the Genesis of Psychic Reality.* Montreal: McGill-Queens University Press.

Mills, J. (2013). Jung's Metaphysics. *International Journal of Jungian Studies*, 5(1), 19–43.

Mills, J. (2014). *Underworlds: Philosophies of the Unconscious from Psychoanalysis to Metaphysics.* London: Routledge.

Mills, J. (2018). The Essence of Archetypes. *International Journal of Jungian Studies*, 10(3), 1–22.

Mills, J. & Polanowski, J. (1997). *The Ontology of Prejudice.* Amsterdam/New York: Rodopi.

York, G. (2017). "Anti-Foreigner Mob Rampages in 'March of Hatred' in South Africa. *The Globe and Mail.* Published Friday, Feb. 24, 2017 12:56PM EST http://www.theglobeandmail.com/news/world/anti-foreigner-mob-rampages-in-march-of-hatred-in-south-africa/article34128998/

Chapter 8

God: The Invention of an Idea

God does not exist. God is merely an idea—a mental object, the invention of imaginative thought championed by reason yet conditioned on desire. We as humanity have devised this myth and it is likely here to stay because world masses cannot live without it. Although there is a rational tenor to predicating God's existence, reason is ultimately mediated by fantasy.[1] God is the product of a collective ideological fantasy fueled by unconscious illusion ensconced in the basic desire for wish-fulfillment. The God hypothesis is merely a conjecture as supposition based on a fantasy principle conditioned by unconscious illusion sustained through social ideology. Although a logical concept born of social convention, God is a semiotic embodiment and symbolization of ideal value. Put concisely, God is only a symbolic thought. Rather than an extant ontological subject or agency traditionally attributed to a supernatural, transcendent creator, or supreme being responsible for the coming into being of the universe, God is a psychological invention signifying ultimate ideality. Here, God becomes a self-relation to an internalized idealized object, the idealization of imagined value. The idea or notion of God is the manifestation of our response to our being-in-relation-to-lack, and the longing to replace natural absence with divine presence. Hence, God remains a deposit of humanity's failure to accept our impending death and mourn natural deprivation or lack in favour of the delusional belief in an ultimate hypostatized object of idealized value.

It is easy to appreciate why the human psyche is compelled to invent the notion of God as an ultimate metaphysical reality, because billions of people have a profound need for God. People want consonance, love, enjoyment, satiation, perpetual peace, joy—no one in

DOI: 10.4324/9781003305958-8

their right mind would deny these universal yearnings! Yet for believers, a secular existence fails to meet this felt necessity. It is deeply comforting to believe in an Ideal Being, for one's anxieties, conflicts, and emotional pain are mitigated by believing in a divine beneficence that promises a satisfying afterlife. This hegemonic fallacy—the belief or faith in such an afterlife—makes personal, daily existence more tolerable with the dream, that deep down, sometime in the future, when you *perish* you will have everything you desire but are deprived of in your momentary life. Death no longer becomes an ending in-itself, but rather an Eden where all cherished wishes and values are realized—the Perfect World. God is a signifier for flawlessness, salvation, everlasting tranquility, or any qualitative value that signifies perennial happiness or bliss. As the product of fantasy life, God is solely a coveted fiction.

Proof and Negation

Every reflecting mind must allow that there is no proof of the existence of a Deity.

—Percy Bysshe Shelley[2]

Certain philosophers may claim that you cannot prove a negation, namely, God's non-existence. But I would ask, How is it that you cannot prove the non-existence of something when by definition there is nothing there to prove? We do not need to prove a negative, especially when there is nothing present. Negation is self-evident by virtue of absence. It doesn't take a natural scientist to demonstrate objective reality. Negation or absence is obvious and indisputable, a plain truism. There is nothing there to predicate other than negation. The burden is in proving how there is something out of nothing, how there *is* when what appears or manifests is *not*, literally no-thing. We do not even have a proper predication because we are positing (concrete) existence (not ideation) in the face of nothingness, a so-called hidden presence when there is salient absence. If the only thing that presents itself is absence, how can the predication of existence negate this apparent negation? In other words, if God is predicated to be yet is occluded, does this not beg the question of what constitutes the properties of existence? If anything, negation is the one thing that you can prove because nothing appears. Here we may side with Hume: "It is an infinite advantage in every controversy, to defend the negative."[3] Translation: that which is not evident needs no coaxing.

The philosopher is never called upon to prove a negative, for the burden is on the one predicating existential affirmation, here God's existence. The laws of induction and inference speak of reasonable and common sense ratios of probability to support likely conclusions based upon evidence some believers wish to categorically disqualify as truth or knowledge because it does not yield absolute certainty. However, is that good justification to negate a negative, let alone a good reason to live one's life by, when there is no evidence (which is missing, hence does not exist) to support such a supposition? Just because something cannot be proved with absolute certainty does not make it *ipso facto* false. Moreover, theists or deists would have us believe: "Because it is not certain that God cannot exist, it is at least equally certain that God exists." According to this way of thinking, any concession to the limits of proving a negation provides proportional (if not equal) logical grounds for positing an affirmation (which at most is an inference, and a poor one at that, based on a non sequitur where the conclusions do not follow from the premises). This reasoning is further based on the value of abstract possibility (itself a mental construction) rather than on mere probability, as if the possible supersedes the probable, especially when there is no tangible data to warrant this leap to metaphysical heaven.

Positing divine being to annul non-being (itself the negation of negation) is to privilege a lop-sided logic that assertion *itself* cancels negation when the assertion is a vacuous statement that lacks a present referential object; while the negative is self-evident by virtue of the fact of nothing being present. Rather than set the bar to zero as a mutual inference based on the laws of induction, the predication of the existence of an absent object does nothing to negate this apparent absence. I do not grant that the proposition of God's existence holds the same level of probability as the apparent nothingness of the (mental) object we are positing. And when philosophers are called upon to prove a negation, they wittingly revert to the proof from *modus tollens*:

$$\frac{P \to Q, \neg Q}{\therefore \neg P}$$

If (p) God exists, then (q) God would not be absent.

(q) God is not present, hence absent.

Therefore, (p) God does not exist.

Although this is a valid proof based on propositional logic, all one has to do is quibble with the premises to manipulate the desired outcome one wants. But here I am appealing to empirical facts: God's lack of presence gives no evidence for God's existence. To quote the new atheists, "the absence of evidence is evidence of absence." Given that most knowledge claims and scientific discoveries are built upon induction and inference, only to be supported or refuted by empirical evidence, does it make logical sense to affirm the existence of a supreme being when no inductive or deductive support can be indubitably established by appeal to all available evidence? Since when does the criterion of absolute certainty garner the respect to warrant the negation of negation in favour of affirmative belief in asserting "God exists!," especially when there is evidence to the contrary, namely, the absence of the very object in question. The burden of proof is on the one proclaiming existence, not on the one questioning whether something exists. Here negation is self-evident because nothing is present; and in order for something to exist, it must *appear* in order for it to *be*.[4]

The Christian philosopher and apologist William Lane Craig states that the theist need not have to appeal to evidence to know God exists, which is brought about through the inner workings of God's "Holy Spirit ... wholly apart from evidence," and by "miracles," one of which he notes is Christ's resurrection from the dead, as well as the canons of natural theology. Instead, rather than offering cogent or plausible proof, he insists that "it is incumbent on the atheist to prove that if God existed, he would provide more evidence of his existence than what we have. This is an enormously heavy burden of proof for the atheist to bear."[5] How so? Apart from this rhetorical challenge, I do not think the presence of nothing requires anymore proof than what is self-evident, namely the absence of an object, which is tantamount to the absence of evidence. Appealing to the subjectivity of belief as epistemological justification for knowing God's existence based on the invisible workings of a divine ghost is not sound (nor even reasonable) evidence to warrant such a conclusion. Neither is the presupposition of miracles that are said to have historically happened, which defy all natural physical laws; nor is scriptural or theological doctrine proffered as good evidence, let alone the imagined intentions or psychological motives attributed to a fantasy object that is presumed to exist. Craig's "proof" is merely the self-projection of his mind. Without providing persuasive argumentation commensurate with verifiable evidence, the theist is simply reasoning in a solipsistic circle.

An assertion of predication is affirmative, but one has the burden of proof. What is it? Where is it? Why does it not stand out or manifest? A proposition is not a proof of itself. And I certainly do not give any credence to Nathan Schneider's definition of proof as "that which makes good,"[6] which relegates evidence, truth, and reason to the scrapheap of relativism. Existence is not a predicate: it cannot be *defined* into actuality. Existence as a hypothetical construct cannot be assigned or unconditionally conferred Being as if it is merely a logical statement that needs no actual proof or substantial demonstration. Logic in itself is a decorous system of abstract inferences that lack substantive properties—an empty formalism, the content of which is arbitrarily supplied by our minds subject to convention. Just because you predicate something does not make it so. One cannot dismiss the request for spatial-temporal location and subsistence when predicating something substantive, such as in the substantive verb *to be*. If we appeal to arguments that God is immaterial and incorporeal, or non-temporal—outside of space and time, ethereal, eternal, and infinite, hence eluding all naturalistic indicators of experiential evidence, then we are positing the presupposition of a being that has never displayed its manifest existence. The premise itself is illegitimate, for there is nothing to predicate other than a missing object, pure nothingness. Here God becomes a hypothetical mental construct that is hypostatized or reified as a concrete subject (a person, no less). If it is only in one's mind, then how can it be real independent of mind? In other words, just because we think it does not make it an extant reality.

At most we can say is that mind as ideation posits a cognitive (mental) object as the subject matter of its predication, but we cannot ontologically justify the leap from internal ideation (even as coherent logical relata) to external actuality. At best God is a hypothesis, an educated guess or speculative conjecture that is empirically unverifiable. Yet thoughts themselves are empirical (experiential) phenomenon, and the parameters of their content and properties can be scientifically studied and objectively recognized. But with the God hypothesis we have no empirical object other than a mental concept, which is not sufficient to justify (let alone establish) the existence of an autonomous object that inhabits a mind independent metaphysical reality.

A negation, on the contrary, has no onus because nothing is predicated. There is no interlocutor engaging a subject, other than one's own mind. Therefore, an affirmative predication is, at best, a psychological object. If you assert that a negation does not provide proof of a possible or potential object to manifest, then by definition it does not currently exist and the whole argument devolves into possible or potential futures that have not occurred, despite the presumption that you cannot rule out their possible future occurrence. But to me this seems to be eluding the present condition of predication and actuality. Possibility is a mental occasion or instance of futurity— pure hypothetical abstraction, while actuality is real presence not limited to a cognitive object of predication.

The main problem in predicating God's existence independent of any tangible evidence is that it relies on a form of argumentation that attempts to deduce existence from the mere concept of existence. These a priori arguments do not rely on sense experience to lend any credibility to the form of argumentation, but rather on an analysis of concepts alone and their logical relations that pretentiously confer the domain of Being to hypothetical objects of thought, which are held to be knowable independent of empirical encounters. Yet these conventions are confined to the domain of ideas: when we deliberate ontology we must separate our conceptual schemes and what they designate from that which is truly extant. Predication and empirical reality are two different things: one is confined to mental operations, the other to facts.

It is generally known that Kant forcefully challenged the ontological argument by claiming that existence is not a property or a real predicate, namely, that the proposition "exists" is not a

properly defining predicate of God.[7] Because existential propositions are synthetic in nature, existence becomes a logical predicate
when such judgements are contingently performed.[8] In other words,
the notion of existence is only meaningful when objects of experience substantiate the predication. A concept alone does not confer
existence: it is impossible for my idea of God to contain any real
properties a priori without an experiential correlate to ground my
epistemic judgement that God actually exists as a real object or
acquires existence outside of my concept alone.[9] In other words,
we cannot conclude that the exact object of my concept exists
independent of empirical reality.

Existential statements typically either affirm or deny that
something exists. Positive existential statements assert existence,
while negative existential statements negate existence. The existential statement "God does not exist" is therefore a negative
one. But we must keep in mind, as we have just shown, that God is
a concept and not an object. There are no good grounds to think
of God as anything but an idea, for there is no counterpart in
material reality that would substantiate God as an empirical object. Therefore, when theists speak of God as existing, they are in
actuality referring to the concept of God as a psychic object. From
this vantage point, there is a special relation that is said to exist in
one's subjective mind independent of the ontological (external)
reality of the concept in question. Therefore, the God posit or
introject can have different functional distributions in a person's
psyche dissociated from the ontological status of God as a real
object, and may serve myriad psychological purposes. Perhaps,
some would argue, this is a sufficient condition to exonerate the
notion of God from the question of ontology. But the God function is still merely a mental relation. It is not a necessary condition
adjudicating the question of the existence of God. If a mental relation is all that is justified to establish a communion with the
divine, then this phenomenon can extend to practically anything,
which potentially imports a whole host of other illusions and
sundry problematics. Despite the fact that the God introject oc-
cupies psychical reality for billions of people, it nevertheless remains a mental construct, the unconscious dynamics of which we
will consider shortly.

As we have elucidated, at most we can say is that any existential statement about God refers not to an ontological object, but to the *concept* of God. And all properties attributed to God are an *instance* assigned to the concept of God. As a result, following Frege's amplification of Kant, the predication of existence can neither be a first order property nor a defining property of God.[10] In short, to reiterate the point, existence is not a defining property or a predicate of God.

Richard Dawkins tells us that it is "almost certain" that God does not exist based upon improbable statistical odds.[11] But I would argue that the God hypothesis is not really an empirical question, because if it were, we already have proof in God's non-existence *via absentia*, for God neither has manifested nor revealed itself directly.[12] Evidence is the *sine qua non* or gold standard by which we base and derive our modern understanding of the world, a condition without which it could not be. If the God question was truly an empirical one, then science has already *proven* that God does not exist, for there is no evidence.

The very notion of existence employs the predicate of identity, namely, that something *is*. The empiricist's criterion of reality is based on the premise of that which is, that which has presence or being (ὄν, *esse*), namely, something actual. The "is" of existence (*There is:*$\exists x$) is an existential instantiation. A (re)presentation and conceptual scheme of existence is further constructed based upon the mode in which an object presents itself, and our mental apparatus uses various existential quantifiers to distinguish among its attributes or qualities. But with the God assertion, we have the converse: a being is predicated to exist based on that which is *not present*, that which does not present itself. Although most sensible people can generally agree that the universe exists because it presents itself to us as a manifold of sense impressions, objects with mass and temporal locations, and natural processes that we are necessarily obliged to participate in and acknowledge as concretely real, the masses often show deference to illogic. Perhaps such tendency towards deference is partly out of conditioning or habit tied to social custom, but also out of sensitivity (if not perspicacity and respect) for the needs of all believers to maintain emotional transcendental illusions that serve discernible psychological functions.[13] But this should not dissuade us from the pursuit of sober truth, no matter how unsavoury we find it. We accept the universe as part of our natural circumstances because we experientially sense it to be real and substantive, what we are thrown into as part of that which is *given*. So why should we not impose the same criterion on the question of God?

The *is*ness of identity refers to a real object that exists and subsists, not merely a cognitive representation of that object, while the *is* of predication refers to a concept or an idea about an object and its representation. Although we may predicate God's existence, such predication signifies a mental (ideal) object—a thought—rather than an extant (real) object, for God is nowhere to be found in the real world, let alone standing out or above other objects. Instead, God's predication would fall into a category of non-being, for the *is* of identity is not demonstrated nor designated to conform to what we customarily experience as that which exists, except only as a psychic projection or hypothesis as ideation the mind generates through the positionality of consciousness towards an ideal state of affairs it wishes to signify or intend.

My assertion that God does not exist is confined to the world of empirical reality. In the realm of psychic reality, this becomes a whole other matter, for, it bears repeating, the God posit is merely an idea. When I refer to God's inexistence as the predication of nothingness or absence, I mean that it does not signify a concrete actuality, for it is merely a formal abstraction with qualities of denial, dispossession, withdrawal, deletion, elimination, erasure, or privation, and so on; hence positing non-existence dialectically stands in relation to being or real presence. Here what is present is the absence of God. Although the presence of absence as lack has a psychological reality, we should not assume that a thing's absence or lack signifies concealed actuality, such as a supreme being justified by an argument for divine hiddenness. We should not presume there is a transcendent deity in hiding, which is concealed and non-manifest, for that which is real should be manifest, revealed, and openly disclosed. To say that God is hidden, undisclosed, or covered-up is to beg the question of God's existence, let alone any attributed motives or presumed intentions to remain hidden rather than transparent, conspicuous, and unconcealed as divine disclosedness. If we adopt the preSocratic notion of truth as *aletheia* (ἀλήθεια) or unconcealment, then God should have disclosed or manifested its being by now. To say God remains hidden to the human world is to say nothing, for absence is not an empirical criterion for being. If this were the case, then anything that has no observational properties, motion, or manifest effects, let alone has never presented itself, could be said to be in hiding. Here the Higgs boson particle may be said to be no different than the God posit, with the exception that physical science can point to tangible evidence even though the detection of subatomic particles largely remains invisible.[14]

In the context of God's non-instantiation as non-materialization, how can we justify the assertion that there is a divine something rather than an apparent nothing? Given the unequivocal fact that the universe exists, shouldn't the God question be asking, Why is there nothing rather than something? If God exists, why does God abstain from revealing itself? Yet this question presupposes that we as mortal humans should assume the existence of a supreme being in the first place that has reasons not to appear or manifest directly, hence imparting a certain intentionality onto God, and projecting a cornucopia of motives which we are not privy to.[15] But this very supposition rests on the presupposition that there is something behind the veil of nothingness (namely, the non-manifested), or more precisely, that there is something *in* nothingness—namely, the inverse of what does not appear. The collective fantasy is that there is a hidden reality—the *Ding an sich*;[16] in this case, a divine invisible presence animating the cosmos.[17]

God as Failed Hypothesis

The very definition of empiricism rests on the notion that something is observable and potentially measurable as revealed to our experiential senses and cognitive faculties. Although one may claim to experience God as the reality of the unseen,[18] in order to escape the charge of a radical or oppressive subjectivism ("It is true because I say so!"), or crass solipsism or idealism ("I think it, therefore it exists!"), experience must be subject to universal (replicable) criterion that gains validity through verification, which by definition transcends subjectivism for objective consensual agreements or calculations, what we typically—and practically—call facts. From an empirical point of view, God does not exist because there is no observable or tangible object/agent that is manifest or present; hence we cannot scientifically study nothing (literally, no-thing) under the rubric or parameters that define the scientific method. Although we may charge science with its own hegemonic agendas,[19] here it may be argued that the God question is not a legitimate scientific topic because it does not meet the basic requisite of falsifiability through testability.[20] In other words, if you cannot falsify a premise through the potential refutation of conjectures, then anything is potentially true. How can you observe, statistically measure, or quantify something that eludes the sensuous world? How can you refute that which does not appear if the presupposition in question does not allow for an empirical assessment? By positing the existence of something that is not observable or manifest, verifiable or falsifiable, one dislocates the object in question away from science to the realm of *thought*. Although thoughts are to some degree introspectively observable and extraspectively recordable, they certainly cannot be dislocated from the thinker or agent entertaining such ideas, even when they become an object of study.

Physicist Victor Stenger claims that the God posit is a failed hypothesis because it does not live up to scientific scrutiny nor pass even simple empirical tests of validity based on all the available data in both the physical and social sciences.[21] If all existing scientific models contain no trace of God, then God would have to appear outside of those models or gaps in systematic observation and measurement. However, this is not a proper scientific argument for it means that the God hypothesis not only defies empirical explanation, it further flouts the possibility of natural description, hence being incapable of providing a plausible account of God as a natural phenomenon. If the God construct fails all attempts to be examined by methodological naturalism through the scientific procedures of hypothesis testing, then science has fertile logical ground to conclude that God does not exist based on lack of evidence. And if the "God of the gaps" or "God in hiding" arguments wish to appeal to supernatural forces as explananda, then the scientific investigation of God is impossible, for such metaphysical postulates are irrefutable by definition because they are not susceptible to empirical falsification.

But abstracting God outside the realm of scientific investigation does nothing to substantiate the existence of God, for abstraction itself conforms to the cognitive and linguistic processes that *define* the laws of predication as human contrivances. Purely logical arguments as language games cannot be equated with the objective (universal) scientific criteria used to arbitrate the circularity of definitions and redefinitions. In the end, science appeals to an objectivist episte- mology that follows a replicable method based on empirical facts as the final judge. As stated before, existence is not a predicate, it is an instantiation. The God hypothesis is not only disconfirmed by the available data, it is contradicted by the fact that no empirical evi- dence for God exists.

The humanities in general, at most a semiotic-hermeneutic science, and the study of religion, theology, and philosophy in particular, are not the same as the natural sciences precisely because they entertain different subject matters and employ different methodologies. Even in contemporary physics, when objects are postulated to exist in- dependent of consciousness, they are still subject to observation se- lection effects (under the influence of anthropic bias) that must pass the test of a replicable method. Yet non-empirical fields within the humanities are comfortable with making ultimate metaphysical truth claims that support the objective realism of God's existence. This is what is generally meant or implied when God is predicated to *be*, that is, to exist as an external entity independent of people's minds. And if we concede that any object of our sense perception, experiential fa- culties, and rational contemplation is necessarily predicated on the hermeneutic interpretation of the natural world—in other words, that *all* experience is mediated by mentation and our faculties of cognition—we cannot epistemologically justify the ontological as- sertion of God's existence independent from mind. In other words, we cannot even conceive of the idea of God's independence and ontological separateness from our own subjective thoughts that, even if shared by others, condition this conception.

Whether we avouch scientific realism, or any of its variants, such as naturalism or critical realism, we are left with the same conclusion: We cannot observe and verify that which does not present itself other than our *ideas* about its lack of presence. This is why the God question, from my point of view, is more properly considered a metaphysical en- terprise.[22] More precisely, the God hypothesis conforms to a particular form of speculative metaphysics that has been largely annexed by theology. Because the God construct lacks a verification principle, its proper investigation and meaning(s) is relegated to a speculative phi- losophy that attempts to lay the theoretical foundations for a grand narrative that allegedly (as *potentia*) lends credibility to a worldview that endeavours to take into account everything as the whole of reality. This Theory of Everything traditionally has centered on the comprehensive understanding, structural interrelatedness, and unification of theology, cosmology, and psychology that systematically attempts to amalgamate the human, natural, and spiritual sciences within a dynamic, coherent complex holism.

Speculative philosophy has its own place in the history of ideas, but we should not compare this with empirical proof. In fact, proponents of logical positivism would say that the God construct is meaningless because it cannot in principle be verified. Yet this assessment displaces the human value attached to the God posit that in itself conveys purpose and meaning to believers. It would be foolish to dismiss its psychological worth as a reified object to humanity, for there is no question that the psychomythology of belief has pragmatic value. God could be said to exist in psychic reality (itself a metaphysical universe), but I would confine these discourses to the realm of human experience, ideation, fantasy, or abstract philosophical ponderings that are purely tentative and hypothetical in nature. They do not conform to the same laws of demonstration or warrant the same determination that we accord the physical universe comprised of the energetic stratification of material substance or informational processing systems that occupy and subsist within spacetime in real tangible (hence observable, measurable, and calculable) forms as quantum states or events.

Granted that an idea is substantive, it is not substantial. Although there are many sophisticated and noteworthy metaphysical schemes that address the synergy of mind and matter, including the governing physical laws regulating the universe itself, these endeavours are reserved for the philosophers and onto-theologists who are invested in chasing a logical rationale for a category of the ultimate or absolute, a fundamental unifying or organizing principle to spirit, nature, and cosmic order, and/or the mystical, transcendental, and numinous resonances that pervade human experience. Here such matters should be reserved for discussion on the phenomenology of spirituality, but not attributed to an ontological force emanating from a godhead.

The Logical Impossibility of God

Speculative metaphysics may posit the ontology of God as an extant entity, but we are only warranted to think of God as a mental object, for no matter how clever one succeeds in providing logical justification, we cannot posit or reason God into actual existence. On the other hand, philosophers have been quite ingenious in their attempts to disprove the existence of God through logic. Disproofs based on deductive arguments have been supported by definitional, doctrinal, and attributional contradictions that nullify the possibility of God. These disproofs include the quagmire of incompatible and contradictory properties, as well as renunciation based on self-contradictory multiple-attributes such as the paradoxes of omnipotence, omniscience, incompleteness, divine freedom and agency, moral perfection, omniconsciousness, and the existence of evil, which are incoherent and lack self-consistency, hence signaling the impossibility of God.[23] Omniproperties (omniperfections) attributed to God are particularly futile arguments that appeal to impossibility in order to ground their alleged possibility, when they are merely self-predicating and circular paroxysms of illogic.

Omniproperty attributions to God rely on a "vicious circle principle" of self-predication, for any property posited either directly or indirectly relates to the divine object in question, hence it is entirely self-referential. Self-predication is not only incongruous and question-begging, it is furthermore *imaginary* because it assumes the *actuality* of the property, capability, or function itself, such as omnipotence, where by definition there are *no limits* to one's powers.[24] Superheroes inhabit the cartoon world of comic books and cinema, not reality. These arguments are reflexively circular and appeal to a self-relation to justify their self-predicating existence, such as the predication of God as *causa sui*, the very thing that is in dispute. The premise of omniattributes is illegitimate to begin with because it presupposes the very thing it must set out to prove or demonstrate.

Recently Colin Howson argues that an omniscient God does not and cannot exist based on the application of Tarski's indefinability of truth theorem,[25] which logically proves the impossibility of complete knowledge or truth; not to mention, in surpassing Dawkins' statistical improbability thesis, the probability of God's possible existence,

Howson argues, should be set to zero based upon (a) the incoherence and inconsistency of God's so-called a priori omniproperties and (b) the posterior odds relative to all the evidence especially due to the prevalence of evil and innocent suffering in the world.[26]

Here the armory of extremely compelling evidence for the impossibility of God's existence is hard to legitimately rebuke let alone logically dismiss. But just as logic cannot produce an extant God out of nothing, one could argue that it cannot rule out such a possibility *in toto*. Because logical "proofs" and "disproofs" apply only to those who accept certain premises, are willing to grant certain conventions and follow specified rules of argumentation, and adopt their terms, usages, methodologies, and systems of reference, it is not too difficult to evade or reject certain truth premises, or question the validity of ascertained conclusions when the senses of certain terms and their meanings, forms of reference, and rules of demonstration are drawn into question, especially when God is purported to be disproven *a fortiori* based on so-called "fuzzy math." What is interesting to analyse psychologically, however, is why anyone would think that such a possibility of a divine artificer is itself even possible. Here the stronghold of unconscious fantasy overrides the dubious and tenuous nature of our existence and the cognizance of our epistemic uncertainties.

The idea of possibility does not in-itself mean to imply that *anything* is possible, only that it signifies a conditional set of indexicals (such as self-instantiated propositions indexed to a person and facts conforming to natural laws) that rationally apply to particular contexts and contingencies within the natural world. This means that the forms of possibility must conform to the descriptive laws of nature, which cannot be suspended because they are given or determined. Here the laws of nature do not require a lawgiver. If we accept the premise that the universe participates in and is governed by natural laws, then whatever is possible must transpire within the confines of those laws. If the universe is denied an autonomous existence of its own, hence that it cannot be an open, self-supporting system of contingent facts with statistical variances as essentially incomplete and ultimately impersonal because it depends upon the existence of a supernatural architect that lies beyond or above the natural world as a transcendent being, then God cannot exist because it is logically impossible to stand above and control the whole of nature without also being part of nature itself as a naturalized fact subject to its laws.

If God is said to have willed the universe into existence and it is sustained by this will, then this succumbs to contradiction because God could not remain independent of and permeate the universe at the same time, hence reside outside of nature and not dependent upon its laws, which are the very laws God is purported to have instituted. Furthermore, if God could impose its will on the world it would *necessarily* conform to natural laws because whatever is willed would naturally occur. It may be argued that this is a logically more fundamental fact over any choices God may allegedly will,[27] because any act of will presupposes events that already conform to natural laws, for they would not nor could not occur in the first place. Just as nature cannot be explained by an appeal to something that is not natural, by definition the universe cannot depend on anything that is not a natural fact of the universe.

The abstract (hypothetical) notion of pure possibility only gains popularity as a thought experiment, often designed for amusement by the intellect. The so-called omniattributes and divine properties supposedly bestowed to God such as absolute perfection, omnipotence, omniscience, moral flawlessness, and so forth are the fabrications of human fantasy. They do not and cannot exist in any creature due to their logical incredulity and sheer impossibility. The point I wish to make is that it is not remotely possible to grant the notion of unbounded or unconstrained possibility any rational acceptance. It is the power of imagination that generates the fantasy of omniproperties special to God and lends them currency nourished by emotional unconscious factors that inform the cognitive basis for bequeathing them to a supreme being in the first place. This psychological disposition is inherent to man as a wishing animal and nurtures the belief in a rationalized (albeit fictional) account *qua* intellectualized fantasy of potential possible realities that surpass our limitations we are condemned to encounter as fate. The fantasy of a *potentially possible reality* (e.g., God's existence or possible future manifestation) involves a teleological suspension of the laws of nature where no limits, bounds, or restrictions are operative, hence a fantasy of omnipotence. Although we can imagine omnipotence as an abstract idea or object of fantasy, by definition it is impossible because it violates natural laws that govern the world we experience.

One such fantasy is the possibility of futurity that transcends death and the finitude of our natural confines or restrictions, such as our organic embodiment or cultural environs. Futurity is a felt existential anxiety we wish to safeguard against for it is always encroaching upon us like foul weather. The qualia of self-asserted possibility provides the psyche a bit of relief for it endows experience with the felt-intuition or attitude of what things seem to be like or mean to us on a qualitative basis. We often confound our qualitative subjective experiences for quantified objective facts that transcend our personal lives. God's omniperfections and a possible future world of salvation attributed to a Heavenly Father are examples that assuage our nervousness about accepting life and death on their own terms. But the notion of possibility itself is always a bounded concept demarcated by the constraints of reality. There is no absolute condition of unbounded possibility: pure *potentia* is itself a mere fantasy.

The abstract form of potentiality is a theoretical abstraction that does not conform to the demands of objective reality, but it appeals to the subjective finite agent only on the condition that it breaches all conditions. Because it defies logic and conditionality, it is granted an exalted status in the imagining mind. Here the realm of the imaginary confers a certain psychic actuality that defies reality itself, and hence surpasses the limits of reason alone. Although authentic, it is nevertheless a purely subjective act of constructing reality in accord with the wishful fantasies embraced by societies throughout the world. We may refer to this psychological proclivity as the *freedom of fantasy*, but one that remains ensconced in its own illusions. No matter how imaginative (and satisfying) such possible projections of the future may be, we are all obliged by the parameters of our finitude. Here the God posit is the product of dissociation as avoidance of the inevitable we wish were not true, a fundamental denial most of humanity will not and cannot rightfully own because it is too painful to bear.

The God question is really a question of natural wonder. As psychological beings we yearn and speculate that there must be something greater out there, such as an encompassing process, unifying force, and/or an ultimate source to the universe that permeates all reality and binds all phenomena into a synthesizing milieu, which may be proffered via an impersonal metaphysics or natural science. But most of humanity psychologically posits a divine deity as creator and ruler of all. This is a curious artifact of human nature that requires our analysis, for it speaks to a greater collective process that exceeds the lone individual bound to esoteric subjectivity. Here I am intimating the notion of a *subjective universality* that is oriented towards generating meaning structures that point beyond the human mind and given natural world as an explanandum, thereby becoming an inspiration of hope and awe that propels human thought, desire, and action, yet one based nonetheless on a *focus imaginarius*. The ancients referred to this as a cosmic animating principle or vitalism inherent in all things, what we may compare to Plato's *chora*, the womb of all becoming, or Jung's collective unconscious as a transpersonal psyche, the condition and ground of existence, World Soul (*anima mundi*). But what conjoins us in commonality is the substance and sustenance of consciousness, the universality of mind in search of meaning and contentment.

The psychological tendency to project anthropomorphic elements into all objects of thought and experience is an unavoidable onto-structural condition of our psychic constitutions for the simple reason that we are human. We project the intrapsychic dynamics and minutia of our minds into objects of lived experience because the psyche postulates and mediates all metaphysical assertions as propositional dispositions advanced by its own internal nature. The anthropic dimension to the God posit is an extrapolation or natural extension of wonder based upon the human tendency to compare all perceived or imagined things with ourselves, despite the fact that it is a logical error based on a category mistake. Yet from an emotional or unconscious factor, this makes perfect sense. We relate to all objects of thought (whether perceived or imagined) as though they are real and filter external variants through our own inner apparatus and perceptual schemas of reality. Although there are multiple dimensions to reality that structure and color our experience and perceptions of the world, these do not confirm, let alone necessitate, the existence of a supernatural ordering to the universe. All we can reasonably conclude is that the conjecture of any ontological ordering is based on an intractable psychologism that underlies our desire to find meaning and make sense out of natural phenomena, the desire to know.

The Problem of Infinite Regress

Theologians and philosophers of religion often fixate on cosmological arguments for the existence of God to explain the structure of the universe, the complexity of life, and how the cosmos came into being. Cosmologists and astrophysicists equally attempt to answer these conundrums. Both sides must contend with the problem of infinite regress. When the point of origination is said to lie in God's creative act or the big bang, each postulation has the onus of explaining pre-beginning, namely, the prior conditions that would bring about the creation of the universe itself. This appeal to earlier conditions must contend with a further appeal to preconditions *ad infinitum*. In the end, either God exists and has always existed or is self-caused, or the universe has no proper beginning and has always existed or is self-generated. In both instances, either a supreme creator or an impersonal universe has *always existed* in some form as an unswerving constant that is eternal and infinite: something rather than nothing is presupposed as the origin of all that is.

In all versions of the cosmological argument, a necessary existence (hence not contingent or accidental) must be posited in order to escape an infinite regress as the entreaty to an endless or interminable chain of causal events that at some point gives rise to existence itself, which is an incessant trace to earlier antecedent occasions that are said to spark and infiltrate each current moment. Theologians tend to favour some variation of an anthropic argument, which is that the basic facts about the existence of the universe are best explained by appealing to God as the cause of existence, while physicists would attribute causality to processes inherent within the cosmos itself. Here the claim is that the universe was caused and came into being by a cause (hence it *began* to exist), and this cause is God as the First Cause that is itself uncaused (hence not conditioned on prior causal events that brought about the initial cause of existence per se) because God is unconditioned or self-caused.

Setting aside for the moment that this argument presupposes the very thing it must set out to prove, namely, that a causal agent can be its own cause without being caused or conditioned by prior antecedent events or material-efficient-formal-telic processes that would bring about its self-organizational complexity, even if such circumstances are over-determined, how do we explain the final cause of causation without reverting to circularity or imposing a self-instituted terminus? Even if the theist concedes to the epistemological limits of knowing the details of God's so-called miraculous powers of self-creation, the unbroken chain of circularity and self-referential premising provides us with no sound justification for positing omnipotent self-causation. Appealing to an omniproperty to explain the omni-act fails to explain how the omni-act is remotely possible, let alone how one acquired the omniproperty to begin with or the mechanisms of how it is self-constituted because it relies on its self-instantiation to justify its presupposed existence, which is the very thing that is in question.

Richard Swinburne summarizes the cosmological viewpoint nicely:

> Arguments for the existence of God have a common character-istic. They all purport to be arguments to a (causal) explanation of the phenomena described in the premises in terms of the action of an agent who intentionally brought about those phenomena. A cosmological argument argues from the existence of the world to a person, God, who intentionally brought it about. An argument from design argues from the design of the world to a person, God, who intentionally made it thus. All the other arguments are arguments from particular features of the world to a God who intentionally made the world with those features.[28]

From this synopsis, we may see that the entire structure of a cos-mological argument is circular and self-referential, which ultimately hinges on the teleological notion of divine intentionality. In order to explain the existence of the natural world and its phenomena, God is presupposed as an intentional agent (a "person" nonetheless) who caused it all. Rather than appealing to the phenomena of the world itself, God is predicated to be the designer and architect of all that *is* despite hiding behind an anthropic curtain. Notwithstanding the circularity of the argument, presupposing the very thing that is in question as the ultimate cause and explanation of causality itself (one without a cause, mind you) does not explain away the problem of infinite regress. Merely asserting that God is self-caused does not explain how that is possible any more than asserting the universe is caused by the big bang or dark energy or the Higgs field without addressing the question of genesis or the preconditions that brought about the big bang in the first place. Appealing to God may be a satisfying answer for Christian philosophers like Swinburne, Craig, and other apologists, but it does not offer a solution to the question of origins. In a nutshell, the cosmological argument is simply begging the question.

The big question that baffles theologians and physicists alike is the problem of origins. Is there an *absolute* point of origination as creation of the universe, or was something always here? Was there a pre-beginning to beginning? Were there certain a priori conditions that were operative and causally necessary to bring about a beginning? Did the world truly begin, or is science only able to observe and measure its effects or statistical variances through mathematical models to infer a particular point in spacetime when the big bang occurred? Can we infer a prior state of affairs that precedes the big bang or act of creation? Is it a necessary and/or sufficient condition to posit a point of derivation where energy, mass/matter, space, and time came into being, or do we need to appeal to a grand designer that brought about such occurrences? If the universe truly had a beginning, did it arise from pure void or nullity? How? What about pre-origins?

Theistic responses to these questions often rest on arguments from fine-tuning, what is said to rely on an anthropic principle, which claims that the laws of physics are finely adjusted to such a degree that the universe could never have come into being nor supported carbon-based life without divine intervention. Put laconically, the arguments from fine-tuning proclaim that because it is so statistically improbable that we are here, that there could even be a life-sustaining universe as the one we inhabit, that there could ever be constants we customarily define as natural causal laws (such as gravity), and that these laws must arise from initial conditions — the conclusion is, "It must be designed." But rather than situate the design argument to the unimpeded and internally derived organizing principles inherent within the universe and organic life itself, where the teleology of nature displays purpose without having to have an *initial* cause, the theist prematurely jumps to the intelligent designer hypothesis where God is said to have created the universe just as we find it, and generously bestows unto God additional omniproperties to boot!

The anthropic argument may be put in the following way:

It is a miracle that we are here—that there is a universe that allows and supports life.

The fundamental constants and laws of nature that permit and sustain life are so delicately balanced, statistically remote, and existentially improbable that we need to account for how this is possible.

Due to such complexity, improbability, and the infinite possibilities or variety of ways we could have turned out, the mystery of existence resists an explanation by chance.

It makes no sense that a life-sustaining universe could exist in the absence of an intentional creator.

Therefore: The universe was designed by God.

Is this conclusion warranted? We would have grounds to expect that a universe that permits human life would surely allow for observers to discover the laws of nature, for what else would we expect to observe? What we expect to observe would necessarily be restricted by the conditions of existence that allow for observers. In the words of philosopher Robin Le Poidevin, "So *of course* the fundamental constants will be such as to permit the development of life."[29] The more controversial claim, however, is that the universe had to be this way in order to permit life and that it was *intended* to be this way by God. Here the cosmological argument is augmented by a teleological explanation that implies that the conditions that allow for the production of life reveal an inherent design or purpose to the universe and that the presence of natural laws is part of the instantiation of that design. The theist is eager to posit the agency of God as designer of the design, however, following Aristotle, a very impersonal account of teleology may be extended to the cosmos characterized by evidential purposes behind quantum events as organized processes inherent to non-conscious entities and organisms but without importing conscious intent. And, for sake of argument, even if we cannot successfully defend an impersonal teleological account of the universe, it still does not justify us positing intelligent design by an intentional designer.

For the believer, the values that define the various physical constants that are necessary for life and consciousness to emerge cannot possibly rely on randomness or coincidences, but rather must be chosen and willed by a cosmic intelligence that wanted life to evolve in precise fashions as we know it today. Just because science and the humanities have no absolute answers to why the physical universe is the way it is, does not warrant inventing a supreme entity to explain it all. Not only is a divine Fine Tuner heralded as the solution to why there is something rather than nothing, but that it was deliberately planned to be this way. Even if we were to concede the premise that there is an intelligent design to the universe, it begs the question to assume that there is a grand designer let alone any assumption that a personal being with intentionality is behind the backdrop of creation. How could anyone possibly know that? This view is neither necessary nor sufficient to explain the universe: it is a leap of faith—itself a theological wish with no grounds for proof, even if such "proof" is produced by mathematical formulas or theorems designed to manipulate desired outcomes, which is then passed-off as serious science, such as we may see in some corners of contemporary theoretical physics where incomprehensibly complex equation models dangle a carrot in front of the dumfounded believer, or in probability, propensity, and confirmation theories, which often give the appearance of an exact science but in the end bake no real bread. Once again, a logical proof or mathematical equation cannot produce God's existence out of whole cloth.

Proponents like Swinburne and Craig argue that the universe has an ontological dependence on God, but as we have just shown, this collapses into circularity. This claim not only presupposes God's self-predication, namely, that God constitutes the subject of its own action, but further that the universe could not be occasioned or self-begotten from its own natural configurations and laws. Comparing the origin of the universe to analogies such as Paley's watch or Hume's factory (where an intelligent designer or manufacturer is assumed to set up the complex machinery of the cosmos) is not only a categorical error, because we cannot sufficiently equate a manmade artifact to the structure of the universe, but this position further manufactures a case for the *necessity* of an extrinsic designer by ignoring the naturalized phenomena of self-generation underlying all processes of becoming as a necessary condition of existence. As Keith Parsons puts it, "In nature ... order *always* arises from spontaneous self-organization brought about by impersonal causes intrinsic to nature itself."[30] We do not need to go beyond a naturalized account of being and becoming to explain what we can scientifically observe and rationally infer. God is superfluous.

Instead of endorsing the viability of naturalized accounts, theologians prefer the argument from *creatio originans*, namely, that the world was originally created out of nothing by divine action. William Lane Craig explains:

> Now the question is, what could conceivably transform an event that is naturally impossible into a real historical event? Clearly, the answer is the personal God of theism. For if a transcendent, personal God exists, then he could cause events in the universe that could not be produced by causes within the universe. Given a God who created the universe, who conserves the world in being, and who is capable of acting freely, miracles are evidently possible. Only to the extent that one has good grounds for believing atheism to be true could one be rationally justified in denying the possibility of miracles. In this light, arguments for the impossibility of miracles based upon defining them as violations of the laws of nature are vacuous.[31]

There is nothing "clearly" about it. Whether one finds this comical, persuasive, or a garrulous tapestry of sophistry, let us try to unpack this argument for a moment. The "real historical event" Craig's claim applies to is the big bang as the presumed singular point of origin of the universe. In espousing a deterministic model, Craig centers his thesis on the spontaneous generation of a creative act that is issued by a divine personal creator responsible for both originating the material existence of the universe and for conserving Being, all of which challenge our current understanding of natural laws, for how can something simply materialize from pure nothingness and be sustained by an invisible entity that fractures *and* regulates the physical laws of nature at will? Craig's solution: It could only be a miracle.

Creationists like Craig base their arguments on an appeal to miracles to explain the so-called miraculous while they deny the atheist the right to insist that all events must be explicable from a natural science framework that by definition excludes the miraculous *unless* such said events can be objectively verified or confirmed to violate natural laws. If I interpret Craig correctly here, the theist leaps to the extraordinary explanation when naturalized accounts fail or are truncated in providing an explanation, while the atheist refuses to concede (in principle) to the possibility of extraordinary metaphysical causation that defies naturalism. Here his point that there *could* exist a metaphysical process that currently eludes physical science should be acknowledged.

Theologian David Bentley Hart wishes to extricate himself from the typical view of God as a supreme "agency," yet he upholds the traditional view that God is the supreme "creator" *and* "the infinite ocean of being that gives existence to all reality ex nihilo."[32] Notice here that Hart equates creation with "being itself," whereby being is assigned the properties of *action* out of nothing. This is a logical contradiction, for any creator that acts must have agency to enact events we would properly attribute to the products of creation. If God is merely Being, which is said to be the ground of all existence, then God could be viewed as being no different than Nature itself, a nature that gives rise to itself and all objects in an eternal universe. If we define God as the infinite source of all things and is eternal, un-caused (viz. that it does not depend on anything else for its existence), and is Being itself (in which all subsequent forms of being are necessarily conditioned by its infinite force), then this view of God is no different (in principle) than attributing divinity to the universe itself. What differentiates the theistic position, however, from the impersonal being of nature is that nature is created out of nothing by a presumptive creator.

Hart wants us to believe that existence cannot be explained without an appeal to a timeless a priori supernatural cause he equates with Being that is responsible for "the very possibility of existence as such," which "logically and necessarily" precedes the material universe and produces all physical laws and events in nature, "for neither those laws nor those states could exist of themselves."[33] But we may naïvely ask, Why not? Do we need to appeal to a supernatural realm to explain what lies before us? Obviously science has come a long way to offer reasonable explanations of natural phenomena through the discovery of fundamental physical constants, such as the processes of gravitational energy, nucleic and electromagnetic force, the speed of light, and so forth. Yet Hart goes so far as to challenge (with great hubris, I might add) that "there simply cannot be a natural explanation of existence as such: it is an absolute logical impossibility."[34] No it is not. The most obvious rebuttal is that existence is simply *given*, part of our natural thrownness, and that existence per se is not caused, rather it is causal. Although this may not be a very satisfactory explanation, it is by no means logically impossible, for if that were true we could offer no explanation at all. Here Hart is merely begging the question of origin.

What does science have to say about the matter? Does it fare any better? Most theists think that we must summon a grand agent that creates the big bang out of nothing, but God is presumed to exist as something. In order to avoid an infinite regress, the scientist focuses on what we can reasonably say about beginning. But no matter what theory is advanced, we still have the same muddle of explicating how something comes into being, and more mysteriously, how something comes from nothing. Recently theoretical physicist Lawrence Krauss has put forth the thesis that the universe comes from nothing, when in fact he posits that energy comes from "empty space," which is essentially *latent* energy that creates all matter mediated by physical laws. Krauss unconvincingly attempts to persuade us into thinking that "nothing" is merely a semantic definition subject to linguistic construction, which is interpreted differently by a scientist, when he in fact displaces all of Western metaphysics by denuding the meaning of "nothing" as being merely a relative term. For example, he rhetorically opines that "'nothing' is every bit as physical as 'something'" for both have physical "quantities."[35] Because Krauss redefines nothing as physicality with quantifying properties, he has invented his own frame of discourse. "Nothing" in the metaphysical sense has always referred to an ontological principle of non-being that signifies *complete absence*, hence, no space, no time, no energetic stratification of matter, no mass, no corporeality or substance, no discernible or inferred empirical properties, and no force or quantum mechanisms whatsoever, which cannot be equated with physicality no matter how clever (or sensationally deceptive in garnering publication in a trade press that was a national bestseller) one is at redefining meanings traditionally held in the history of philosophy to suit self-purposes under the rubric of science. For Krauss, "space exists, with nothing at all in it,"[36] which is the pre-condition for the spontaneous generation of our inflationary universe. Yet space has energetic processes with physical properties and gravitational forces and pressures, therefore it is not an absolute zero-point of pure nothingness. Here I must concur with the consensus opinion held by philosophers and theologians that even empty space devoid of content still qualifies as something, even if it exists in a quantum vacuum.

We must not confound the field of physical science, which relies on empirical (experimental-observational) and theoretical (mathematical-statistical/simulation) paragons, with the subfield of metaphysics that employ wholly separate methodologies, usually grounded in speculation, logic, abduction, and hermeneutics. Despite the inevitable overlap in physics and philosophy, we must respect categorical distinctions in meaning and methodology that differentiate these two broad disciplines rather than collapsing philosophy entirely into natural science by "operationally" redefining what we mean by our terms in order for them to (nicely and conveniently) fit into a contrived empirical or computational framework where the researcher or subject is dislocated from the research or subject matter under investigation. One could claim that the field of physics is simply trying to substitute the God function for a similar cosmological corollary when positing the Higgs field as an invisible background permeating all of spacetime, which is responsible for dark matter/energy in their spontaneous acts of creation scientists observe in the lab when particles materialize or are inferred based on statistical equations that crunch enormous amounts of data into meaningful units of information. If the Higgs is always there yet hidden in empty space, and is responsible for the generation of all that exists today, including the inflationary big bang, then is this any different from the theological functionality of the God posit? Perhaps this is a good example of wonder at work in both science and philosophy, for in the lab, on the computer, or just pondering intractable questions, the human mind wants to know.

If empty space is said to *preexist* prior to the materialization of the universe, then Krauss inherits a set of conundrums facing the question of infinite regress. Here he is saddled with the same problem as the theologian in his attempt to expound how something comes from nothing. A point of energy before it explodes in rapid exponential inflation in a tiny fraction of its first second of life,[37] which is the premise behind the modern inflationary big bang theory, still needs an explanation of how that energy was derived in the first place out of a sea of nothingness. Victor Stenger argues that the inflationary big bang thesis has passed all stringent empirical tests to date that could prove it false,[38] but this still does not mean that we have solved the riddle of pre-beginning. This energetic organization is propounded to exist prior to the big bang and before it undergoes inflationary eruption, which is averred to bring it about, but it does not answer to how such energy came into being prior to its expansion. Moreover, it does not address the specifics of the preconditions for energy to emerge. In other words, how is the void, nothingness, or empty space organized in such a way as to bring about energetic expressions, not to mention that the *appearance* of energy, namely, what is physically observed, measured, or calculated, may be distinct from its original nucleus or structural process that eludes current empirical classification?

Stenger offers his own view that we have reason to believe that the universe did not in fact begin with the big bang, but rather prior conditions existed that brought it about, including the possibility of a prior universe.[39] Using theoretical equation models of cosmology based on the notion of "quantum tunneling" or fluctuations,[40] he posits that it is conceivable that our current universe materialized from a preexisting one, which draws into question the notion of an absolute beginning or point of birth of the cosmos. Here Stenger favours the "no boundary model" of James Hartle and Stephen Hawking who claim that the universe has no beginning or end in space and time.[41] This view is in opposition to William Lane Craig's who challenges such a declaration,[42] instead insisting that the universe began from an initial singularity and has a finite past, hence had an absolute beginning, which he works out in obsessional detail in his kalâm cosmological argument,[43] what Stenger dismisses as an erroneous appeal to a predetermined model of causality, when physical science makes no claims in its controlled observations of atomic and subatomic activity, which are often spontaneous productions without any evident cause.[44] In Stenger's model, using mathematical calculations, he speculates how our world could have tunneled through a previous universe that has "existed for all previous time."[45] Yet here we have the same concerns about infinite regress. Even if we posit a prior universe or universes that conditioned the coming into being of our current one, we will still need to address the notion of what brought the preexisting universe(s) into being. Positing a metaverse or multiverse only extends the regress farther back in time and down the fox hole.

If the cosmos is considered to come from nothing, either from a God that is said to be the initial cause but is and has always been *absent*, or as energy derived from empty space, we are still not likely to find this a sufficient proof for a theory of *creatio ex nihilio* as it fails to explain how the physical universe can just appear from *no prior state of being*, and moreover, how this transpires *naturally*, viz. as an objective certainty explaining the process of empirical phenomenon— not as metaphysical speculation, logical induction, or statistical (mathematical) manipulation that dislocates the phenomenon in question from its natural occurrence. In other words, how can the whole universe just pop into existence as though it is a rabbit pulled from a magician's hat, especially when the magician or the hat is nowhere in sight? If we could irrefutably offer this explanans, then this could be arguably called a miracle.

The problem with temporal and modal cosmological arguments is that they always beg the question of causation and specifically the notion of a *first cause*.[46] And because causation is a temporal concept, that is, it relies on predicating antecedent conditions, events, and outcomes that happen at particular instances and places, we cannot posit an original causation that precedes itself in time. Furthermore, if we insist on the notion of a beginning to the universe from a first cause, then time itself would have a beginning. But if this were the case, then the universe cannot have a cause, at least not in any ordinary sense of the word, because this would imply a time that existed *before* the universe began to exist. Nothing could have occurred before this time, that is, before the universe started to exist. This would mean that time itself has a beginning, and hence a cause. But time cannot be the cause of itself nor precede itself, for nothing is said to exist nor occur before time itself. Here time cannot have a cause of its own existence for the circularity of these propositions hinge on the premise that everything that *begins* to exist has a cause. In other words, because nothing can occur before time exists, time cannot have a cause.

While the exact nature of the origin of the universe remains an open indeterminate question and is foreclosed from current scientific knowledge, we neither have to posit nor prove the parameters of the conditions that make the existence of the universe possible to make my case that there is no evidence of an agentic God who teleologically created matter and the laws of physics, nor do we have to appeal to a supraordinate causal creator when there is no cosmological footprint of God's existence. Most physicists agree that the natural constellation of events on macro and micro levels is something rather than nothing. As Stenger puts it, "an empty universe requires supernatural intervention— not a full one. Only by the constant action of an agent outside the universe, such as God, could a state of nothingness be maintained. The fact that we have something is just what we would expect if there is no God."[47] It is more plausible to assume that the universe has always existed in some form, even if it had arisen from previous rudimentary cosmic fluctuations within its sea of eternity, as well as underwent violent change, transmogrification, and expansion, for it is the nature of process reality that allows for transmutational variations and evolutions to instantiate over time. Although I do not claim to resolve this paradox, we need not conjure a supernatural entity to explain the magisterium of natural existence.

Notes

1 This is a major tenet of psychoanalysis, however, it may be said to originate in antiquity. Aristotle anticipates Hegel's psychology when he suggests there is a sort of unconscious intelligence at work that mediates images and stored objects within the abyss of the mind. Originally laid down and retained as sensations, "after-images" can take on a life of their own, as we may observe in dreams and fantasy, and are reproduced by the faculty of imagination as re-presentations that are unconsciously derived. This is why Aristotle states: "Thinking is different from perceiving and is held to be in part imagination, in part judgment" (*De Anima*, 427b28–29). Notice that imagination and thought intermingle. Here we may appreciate why Hegel (1817) claims, even with stipulations, that "phantasy is reason" (*EG* § 457). In other words, unconscious valences intervene during any act of thinking, especially in fantasy formation. Because reason is a developmental achievement, it is grounded upon our natural embodied

constitution that acquires advanced forms of cognition through human maturation. Therefore, reason is the epigenetic evolution of its prior shapes that transform yet derive from our natural corporeality as desire, sentience, affect, and the life of imagination (see Mills, 2010).

2 This was the final sentence of his 1811 anonymously published pamphlet, "The Necessity of Atheism," for which he was expelled from Oxford for refusing to denounce authorship to the university authorities.

3 David Hume (1755), "Of the Immortality of the Soul," (p. 598).

4 Recall Hegel's equation of appearance as essence, for nothing could exist unless it is made actual. From the *Encyclopaedia Logic*, Hegel (1817) says: "Essence must *appear*. Its inward shining is the sublating of itself into immediacy, which as inward reflection is *subsistence* (matter) as well as *form*, reflection-into-another, subsistence *sublating itself* ... . Essence therefore is not *behind* or *beyond* appearance, but since the essence is what exists, existence is appearance" (*EL* § 131). Also compare with the *Phenomenology*, § 147.

5 Craig (2007), "Theistic Critiques of Atheism," p. 70.

6 See *God in Proof* (2013), p. xi. Schneider's redefinition of proof allows him to take poetic liberty with ordinary experiences we would not typically classify as proof. For example, he surprisingly opens his book with a so-called self-acclaimed proof in God: "One almost-gone afternoon in November, as I stepped out into what sun remained in the day, a proof for the existence of God took hold of me. I was a freshman in college and had just finished a meeting with a teaching assistant. The department house's heavy wooden door thudded shut behind me. Light; truth" (p. ix). Was it the sound of the door slamming, or perhaps the meeting with an attractive teaching assistant that struck this young man's fancy? Since we do not have first-person epistemic access to his thought processes, we will never know. But if this vague, quasi-mystical, and entirely subjective ineffable form of the numinous constitutes proof in God, then practically anything could constitute proof based upon the idiosyncratic nature of relativized experience imagined by anyone. "I ate a donut. Light; truth." Hardly a defensible criterion of proof. But in all fairness to Schneider, you can glean from his writing that he is a genuinely good soul. His book showcases (like no other I have read) a very authentic, humane, and emotionally open struggle with the God question by someone who craves the spiritual, the good life, and the best for collective humanity; yet he is epistemologically uncertain about his faith despite his belief in God (see p. 227). I applaud him on his individuation process, as we all must travel our own path.

7 See *Critique of Pure Reason*, Ch.3, Sec.4, "The impossibility of an Ontological Proof of the Existence of God."

8 *Ibid*, A 598/B 626.

9 *Ibid*, A 600/B 628.

10 Cf. Nicholas Everitt (2004), p. 54.

11 *The God Delusion*, p. 137.

12 Here God's lack of manifestation should be understood as the failure to directly appear as a substantive (although possibly immaterial) being, not merely revealed or made manifest in the mind of a subject, which can be entirely subjective and construed to be whatever an individual interprets manifestation or revelation to be. Admittedly, it is hard for me to fathom how this manifestation would transpire if God were to appear as anything but a substantive entity. Jung and the post-Jungian spiritual movement have attempted to make God unconscious, and hence one could argue (if you accept Jung's theories) that archetypal appearances from a collective unconscious may qualify as a form of manifestation, albeit it would be entirely confined to subjective experience and interpretation, such as the content and hermeneutics of dreams. Yet this would still confine God to an intrapsychic materialization and not an external (objective) one. My fantasy is that God would have to pervade the senses of all peoples on earth as an experiential certainty in order for God's manifestation to be considered actual; however, we would still have the messy epistemological and empirical criteria to deal with. I could also imagine that if something remotely possible as divine manifestation were to materialize, then there would be a mass hysteria or collective psychosis that would paralyze humanity. Because the bounds of imagination have no bounds, I am content with leaving this thought experiment unexplored for the moment.

13 Living as an outspoken atheist is a tough row to hoe as a minority in societies that condemn free speech and inquiry. But social discrimination and marginalization abounds in free societies as well. Those who question others or speak unabashedly about religious disbelief are often lambasted for their deviant convictions and lack of observance to social decorum. Moreover, we are quick to be labeled as radicals, heretics, or antisocial who thrive on creating interpersonal discomfort in others. We should challenge this political hegemony and militate against it. Yet this may come with certain costs. An inevitable social distance and alienation occurs when a lack of tolerance for difference in belief systems is experienced by atheist and theist alike. Cryptic discriminatory practices are prevalent on all stratifications of culture, economic class, and political dynamics operative within social organizations, from tiny cliques to large political bodies that collectively determine almost anything, from the fate of how one is treated interpersonally by others to social policy. This is why many atheists are cautious about offending others because their authentic, uncensored views could have tangible consequences that encumber the concrete quality of their lives. This is quite conspicuous in smaller communities where anonymity is limited or nonexistent, which influences everything from social gossip, exclusion or expulsion from group membership, to ostracism in public schools, business, and communal practices. It is likely that with increased education, awareness, and social dialogue these emotional prejudices will acquire reform within democratic countries.

14 Recent new evidence in support of the Higgs boson was revealed at the world's largest and highest energy particle accelerator, the Large Hadron Collider, which is located in a 17-mile tunnel near the Franco-Swiss border near Geneva, and is

224 God: The Invention of an Idea

operated by CERN, the European Organization of Nuclear Research. The ATLAS and Compact Muon Solenoid calculators detected unusual particles that *manifested*, hence popped into existence, after these collision experiments occurred (see Carroll, 2012; Landau, 2013).

15 In *Breaking the Spell* (2006), Daniel Dennett views the concept of God as an "intentional object." Here I wish to emphasize that the intentional stance or object is in fact the human subject whom cannot help but project their own internal human attributes (and dynamic conflicts) onto the *idea* of what is construed to be God.

16 Cf. Kant's (1781) discussion of "Things-in-themselves" as unknowable but thinkable, pp. 27, 74, 87, 149.

17 Stephen Maitzen (2006) argues that according to the argument of divine hiddenness, "God's existence is disconfirmed by the fact that not everyone believes in God" (p. 177) based on an uneven distribution of theistic belief due to a dwindling reduction in the demographics of theism.

18 See William James (1902), *The Varieties of Religious Experience*, Lecture III, p. 53.

19 One can argue that science fundamentally rests on statistical hypotheses that are in principle unfalsifiable and based on induction; therefore, in practice the scientific method almost never employs falsification and is only concerned with reporting statistically significant results that drive and legitimize the political world of scientific publishing.

20 See Karl Popper (1959), *The Logic of Scientific Discovery*, "Falsifiability as a Criterion of Demarcation," Ch. 1, p. 1.

21 Stenger (2007), *God: The Failed Hypothesis*, pp. 11–18, 34, 233, 237.

22 In contrast, the linguistic, postmodern turn in Continental philosophy, which developed contemporaneously with Anglo-American analytic philosophy, reduces all propositions to linguistic predications governed by social construction and the conventions of grammatical discourse. In essence, what we *think* is a product of our socialization practices grounded in language. The original content of our thoughts—what we posit, conceive, imagine, or hypothesize about—does not ensure a direct correspondence between the object of thought and an external independent reality. Instead, all ideas are cultural-linguistic mediations. Here the stability of the modern notions of truth, reality, objectivity, and absolutism are overturned by the context and contingencies of society, history, cultural relativism, and linguistic construction. From this perspective, metaphysics is untenable.

23 For a nice overview of these detailed arguments see Martin & Monnier (2003), *The Impossibility of God*.

24 Cf. Spinoza, *The Ethics*, Proposition XV, Part I.

25 Howson (2011), *Objecting to God*, pp. 199, 200, 203, 208.

26 *Ibid*, p. 133.

27 Cf. Gilbert Fulmer (1977), p. 113.

28 *The Existence of God*, p. 20.

29 Le Poidevin (1996), p. 55, italics in original. See his comparison between weak and strong anthropic arguments, pp. 54–56, 59–61.
30 Keith M. Parsons (2013), "Problems with Theistic Arguments," p. 491.
31 William Lane Craig (2013), "Creation and Divine Action," p. 386.
32 *The Experience of God: Being, Consciousness, Bliss*, p. 36.
33 *Ibid*, pp. 40–41.
34 *Ibid*, p. 44.
35 Krauss (2013), *A Universe from Nothing*, p. xxiv.
36 *Ibid*, p. 149.
37 See Alan Guth (1997), *The Inflationary Universe*.
38 *God: The Failed Hypothesis*, p. 117.
39 *Ibid*, pp. 125–127.
40 See Atkak & Pagels (1982) and Vilenkin (1983).
41 See Hartle & Hawking (1983). Cf. Stephen Hawking (1988), *A Brief History of Time*, where he says: "if the universe is really self-contained, having no boundary or edge, it would have neither beginning nor end; it would simply be" (pp. 140–141).
42 See Craig (2013), p. 381.
43 Craig (1979), *The Kalâm Cosmological Argument*.
44 *God: The Failed Hypothesis*, p. 124.
45 See Stenger (2006), *The Comprehensible Cosmos* and *God: The Failed Hypothesis*, p. 126.
46 Robin Le Poidevin (1996) provides a nice critique of the temporal and modal arguments that ultimately rely on a notion of causality incompatible with our contemporary knowledge of determinism (see pp. 5–15).
47 *God: The Failed Hypothesis*, p. 133.

References

Aristotle. (1984). *De Anima* (On the Soul). In J. Barnes (Ed.), *The Complete Works of Aristotle. 2 Vols.* (The revised Oxford trans.) Princeton, NJ: Princeton University Press, pp. 641–692.
Atkatz, D., & Pagels, H. (1982). Origin of the Universe as Quantum Tunneling Event. *Physical Review*, D25: 2065–2067.
Carroll, S. (2012). *The Particle at the End of the Universe: How the Hunt for the Higgs Boson Leads Us to the Edge of a New World.* New York: Penguin.
Craig, W.L. (1979). *The Kalâm Cosmological Argument.* London: Macmillan.
Craig, W.L. (2007). Theistic Critiques of Atheism. In M. Martin (Ed.), *The Cambridge Companion to Atheism* (pp. 68–88). Cambridge: Cambridge University Press.
Craig, W.L. (2013). Creation and Divine Action. In C. Meister & P. Copan (Eds.), *The Routledge Companion to Philosophy of Religion*, 2nd Ed. pp., 378–388. New York: Routledge.

Dawkins, R. (2006). *The God Delusion*. New York: Mariner Books.

Dennett, D. (2006). *Breaking the Spell: Religion as a Natural Phenomenon*. New York: Penguin Books.

Everitt, N. (2004). *The Non-Existence of God*. London: Routledge.

Fulmer, G. (1976/77). The Concept of the Supernatural. *Analysis*, 37, 113–116.

Guth, A. (1997). *The Inflationary Universe*. New York: Addison-Wesley.

Hart, D.B. (2013). *The Experience of God: Being, Consciousness, Bliss*. New Haven, CT: Yale University Press.

Hartle, J.B., & Hawking, S.W. (1983). Wave Function of the Universe. *Physical Review*, D28: 2960–2975.

Hawking, S.W. (1988). *A Brief History of Time*. New York: Bantam.

Hegel, G.F.W. (1807). *Phenomenology of Spirit*, Trans. A.V. Miller. Oxford: Oxford University Press, 1977.

Hegel, G.F.W. (1817/1827/1830). *The Encyclopaedia Logic*. Vol. 1 of *Encyclopaedia of the Philosophical Sciences*. Trans. T.F. Geraets, W.A. Suchting, & H.S. Harris. Indianapolis: Hackett Publishing Company, Inc., 1991.

Hegel, G.F.W. (1978). *Hegel's Philosophy of Subjective Spirit [Hegel's Philosophie des subjektiven Geistes]*. Vol. 1: *Introductions*; Vol. 2: *Anthropology*; Vol. 3: *Phenomenology and Psychology*. Ed.M.J. Petry. Dordrecht, Holland: D. Reidel Publishing Company.

Howson, C. (2011). *Objecting to God*. Cambridge: Cambridge University Press.

Hume, D. (1755). Of the Immortality of the Soul. In E.F. Miller (Ed.), *Essays: Moral, Political, and Literary*. Revised Edition (pp. 590–598). Indianapolis: Liberty Fund, 1985.

James, W. (1902). *The Varieties of Religious Experience*. New York: Modern Library.

Kant. I. (1781/1787). *Critique of Pure Reason*. N.K. Smith (Trans.). New York: St. Martin's Press, 1929.

Krauss, L. (2013). *A Universe from Nothing: Why There is Something Rather than Nothing*. New York: Atria.

Landau, E. (2013). Scientists More Certain that Particle is Higgs boson. CNN, updated 10:45 AM EDT, Sat March 16. http://www.cnn.com/2013/03/14/tech/innovation/higgs-boson-god-particle

Le Poidevin, R. (1996). *Arguing for Atheism*. London: Routledge.

Maitzen, S. (2006). Divine Hiddenness and the Demographics of Theism. *Religious Studies*, 42, 177–191.

Martin, M., & Monnier, R. (Eds.) (2003). *The Impossibility of God*. Amherst, NY: Prometheus Books.

Mills, J. (2010). *Origins: On the Genesis of Psychic Reality*. Montreal: McGill-Queens University Press.

Parsons, K.M. (2007). Some Contemporary Theistic Arguments. In M. Martin (Ed.), *The Cambridge Companion to Atheism* (pp. 102–117). Cambridge: Cambridge University Press.

Popper, K. (1959). *The Logic of Scientific Discovery*. London: Routledge.

Schneider, N. (2013). *God in Proof*. Berkeley, CA: University of California Press.

Spinoza, B. (1992). *The Ethics, Treatise on the Emendation of the Intellect, and Selected Letters*. S. Shirley (Trans.) & S. Feldman (Ed.). Indianapolis: Hackett.

Stenger, V.J. (2006). *The Comprehensible Cosmos*. Amherst, NY: Prometheus Books.

Stenger, V.J. (2007). *God: The Failed Hypothesis*. Amherst, NY: Prometheus Books.

Swinburne, R. (1979/2004). *The Existence of God*, Rev. 2nd Ed. Oxford: Clarendon Press.

Vilenkin, A. (1983). Birth of Inflationary Universes. *Physical Review*, D27: 2848–2855.

Chapter 9

Towards a Theory of Myth

The term "myth" is derived from the Greek *muthos* (μῦθος), meaning *word, speech*.[1] The term was used frequently by Homer (see *Odyssey* II.561; *Iliad* 9.443; 19.242) and other ancient poets, especially referring to the *mere word*. It is also referred to as *public speech* (*Odyssey*, I.358) as well as *conversation*. When combined with the word *logos* (λόγος), such as in the compound *muthologia* (μυθολογία), myth becomes a discourse on narrative. Myth as word, speech, discourse generically refers to the *thing said*, as *fact*, or *matter* at hand, as well as the *thing thought*, the *unspoken word*, revealing its *purpose* or *design*. This may be why the migration of the term was closely associated with the process of thinking itself: i.e., in Old Slavic, *mysle* is equated with thought, as is *smūainim* in Old Irish, hence *I think*, perhaps derived from the Indo-European *mudh-*, to think, to *imagine*.

When Heidegger (1927) discusses the concept of logos and truth (ἀλήθεια), he tells us that "discourse" as logos "lets something be seen" by making it manifest and accessible to another party (§ 7, B). Like muthos, logos is a convoluted concept that has acquired many different meanings throughout the history of philosophy. Λόγος is customarily translated as "reason," "meaning," "judgement," "intelligence," "concept," "word," "definition," "assertion," "ground," and "relationship," which means it always succumbs to interpretation. Heidegger argues that its original, basic signification is "discourse." In fact, Heidegger specifically refers to the logos that transpires in the speech act between interlocutors as the space where signification is acquired "in its relation to something in its 'relatedness'" (p. 58). Here "interpretation" unfolds within a "relationship"

DOI: 10.4324/9781003305958-9

where potential multiple meanings surface from a clearing based on a certain setting forth, exhibiting, laying out, recounting, and so forth, which transparently applies to any discourse on myth.

On the Signification of Myth

The transliteration of muthos as myth has acquired various significations, many of which have centred around a story, tale (see *Odyssey* 3.94; 4.324), saying, legend, or proverb. But unlike in Homer (800 B.C.E.), where there is no distinction of true or false narratives (*Odyssey* II.492), modern and contemporary references to myth have acquired a pejorative meaning that stand in relation to derived etymologies from antiquity where discourse on myth began to be viewed as fiction and fable (Plato, 1961a, *Phaedo*, 61b; 1961b, *Republic*, 377a; Aristotle, 1984, *Meteorology*, 356b1). Like logos, muthos implies no reference to the truth or falsity of a narrative,[2] it is merely the reason, the ground of discourse, as matter of fact. Perhaps this is why when Robert Segal (2004) defines myth as "a story" (p. 4), he refrains from passing judgement on the truth or falsity of its claims (p. 6).

Given that words, hence myths, stand in relation to a string of signifiers where meaning is always descended from and connected to other signifiers in an ontic chain of relations to various experiential things that are signified in thought, myth will always retain a mercurial sense of undecidability. It is only when we assign a circumscribed determinate meaning that is conventionally adopted as a linguistic signifier or semiotic operative within a particular discourse, culture, or socio-symbolic structure that such undecidability is occluded. But this is merely a formal imposition of grammar that does not erase the aporia or uncertainty of the term itself and its chthonic ambiguity of meanings left open to interpretation, impasse, and deferral to a web of unconscious relations where semiotic properties are virtually infinite and indeterminate. It is for this reason that we prescribe social conventions of meaning and construct operational definitions in order to provide a structural template of fixed determinations of the signification of certain words, while all along ignoring the relativity and fluidity of discourse. Here mythos is just as much an affront on truth as is any other mode of discourse, including science, with the exception that some discourses are more persuasive than others.

If we accept the premise that any discourse by definition imports an overdetermination of meaning, where undecidability, relativity, and an infinite chain of semiotic deferrals leave an etymological uncertainty, or have undergone historical transmogrifications and variations when applied to other languages and cultures that efface the true question of origins, then the most we can hope for in detecting any original meaning is the derivative, the trace. This leads us to ask, What is the essence of myth? Can it be deconstructed, so to speak, or analysed in a manner that can advance our ways in which we theorize about the theory of myth?

Towards a Theoretic Typology of Myth

If we adopt the principle of sufficient reason, namely, that every mental object must stand in relation to an archaic event derived from an original ground *in illo tempore*, then myth, like all psychic experience, must stand in relation to its origins. In other words, how is myth derived from archaic ground *ab origine*? It may appear strange to ask about original meaning, but if you change original meaning then a theory of myth becomes *presumed*, hence given, when this conclusion is a displacement of origins that is *subsumed* in any contemporary discourse on myth.

Why do we need a theory of myth? Because no systematic theory exists, let alone a consensus. If no agreement exists on what myth is or signifies, then expressive and representational approaches to language and ontology are merely relative or devolve into circularity, tautology, or are simply begging the question. What I am particularly interested in addressing are not specific theories of myth, or specific myths themselves, but rather what constitutes a good theory. In particular, throughout our investigation I hope to illuminate what a proper theory of myth would be expected to offer. But before we get there, we need to prepare the groundwork in anticipation of our conclusions.

As Segal (1999, p. 1) points out, myth is an applied subject that always appeals to broader categories that are then in turn applied to the case of myth. As a result, comparative and discipline-specific analyses of myth tend to be dubious due to the arbitrary and turbid nature of the way in which they vary in their approach to investigating myth. Furthermore, a particular approach to theorizing already imports certain epistemological assumptions about the very nature of the subject matter, such as what the theory is supposed to do or be used for, or what it is about, or accounts for, or signifies, what it is supposed to describe, and so on. For this reason, many of the leading modern theorists of myth introduce explicit presuppositions about the way things are in their very approach to myth, such as myth is a subset of religion, accompanies ritual, serves a practical function, is an ethic or conviction, is the primitive counterpart to science, or is a proto-logical view of describing and explaining the physical world, the cosmos, gods, society, the mind and human relations, the process of civilization, cultural artifacts and values, and so forth (for an overview see Chase, 1949; Feldman & Richardson, 1972). Here Segal (1999, p. 2) argues that comparative theories of myth often engage answers to fundamental questions such as, What is the (a) origin, (b) function, (c) subject matter or referent, and (d) meaning of myth?

Let us attempt to expound upon this typology or principle of categorization. First, *What is myth about?* Any reference to subject matter already presupposes various ontological assertions, so let us begin with *origin*. Origin is about foundations, archaic ground, hence history and genesis. So whatever myth refers to, it must engage a point of origination, which signifies both meaning and function, and is therefore overdetermined in surplus and value on any discourse we adopt on myth. If we begin with history and archaic ontology, where myth emerged, then we are by definition adopting a discourse about *being human* even if we are attempting to define a particular feature, function, and/or reason for positing myth. If myth is always *about* something, then it imports ontology, namely, the material world, culture, anthropology, cosmogony, the supernatural, and so on despite the sociological and psychological functions they serve. So first of all, myth is about ontology—what is purportedly real—even if only symbolic or bears out to be a false claim.

The *function* of myth is varied, sociologically diverse, and ultimately idiosyncratic to individual persons despite participating in common collective beliefs and practices. Functions of myth may be designed to bind social collectives, such as in religion, facilitate roles and rituals, or have applied personal purposes and delineations, but they often serve a job or pragmatic task, such as a utilitarian description, interpretation, observation, deliberation, way of being, explanation, and/or expression of human phenomena, even when the subject matter is not about the human being. In this way, myth is about utility, service, helpfulness, and efficacy.

The *meaning* of myth can be (a) literal, (b) figurative, (c) metaphorical, (d) symbolic, (e) semiotically circumscribed, such as in a creed, doctrine, or ideology, and (f) imaginative, as suggested by its etymology, which is always open to hermeneutics and fantasy. In this way, myth can be personal and collective, hence universal regardless of its form and content, and open to an infinite chain of significations, meaning relations, and referents without being predetermined or confined in its ostensive definition or purpose. In this way, both function and meaning may be interdependent within a rubric of irreducibility. Although function and meaning may operate outside of the ontic conditions of archaic ground, they are not ontologically independent from origin. As previously stated, every event or appearance must stand in relation to its archaic derivations, in this case, the phenomena of myth.

Although the nature of theory has been subjected to critique in the sciences, the social sciences, and conceptual research (Corley & Gioia 2011; Estrada & Schultz, 2017; Gibbs, 1990; Shalley, 2012; Van Lange, 2013), where the characteristics of accuracy, consistency, scope, simplicity, and fruitfulness (Kuhn, 1974) have enjoyed dominant attention, which often involve a limited adoption of logical empiricism (Ye & Stam, 2013), the role of imagination objectively grounded in data and practicality (Calder & Tybout, 2016) that focus on reliability, precision, parsimony, generality, falsifiability, and progress (Gawronski & Bodenhausen, 2015; Gieseler, Loschelder, & Friese, 2019; Popper, 1965) informs our current discourse. Critique of theory is often not discussed in the humanities: theory is merely presumed according to discipline-specific norms. The same applies to studies of myth, and theories about theoretics that are taken at face value rather than critiqued for their disposition, structure, methodology, epistemological verity, and viability as an explanatory model of knowledge. This becomes even more nebulous if we concede that theory itself is a limited medium to access the meaning of myth. Rather than critique the value and limits of studies in mythology, we may see how sound theory is a necessary requirement that guides research methodology. In general, theory of myth should be:

1. Descriptive/precise,
2. Coherent/consistent,
3. Expository/explanatory,
4. Generalizable/broad,
5. Meaningful/expressive, and
6. Pragmatic; namely, useful or progressive.

The more clearly defined concepts and operational definitions are that allow for descriptive precision, coherency of presentation and argument, logical structure, form, and consistency, explanatory scope and depth that are generalizable or widely applicable in meaning and breadth, and that have utility, hence inspire or promote new research or theoretical progress, the more sophisticated a theory becomes. While the criteria of parsimony, falsifiability, and prediction often apply to the sciences, they do not necessarily apply to the humanities, let alone studies of myth for the plain reason that theory can be quite complex or profound, hence far from simple, not to mention they do not necessarily conform to empirical or real-world events; therefore the criteria of replication, falsification, or refutation of conjectures through testing and experimentation do not readily apply to theories of myth, which do not require empirical reality to lend them meaning or credibility when the subject matter, referent, and function lay outside of natural observation. This does not mean to suggest that research methodology is lacking in refinement and validity just because it does not conform to the parameters of empirical science. On the contrary, the theoretical humanities may often be far more intricate and erudite, which the principle of parsimony occludes or dislocates from its scope of investigation.

To what degree is theory and method arbitrary, contextual, contingent, relative, personalized, exploratory—hence experimental, and non-conclusive? Does theory only provide parameters for explanation and meaning, or does it guide method? If so, are theory and method virtually the same thing, or merely closely related even though they are subject to categorical distinctions? If one is the framework in which meaning is created and the other its application, then identity and similarity must be differentiated by their modes of instantiation. When a method or application is followed and posited to derive from and/or engender theory, then the dialectical ontic nature of theory and method become more difficult to differentiate as they are mutually implicative, and hence interrelated. And if this is the case, how do they stand in relation to individual and cultural differences, social and anthropological discrepancies, historical and gender variances? And can a methodological approach to myth, in theory, transpire without relying on theory? In other words, can a methodology actually be executed devoid of any theoretic directing the method or procedural actions themselves?

Every discipline has a set of theoretical orienting principles guiding inquiry, research, and methodological process, whether presumptive or not. Is this notion of criteria any different for the humanities versus the empirical researcher? Perhaps this binary is unnecessary to evoke, for we may make empirical observations on the social objectivity of the existence of myth, but not necessarily on its cultural meanings, although we can generally agree that the study of myth reflects the human, semiotic, and hermeneutical sciences without devolving into the discourse of natural science.

It was Dilthey (1883) who proposed the distinction between the human sciences based upon investigating and understanding the motivations and meanings inherent to the experiential subject or human being versus that of the natural sciences, which is concerned with the impersonal forces and organizations of nature. Whereas the *Geisteswissenschaften* focus on the science of mental processes and social systems within a class of human events, the *Naturwissenschaften* focus on the domain of the natural world. Therefore, the bifurcation that is often forged between the human and natural sciences takes as its premise that nature and human experience are mutually exclusive categories. However, the distinction lies in the methodology and discourse each discipline employs. What was crucial for Dilthey in positing distinctions between the natural and human sciences is the pivotal concept of "lived experience" (*Erlebnis*), the irreducibility of subjectivity that prereflectively (unconsciously) encounters the immediate presence of reality, that which is present "to me" as an internal sense, not as a given external object or datum of consciousness, but as an immediate internal mediacy. Here the subject-object distinction is obscured, if not sutured: Psyche is the lifeworld (*Lebenswelt*).

Although this nature versus human science differentiation was met with criticism due to the fact that human subjectivity and sociality are part of the natural world, and that critics (from neo-Kantians such as Wilhelm Windelband and Heinrich Rickert, as well as Freud) would claim are equally open to scientific scrutiny and can, in principle, find simpatico, this categorical distinction has nevertheless often been employed to distinguish the humanities from the physical sciences. But regardless of which approach we adopt, we cannot evade making ontological assertions. To say that a linguistic, semiotic, or scientific paradigm describes or explains a phenomenon, even if mired in uncertainty and impasse, is to evoke a referent that it is still *about* something, whether a corporeal object, a mental concept, or imaginative (immaterial) state of affairs (as fantasy) derived from representational (experiential) consciousness. The mode of discourse does not displace the signified object(s) in question, which always engages the question of ontology. In other words, we cannot elude the question of truth and realism no matter what discourse we adopt. Metaphysics always has a way of coming back to bite us in the backside.

The subject matter within a human science model is that of the experiential person and collective social life contextualized within a genus of human events; and impersonal aspects of the natural world are not typically part of its scope or locus. But myth has very often been historically offered as statements of explanation about the natural world. Yet, because human sciences are interpretive and target the meaning of experience, by definition they become hermeneutic. Because myth is necessarily predicated on human speech and language, as is noted by the ancients, and involves the pursuit of understanding human motivation and constructing meaning through interpretive intersubjective exchange, it may be considered a hermeneutic science.

For Dilthey and others, interpretation, understanding (*Verstehen*), or comprehension becomes a method for investigating the human sciences in relation to life-contexts, while the natural sciences are confined to sensory observation, description, testing, and explanation of causality and their effects. However, this distinction is not devoid of certain problems especially when rules or criteria for understanding may become opaque or overlap, as they do in the social sciences where methods of comprehensibility straddle the two methodological domains. Here it can be argued that hermeneutics never fully escapes the charge of slipping into relativism or recalcitrant subjectivism, given that, following certain rules of discourse versus what someone "really meant," can easily be two different things. The same applies to the scientific method where testability, verification, and falsifiability are subject to epistemic interpretation rather than pristine explanatory objectivity. Likewise, exegetical interpretation of a text or deconstructive praxis, and the application of that interpretation, may readily transform or alter it from its original meaning or purpose, even if we presuppose a hermeneutic circle. In other words, the very act of translation itself institutes reinterpretations of interpretations that can potentially spin on in circularity or regress to a point that meaning is foreclosed from its original signification.

Segal on Myth

Robert A. Segal is arguably one of the most accomplished contemporary scholars of myth. Throughout his vast writings on the topic, Segal's stylistic approach to theorizing about myth is to assume and exegetically articulate the positions of various theorists on myth, particularly those after the rise of modernity, only to add his own critique. He generally shies away from taking a stance on the truth or falsity of myth, instead focusing on its origin and function, but there is a tension in his thinking influenced by his affinity for exactitude and science. Segal has largely adopted methodologies derived from Anglo-American analytic philosophy, logical positivism, and the philosophy of science with particular historical resonances to Russell, A.J. Ayer, Quine, Kuhn, Popper, and Grünbaum, which he has applied to his studies on myth, anthropology, and religion. He particularly focuses on distinctions between explanation and interpretation championed by R.G. Collingwood (1946), William Dray, Peter Winch, and Gilbert Ryle (1971) as they are related to natural, social, and human science categories.

Although Segal generally analyses why myths arise and examines the purpose they serve, he also becomes preoccupied with how theorists offer either interpretations or explanations about the structure and verity of myth. For example, the views of E.B. Tylor (1832–1917) and James G. Frazer (1854–1941) who claim that myth is the primitive counterpart to modern science make myth incompatible with science, which is assumed to be true, and so hence makes myth false, despite the fact that they both serve different functions. Myth here is taken literally. By contrast, the view of myth as anything but archaic or prescientific either sidesteps the question or else makes myth true, but only true symbolically or psychologically. In other words, this form of truth only applies to human nature or society, but not the physical world. Mircea Eliade (1907–1986), Bronislaw Malinowski (1884–1942), Rudolph Bultmann (1884–1976), Hans Jonas (1903–1993), Sigmund Freud (1856–1939), and Carl Gustav Jung (1875–1961) would mainly fall into this camp. So here myths are not about material reality, only psychic reality; whether individual or collective is a matter of emotional identification with the subject matter mediated through imagination.

Regardless of the historical origins and functions of myth, much of Segal's analyses revolve around myth as an explanation of the world, whether antiquated, incorrect, or simply a false claim in relation to science is moot. But why does myth have to meet the challenge of science? Science merely explains while myth may serve many functions science cannot. But this all depends upon what we mean by science, hence to *know* (< Lat. *scientia*, from *scire*, to understand). In psychoanalysis for instance, to see an example from the social sciences, to offer a theory that explains psychological conditions and states of mind within social collectives, myth attempts to present the complexity of intrapsychic, intersubjective, and communal arrangements within a given culture, an unconscious manifestation of the need to make the unconscious conscious. For psychoanalysis, myth reveals in disguised forms all of humanity's desires, conflicts, defences, emotions, traits, dispositions, longings, and complexes that expose the personal and collective plight of humankind. Here myth has psychological significance for masses and functions in psychic economy unconsciously. Myth serves to symbolize culture and the symbolic value inherent in culture. In this way, myth as functionalism serves the overdetermined systems of society, and provides regulation to constant change, such that there is order, purpose, and structure to sociocultural networks via the narrative. A narrative in turn provides meaning, which is at once open to interpretation, even when attempts at explanation fail. Yet the notion of explanation is itself controversial.

For Segal (2014a), "Explanation provides causes. Interpretation provides meanings" (p. 25). In comparing Max Weber, Clifford Geertz, and Paul Ricoeur, he notes an "ontological" difference between explanation and interpretation: causality is physical, while meaning is mental or psychical. Although Weber (1968, v1, pp. 4–5; 21–21) collapses the distinction and makes mentation a causal process in its own right, akin to psychoanalysis, whereas psychic meaning is determinative, Geertz maintains a division on their incompatible ways in which they account for intentional behaviour and their consequential effects. For Geertz (1973, p. 43), interpretation applies to a particular, while explanation applies to a universal or generality. Ricoeur (1981, pp. 155, 158, 161), on the other hand, wants to maintain the reconcilable compatibility or consilience between explanatory and interpretive methodologies because they harmonize one another and provide answers to different questions, at once explanatory as well as interpretive (Segal, 2014a, p. 29). In the end Segal believes that Ricoeur's conciliatory attempt fails because he fails to keep the distinctions apart: reconciling meanings with causes becomes our task at hand, and Segal (2014a, p. 33) seems to be more comfortable with reducing meaning to cause.

According to Segal (2014b), "Any explanation starts with the effect and works backwards to the cause" (p. 93). But why should explanation predicate causality? For Segal (2009, pp. 69–72), if I read him correctly, an explanation is a reference to "proof" and "causality," which requires "testing," hence a privileging of empiricism, objectivity, and the scientific method, while other theories of explanation may rest on metaphysical foundational principles wedded to logic, non-contradiction, and internally coherent argumentation. Sometimes theories of explanation clash with one another, especially when they do not conform to the tenets of scientific experimentation, testability, verification, falsifiability, validity, replication, and reliability of measures. But this privileging of one method over another may simply be begging the question of a master discourse on method, especially when science reiterates its own ideologies when it fails to explain phenomena outside of its narrow scope of empirical observation, description, and experimentation that cannot control for variables, environments, and measurements that fall outside of the laboratory (Mills, 2015). That is why myth is part of the humanities and not the natural sciences.

As the gadfly of the Jungian world, Segal has offered a sustained critique of Jung. Recently he has applied his scheme of scientific critique using the categories of explanation versus interpretation to interrogate Jung's theory of myth, but it is the scheme that I wish to examine here rather than Jungian theory, as I find it applicable to any critique of myth. Segal (2014b, pp. 82–84) believes that any good theory that is scientific must be testable, and that we simply cannot assume tenets or propositions without arguing for them. Nothing serious or worthy of merit is to be presupposed. Nor are they applicable (hence generalizable) without solid grounds for accepting them. And they must be predictive, not post hoc or ex post facto constructions. At the very least, an *internal criteria* must be met that satisfies the framework of a good theory, and this is what I would impart to internal consistency that is coherent and non-contradictory, which conforms to the parameters of what I would consider to be a sound theory of myth. But a certain degree of *external criteria* must also be met, according to Segal, to make it generalizable, hence valid. Not only is a good theory applicable and subject to the probabilistic laws of predictability, any test would have to address the viability of the theory: here testability automatically assumes the theory will be subject to scrutiny. Will it pass muster? Segal is also demanding evidence. No proposition is proof of itself. Nothing can be predicated into existence, let alone assume others will buy its applicability, meaningfulness, or pragmatic value. Evidence is inexorable. It is an essential requirement, a necessary condition for any theory to be true. But is it a sufficient condition? And what about predictability? Should this be a defining theory of myth like it is of science? Is this not a category mistake?

Segal (2014b) makes an important claim: "an interpretation must be supported by an explanation" (p. 83). But we may ask, Why? And if so, is there any real difference between the two? Segal singles out the criterion of "persuasiveness" as a central feature in how a theory is applied. It seems to me that both an interpretation and an explanation must satisfy the criterion of persuasiveness if a theory is to have any merit. For Segal (1992), as for the hermeneuticists, an interpretation applies to meaning, while an explanation applies to the question of origin—why a myth was created and lasts. But a meaningful interpretation may also apply to an explication of the accounts of origin. They need not be binary categories or antinomies. They may be mutually implicative and ontically interdependent, what Segal calls "interlocking." There is no need to cleave them off from each other as they are both operative within any meta-representational framework that addresses the meaning, origin, and function of theory.

When Segal (2014b) defines the meaning of "explanation," he is referring to "the account—of mind, the world, culture, or society—that is presupposed by the interpretation" (p. 83). So here explanation and interpretation are not bifurcated even though we could argue that an interpretation is an attempt to provide a meaningful explication of events or a state of affairs, while an explanation is a cryptic form of interpretation disguised as certitude. In the end, Segal insists that a good theory of myth be justified, is generalizable, and predictive, not simply the ability to interpret a story.

From *Explanandum* to *Explanans*

Despite the long tradition in the natural, social, and human sciences that have historically attempted to separate the notion of explanation from interpretation (Lipton, 2004; Ricoeur, 1971; Bergström, 1990; Faye, 2011; Roubekas & Ryba, 2020), we have good reason to believe this bifurcation is a false dichotomy. An *explanandum* describes a phenomenon to be explained, not the phenomenon itself, while an *explanans* seeks to adduce an answer or explanation to account for the phenomenon—its reason(s), purpose, origins, and so forth. While the *explicandum* is that which gets explicated, the *explicans* is that which gives the explication. Although an explanation attempts to account for the coming into being of a phenomenon, it is more than that. It always implies, if not literally evokes, the question of causality by attempting to explain the ground or preconditions that bring something about, such as certain antecedent events or the necessary conditions (not sufficient ones) that are temporally and materially a priori. So contrary to predicate or propositional logic, which is merely concerned with the meaning of words or expressions and their formal systemic relations and operations, or statements that make something comprehensible, an *explanans* is much more far-reaching—it is about ontology.

On the one hand, an interpretation is an attempt to describe a phenomenon, on the other, an explanation attempts to offer more, that is, how and why a phenomenon occurs. But so does an interpretation—each are about explication. So how does an interpretation differ from an explanation? When applied to the question of myth, I argue that both interpretive and explanatory models are equally making ontological claims, even if they are tarrying in epistemic uncertainty when it comes to the question of causality. Recall that for the ancients, a cause (αιτία) was the reason or explanation for something happening, which is always overdetermined.

If myth is a declarative attempt to make phenomena comprehensible, then we must contend that it is offering an explanation of phenomena, even if contestable, or it would not have any currency to grant meaning to the human mind. Whether it is true or false is another issue, one we should adjourn for now. The prowess of myth over the eons seems to coalesce into many different meaning structures that wed interpretation, explanation, emotion, feeling, aesthetics, parable, morality, spirituality, and higher rational insights into a psychic medium that is historically and culturally enshrined within the development of human civilization. To say that myth is merely about one thing, or serves merely functions—psychological, sociological, anthropological, and so on—is to miss the point that myth is ultimately about ontology, about what it signifies, that which is ultimately real, even if presented as fiction or fantasy. In other words, the imaginary is real. And anytime we evoke the notion of what is really real, we cannot bracket or suspend the question of determinism. But why should we grant the narrative—the "story"—the status of offering a theory of causality? Why should we assume an *explanans* has anymore epistemological weight or verity to phenomenal description—to the *explanandum*? Does not an explanation have multiple threads, multiple significations, hence an overdetermination and surplus of meaning and value, not to mention causal-semiotic strands of deferral to an infinite chain of associations and signifiers? This logically implies that no single explanation is ever complete or unequivocally valid, rather only a partial attempt at conceptualizing and describing phenomena.

The Truth of Myth and the Myth of Truth

Eliade (1963) adopts a particular view held by archaic societies that myth means a "true" story, whether literally or a narrative believed to be true by relevant social collectives, which holds sacred socio-religious significance of transcendental spiritual value explicating "beginnings" or the coming into existence of reality itself by supernatural provenance. Since the Western epistemological turn in modernity, and the hermeneutical narrative turn in more contemporary postmodern times, we may concede that our understanding and consensus of the meaning of "truth" remains hotly contested. Whether we adopt Eliade's affinities for supernaturalism or not, his position that myth narrates sacred history is itself an explanation, for it attempts to delineate a causal factor in positing an account of "creation"—the ground of archaic ontology from which myth arises. Here Eliade may be accused of obfuscating truth with reality.[3] One person's truth may be their psychic reality subject to relativism, illusion, projection, and fantasy, if not delusion, hence their phenomenal experience of the world, while another demands that reality must conform to the stronghold of objective (demonstrated and proven) empirical and material facts in order to be flown under the banner of truth, a debate we do not have to continue at length here.

If interpretive and explanatory models are used to describe and lend understanding to phenomena, which always evoke the question of ontology, as I argue, then they inevitably engage the questions of truth and epistemology, even if unintended or silent on the matter. What does this imply? This would suggest that any discourse on myth simultaneously speaks about epistemic verity and/or the truth or falsity of its predications or claims. But what do we mean by truth? If mythos and logos cannot elude the question of truth, then would not any discourse on truth equally imply that a certain mythology is at play? The myth that there is Truth, as if it were a single, unified condition, entity, or unquestionable empirical state of affairs that transcends all phenomenal realities and fulfills every epistemic criterion imaginable is simply a fantasy. If this were otherwise, then no one would be debating the question, scope, and meaning of truth. It would simply be accepted as *given*, as part of our natural thrownness. As I have critiqued elsewhere (Mills, 2014), discourse on truth is not about "correctness" or so-called empirical facts, rather it is about what phenomenally *appears* in the real world of ontic relations. Both the methods of interpretation and explanation are making propositional assertions about truth-claims, and truth-claims stand in relation to what they ultimately signify or represent, namely, onto-phenomenal conditions.

Truth may be better understood by revisiting the ancient notion of *aletheia* (ἀλήθεια), where truth is defined as a process of disclosedness or unconcealedness. Truth appears as the manifestation of particularized expressions of the psyche-in-society that have their source in an unconscious ontology teleologically motivated to disclose itself. This applies to myth, or humanity would never have invented such discourse to begin with, for it *speaks* to a collective need to understand and recapitulate archetypal experience of-and-in the world. Here the very conditions for truth to be disclosed must be conditioned on unconscious experience. Myth as disclosure through discourse reveals the unconcealed longings of the human race to describe, interpret, and explain human experience that could not be articulated otherwise before the age of reason and science. But even today, such mythic language can never be replaced by the antiseptic discourse of science, for staid or stolid approaches to explicating lived experience never live up to the psychological needs for satisfaction, emotionality, and enjoyment. It is a primal phenomenon arising from the pulsional desire to interpret, expatiate, and know the world.

The truth of myth is both a universal and particularized form of disclosedness—an appearance of a much more complex process that may only reveal itself a bit at a time as partial unconcealment—as event, a moment, an instance. We must graft more meaning structures onto our interpretations to expand and complicate them, where there are richer and more robust and variegated theories that fall under the categorical rubric of what we call explanation.

For example, the theory of evolution is an interpretation of human origin, but is it not an unqualified explanation, albeit plausible and scientifically probable. It is very much a scheme or set of hypotheses that have explanatory power. Evolutionary biology may very well be a necessary condition but not a sufficient one to explain human origins. The same equally applies to myth. Myth, like religion, attempts to answer to origins—to ontology—as does physics and evolution, only on the condition that it is a narrative *about* origins, hence an interpretation of human experience and valuation—itself a phenomenon or appearance of our psychic expressions signifying something that is purportedly attempting to transcend human subjectivity, namely, archaic ontology. But given that myth is universal to humanity, only the particularities vary, any theory of myth must concede that it is merely a partial *explanans* of the *explanandum*.

Can a myth be true, or is it by definition false? Notice the binary logic involved in the question, presuming that the predicate "true" is valued over that which is "false." This question always stands in relation to epistemology and the discursive or procedural methods we adopt, as well as the definitions we attribute to the signifier "truth." Is truth merely about correctness, internal consistency, logical form? If so, this conforms to a theory of discourse we as collectives or cultures define through semantic or linguistic convention. Or is it about fact? But how do we determine fact and evidence independent of human consensus? Even scientific models of metaphysical realism that profess to "discover" truth and "natural laws" cannot escape from our human subjectivity in offering interpretations of those laws, even when submitted to rigorous testing exposing the problems of verification, falsification, replication, reliability, validity, observation selection effects, anthropic bias, and refutation of conjectures. All constants evolve, change, mutate, and rematerialize in other forms— the transmogrification of reality. From physics to myth, humanity cannot help but invent and reinvent its own so-called truths. Explanation is as much a myth at explicating causality as is science; yet the matter becomes not truth, but rather plausibility based on statistical probabilities and predictive validity, the gambling intellect that places value in attempting to predict possible future conditions and events. Science predicts as it explains, while myth is an explanation of interpretation, itself predictable.

The Essence of Myth

A proper theory of myth must have several components. We have identified four thus far: (1) referent, (2) origin, (3) meaning, and (4) function. Setting aside the subject matter, let us start with origin, and I will compare this to archaic ontology appropriating Aristotle's categorization of causality as our guide. I wish to avoid the, at times, simplistic (parsimonious) models of science, but they are subsumed in a more comprehensive explication of determinism, or more appropriately, overdetermination (Mills, 2013), so I will include them here without succumbing to reductionism.

A myth must have a (1) source, (2) force, (3) form, (4) object, and (5) goal. Because mythology is archetypal, that is, it is rooted in the archaic development of civilization and language, it is by definition a human invention, hence a cultural phenomenon that makes attempts to explain via consciousness (interpretation) origins, that is, the cosmos, gods, Being, and so forth. Although the *source* is, strictly speaking, mediated through human cognition, it attempts to answer to the question of fundamental ontology. The *force* or essence of myth is process, or the revealed organizing principles behind the narrative. The *form* is the organizational style, typology, categorization, formula, patterning, and/or genre of the story, often poetical, metaphorical, aesthetic, moralistic, and brimming with latent meanings, usually revolving around the development of characters and plot within metanarratives and meta-representations. As human linguistic inventions, they are psychologically mediated through imagination, so imaginal properties suffuse mythic structure. The *object* of myth refers to contents, properties, place, context, contingencies, and fantasies, as by contemporary definition myth is a fictional or illusory product of the imagination, although it can be taken as real, literate, material, significatory, and/or suggestive of a greater transcendental object or reality. But to a minor degree, the object of myth (the overarching narrative or meta-structure) is intimately linked with its *goal*, namely, its purpose. The purpose or aim is both to interpret and explain—hence to assign meaning and value to—the narrative.

Myth furthermore discloses an intent or *telos*, even if supple, hence revealing the agency behind the story. Here the meaning of myth reveals the emotional mind, and often has aesthetic and ethical dimensions and utilities in conveying a message(s) that reverberates in the psyche and in social collectives through identificatory unconscious resonances. Hence a myth conveys or expresses the human soul. It is only the human being who can generate and understand myth, even if professed to be about genesis or come from an original cause outside the human mind.

As human creation, myth may be said to be socially constructed as the ethos and expression of culture, or it can be solely individualistic, subjective, and private. Although it is unconsciously motivated, and displaces the vast array of human affects, conflicts, desires, defenses, fantasies, and their compromises, it ultimately has a telos, purpose, or objective, the goal of which is to communicate internal experience, discharge pulsions, contain anxiety, and engender meaning that usually transcends mere conscious intent. Here myth is overdetermined, that is, it provides meta-meaning and has multiple functions that resonate on many parallel processes of mentation.

With stipulations, it may also be argued that meaning and function are equiprimordial, but without equating the two or collapsing them into the same category: while all functions convey meaning they may not be meaningful. They may be understood, have a practical structure, reason, and so forth, but they may offer little or no psychological solace. Functions may serve a purpose or have practicalities but may be devoid of value to the psyche. Myths logically must transcend mere function, or they would cease to lose all value, unless we were to concede that masses remain largely unconscious of their need for myths and simply are conditioned sheep in the meadow. But even if we were to yield this hypothesis, the sociological organizations that promulgate and keep mythic discourse alive speak to greater communal narratives of how myth serves both utility and meaning in collectives, or it would have disappeared from socialization practices altogether. The prime example is religion. Religion will never disappear because it serves equiprimordial needs and meaning for humanity.

Myth is an inherent and indispensable aspect of human civilization that disperses its particularities into the social fabric of every culture, which has its own regional contents, contexts, and intent, yet it cannot stand outside of its own origins, namely, human consciousness, even when its subject matter is about cosmos, theos, and prebeginnings. Yet given that consciousness is conditioned by unconscious process, following Freud and Jung, we may conclude that myth is a collective unconscious projection of its own mythical character. Because myth is the exteriorization of interiority, myth becomes the realization of archaic unconscious ontology. As the self-externalization of its own internal lived-value, conscious identification with myth both validates and fulfills the felt-qualia of one's living interior or feeling soul.

Hence *qua* myth annuls any claim to pure epistemology and objectivity, even in science, because models of human knowledge by necessity contain their own mythic structure. Here the meaning-making powers of myth find their way into every conceivable venue in which we construct, explain, and experience the world. Because myth is always the expression of human imagination, and specifically unconscious fantasy, we may conceive of myth, like the dream, as a symptom of humanity. Myth communicates something to us and for us, hence it has a sense. Not only does it have a function, meaning, and purpose, it makes sense. In its essence, myth is a form of inner sense.[4]

Notes

1   Initiated in the 19th Century, and now in its 9th revised edition, Liddell and Scott's (1843) *Greek-English Lexicon* is generally considered among classicists to be the finest compilation to date of the classical works of antiquity where the etymological sources of ancient words derive and correspond to contemporary linguistics and modes of discourse. All references to μῦθος begin on p. 1151, Vol. 2.

2   See Anderson (2004, p. 61) for a discussion.

3   Eliade (1963) asserts that "the myth is regarded as a sacred story, and hence a 'true history,' because it always deals with *realities*. The cosmogonic myth is 'true' because the existence of the World is there to prove it; the myth of the origin of death is equally true because man's mortality proves it" (p. 6). Here we may say that Eliade is conflating myth with an actual portrayal of history and that such a portrayal conveys actual realities, which needs defined and demonstrated, hence proved. A myth may be true insofar as it is an artifact of culture, but it does not mean that it signifies a true reality apart from the experience of the subject or social collective. And just because the world exists does not make the myth real or true apart from the believer. The existence of the world does not remotely prove the reality of the myth other than it is an anthropological occasion or

psychological projection. Projections do not necessarily correspond to objective reality. And just because we are mortal and die, does not mean that a myth of the origins of death proves it any more than the biological fact that we cease to be, as any anatomist or mortician will tell you.

4 Earlier versions of this paper were given as a conference presentation under the title "Listening to the Other: On the Theory Versus Research Debate in Psychoanalysis" (Mills, 2019) and appeared later as "The Essence of Myth" (Mills, 2020).

References

Anderson, A.A. (2004). Mythos, logos, and telos: How to regain the love of wisdom. In A.A. Anderson, S.V. Hicks, & L. Witkowski (Eds.), *Mythos and Logos: How to Regain the Love of Wisdom*. Amsterdam: Rodopi.

Aristotle (1984). *Meteorology*. In J. Barnes (Ed.). *The Complete Works of Aristotle*. 2 Vols. (The revised Oxford trans.). Princeton, NJ: Princeton University Press, pp. 555–625.

Bergström, L. (1990). Explanation and interpretation of action. *International Studies in the Philosophy of Science*, 4(1): 3–15. DOI: 10.1080/026985 99008573342

Calder, B.J., & Tybout, A.M. (2016). What makes a good theory practical? *AMS Review*, 6: 116–124. DOI: 10.1007/s13162-016-0084-1

Chase, R. (1949). *Quest for Myth*. Baton Rouge: Louisiana State University Press.

Collingwood, R.G. (1946). *The Idea of History*. T.M. Knox (Ed.). New York: Oxford University Press.

Corley, K., & Gioia, D. (2011). Building theory about theory building: What constitutes a theoretical contribution? *Academy of Management Review*, 36: 12–32.

Dilthey, W. (1883/1923). *Introduction to the Human Sciences*. R.J. Betanzos (Trans.). Detroit: Wayne State University Press, 1979.

Eliade, M. (1963). *Myth and Reality*. New York: Harper & Row.

Estrada, M., & Schultz, P.W. (2017). The use of theory in applied social psychology. In A.P. Buunk, K. Keizer, L. Steg, & T. Rothengatter (Eds.), *Applied Social Psychology: Understanding and Managing Social Problems*, 2nd Ed. (pp. 27–51). Cambridge, UK: Cambridge University Press. DOI: 10.1017/9781107358430.002

Faye, J. (2011). Explanation and interpretation in the sciences of man. In D. Dieks, W. Gonzalez, S. Hartmann, T. Uebel, & M. Weber (Eds.), *Explanation, Prediction, and Confirmation: The Philosophy of Science in a European Perspective, Vol 2* (pp. 269–279). Dordrecht: Springer.

Feldman, B. & Richardson, R.D. (1972). *The Rise of Modern Mythology, 1680–1860*. Bloomington: Indiana University Press.

Gawronski, B., & Bodenhausen, G.V. (2015). Theory evaluation. In B. Gawronski & G.V. Bodenhausen (Eds.), *Theory and Explanation in Social Psychology* (pp. 3–23). New York, NY: Guilford Publications.

Geertz, C. (1973). *The Interpretation of Cultures*. New York: Basic Books.

Gibbs, J.P. (1990). The notion of theory in sociology. *National Journal of Sociology*, 4: 129–159.

Gieseler K., Loschelder D.D., & Friese M. (2019). What Makes for a good theory? How to evaluate a theory using the strength model of self-control as an example. In K. Sassenberg & M. Vliek (Eds.), *Social Psychology in Action*. Cham: Springer.

Heidegger, M. (1927). *Being and Time*. J. Macquarrie & E. Robinson (Trans.). San Francisco: Harper Collins, 1962.

Homer. (800 B.C.E.). *The Odyssey*. S. Butler (Trans). http://classics.mit.edu/Homer/odyssey.html

Homer. (800 B.C.E.). *The Iliad*. S. Butler (Trans). http://classics.mit.edu/Homer/iliad.html

Kuhn, T.S. (1974). Objectivity, value judgment, and theory choice. In T.S. Kuhn (Ed.), *The Essential Tension: Selected Studies in the Scientific Tradition and Change*. Chicago: University of Chicago Press, 1977.

Liddell, H.G. & Scott, R. (1843). *A Greek-English Lexicon*. 2 Vols. Oxford: Clarendon Press.

Lipton, P. (2004). *Inference to the Best Explanation*. London: Routledge.

Mills, J. (2020). The essence of myth. *Journal of Indian Council of Philosophical Research*, 37(2): 191–205. DOI: 10.1007/s40961-020-00198-3

Mills, J. (2019). Listening to the other: On the theory versus research debate in psychoanalysis. Paper presentation for panel: [Re]Claiming a Space for the Voice of Research in Psychoanalytic Discourse. Society for Psychoanalysis & Psychoanalytic Psychology. Division 39 of the *American Psychoanalytic Association*, Philadelphia, PA, April 5.

Mills, J. (2015). Psychoanalysis and the ideologies of science. *Psychoanalytic Inquiry*, 35: 24–44.

Mills, J. (2014). Truth. *Journal of the American Psychoanalytic Association*, 62(2): 267–293.

Mills, J. (2013). Freedom and determinism. *The Humanistic Psychologist*, 41(2): 101–118.

Plato (1961a). *Phaedo*. In E. Hamilton & H. Cairns (Eds.), *The Collected Dialogues of Plato*. Princeton: Princeton University Press, pp. 40–98.

Plato (1961b). *Republic*. In E. Hamilton & H. Cairns (Eds.), *The Collected Dialogues of Plato*. Princeton: Princeton University Press, pp. 575–844.

Popper, K.R. (1965). *Conjectures and Refutations: The Growth of Scientific Knowledge*. New York: Harper.

Ricoeur, P. (1981). *Hermeneutics and the Human Sciences*. In Thompson, J.B. (Trans. & Ed.). Cambridge: Cambridge University Press.

Ricoeur, P. (1971). What is a Text? Explanation and Interpretation. In D.M. Rasmussen (Ed.), *Mythic-Symbolic Language and Philosophical Anthropology* (pp. 135–150). Dordrecht: Springer.

Roubekas, N. & Ryba, T. (Eds.) (2020). *Explaining, Interpreting, and Theorizing Religion and Myth: Contributions in Honor of Robert A. Segal*. Netherlands: Brill.

Ryle, G. (1971). *Collected Papers*. 2 Vols. London: Hutchinson.

Segal, R.A. (2014a). Weber, Geertz, and Ricoeur on explanation and interpretation. *Bulletin for the Study of Religion*, 43(1): 25–33.

Segal, R.A. (2014b). Explanation and interpretation. In R.A. Jones (Ed.), *Jung and the Question of Science* (pp. 82–97.) London: Routledge.

Segal, R.A. (2009). Religion as ritual: Roy Rappaport's changing views from Pigs of the Ancestors (1968) to Ritual and Religion in the Making of Humanity (1999). In M. Stausberg (Ed.), *Contemporary Theories of Religion: A Critical Companion* (pp. 66–82). London: Routledge.

Segal, R.A. (2004). *Myth: A Very Short Introduction*. Oxford: Oxford University Press.

Segal, R.A. (1999). *Theorizing About Myth*. Amherst: University of Massachusetts Press.

Segal, R.A. (1992). *Explaining and Interpreting Religion*. New York: Lang.

Shalley, C.E. (2012). Writing good theory: Issues to consider. *Organizational Psychology Review*, 2(3): 258–264. DOI: 10.1177/2041386611436029

Van Lange, P.A.M. (2013). What we should expect from theories in social psychology: Truth, abstraction, progress, and applicability as standards (TAPAS). *Personality and Social Psychology Review*, 17: 40–55. DOI: 10.1177/1088868312453088

Weber, M. (1968). *Economy and Society, Vol. 1*. E. Fischoff (Trans.); G. Roth & C. Wittich (Eds.). New York: Bedminster Press.

Ye, H. & Stam, H. (2013). What is a good theory? A perspective from theoretical psychology. *Acta Psychologica Sinica*, 44: 133–137. DOI: 10.3724/SP.J.1041.2012.00133

Deconstructing Hermes: A Critique of the Hermeneutic and Phenomenological Turn in Psychoanalysis

In Plato's dialogue *Cratylus*, Socrates tells us that "Hermes has to do with speech, and signifies that he is the interpreter (ἑρμηνεύς), or messenger, or thief; or liar, or bargainer; all that sort of thing has a great deal to do with language ... he is the contriver of tales or speeches" (408-a-b), where "speech signifies all things" (408c). Here Plato inaugurates the role of language and speech through the act of interpretation as the usage of words and creation of meaning within the linguistic field. He also alludes to the inherently misleading, deceitful, and manipulative nature of words and the contortion of meaning, in which Hermes is "always turning them round and round" (408c). What is remarkable is that Plato prefigures 20th century continental philosophy by 2300 years. Hermes becomes our postmodern man, the inventor of language, the quintessential interpreter of meaning through the linguistic determination of thought and understanding.

Today hermeneutics is broadly classified as the analysis or process of interpretation and the possibility of its conditions. The general or systematic fabric of language, and the particular acts of interpretation, therefore generate the semiotic conditions or ground for the possibility of all understanding. This is the postmodern platform for the linguistic turn in philosophy spearheaded by many German and French hermeneutic traditions. Interpretation intervenes on the representation of its object, its relation to the object, and our relation(s) between our interpretations or commentaries and the object itself (Ormiston & Schrift, 1990). Here interpretation/interpretant as interjection is wed to context and takes as its object its own

DOI: 10.4324/9781003305958-10

participation as part of the aims, methods, and techniques of analysis. Hermeneutics therefore takes as its task and object the question of interpretation itself in an attempt to understand the discourse of others and the very condition or ground of discourse itself, leading Kristiva (1990) to conclude that hermeneutics is "a discourse on discourse, an interpretation of interpretation" (p. 99). Following Derrida (1974), interpretations are always instituting re-inscriptions of interpretations.

The proposition that "there are only interpretations of interpretations" leads to an inescapable circularity whereby each interpretation could be perennially begging its own question of what interpretation is really about, not to mention *what* interpretation is superior to others, contains more value, is more precise, definitive, or claritive, and so on, because it lacks a referent or criterion for which to anchor meaning. If we follow this proposition through to its logical end, this ultimately collapses into relativism because meaning is relative to its interpretive scheme, which further relies on other interpretative schemata for which there are no definitive definitions, conclusive consensus, or universal laws governing interpretation.[1]

In the very act of asserting an interpretive truth, or the condition of truth, we are engaged in the search of absolute ground, even when there is none to be found; and hence *all* conditions could be overturned with hermeneutic discourse—itself a condition of the ground of grounds. Yet this pursuit becomes a metaphysical enterprise, the quest for first principles. Hermeneutics conditions its own conditions and displaces its conditions in the same breath. If there are only interpretations of interpretations, then objective science is bankrupt because any discovery of the extant world would be solely subject to interpretation rather than accepted as uncontested fact.[2] In other words, if observable reality itself is merely an interpretation or construct, then there can be no facts apart from interpretation. Taken to the extreme, if everything is an interpretation, then there is no such thing as facts.[3]

But let us challenge this assumption for a moment. Is it merely an interpretive hypothesis that ordinary table salt contains oxidized sodium chloride? Although a mountain has various perspectives in shape and perceptual attributes, this does not annul the fact that it has a certain mass and size. Are there not certain analytic statements,

as opposed to synthetic statements, that are not, by definition, unquestionably true, such as "All bachelors are unmarried men," or
"A triangle has three sides?" Perhaps the hermeneutist would reply:
It is precisely through language that such definitions are possible
and form a consensus of agreement that necessarily requires linguistic
interpretation in order to make such statements meaningful to begin
with. Mathematicians and chemists have their own language just as
do other disciplines, where they provide certain interpretive truths
under the influence of grammatical relativism.

But when interpretations devolve into other interpretations, or
descend the deferral chain of linguistic signifiers into a combinatory
of indetermination as indiscriminate meaning, are we not headed
towards the abyss of infinite regress? Are we not arguing in a
circle—yet one contained? Both a one and a null—its inconclusive
openness and its end, hence its closure? For example, if we say: *this*
means *that*, then one can say, but that *really means* this, ad infinitum.
If every interpretation is based on another interpretation, then one
can never elude the circularity of interpretation.

We cannot ignore the potential problematics of the hermeneutic
turn, despite the fact that we all rely on interpretations to function in
the world. Unlike explanation, which sets as its task the function of
providing descriptions of events and their cause, interpretation conveys and confers meaning.[4] Interpretation mediates between object
and meaning, but it can equally obfuscate our understanding, especially our experience of interpretation. When one raises the question
of interpretation and its conditions, that is, the possibility of interpretation, the question itself is already circumscribed and refractory,
leading Foucault (1990) to observe that interpretation must always
"interpret itself" for it "cannot fail to return to itself" (pp. 59, 67),
hence undermining its own conditions and claims to truth.
Furthermore, because we mediate, translate, and impose interpretations in accord with our dissimilar and competing desires, intentions,
and personal agendas, we may observe Gadamer's (1960) insight that
all methodologies of discourse are potentially laced with prejudice.

Frank Summers (2008) makes the claim that "the very nature of
psychoanalysis is hermeneutic" because it is an activity engaged in
"understanding people" (p. 422). This definition by necessity
would make any discipline hermeneutic by virtue of the fact that

understanding is an intersubjective enterprise whereby the presence of others are internalized and mediated through self-relation and language, which gives rise to interpretation, understanding, and knowledge even if the scientific object in question is not a human being.[5] But the distinction he wants to emphasize is between psychoanalysis as intrinsically engaged in understanding human subjectivity versus the natural world, the former requiring interpretation, the later observation. Summers (2004) sees hermeneutics as particularly attractive because it leans towards a human science model where the main goal of analysis is to explain human motivation and uncover meaning, rather than take an observational stance concerned with discovering relationships among observable facts (see Ricoeur, 1970), which privileges an objectivist criterion. He concludes: "Psychoanalysis is a paradigmatic hermeneutic science because its target is the meaning of experience" (p. 123). Following Dilthey, Husserl, Heidegger, Ricoeur, Gadamer, and others, which he tends to lump together under one umbrella, psychoanalytic inquiry is first and foremost concerned with the experiential subject whereby human experience should be the primary object of investigation "as *opposed* to nature," which is the subject matter of the natural sciences (p. 123, italics added).

I would argue that it is not necessary to create a binary between experience and nature, for clearly human beings are part of nature and inclusive of anything we classify as natural or belonging to the natural world—namely, that which is *given*. Just as surely as we are embodied organic beings where we come to take our own nature as its object (i.e., the realm of self-consciousness as metarepresentation), we need not negate human experience as a natural phenomenon, nor contribute to the hegemony that science constructs in its insistence on the superiority of observation, fact, experimentation, and measurement as opposed to meaning analysis. Although Summers wants to champion hermeneutics as a science, "the methods of which involve rules of interpretation, not observations or their manipulations" (p. 123), I believe it is not possible to ontically separate the two human activities because observation and interpretation are co-extensive-simultaneous facets of mental activity, whether they apply to systematic/semantic rules of interpretation or observational/empirical procedures. And psychoanalytic method necessarily requires observation in order to offer interpretations that convey meaning and understanding. We observe by listening, hence focusing on the nuances of the speech act, pointing out patterns and inconsistencies with attention to inter-relationships and their correspondent inner-relations between thought, feeling, and fantasy, all of which are illuminated through mutual dialogue that aims towards meaning construction.

Equally, "meaning" and "motivation" are not merely "uncovered" or "discovered," which contrarily to Summer's thesis, invokes a natural science paradigm of acquiring knowledge and understanding through engagement with the external world where facts are to be accumulated and catalogued. Rather, there is a simultaneous process of creating the found world, to re-appropriate Winnicott, whereby there is a contiguous procreativity or generative production belonging to and instituted by the agentic ego. This generative creativity is co-extensive with the act of discovering psychic data or unraveling truth (*aletheia*) as unconcealment or disclosedness, namely, that which appears as phenomena (φαινόμενον). Here human experience becomes an overdetermined quest for the desire to know and understand the found given, as well as agentically create, construct, and shape meaning via human dialogue.

It was Dilthy (1883) who proposed the distinction between the human sciences based upon investigating and understanding the motivations and meanings inherent to the experiential subject or human being versus that of the natural sciences, which is concerned with the impersonal forces and organizations of nature. While the *Geisteswissenschaften* focus on the science of mental processes and social systems within a class of human events, the *Naturwissenschafhten* focus on the domain of the natural world. Therefore, the bifurcation that is often forged between the human and natural sciences takes as its premise that nature and human experience are mutually exclusive categories. However, the distinction lies in the methodology each discipline employs.

The subject matter within a human science model is that of the experiential subject and collective social life contextualized within a genus of human events, while impersonal aspects of the physical world are not typically part of its scope or locus. Hence, because human sciences are interpretive and target the meaning of experience, by definition they become hermeneutic. Because psychoanalysis is necessarily predicated on human speech and language, and involves the pursuit of understanding human motivation and constructing meaning through interpretive intersubjective exchange, it may be considered a hermeneutic science.

For Dilthy and others, interpretation or *Verstehen* becomes a method for investigating and understanding the human sciences; however, this is not devoid of certain problems especially when rules or criteria for understanding may become nebulous. Here it can be argued that hermeneutics never fully escapes the charge of slipping into relativism or recalcitrant subjectivism, given that, following certain rules of discourse versus what someone "really meant," can easily be two different things. Likewise, exegetical interpretation of a text or deconstructive praxis, and the application of that interpretation, may readily transform or alter it from its original meaning or purpose. In other words, the very act of translation itself institutes reinterpretations of interpretations that can potentially spin on in circularity or regress to a point that meaning is foreclosed from its original signification.

How can hermeneutics escape the charge of circularity, infinite regress, negation of universals, its tacit relativism, and the failure to provide a consensus or criteria for interpretation? How is psychoanalysis able to philosophically justify interpretative truth claims when they potentially inhere to a recalcitrant subjectivism while claiming to be objectively valuative?

Despite the ubiquity and centrality interpretation plays within the psychoanalytic edifice, and the unequivocal significance the hermeneutical turn has had on our field, we are left with the conundrum of explaining how interpretation follows a logic that attempts to offer a compelling case for meaning construction based upon a stylized (contexual), particularized (individual) method that purports to follow an objective (replicable) pattern of analysing human experience, while at the same time eluding any concrete (universal) criteria on which to judge its epistemological foundation and efficacy.

In response to the historical tensions and pitfalls associated with the science versus hermeneutic debate in psychoanalysis, Marilyn Nissim-Sabat (2009) offers an appealing and cogent series of arguments for adopting Husserlian phenomenology as the foundation of a new psychoanalytic science that displaces the positivism of a natural science framework and the potential relativism and subjectivism inherent in a purely hermeneutical approach to psychoanalytic inquiry. Given that contemporary psychoanalysis has largely adopted the postmodern turn and has found many traditions within continental philosophy appealing for rethinking psychoanalytic theory, it is surprising that phenomenology has not been given more attention. Nissim-Sabat fills that gap and provides the first sustained argument for why the field should adopt a Husserlean perspective.

Although proponents of phenomenology are diverse in theoretical scope and focus, and are by no means homogenous, phenomenology may be said to be first and foremost concerned with the process of experience and how phenomena are disclosed and appear to the human subject via an analysis and description of consciousness. Husserl in particular, and phenomenologists in general, typically admit to a radical difference between the "natural" and "philosophical" attitudes, the latter challenging scientific epistemology. While natural science makes metaphysical assumptions about how things really are in themselves, including discovering objective laws and unchanging "truth," phenomenology suspends its ontological commitments in favour of an epistemological stance that takes concrete human subjectivity and experience as the proper objects of science. For Husserl, this is accomplished by a radical repositioning of our methodological practices that does not privilege the natural science attitude, but rather displaces such an attitude through a purely formal investigation into the structures and disclosedness of subjectivity. Rather than assume the existence of natural objects independent of consciousness, Husserl, following Kant and the German Idealists, focuses on how meanings and their relations, rather than things, are constituted via transcendental subjectivity. Unlike the natural scientific attitude that avouches an unadulterated realism that can be observed and measured, the phenomenological subject is never dislocated from its object of study and hence can only make interpretations and convey meaning through its own relations as immediately experienced in the life-world (*Lebenswelt*). Here there is no distinction or separation of subject from object, for this contrast is united.

Although there is a complicated set of relationships between science and philosophy, Husserl advocates for a foundational role phenomenology plays in the constitution of any science, indeed, in the possibility for there to be any science at all, including psychoanalysis. In order to achieve its task, this requires philosophy to perform a certain reduction or act of withdrawal from the usual assertions we make about what exists or does not exist in the world. The result of this reduction, suspension of judgement, or bracketing is to reveal the world as a correlate of consciousness. In fact, it is just such a reduction or ἐποχή (*epoché*) that makes phenomenology a descriptive science, the science of pure consciousness as such. In what follows, I will briefly discuss the implications of the phenomenological notion of pure consciousness vis-à-vis the psychoanalytic notion of the unconscious.

Nissim-Sabat carefully prepares her arguments by pointing out the precariousness of naturalism, as well as the advantages of phenomenology over hermeneutics. According to Nissim-Sabat, the natural science attitude is full of unwarranted presuppositions about what is real, objective, universal, absolute, unchanging, and causally deterministic, which ultimately devolves into the bane of material reduction. I particularly find instructive her categorization of scientism as adhering to (a) positivism and naturalism, where science is seen as the only source of knowledge; (b) belief in a mechanistic "billiard-ball model" of causation following fixed universal laws; (c) affirmation that material and efficient ontological explanations are a sufficient condition for understanding process and reality, hence privileging (d) realism and (e) a correspondence theory of truth, which ultimately have their substance and existence in matter; and the belief that (f) one can have objective knowledge about the world independent of subjectivity or consciousness (p. 44). Although one may object to her broad generalizations to science in general, and Freudian psychoanalysis in particular, she very eloquently shows how these attitudes have formed an inedible foothold in the theoretical corpus that underlies scientism and naturalized views of epistemology, and that this furthermore prejudices science in its various investigations and methodologies.

Equally interesting is her analysis of hermeneutics, which is frequently associated with a phenomenological perspective, and has been welcomed by many contemporary psychoanalytic theorists.

Despite the fact that hermeneutics collapses the subject-object divide, sees subjectivity as necessary to all interpretations, and generally holds an anti-scientific posture, Nissim-Sabat argues that it is ultimately subject to relativism because of its disavowal of universals, and hence the rejection of the possibility of any scientific law governing interpretation. Another reason, I must reiterate, is that hermeneutics lacks a methodological criterion for which interpretation and meaning are construed and conveyed; hence it cannot escape the circularity of potentially collapsing into a radical subjectivism—or even worse, egoism—where interpretation gives way to subjective caprice guided by self-gratification. Here, she argues, a phenomenological science becomes a more palatable alternative that insulates psychoanalysis from positivism and relativism.[6]

By dismissing the natural science standpoint, or rather, scientism, natural science's own self-misinterpretation, Nissim-Sabat is also able to reconfigure and reincorporate the hermeneutic tradition within a proper phenomenological attitude that governs our sensibilities regarding interpretive theory and practice. Our object of concern should be the lifeworld and all its variations, which is revealed to consciousness through the phenomenological reduction, hence the systematic bracketing or voluntary suspension of all ontological commitments. This disciplined suspension promises to disclose the psychic field of subjectivity "as a self-sufficient sphere, and thus as a proper object of scientific investigation" (p. 63). By reconceiving psychoanalysis as a nonnatural science that places the realm of the psychic as the proper core of psychoanalytic investigations, she hopes to open up an attractive space for psychoanalysis to flourish as a philosophical science of subjectivity.

But in the end, does phenomenology pose its own set of incompatibilities when by definition it centres on the question and structure of subjectivity qua consciousness? Can it provide any clearer window into the processes and components of interpretation when its proper object of study is human consciousness rather than unconscious phenomenology? And does this not pose a new set of limitations when the phenomenological method is supposed to bracket or suspend all ontological commitments, which ultimately applies to our collective belief in the ontology of the unconscious? Here psychoanalysis is no further ahead.

What would the adoption of the phenomenological method entail for psychoanalysis? First of all, we would have to set aside our theoretical biases and intellectual prejudices about our preferred orientations and simply observe mental phenomena as it shines forth or appears. I could envision a technical process where this would be instructive and even complementary to the free associative method, however, it would be very challenging for most of us to set aside our preferred conceptual frameworks, let alone our ontological worldviews that we import into every subjective act of experiencing. But following the spirit of phenomenology, is this not what science should aspire towards when it makes its observations, engages in data collection, and performs statistical analyses? Is it not supposed to be neutral, precise, and unburdened by theoretic bias when observing and classifying phenomena? Are there really any procedural differences between the two methodologies if they are both based on explicating observable phenomena as they appear to consciousness?

But if we adopt the phenomenological stance, what becomes of ontology? When asked to suspend all ontological commitments, is Nissim-Sabat asking us to do something that we are incapable of doing (at least from a practical standpoint) by virtue of the fact that every human action is prefaced and premised on ontological assumptions we import (especially unconsciously) in our subjective engagement with the world and reality? Here she would say "no," because she is merely advocating for the *suspension of judgements* regarding the ultimate ontology of the world, not that there is a denial of Being per se; only that, following Kant, the ultimate nature of the world is in itself unknowable. In fact, she argues, the phenomenological attitude is what is needed in any viable theory and method of scientificity.

If psychoanalysis does adopt Husserl's phenomenological method, will it have to abandon the belief in an unconscious ontology, and unconscious processes in general, like the ubiquity of transference and defense, which are the historical pillars of psychoanalytic knowledge? Does Husserl (1950) himself make certain ontological commitments when he avers the existence of a transcendental ego that pre-reflectively performs the acts of *epoché* as analysis of subjectivity qua subjectivity, something Sartre (1957) outright rejected? Does Husserl's system (like Sartre's) by necessity reject *in toto* the notion of unconscious operations, or can unconscious mentation be explained within the structures of subjectivity? If, by definition, phenomenology is a science of consciousness, this would seem to eclipse any possibility of apprehending or knowing unconscious activity because it is not accessible to conscious experience; and even if it was, it would betray the phenomenological attitude by positing ontological processes beneath (or behind) the veil of consciousness.

But is there any possibility of observing subjectivity that could be conceived as the manifestation or instantiation of unconscious structure? Can we save Husserl from his own contradictions? Husserl (2001) barely mentions the unconscious in his writings; however, a cryptic feature of his analysis of the ego entails what he refers to as "passive synthesis" or "passive constitution," which explains the formal mediating and unifying operations of the transcendental ego, what I have called an agentic unconscious ego-organization responsible for all productions of consciousness (Mills, 2010). Although he did not adequately emphasize passive synthesis as the domain of the unconscious, here we may not inappropriately extend Husserl's method to a proper study of unconscious phenomenology.

Notes

1 One may argue that relativism is necessary since interpretation can only take place within a historical context that relativizes it. I prefer to distinguish the notion of perspectivism from relativism, the former allowing for historical contextualism as well as qualitative variances in subjective experience, while the latter denotes the philosophical doctrine that there are no universal truths or intrinsic characteristics about the world, only different ways of interpreting it.

2 Although science requires interpretation to arrive at understanding and knowledge, it is primarily wed to an objectivist epistemology that would resist hermeneutic constructions of the subject. But because science is not estranged from subjectivity, or more precisely, the individual scientists (subjects) studying the external world (objects), the cognitive processes underlying subjectivity qua mentation must necessarily impose interpretations on objects of study; and in this way the subject-object divide is suspended. In other words, if we were to examine the individual personalities of each scientist or *any* theorist, we would not only conclude that their peculiar subjectivities inform their scientific theories, but structures of subjectivity necessarily participate within universal conditions that make objectivity possible; and this becomes a ground or condition for the possibility of science itself. This is why Husserl (1950) advocates for a foundational

role phenomenology plays in the constitution of any science, indeed, in the possibility for there to be any science at all, including psychoanalysis.

When universal cognitive processes that comprise the generic structure of subjectivity (including all its unconscious permutations) become the focus of intellectual investigation, the subject becomes an object of science. And when the object is viewed as an independent microcosm that radically betrays universal classifications due to self-articulation and stylized particularity based on creative self-definition belonging to the existential agent, the individual ceases to be merely an object. Yet each determination requires procedures of interpretation, what we may traditionally attribute to the field of hermeneutics.

When the question of psychoanalysis as a science versus a hermeneutic discipline is raised, this very question presupposes an incommensurate dichotomy, and hence reinforces a hegemony whereby each side of difference attempts to exert self-importance over the other; when both have failed to observe the dialectic that conjoins such differences within a mediatory process that attempts a sublation (*Aufhebung*) or integrative holism between the two polarities. If psychoanalysis is to achieve some form of consiliatory paradigm, it must be willing to attempt to explain its activities on multiple plains of discourse with sound methodological coherence. Here I am not concerned so much with a dialectical synthesis of the oppositions of science and hermeneutics as I am concerned about preserving the two methodologies and modes of discourse that have legitimacy within their own frames of reference and perspective purposes.

3 We may very well conclude that there are no facts apart from interpretation because our epistemological justifications rest on our cognitive capacities to form judgements about any object in question. We are conditioned to interpret since childhood according to our cultural context and the internalization of others' interpretive schemata, which have been historically and consensually validated.

4 It may be argued that any explanation of events—especially human actions—necessarily requires interpretation, particularly when making claims about facts and their causal connections, which are sensitive to context. In this way any explanation evokes an act of making something intelligible or understandable.

5 Here I am reminded that for Lacan, what is primary is not the individual, but the Other, that is, the symbolic and social functions imbedded within the subject. And for Lacan, the subject is always the subject of the unconscious, and the unconscious is always the Other's discourse. There is always another voice speaking in the patient, a metapsychology of internalized culture, the ontology of symbolic meaning and demand instituted through speech and desire. This is what the Lacanian analyst listens for.

6 Perhaps Nissim-Sabat is taking too much liberty in separating phenomenology from hermeneutics, for they may be viewed as complementary rather than antithetical. If hermeneutics is more interpretive than descriptive, phenomenology is more descriptive than interpretive: it becomes a matter of emphasis rather than difference.

References

Derrida, J. (1974). *Of Grammatology*. G.C. Spivak (Trans.). Baltimore: John Hopkins University Press.

Dilthy, W. (1883). *Introduction to the Human Sciences*. R.J. Betanzos (Trans.) Detroit: Wayne State University Press, 1923.

Foucault, M. (1990). Nietzsche, Freud, Marx. In G.L. Ormiston & A.D. Schrift (Eds.), *Transforming the Hermeneutic Context: From Nietzsche to Nancy*. Albany: SUNY Press, 59–67.

Gadamer, H-G. (1960). *Truth and Method*. 2nd Ed. New York: Crossroad, 1989.

Husserl, E. (1950). *Cartesian Meditations: An Introduction to Phenomenology*. D. Cairns (Trans.). Dordrecht: Kluwer.

Husserl, E. (2001). *Analyses Concerning Passive and Active Synthesis: Lectures on Transcendental Logic*. A.J. Steinbock (Trans.). Netherlands: Springer.

Kristiva, J. (1990). Psychoanalysis and the Polis. In G.L. Ormiston & A.D. Schrift (Eds.), *Transforming the Hermeneutic Context: From Nietzsche to Nancy*. Albany: SUNY Press.

Mills, Jon (2010). *Origins: On the Genesis of Psychic Reality*. Montreal: McGill-Queens University Press.

Nissim-Sabat, M. (2009). *Neither Victim Nor Survivor: Thinking Toward a New Humanity*. Lanham, MD: Lexington Books/Rowman & Littlefield Publishers.

Ormiston, G.L., & Schrift, A.D. (Eds.) (1990). *The Hermeneutic Tradition: From Ast to Ricoeur*. Albany: SUNY Press.

Plato. (1961). *Cratylus*. In E. Hamilton & H. Cairns (Eds), *The Collected Dialogues of Plato*. Princeton: Princeton University Press.

Ricoeur, P. (1970). *Freud and Philosophy*. New Haven: Yale University Press.

Sartre, J.P. (1957). *The Transcendence of the Ego*. F. Williams & R. Kirpatrick (Trans.). New York: Noonday Press.

Summers, F. (2004). The Epistemological Basis for Psychoanalytic Knowledge: A Third Way. In J. Reppen, J. Tucker, & M.A. Schulman (Eds.), *Way Beyond Freud: Postmodern Psychoanalysis Observed*. London: Open Gate, pp. 113–131.

Summers, F. (2008). Theoretical Insularity and the Crisis of Psychoanalysis. *Psychoanalytic Psychology*, 25(3), 413–424.

Chapter 11

Psychoanalysis and the Ideologies of Science

The question and status of psychoanalysis as a legitimate science has been a grave source of controversy. Although Freud (1940, p. 282) insisted that psychoanalysis is a natural science, it has been lambasted on the grounds that it fails to qualify as science (Grünbaum, 1984; Cioffi, 1998) despite the fact that the scientific credibility of psychoanalysis has been empirically investigated since its inception (Fisher & Greenberg, 1977, 1996). Within psychoanalytic research circles, however, there has been an increasing movement to legitimize, revise, and improve psychoanalytic theory and practice through empirical investigations in developmental psychology, clinical psychopathology, attachment processes, cognitive neuroscience, infant observation research, affect theory, defense mechanism research, and therapeutic technique (Bucci, 1997; Cramer, 2006; Fonagy, Gergely, Jurist, & Target, 2002; Luborsky & Crits-Christoph, 1998; Masling & Bornstein, 1996; Mills, 2005c; Shedler, 2010; Shore, 1994; Solms & Turnbull, 2002; Stern, 1985; Wallerstein, 1989; Westen, 1998, 1999). Of course this is good for psychoanalysis as a discipline, especially politically, as it spars with other popular clinical approaches boasting treatment efficacy (e.g., CBT). But in all its apologetics, psychoanalysis has a reason to be worried: it has not kept up with the times. Perhaps this is reflective of its self-aggrandizing nature due to its historical privilege as a major intellectual contribution to the humanities. Now it has to work harder to bake bread. Society wants proof—Where's the beef? Do we go belly-up or join the game? We can no longer afford to resist assimilation into the mainstream if we want to compete for scientific and public respect, which ultimately

DOI: 10.4324/9781003305958-11

effects funding allocations and remuneration from third-party payers, as well as patients' access to extended-health reimbursements.

For all practical reasons, if psychoanalysis does not attempt an aggressive comeback by demonstrating its tangible value, it faces a continual litany of objections from insurance companies, underwriters, and actuaries who operate from a mathematical bottom-line mentality expecting quick and concrete results, which can ultimately determine the financial fate of the profession in America. Some have gone so far as to predict the death of psychoanalysis if it does not adopt a scientific framework as the fulcrum of its activities (Bornstein, 2001). Although there are some proponents of psychoanalysis who are anti-empirical by disposition (Blass & Carmeli, 2007; Hoffman, 2009), instead opting for more clinical, philosophical, and hermeneutic approaches to theory and practice (Mills, 2002a), the field may be said to be splintered between those who value (a) therapeutic work and clinical theory; (b) rigorous empirical systematization; and those who are primarily concerned with (c) theoretical and applied psychoanalysis.

In the "spirit of true science," Patrick Luyten (2015) has recently challenged the field to think critically about several "unholy questions" of psychoanalysis that, he argues, does not live up to empirical scrutiny, namely: (a) the theoretical language of psychoanalysis; (b) treatment, technique, and training; (c) theories of development; (d) attachment and object relations models; and (e) the nature of explanation in psychoanalysis. I will address most of his concerns in turn, which all hinge on the accusation that these five central tenets have not been empirically verified, hence are in need of rectification. But before I do so, I would like to play devil's advocate. I realize that psychoanalytic researchers are concerned about the future state of psychoanalysis and wish to improve its scientific viability. These are noble intentions and worthwhile pursuits. And this is unequivocally good for the profession. Yet the virtues and drawbacks of the conceptual foundations governing the philosophy of science have a long ideological basis that are at times fundamentally opposed and antagonistic towards axiomatic principles inherent to many disciplines in the humanities. It is from this perspective that I shall give voice to traditional criticisms of nomothetic approaches to scientific explanation, positivism, and the scientistic worldview that purports only the empirical method can produce credible theories of truth, replication, and knowledge. Here I wish to offer counterarguments in the true spirit of philosophy that have historically challenged dominant views on scientific paradigms. In doing so, I neither intend to disparage psychoanalytic researchers nor devalue their aims, only to expose certain philosophical concerns that have direct bearing on their explanatory models. In offering this critique, I hope there may emerge a simpatico between psychoanalytic science and the philosophical parameters that inform future research.

Luyten's criticisms fundamentally rest on several assumptions about science as a privileged discourse and superior methodology that the field of psychoanalysis should adopt wholeheartedly and to its betterment; yet I argue this presupposition is inherently problematic and reflective of the ideologies of science as a master discourse. The force of this discourse is built upon a fantasized objectivist epistemology and reductionist framework that is far removed from the human condition and the experiential subject that belies the biases of scientific explanation, which is inferential and speculative at best. Contra Luyten, I will attempt to demonstrate that science lacks true explanation as it artificially reduces the human being to simplistic, naïve theories of parsimony that carry dogmatic ontological assertions about mind, human nature, and behaviour. Such reductive paradigms further ignore the role of theoretics and subjectivity that by definition saturate any empirical method, and hence color its results; not to mention import an inflated valuation of the alleged virtue of empiricism itself, which may be viewed as a supercilious and officious imposition on the human sciences in general.

Science as Master Discourse

Science is a dominant discourse, a discourse of power. It holds a certain sway over mass culture as a master discourse that successfully inculcates (both consciously and unconsciously) the general prosaic belief that it alone holds the touchstone to truth. Here it is often thought that all other disciplines are inferior to science. Although it has propitious advantages in many fields and in contributing to proper domains of knowledge, its hegemony overshadows competing viewpoints and methodologies that enjoy legitimacy in their own right, which may be either compatible with or antagonistic to a scientific *Weltanschauung* depending upon what discipline one consults. Although science facilitates our general understanding of the world, hence allowing us to see and appreciate aspects of reality that fall under its purview, it may also hinder and occlude other inquiries and disclosures that equally contribute to human knowledge. But as a dominant institution, it continually presents the appearance of precision, fastidiousness, reliability, and certainty, when such appearances are in fact political reiterations of a master hegemonic discourse designed to retain power and influence over masses and their economic resources.

Science is held in high esteem by society because it follows a special procedure that often proves to be of merit in furthering the knowledge industry. No sane individual can disparage science for its monumental contributions in improving the human condition: from medicine to technology we enjoy a better existence. When something is given the label "scientific," it tacitly carries with it a stamp of approval based on claims that are particularly well-founded or undisputed, hence offering a privileged stance based on its methodologies. But we may readily question the basis of such authority when we closely inspect what science is actually doing. To begin with, not all scientific endeavours are the same, nor should we assume certain fields fall under the rubric of science even if they identify themselves as such. In politics and practice, certain specialities within the sciences may be adjudicated to be pseudoscientific when their methodologies are carefully examined. Here context is everything. There is partisan infighting in the scientific sector just as there are hierarchical bodies that determine the scope of research projects that should be funded, departmental allocations of resources, and scholarly activities that are deemed "truly scientific" and worthy of support. Science is the gold seal securing economic backing and is therefore the dominant currency regulating most forms of commerce.

Although methodologies vary from discipline to discipline, what is not often said is that all domains of science rely on inductivism, speculation and probability, are theory-dependent, subject to anthropic selection bias, and are susceptible to observational discrepancies in perception, measurement, and calculation based on the nature of the examiner's subjectivity (Chalmers, 1982). Hypothesis testing presupposes theory, as does observation, experiment, and method construction under applications of relativism that suit the particular self-interests and dispositions of researchers. Observation selection effects are well documented in science (Bostrom, 2002), which are subject to biases in sampling techniques, limitations in measuring devises, self-sampling assumptions, methodological pre-scriptions, fallibility of falsification criteria, epistemic uncertainty, and anthropic reasoning that may contaminate data collection and the objectivity of investigative evidence. In fact, a fundamental me-taphysical assumption that underlies science is the belief in a mind-independent world where we can discover, measure, and deduce fundamental physical laws that can then be generalized to all objects in its class, when this assumption begs the question of realism. This hegemonic stance becomes intractable when the subject-object divide institutes firm boundaries between the physical universe on the one hand, which is said to exist independent of all observers, and the human psyche on the other; especially when our apprehension of the external manifold is dependent upon the subjective contingent nature of observation. Scientific realism furthermore presupposes a correspondence theory of truth, where a pure factual world is predicated to exist as objective, actual, and enduring, yet all experi-ence and knowledge is necessarily mediated by mind. A more basic philosophical problem with this argument is the epistemological difficulty of claiming that anything actually exists corresponding to what we think or observe.

As a self-legitimizing discourse, science is keen to indoctrinate other disciplines into its own preferred mode of thinking by perpe-tuating power differentials to the degree that it has become a system of ideologies, the one who is supposed to know—the Big Other. This hegemonic symbolic matrix we call "science," often thought of as "pure" knowledge, is in fact a cacophony of guesses we call "experiments" in chase of knowledge, something it has no possession of until it is encountered *or* manufactured, then passed-off as truth corresponding to an objective reality.[1] Of course this is not how science truly functions, which is very limited in its scope and ability to offer generalized explanations, but its mystique and illusory promise of offering ultimate answers to metaphysical questions maintains a stronghold over human consciousness, especially when offering causal attributions, hence insinuating—This is the way things really are! Because the very word carries the semiotic equivalence of knowledge and authority, this means that the institution of science is simultaneously a political enterprise where systems of abstract thought are manipulated, systematized, and applied to public matters in such a way as to become a master discourse affecting the intellectual, political, and economic constraints of a given society. Here the ideologies of science have infiltrated the world, which may be said to have an unconscious grip over the very way we approach the question of knowledge.

Let's start with basics: What exactly do we mean by science? Historically, the term signifies knowledge acquired through experience (< Lat. *scientia*, from *scire*, to know). Contemporarily, it refers to the observation, identification, description, empirical investigation, and theoretical explanation of natural phenomena derived through experimental measures. We tend to use the term in a pedestrian fashion to signify a disclosure or truism about the natural world as a discovered *fact*, but this hardly happens in the behavioural and social sciences, which is the proper domain of both psychoanalysis and empirical psychology. Like any discourse, we need to define our parameters. Within psychology, human experience is not studied as it purely happens, such as in phenomenology; rather it is dislocated, redefined, and reframed from the vantage point of a contrived method and conceptual framework conducive to the imposed needs of the so-called scientist as the one who supposedly knows. This convention is superimposed *ex cathedra* on the object or issue in question simply because academic, industry, or corporate (political) custom has historically sanctioned this preferred discourse that continues to dominate majority opinion conditioning public sensibility. When mass world discourse is dictated by the language of science, it is understandable that psychology would not want to be left out of the fold. Will divine truth be illuminated by holy science? Or is this a psychomythology born/e of social convention designed (sometimes with great hubris) to appease our anxiety to know by offering "hypotheses" disguised as truth, which continue to subjugate the masses to ideology? Yet this propaganda inevitably comes up short, for science is always changing its mind, hence shifting the strictures of what it claims to know.

Today science is arguably equivalent to religion as a master discourse, which has equally put a spell over uncritical thinking members of society in desperate need of easy answers and quick cures. As such, the populace has been conditioned like dogs to accept whatever is spoon-fed to them as truth, whether it be a new medication, a fad in technology, or an insurer ready to financially support a particular service, pill, or product over another simply because it has the requisite stamp of "scientific" approval. Here we may observe an entrenched unconscious subjugation of reason, for much of society heedlessly trusts in anonymous authority under the stranglehold of scientific patriarchy.

Although science (in espousing naturalism) is grounded in empirical methodology, observation, measurement, verification, falsification, and replication, it employs explanatory models relevant only to specified research across a whole host of disparate domains. The nuanced methodologies in the natural sciences, such as in experimental particle physics or biochemistry, are vastly different than ones employed in the social and behavioural sciences; yet we often have a tendency to view *all* disciplines that identify themselves as "scientific" to be equivalent in scope and explanatory power, when this is not the case. In fact, there is a pecking order in the scientific community where "true" or pure experimental methods and observation inherent in naturalized approaches may devolve into manufactured situations that have nothing to do with the natural phenomena in question. Here it becomes rather easy to reconfigure "nature," where mathematical models create statistical manipulations that derive statistically significant results rather than actually contributing anything to our understanding of the phenomenon in question.[2] This is much of empirical research today in behavioural science: it advances trite (if not worthless) hypotheses and theses about the human condition based on inference, speculation, and the pet theories of researchers—not on deduction or indisputable states of affairs; and then creates an artificially controlled set of variables that extract the true subject from its subject matter.[3] This fabricated approach dislocates the complexity that actually comprises the research subject in question by reducing it to artificial principles, which it statistically analyses to get the magic numbers it can then generalize to all subjects in its class, proclaiming all along it corresponds to an objective realism. Here lies the ideology of scientism: we may only have "pure" knowledge through the scientific method.

In reality, research presents its own versions of truth as a circumscribed discourse or talk (ἀπόφαυσις), nothing more. The broader discourse of *logos* (λόγος) far exceeds the scientific method by virtue of the fact that science (by its own definition and kerbing scope of inquiry) may only offer a window into a particular slice of truth it has carved off by the delimitations generated through its own methodology. A perfect example of this is how a social or behavioural researcher "controls" for "variables" by creating a false environment—one completely removed from the real world, where all the variances that compose human reality are arbitrarily removed, hence extracted or displaced from the pure phenomenon in question, and reduced to a simplified paradigm that is said to represent such reality. All results merely point towards conclusions culled from the limited parameters of the manufactured research project itself, not the real object(s) it attempts to study. Here behavioural science is destined to remain self-alienated and isolated through its very method from studying the complex holism that comprises the human situation. In the end there is analysis of "data" selectively extricated from the whole rather than a comprehensive unifying analysis of the whole itself. In more metaphorical language, we get snapshots enclosed by frames, but never the whole picture itself. This is the royal scam: pretend and promise objective truth culled through "experimentation, data collection, and results" (that are statistically manipulated to get desired outcomes) as a general procedure that is then generalized to universal situations and outcomes, and because the public is "ignorant" of the language games and illegitimacy of making such hasty generalizations, the lingo of science pulls the wool over the masses under a transference unto authority.

The Languages of Psychoanalysis

Luyten (2015) begins his critique of psychoanalysis with a false scenario when he claims that the field shies away from asking tough questions of itself and fails to embrace novelty and change. There are a few of us in recent times who have embraced internal critique as a way of advancing the specialty (Eagle, 2003; Eagle,

Wolitzky, & Wakefield, 2001; Masling, 2003; Mills, 2005a,b, 2012, 2014; Summers, 2008), and the relational movement is a recent good example of introducing theoretical and technical reform; but I must agree with Luyten that critique often breaks a taboo inherent in our professional culture to the degree that psychoanalysis largely comprises an assemblage of factions holding onto their preferred theoretical customs. But he soon compares our discipline to the natural sciences such as biology, which is a category mistake, and claims that the core ideas of psychoanalysis have a "shaky conceptual and empirical foundation." His main point is that in order to be progressive, such theories should be replaced by new and more comprehensive models aided by science. This of course begs the question of what it means to be progressive and comprehensive, of which many analytic traditions would claim they are.

Luyten accuses psychoanalysis of employing metapsychological concepts that are "hindering the advance" of the field due to their "descriptive, rather than explanatory, nature" (p. 7). But nowhere does he define what he means by *description* versus *explanation*. While he does give examples from evolutionary biology through discourse on genetic and neuronal reduction, which I will comment upon shortly, he does not delineate his premises. Through a meandering series of straw man arguments, where he positions psychoanalytic concepts in such a manipulative way as to attack their validity, his conclusion is that psychoanalytic theories "are often sophisticated, metaphorical and circular descriptions rather than *true* explanations" (italics added). Here he imports the notion of truth, as though science has the proper explanatory answer. Once again, without defining his terms, he immediately jumps to accusations that psychoanalysis— and he is painting with a broad brush—fails to demonstrate a "*causal link*" between theory and actuality, thereby declaring, "analysts have explained nothing" (p. 7). Here Luyten reveals his cryptic agenda: science offers causal explanations, while theoretics are fanciful, linguistic narratives that have little to do with "why or how" things really happen.

It is important for us to define the nature of description versus explanation, as this invented binary seems to be important enough to Luyten to use it as a rally cry against the scientific status of psychoanalysis. Parenthetically, it should be noted that much of his critical rhetoric relies on the empirical work of Peter Fonagy and his research colleagues in Britain, Europe, and the United States, of which Luyten is part of his "team." I do not begrudge these "new empiricists" for self-promotion, as their work has influenced my own thinking in many appreciative ways. Yet the curious silence of value assigned to explanation over description deserves our close attention. Recall, Luyten does not define these terms; they are simply presumed. But these terms mean different things to different disciplines. Explanations are typically thought of as warranted assertions about the causality of events, when they are actually *statements of interpretation* of facts that clarify events and their presumed causes, which necessarily rely on descriptions of events or actions in order to do so. Explanations necessarily require descriptions in order to offer any understanding of the phenomena in question, and as such demonstrate the link between explication and fact. Descriptions by themselves are attempts at providing a narrative of what was observed or recorded and to depict or give an account of factual events, but its narration, exposition, argumentation, and meaning are dependent upon definition.

Philosophically, descriptivism is the notion that evaluative statements aim to be purely factual in nature and are determined in relation to their truth conditions. In symbolic logic, for example, a theory of descriptions (introduced by Russell [1919] but refined by Strawson [1950; 1952; 1959] and Donnellan [1966; 1978]) pertains to analysis of sentences containing definite and indefinite descriptions. Here descriptions are only meaningful in the context of attributive and referential statements and their symbolic relations inherent in sentence structure. Explanation, on the other hand, makes something intelligible or understandable by explaining why or how something happened, such as impersonal events or human actions. There are several types of explanations that may be causal, teleological, inductive, deductive, reductive, methodological, subsumptive, and so forth. Like descriptions, explanations are contextually derived and contingent upon multiple factors. Luyten accuses psychoanalysis of only offering descriptive theories rather than "true" explanations, but there is nothing from his argument that supports this conclusion. Descriptions and explanations are inseparable as explanations necessarily rely on descriptive events (offered as evidence) and their mutual *relata* in order to confer meaning.

One such example he gives of nebulous psychoanalytic theory is the claim that "the patient's depression is related to his severe superego," which he says "does not explain vulnerability for depression" (p. 7). But notice here that he evokes a *relation* between an actual condition (depression) and a state of mind (severe superego), only to then say that this does not demonstrate a causal connection, when this may readily be offered as a causal explanation, albeit an incomplete one; just as early socialization practices or genetic predisposition are insufficient (hence incomplete) as explanations, not to mention palpably reductive. Here behavioural science research is in no better a position to offer viable explanations than psychoanalytic theory because it invariably reverts to inference when addressing the relationship between description and causation. Do "genes" or "socialization history" cause depression over superego severity, when by definition superego theory points to the internal phenomenology of depressed states of mind (viz. excessive guilt, feelings of worthlessness, need for punishment, etc.)? You can no more prove that genes or the environment cause depression than internal dynamic processes, even when we postulate interaction effects, because this presupposes that causation is reducible to material and efficient forces that trump the principle of overdetermination as causal complexity; not to mention the obvious fact that intrapsychic dynamics are operative in all forms of depressive phenomenology.

These naïve accounts Luyten endorses furthermore trivialize the sophistication of mental functioning that psychologically mediates between our embodiment and cultural environs that influence our experience of the world. What we are ultimately debating about is the question of causation, not description, and here so-called "scientific" explanations far no better than psychoanalytic theory. Recall that the ancients used the term *cause* (αιτία) to mean the reason for something happening. In fact, with psychoanalytic explication, you have a far richer and robust attempt to explain complexity, whereas the simple causal reductive paradigms endemic to behavioural science remain a philosophical embarrassment.

One of Luyten's main criticisms of psychoanalysis is its reliance on the language of "poetics" or metaphor rather than the so-called scientific language of "schematics." Here he presupposes that discourse on the human condition should be circumscribed to a scientized (often mechanistic) framework rather than view the range of human expression as encompassing a vast use of ideational, emotional, desirous, and valuational language that more properly symbolizes the complexity of being human. Furthermore, he imports a higher valuation in the use of more technical (presumably objective) language that supposedly characterizes the sciences. But all descriptive and explanatory language is a semiotic enterprise that signifies a whole range of signification practices based on observed linguistic conventions, hermeneutic contingencies, and grammatical relativism that convey meaning within formalized systems of discipline-specific discourse. Here a variety of languages are used to suit their contexts. In the end, all explanations are semiotic descriptions of meaning.

Luyten's reference to the poetics of psychoanalytic language is meant in a pejorative fashion, rather than as an aesthetic achievement expressing the interior emotional qualities of the soul (*Seele*) or metaphorical mind. In his estimate, it does not always speak to the "realm of justification" following the law of "parsimony" customary of science. But why should we adopt such antiseptic models when explaining human experience, let alone assume parsimony is superior to metaphorical attributions of meaning? This was certainly not a problem for the ancients who revered *both* the notions of schematics as *idea* or form (ἰδέα) and aesthetics, which were realized through psychological expressions via poetics (ποιητικῆς)—such as in drama, literature, and art, as well as moral and spiritual activity of the human psyche. Although Luyten does acknowledge the interdependence of metaphor within scientific paradigms, he does nevertheless believe that science is a superior discourse of "comprehension" and "understanding," when the humanities in general would beg to differ. In fact, this juxtaposition between human studies (as a semiotic science) and empirical psychology (as a natural science) is simply begging an old question, and one that is not very original at that. The same banal argument is offered over again: science has the potential to offer a more complete and comprehensive understanding of human phenomena that demonstrates its efficaciousness while psychoanalytic theory does not. Says who? Says science, he would retort, based on its own self-legitimizing propositions, the very legitimacy of which are in dire need of an argument to warrant such predications without running the risk of collapsing into a *petitio principii*.

It can be argued on a priori grounds that no discourse is in itself complete: neither the scientific method nor psychoanalytic theorizing have cornered the market on truth. And nor is it accurate or helpful to perpetuate this false dichotomy: psychoanalysis is as every much empirical as it is theoretic because it addresses the observations, scope, and limits to human experience as they are clinically encountered in the consulting room. This methodological approach to working with patients in the real world is no less valuable than contrived research programs that change the parameters of the real life situation in which clinicians immerse themselves in every day.

Theoretical Myopia in the Age of the Brain

Luyten is enamored with the master discourse of science and advocates for a reductive theory of mind rooted in the neurosciences. He states, "The more analysts learn about the brain, and neuro-circuits involved in explaining psychological phenomena, the more they need to change their language" (p. 8). But we may ask, Why? Not only is this a non sequitur, it fails as an argument for why parsimony would require us to change our modes of discourse. Relying on the language of genetics, evolutionary biology, environmental determinism, and neuroscience, Luyten believes that "inbuilt capacities" for self-other "mapping," the "mirror neuron system," "activation versus deactivation patterns," our "genetic make-up," "vulnerability," and "gene expression," "evocative gene-environment correlations," "interactions" and "effects," and general references to the brain somehow are proffered as a better way to explain human psychological phenomena, when these are presumptive, narrow assertions that fail to fully capture the meaning of felt experience and the qualia of psychic reality. Furthermore, they are ontologically reductive. Take for example Luyten's explanation that "a cortical midline system is *responsible for generating* the experience of self as distinct from others" (p. 17, italics added). This is material reduction at its finest. This statement captures perfectly the anthropic bias in science: material-efficient substrates of the brain *cause* mental phenomena, when there is no sound justification for this conclusion. It is merely *doxa* based on simple-minded versions of determinism. Here Lutyen invents his own mythology by importing causality into the phenomena he describes rather than simply highlighting their correspondence to physical-energetic processes in the brain. This *correlation-causation confound* is lush in the sciences and perpetuates a flagrant myopia devoid of critical thinking rampant in empirical psychology.

By reappropriating the language and procedures of generic (hence non-contextualized) science, which are often ad hoc, and fortifying metaphysical commitments to reductionism as an *explanans* for the *explanandum*, behavioural science research is overstating its *actual* contributions to knowledge. This exaggeration of credibility, which is simultaneously a political self-posturing, furthermore sustains the false consciousness of scientific ideology as the one who is supposed to know. Not only does our generic scientist foray carelessly into making causal assurances that have multiple layers of ambiguity and uncertainty, there are other ontological ramifications that become philosophically problematic for the empiricist to answer. Reductionism (1) commits the fallacy of misplaced concreteness; (2) makes a mereological attribution error; (3) ignores the metaphysics of overdetermination; (4) overvalues the notion of Occam's razor; (5) succumbs to a rudimentary model of mind; (6) is unable to adequately address the question of qualia or the phenomenology of lived experience; (7) is incapable of resolving the notions of self and psychic holism; and (8) fails miserably to account for agency and human freedom (cf. Mills, 2002b). Talking about neuronal activation patterns does nothing to explain the experiential stream of consciousness or the phenomena of awareness as it is happening moment to moment: conscious and self-conscious experience cannot be reduced to biochemical transactions in the brain as this explains nothing about our conscious intentionality, feelings, meant objects, or lived meaning we generate through psychic experience.

When researchers make such causal attributions to brain organization, they appear to be unaware of the philosophical consequences. The founders of phenomenology long ago rallied against this reductionist attitude inherent in materialism and positivism, which was simultaneously a political protest against the scientific hegemonic positioning of their day. How can molecules, cells, and genes actually cause the conscious act of perceiving and intentionally conveying emotional and symbolic meaning? These are higher order developmental achievements belonging to a sophisticated psychological organic process. Reducing the unique qualitative aspects of perception to genetic determinism is a meaningless proposition when a non-perceptive cell does not apprehend an object of conscious experience or awareness like a human agent does. A non-conscious entity, such as a particle, is not capable of causing a higher order organic activity or function that is derived from a complex systemic organization, yet the fallacies of scientific reduction govern our discourse on causation. How can an imperceptible atom cause intentional conscious activity when this tiny speck of enmattered energy has no capacity to experience, emote, think, or perceive the conscious world we inhabit? How can particles grouped into neuronal clusters actually *instantiate* the multifarious acts of consciousness? Logically they cannot, for only an evolved organic holistic system that is irreducible to its parts is capable of such intricate mental activities, for consciousness (not to mention self-consciousness) is a cultivated phase of natural order.

One of the main problems with the reductionist perspective in neuroscience and biosemiotics is that it is unable to account for human freedom (see Mills, 2010, p. 275n7). One notable exception is Ansermet and Magistretti's (2007) claim that the "neuronal apparatus" is actually based upon a biology of freedom that allows for neural plasticity or modification in how it unconsciously encodes experience. They tell us:

> The concept of plasticity means that experience can be inscribed in the neuronal network. An event experienced at a given time is marked at the moment and can persist over time. The event leaves a trace, and simultaneously, time is embodied ... [T]he fact of plasticity thus involves a subject who actively participates in the process of his or her becoming (p. 13n3).

Their attempt to wed *bios* with *psyche* is to be applauded, especially when they speculate on the possibility to "conceptualize a psychic causality capable of shaping the organic" (p. 7). However, there still remains the question of agency. Ansermet and Magistretti repeatedly situate the locus of agency within the "mechanisms of plasticity" (p. 47), which they reduce to neuronal processes.

Thus they inadvertently collapse agency into biological structures without properly accounting for the agent directing these agentic functions. Here they commit the mereological attribution error of assigning agency to a part or subsystem of the brain rather than addressing the human subject as a complex systemic whole. If agency is reduced to neuronal (and specifically, "synaptic") plasticity rather than being co-extensive with and directing neural modification, then mind becomes an epiphenomenon with no real causal powers of its own.

Rhetorical phrases Luyten employs, such as "studies suggest," "research shows," there is "growing evidence" which "is congruent with neuroscience findings," are informal fallacies of logic that appeal to authority and consensus among a subgroup of researchers interested in promoting their own way of thinking. This is neither proper justification nor does it demonstrate causality. Just because a group of professionals adhere to a thesis about human phenomena does not make it true. Explanations require strong argumentation and demand *demonstration* based upon evidence. The evidence of observation conveyed as description cannot be passed off as an *explanans*. It is one thing to locate neuronal functionalities, biochemical processes, and physical structures of the brain, but it is quite another to conclude these are the causal apparatuses behind higher psychological organizations we call mind. We may ask, How do you know that? Are there plausible alternatives to material reduction? Why could it not be the other way around: mind produces, hence causes, alteration in brain activity and the neural mechanisms we think are "responsible for generating" mentation and thought? Even the fiercest proponents of material ontologies of mind concede to the limitations of their hypotheses. And a truly scientific attitude would be open to alternative explanations, not self-satisfied with reductive paradigms.

Notwithstanding the contributions of naturalized explanations in evolutionary biology, neuroscience, and the study of the brain, it has become all too superficial and one-dimensional to collapse mental processes into neuronal patterns rather than see how the sophistication of consciousness as a self-organized systemic achievement can produce neurochemical-biologic effects of its own. Just because the brain may be scientifically observed and measured by technological methods and neuroimaging techniques such as functional magnetic resonance imaging (fMRI) and positron emission tomography (PET) scans does not mean that mind is equivalent to its physical locality. In other words, we should not simply assume a linear one-way causal relation among brain processes that determine the productions of consciousness as an epiphenomenon, but rather human consciousness should be conceived as an evolved organic matrix that equiprimordially and reciprocally determines physical effects that transpire in the brain as a dialectical two-way, causal systemic informational and relational exchange of events that leave their reverberations on neuronal activity. We cannot justify the belief in absolute (hard) determinism when it comes to biological organisms without shouldering a presumptive causal bias (Mills 2013a), especially when the complexifications of consciousness may exert a causal influence on how the manifestations of brain activity are understood.

Proponents of mental determinism that rely on reductive epistemologies based on brain discourse grounded in neuro-ontology commit a mereological fallacy (Bennett & Hacker, 2003) by demoting psychic complexity to its material constituents alone, not to mention being guilty of the fallacy of simple location or misplaced concreteness where human consciousness is said to be found in a reducible particle (Whitehead, 1925).[4] Here the intricacy of an organic whole or gestalt is reduced to its parts as neuroscience mistakenly conceives of mind *as* brain. Yet this naïve determinism supporting the conclusion that mind equals brain still continues to infect contemporary science. While the brain is a necessary condition for mind, it is far from a sufficient one: mind cannot be reduced to brain states alone, for mind is a higher-order developmental and epigenetic organic process that transcends simple equations.

In Defense of Theory

Theory is never purely divorced from method, yet we may categorically (logically) separate out descriptive events from theoretical explanations. Luyten charges much of psychoanalysis with espousing an "obsolete model of the mind" (p. 9) by holding onto outdated theoretical orientations inherited from tradition. It is true that some theories are antiquated and need to be aborted, as certain techniques need to be refined, expanded, or displaced for more appropriate interventions that are tailored to the patient's needs and the unique contingencies of the analytic dyad; but once again he paints with a broad brush. It is important to remember that there are many post-classical movements within the psychoanalytic domain that have developed since Freud's time, hence introducing redirecting shifts in emphasis, reformed approaches to theory and praxis, and the out-right rejection of earlier models. This obvious fact is not mentioned in his critique, yet Luyten does pick and choose various concepts to criticize from Freudian, Kleinian, and Lacanian theory, as well as general principles of object relations and ego psychology. Given I have offered my own critique of many of these approaches (Mills, 2012; 2014), we share similar views on outdated developmental models and some theories of psychopathology, as well as how theory guides practice and how it is a useful clinical heuristic. But some of the claims Luyten makes with regards to core psychoanalytic constructs deserve special attention.

I have already argued that the languages of science, which are largely procedural, cerebral, non-emotive, and so forth, merit no special consideration as a superior type of discourse because all language is imbued with meaning and anthropomorphic properties that infiltrate every discipline. As such, Luyten's argument that me-taphorical or poetical portrayals of human experience are inadequate in comparison to scientific terminology (Cf. Bornstein & Becker-Matero, 2011) fail because we cannot step outside of semiotic classifications of meaning construction every discourse conveys in some fashion. The issue becomes, for what purpose and context is a said discourse applied? Different definitions, goals, aims, etc. will determine a particular approach to methodology, interpretation, and explanatory conclusions derived. Taking as surprising examples, Luyten challenges the canonical notions of "projection," "splitting," and "representation." Relying on his close collaboration with Fonagy (e.g., Fonagy & Luyten, 2009), Luyten proclaims that the process of projection or projective identification "does not actually involve the projection of internal mental states in the mind of someone else (how would that work?), but rather precisely the *opposite* process: that the supposed receiver of the 'projection' resonates with internal mental states because of our inbuilt capacity for self-to-other and other-to-self mapping" (p. 8). Setting aside the geographical language (which employs a spatial metaphor), Luyten at first denies that the subject could project their own internal thoughts onto another, but then claims that the other really does not receive these thoughts, rather it triggers the "mirror neuron system," which "starts to feel like the other person (who purportedly 'projects'), because he or she is unable to inhibit his or her attempt to map the self on to the other" (p. 8).

Here I see no contradiction with classical theory. Unless one is prepared to reject the whole history of modern philosophy, phenomenology, and the philosophy of mind, it is an uncontested fact that the internal subjectivity of a thinker directs thoughts onto objects (as either external to oneself and in the sensuous world, or as internalized relations derived from personal experience). Of course this is a two-way reciprocal relation when we encounter another human being, which is also characteristic of transference. At the very least, we must concede that when two subjects encounter one another, separate psychic processes are activated in each subject, yet they are mutually implicative and transpire on parallel levels of mental functioning. To imply that one is not projecting and the other is not really receiving a projection, but instead becomes confused when they see the face of the other, which then triggers internal events based on a confusion of internal circuitry and a disinhibition of self-other mapping is simply a circular argument that betrays the dialectical nature of subjectivity. Reducing projection to brain processes is not only ontologically diminutive, it furthermore serves no clinical utility when encountering projective identificatory processes in the office. What would you say to a patient?—I think your mirror neurons are misfiring!

The point I wish to clarify is that a subject is not really inserting thoughts into another person's mind, of which Luyten would presumably agree, but this does not annul the dynamics of projection or projective identification. Each individual assumes a complementary dialectical (inverse) relation to another, with mutual psychological processes potentially operative at any given moment (which in scientized language is referred to as "activated" or "deactivated"—recall Freud prefers the terms "inhibition" and "disinhibition"); therefore, the subject is always engaged in a simultaneous process of projecting internal contents onto others and identifying with various aspects of others' states of mind that are expressed, articulated, instantiated, or inferred through their behaviours, utterances, affect, non-verbal body comportment, and so on, which is then either negated, unformulated, dissociated, or sensuously taken up by the other (even if only partially) as an internal experience of their own related to their own unique intrapsychic configurations. The other's behaviour stimulates (activates) internal experiences in ourselves that we attempt to mediate and make sense of through meaning attributions in self-other representations, not that we can read others' minds or that others can directly place their thoughts into our minds. If anything, we are always projecting our own thoughts onto others as meant objects whether they identify or resonate with our inner experiences or not.

Luyten makes similar sweeping dismissals of select (cherry-picked) aspects of psychoanalytic theory, such as "there is no such thing as a state of primary narcissism or an autistic stage, as infants are oriented towards others from the very first stages of life" (p. 9). But he fails to appreciate how these theoretical terms are utilized to denote functional properties or as experiential modes of self-relation inherent in infantile development: orientation to others does not negate the intrinsic interrelations of mind nor address the question of self-organization that is indisputably internally derived from intrapsychic configurations that logically transpire before birth as unconscious presubjectivity (see Mills, 2010). Just because infants are adapted towards the world and their caregivers from birth does not mean that their inner experiences and correspondent self-relations (even if biologically driven) do not conform to the semiotic equivalent of a solipsistic or primary self-enclosed state of self-orientation in the face of external reality characteristic of Freud's or Ogden's theoretical explanations as an attempt to label the inner phenomenology of mind at this incipient stage of development.

Luyten also opines that "defense mechanisms are not activated by intrapsychic conflict," which "does not seem to correspond to what is actually happening" (p. 9). Then what is actually happening? According to Luyten, it is simply a matter of automatic learned responses corresponding to neural circuitry. This absurd behaviourist oversimplification of unconscious experience does not remotely come close to offering a cogent explanation of inner phenomena simply because it cannot capture the qualitative dimensions to internal life, let alone address the functions, motives, and conflicts involved in the "activation" of defenses to begin with. The same lame argument applies to the phenomena of "splitting or conversion," which Luyten believes is "implausible." He asks us rather naïvely and concretely, "what would exactly be split in splitting? Do we really believe that a representation is split in two or more parts? Or that one part of the representation is kept unconscious (i.e., is defended against)?" (p. 9). While offering no substantial arguments of his own, instead reiterating the notion that these are not "parsimonious" accounts customary of empirical methodology, and that they participate in an antiquated model of the mind, which is tantamount to saying they do not conform to a scientific way of thinking, Luyten is convinced that his false binary assertions are justifications for dismissing standard psychoanalytic discourse as mere lore.

Defenses by definition are internally instituted by unconscious or preconscious processes (even if they are stimulated by environmental forces or acts of consciousness) with teleological motives aimed at achieving particular psychic functions and ends. This may be explained within a naturalized framework consistent with evolutionary biology and contemporary neuroscience without devolving into a mechanistic explanation that strips away the affective and experiential quality of mental life. Splitting is a description of an internal process of division, negation, and fracturing by partitioning off particular aspects or spacings of interiority as *mental relations* to objects, which may contain many elements such as sentience, affects, images, fantasies, thoughts, and other apperceptive experiences retained in memory (or memorialized within somatic processes) and related to as internal objects, which are the re-presentations (*Vorstellungen*) of sensuous experience re-collected from the unconscious abyss (Mills, 2002c). The crass rejection of these core psychoanalytic ideas via negation without providing any proper argumentation is fallacious.

Lutyen continues his critique of psychoanalytic developmental theories beginning with an overly simplified misrepresentation of Freudian theory, only then to generalize it to postclassical thought by summoning the nature versus nurture debate in a pedestrian dichotomous fashion. The conceptual move Luyten makes is to proclaim that the language of "evocative gene-environment correlations" somehow better captures what is *really going on* when we posit developmental processes and their intervening psychopathologies. It is beyond embarrassment that in this day and age the nature-nurture-interaction discourse of the 1960s is being reintroduced under new pretenses, when this simply perpetuates an unsophisticated paradigm of causation. Propositions of epigenetic mechanisms altering gene expression, genetic vulnerability to particular environmental stimuli, gene-environment effects, and synergistic interaction all presuppose reductive causal models that do not sufficiently take into account complex interactive patterns inherent to overdetermination; such as the nature of phenomena influencing qualia and one's subjective experiences of the world, transgenerational transmission repetitions, and unique cultural factors that define the history, retention, and environs of certain group or ethnic socialization practices, all of which affect unconscious agency, personality formation, and personal freedom of choice regardless of so-called gene-environment correlations, which are speculative hypotheses at best. Moreover, these theses don't really explain anything. How can a gene or an external object account for (hence produce the complexity of) consciousness? A gene is not a conscious agent, neither is any environment a conscious being. The presupposition that human mental activity is reducible to these basal conditions extricates the human being from its own essence. Our genetic predispositions, history, or environmental facticity are merely generic substrates of biological life and the cultural contingencies that we are thrown into as pre-given ontological structures that inform our being in the world. They are necessary conditions, but far from sufficient ones.

If behavioural science would refrain from importing causal attributions into their explanations, and merely stayed within the parameters of their research models, perhaps much of these disagreements would be dispensed with, or at least bracketed. In any event, the point is these causal implications should be deferred. But Luyten continues to mischaracterize psychoanalytic theory when he declares that behavioural scientists "question one of the most basic assumptions of object relations and attachment theories, namely that parental behaviour largely *determines* child development" (p. 15, italics added). Notice the simple one-way causal relation he attributes to these broad theoretical schools within psychoanalysis, when this is simply a straw man. He provides no original textual references to any pivotal theorist in the object relations movement that says parents' behaviour causes child development, yet we should all assume it does. Luyten's solution is to replace this so-called environmental determinism with evocative gene-environment lingo as a more appropriate explanation, which is merely a clichéd reiteration of antiquated dichotomous rationale replete in empirical psychology. This blinkered framework of thinking that guides theory and procedural methodologies in behavioural science is itself a form of professional mythology I like to call *bioideology*.

When Luyten continually uses the flagship phrase "there is growing evidence," or "research supports" as a justification for *why* we should believe the verity and validity of his arguments that genes, the environment, or both cause the human being to be, relate, feel, act, and experience, he is merely putting a new spin on old ideas using the rhetoric of science. One such example is that attachment processes may be attributed, hence caused, by the presence or absence of DRD4 7-repeat allele, which epitomizes the fallacy of simple location. Such complexities in psychological processes cannot be logically reduced to these factors alone without committing a mereological error under the seduction of positivism. I suppose the inability to think critically about causal complexity is conditioned by how science successfully imposes its master discourse on the educational process, much like how the CBT and empirically-supported treatment movements prescribe a rote set of procedures for all treatment populations across the board *as if* all people in that group are the same, when this is a category mistake that fails to appreciate the fact that "the only statistically pertinent sample is $N = 1$" (Mills, 2012, p. 178; also see Verhaeghe, 2004). Making grand universal generalizations to "groups" assumes everyone in that group is the same or possesses similar characteristics to be pigeonholed into some class, when this presumption strips away subjectivity from the subject, the unique experiential field that composes the lived quality of a person's inner life in relation to their personal history, and lumps them into an impersonal classification that may have little to do with how they actually think, feel, and perceive the world. Of course this is passed off as "objective" evidence, when it is more properly based on the hegemonic agenda of scientism pretending to be the one that knows.

To illustrate the brazen pronouncements of hubris Luyten upholds under the banner of science, he is willing to deny the internal reality of representations in the mind, which he claims "are no longer in line with what *we now know* about representational processes: *Representations do not exist*; they thus cannot be split or integrated, and they cannot be hierarchically organized" (p. 16, italics added). In the history of philosophy—from Aristotle to Husserl, representations are essential to the internal workings of the mind. With Kant's introduction of the epistemological turn in late modern philosophy, through to Fichte, Hegel, and Schopenhauer, Luyten's brash dismissal of such an important psychological process in the history of ideas is most incredulous. Instead, he says representations are "*states of mind.*" But of course they are: they are internal spacings of internalized sensuous experiences that have been mnemonically imprinted and organized in the unconscious mind, recollected through the mediatory processes of memory and imagination, and realized in lived phenomenal time as intrapsychic qualitative states of psychic reality, as the whole history of modern philosophy has already explained through various standpoints from the British empiricists to the German idealists. Here Luyten is reinventing the wheel and attempting to pass it off as a "new" discovery. He believes the language of representation is guilty of "reification" when this is the very thing he commits when he condenses complex mental processes to "neural circuits" characteristic of material reductionism. Representations are far from being reified; rather, they are fluid *processes* with variable contents as sentience, affect, and imago are distilled within various schemas mediated by memory, imagination, and cognition (Mills, 2002c; 2010).

How is this neuro-language of brain circuitry helpful in offering an explanation of the phenomena of representation? It is not, because it dislocates phenomenology from the phenomena in question. When we attempt to dissect phenomenology, we kill it. The mechanical rendition of the *awareness* or *presence* of lived experience to biochemical and physical structures in the central nervous system is an unwarranted ontological predication that has no bearing on lived psychic reality. The proverbial joke becomes—"Just use some fancy science-language and others will pretend they understand it. And we can sell them something to boot!" A profound explanation indeed.

A redundant form of straw man reasoning is used again and again by Luyten in attempting to manufacture a bifurcation between concepts or phenomena when they do not exist. Not only does he do this by making the concept "representation" a reified object, opting instead to import a process account—as if that is an original idea, he further pulls this move by claiming "people do not *have* a self or identity or personality; rather, they have the ability, to a greater or lesser extent, to activate a more or less consistent, coherent, and differentiated *feeling* or *experience* of coherence and stability" (p. 17). Notwithstanding the current pomocentrism that is popular in some forms of contemporary psychoanalysis, this position denies selfhood yet evokes the *agency* of the subject as possessing the "ability ... to activate" feeling states and personal experience. But if you do not have a self, identity, or personality, how can you activate anything? Does this just magically come from neurotransmitters firing randomly in the brain that gives the illusion that *I* have internal thoughts, feelings, desires, and so forth, which influence my conscious awareness of *my experience* of these internal events, or does this not require an agent performing such activities, even if these modes of thought are unconsciously constituted? By definition, self-consciousness (as self-reflectivity) necessarily requires an internal point of reference that we typically call the self, even if we view the self as a fluent and transient process of becoming.

This false antinomy between the self as a static thing versus a process system of change unfolding within universal invariances inherent to mind dates back to the pre-Socratic antipode of being versus becoming. It is merely old wine in new bottles, which have now turned to vinegar. Luyten's apparent lack of knowledge of the history of philosophy, not to mention his cavalier attempt to snatch the credit for introducing a so-called "new" perspective, deserves what Plato refers to in his dialogue *Gorgias* as a refutation by laughter (cf., 473e). This is a good example of why empirical psychologists should humbly refrain from veering too far from their path of expertise.

On Explication in Psychoanalysis and Operationalization in Science

Lutyen's critique of five central tenets of psychoanalysis ends on a denunciation of its explanatory powers in favour of the empirical tradition. Luyten believes that due to the complexity of psycho-analytic theory that relies on metaphorical discourse, this "hinders operationalization" in science. The implicit assumption here is that psychoanalysis should concern itself about empirical operations. But why should operationalization matter to the psychoanalyst who does not believe in science as a privileged discourse, let alone care about matters that have nothing to do with working with patients, especially when other methodologies in the humanities and in clinical praxis are more relevant? Without proper justification, Luyten further harangues that psychoanalytic frameworks fail to develop a "comprehensive understanding of the human condition" (p. 18). Just because the overspecificity and complexity of theory do not easily fit into sanitized, artificial, and arbitrarily operationalized approaches to behavioural science research does not mean there is no comprehensive explanatory scaffolding about the human condition. He provides no argument, only the non sequitur that what psychoanalysis offers is not "true" explanation, hence, once again, begging the question on truth. The insipid conclusion is the reiteration that psychoanalysis has faulty assumptions that belie empirical verification. But what he specifically hones in on is drive theory, thus proclaiming "the notion of drive is obsolete." On one hand he embraces the field of genetics and evolutionary science, and on the other he negates human *Triebe* or instincts, itself a most blatant contradiction.

It is unfathomable, both logically and empirically, to negate the ontology of drives as embodied organic processes that evolutionarily inform human desire, affect, cognition, and behaviour. These innate instinctual impulses or biological processes are in today's lexicon often equated with genes that have built-in teleonomic pressures (Mills, 2010), which orient and motivate the organism to action and ensure its survival. The psychophysiological instantiation of drives or genes in no way cancels out our relational natures and object seeking attachments (Mills, 2012), rather they are the biological substrate within an unconscious agentic organization that makes relatedness to others possible (Mills, 2010). Jettisoning drive theory is tantamount to denying the basic instinctual systems inherent to animal bodies. To displace the primacy of sex and aggression in the human condition violates the laws of nature, not to mention the empirical fact that sex and aggression are two of the most salient aspects of social existence

in all spheres of human affairs. This is evinced by the fact that por-
nography is the number one industry on the world wide web, just as
sex unconsciously fires human material production in all forms from
economics to fashion, cosmetics, advertising, and gendered socialization practices; not to mention the indisputable fact that all cultures
manifest human aggression: from the nursery to every community
worldwide, domestic, national, and global (military) conflict saturates
our daily consciousness throughout the planet (Mills, 2013b).

When you look closely at the tenor and posturing of Luyten's
arguments, they are designed to create the impression that psychoanalytic theory fails because, as Luyten accuses, it is "overly simplistic about the complexity of developmental processes," adhere to
a "naïve environmentalist position," and that they have "limited
predictive effects" because there is "more to development" than object relations and attachment mechanisms. But of course there are:
this bald fact underscores the complexity of psychoanalytic theory.
Luyten is not remotely justified in lumping all psychoanalytic approaches to theory and method into the same basket, and his perennial mischaracterizations are a continuation of his use of informal
fallacies. Nowhere do we find in Freud, for instance, *any* statement
that commits him to either a simple biological *or* environmental determinism. He accounts for inner and outer, hence the intrapsychic,
intersubjective, and the social, and meticulously details the workings
of drive, wish, and defense, identification, object attachments,
semiotics, the process of civilization, and the cultural environs that
influence individual and collective development. Luyten's main
agenda here is in fortifying the illusion of the "predictive" promise he
thinks science is able to deliver in its explanatory models, when experimental psychology is no more predictive of human behaviour
than psychoanalytic sensibility. Are gene-environment-interaction
(statistical) probabilities anymore capable of predicting future
events than a thorough understanding of the phenomenology of a
person's developmental history and life experience? No, because
we are simply not causally determined in such rote fashions by these
categorically reductive automations. On the other hand, we may
be more justified in predicting possible future occurrences from
people when we understand their psychic lives and developmental
history because inner phenomenal experiences motivate human

activity. Here the scientific method is no more likely to predict future events than the phenomenological method. Once again, we may smell old propaganda under the political hegemony of empiricism.

Luyten's solution is to return to the evolutionary lingo driving theories of explanation in the biological sciences, where the complexity of human cognition, emotion, motivation, and behaviour devolve into perfunctory involuntary processes that strip the human being of its psychological and experiential sophistication. He overstretches the explanatory nature of his preferred holy science, and is quick to devalue the broad domain of psychoanalytic treatment as offering "nothing unique." If this were genuinely the case, then we would be a bankrupt discipline, and as such, practitioners would no longer be in business. Although the psychoanalytic landscape has changed in terms of both theory and praxis, analytic practitioners continue to employ modified psychoanalytic principles in their varied clinical activities regardless of the pressures for mainstream treatment approaches or the hyperbole of scientific psychology. Such political posturing exemplifies the master discourse attempting to sell us something novel, when this is merely the recapitulation of its well-entrenched ideology.

Concluding Unscientific Postscript

For the record, I am not against science, nor am I an anti-empiricist; I am merely critical of the way the so-called scientific method has been politically annexed by empirical psychology eager to join the ranks of high authority in a privileged position of determining what constitutes so-called knowledge and *how* we should conceptually frame a *philosophy of explanation*. In my opinion, empirical psychology does not offer a philosophy of explanation, rather it offers a method that produces tangible results that enlist and describe data, which are then converted into an *explanans* as a conflation of the *explanandum*. Scientific psychology has the onus of proving itself in the world of academia and public affairs, where research grants, publication numbers, and the procurement of external funding determine its worth. But it is not remotely commensurate to the specialized fields that compose the proper domain of the natural sciences where precise observation, experimentation, and discovery of natural laws and their processes are much more systematized and rigorously investigated. Sadly, empirical psychology suffers from an inadequate conceptual framework on how to philosophically approach its methodology when constructing explanatory models. Resorting to reductive paradigms of causation does not help its position, for it becomes tautologically ensnared by its own presuppositions fueled by circular reasoning.In order to avoid begging the question of causation via reductionism, empirical psychoanalytic psychology should consider developing conceptual models of explanation that take into account the complexifications of over-determination and human agency.[5]

The ideologies of scientism continue to condition our conventional modes of discourse on causal explication and human knowledge. The humanities in general, and continental philosophy in particular, continue to challenge the Cartesian, logocentric, positivist, and physicalist frameworks underlying the scientistic hegemony of Western thought, yet the preponderance of science as a master discourse totes the potential for both discovery and mastery over natural order, whereas the humanities typically do not. To what degree the promise of science is based on illusion or even sophistry continues to fragment professional disciplines in debate. Within psychoanalytic inquiry, camps continue to remain divided as well based on differing methodologies and theories of explanation. This is largely based on, I suggest, an ingrained worldview that is split in terms of its epistemological claims and capacity for prediction governing its elucidatory models. Although psychoanalysis as a discipline has much to gain by empirically validating its theoretical premises and technical procedures, it remains in need of a philosophically coherent framework of explanation that resists the reductive ontological commitments expounded by contemporary science. Parsimonious approaches to theory and operationalization only complicate the matter by perpetuating shallow explanations rather than answer to the conundrums generated by complexity. A more vibrant psychoanalysis could conceivably emerge if researchers and scholars attempted a consilience between science and philosophy.

Notes

1 To be fair to my research colleagues, many thoughtful empiricists recognize the limits to empirical measures and the dangers of over-generalizability of results, which are typically more measured, contingent, qualified, and less deterministic. It is within the traditional philosophical debates against scientism as an epistemological and political

movement lambasting or disqualifying other legitimate discourses that these criticisms are directed.

2 Although intended for another context, physicist Victor Stenger (2007) makes the interesting and perspicacious observation that "A number of studies have claimed to be able to overcome the lack of statistical significance of single experiments by using a technique called 'metanalysis,' in which the results of many experiments are combined. This procedure is highly questionable. I am unaware of any extraordinary discovery in all of science that was made using metanalysis. If several, independent experiments do not find significant evidence for a phenomenon, we surely cannot expect a purely mathematical manipulation of the combined data to suddenly produce a major discovery" (p. 93). And this is coming from an academic astrophysicist.

3 This is one reason why the fields of phenomenology and hermeneutics reproach scientific methodology for its lack of reflectivity and for not examining the true object in question in its native form and as it exists in its phenomenal moment or modes of appearance. These philosophical criticisms of the scientific method also extend to the subjectivity of the researchers who assume they can extricate themselves from their subject matter under the guise of pure objectivity. These are axiomatic challenges—hence categorical arguments—directed towards the philosophical frameworks informing scientific paradigms that rely on the control and manipulation of experimental variables, hence they are ideological oppositions to the essence of science. The controlling of variables that lead to reduction and simplification of the phenomenon in question in the service of avoiding logical or inferential errors begs the question of the accuracy and generalizability of results if they do not reflect a pure analysis of the actual phenomenon itself. This is why philosophy has historically always offered alternative models of explanation that originally rely on metaphysics, which are speculative, abductive, and empirical in scope, beginning with the ancient's preoccupation with mind and matter, later refined by the modern philosophers, advanced more by the German and British idealists, and culminating in the phenomenological and hermeneutic traditions of 20th century Continental philosophy. Given that human behaviour and mental processes are far more complicated than studying organic matter in a test tube or under a microscope, such as in biochemistry, the ideological challenge to scientism from phenomenological hermeneutics stands as a valid criticism towards many branches of empirical psychology today.

4 See my discussion and critique of reductive material ontologies (Mills, 2010), pp. 10–12, 251, 263n9.

5 With the exception of Ansermet & Magistretti's (2007) work, I am unaware of any contemporary empirical research in neuroscience or the philosophy of mind that attempts to address the question of causality, agency, and human freedom that does not devolve into material reduction, epiphenomenalism, and brain or evolutionary discourse. The fundamental problem here lies between ontology and phenomenology: the former is primarily concerned with foundational aspects or first principles and the question of ultimate reality, while the latter is concerned

with preserving the source, force, and independence of lived experience and its qualitative manifestations. Because science employs reductive models while the humanities resist such tendencies, I am afraid there will always remain an ideological clash of theoretical assumptions and their imported values.

References

Ansermet, F., & Magistretti, P. (2007). *Biology of Freedom: Neural Plasticity, Experience, and the Unconscious*. New York: Other Press.

Bennett, M.R., & Hacker, P.M.S. (2003). *Philosophical Foundations of Neuroscience*. Oxford: Blackwell.

Blass, R.B., & Carmeli, Z. (2007). The Case Against Neuropsychoanalysis. *International Journal of Psychoanalysis*, 88(1): 19–40.

Bornstein, R.F. (2001). The Impending Death of Psychoanalysis. *Psychoanalytic Psychology*, 18(1): 3–20.

Bornstein, R.F. & Becker-Matero, N. (2011). Reconnecting Psychoanalysis to Mainstream Psychology: Metaphor as Glue. *Psychoanalytic Inquiry*, 31: 172–184.

Bostrom, N. (2002). *Anthropic Bias: Observation Selection Effects in Science and Philosophy*. London: Routledge.

Bucci, W. (1997). *Psychoanalysis and Cognitive Science: A Multiple Code Theory*. New York: Guilford Press.

Chalmers, A.F. (1982). *What is this Thing Called Science?* (2nd Ed). St. Lucia: University of Queensland Press.

Cioffi, F. (1998). *Freud and the Question of Pseudoscience*. Chicago: Open Court.

Cramer, P. (2006). *Protecting the Self: Defense Mechanisms in Action*. New York: Guildford.

Donnellan, K.S. (1966). Reference and Definite Descriptions. *Philosophical Review*, 77: 281–304.

Donnellan, K.S. (1978). Speaker Reference, Descriptions, and Anaphora. In P. Cole (Ed.), *Syntax and Semantics 9: Pragmatics*, New York: Academic Press, 47–68.

Eagle, M. (2003). The Postmodern Turn in Psychoanalysis: A Critique. *Psychoanalytic Psychology*, 20(3): 411–424.

Eagle, M., Wolitzky, D.L., & Wakefield, J.C. (2001). The Analyst's Knowledge and Authority: A Critique of the "New View" in Psychoanalysis. *Journal of the American Psychoanalytic Association*, 49: 457–488.

Fisher, S., & Greenberg, R.P. (1977). *The Scientific Credibility of Freud's Theories and Therapy*. New York: Basic Books.

Fisher, S., & Greenberg, R.P. (1996). *Freud Scientifically Reappraised: Testing the Theories and Therapy.* New York: John Wiley & Sons.

Fonagy, P., & Luyten, P. (2009). A developmental, mentalization-based approach to the understanding and treatment of borderline personality disorder. *Development and Psychopathology,* 21(4): 1355–1381. doi: 10.1017/s0954579409990198

Fonagy, P., Gergely, G., Jurist, E.L. & Target, M. (2002). *Affect Regulation, Mentalization and the Development of the Self.* New York: Other Press.

Freud, S. (1940 [1938]). Some Elementary Lessons in Psycho-Analysis. *Standard Edition,* 23: 281–286.

Grünbaum, A. (1984). *The Foundations of Psychoanalysis.* Berkeley: University of California Press.

Hoffman, I.Z. (2009). Doublethinking our Way to "Scientific" Legitimacy: The Desiccation of Human Experience. *Journal of the American Psychoanalytic Association,* 57(5): 1043–1069.

Luborsky, L., & Crits-Christoph, P. (1998). *Understanding Transference: The Core Conflictual Relationship Theme Method* (2nd Ed.). Washington DC: American Psychological Association.

Luyten. P. (2015). Unholy Questions about Five Central Tenets of Psychoanalysis that Need to be Empirically Verified. *Psychoanalytic Inquiry,* 35: sup1, 5–23. doi: 10.1080/07351690.2015.987590

Masling, J. (2003). Stephen A. Mitchell, Relational Psychoanalysis, and Empirical Data. *Psychoanalytic Psychology,* 20(4): 587–608.

Masling, J.M. & Bornstein, R.F. (Eds) (1996). *Psychoanalytic Perspectives on Developmental Psychology.* Washington, DC: American Psychological Association.

Mills, J. (2002a). Reexamining the Psychoanalytic Corpse: From Scientific Psychology to Philosophy. *Psychoanalytic Psychology,* 19(3): 552–558.

Mills, J. (2002b). Five Dangers of Materialism. *Genetic, Social, and General Psychology Monographs,* 128(1): 5–27.

Mills, J. (2002c). *The Unconscious Abyss: Hegel's Anticipation of Psychoanalysis.* Albany, New York: SUNY Press.

Mills, J. (2005a). A Critique of Relational Psychoanalysis. *Psychoanalytic Psychology* 22(2): 155–188.

Mills, J. (2005b). *Relational and Intersubjective Perspectives in Psychoanalysis: A Critique.* Northvale, NJ: Aronson/Rowman & Littlefield.

Mills, J. (2005c). *Treating Attachment Pathology.* Lantham, MD: Aronson/Rowman & Littlefield.

Mills, J. (2010). *Origins: On the Genesis of Psychic Reality*. Montreal: McGill-Queens University Press.

Mills, J. (2012). *Conundrums: A Critique of Contemporary Psychoanalysis*. New York: Routledge.

Mills, J. (2013a). Freedom and Determinism. *The Humanistic Psychologist*, 41(2): 101–118.

Mills, J. (2013b). Civilization and its Fate. *Studia Philosophica Wratislaviensia*. Supplementary Volume: English Edition, pp. 195–222.

Mills, J. (2014). *Underworlds: Philosophies of the unconscious from Psychoanalysis to Metaphysics*. London: Routledge.

Plato. (1961). *Gorgias*. In E. Hamilton & H. Cairns (Eds.), *The Collected Dialogues of Plato* (pp. 229–307). Princeton, NJ: Princeton University Press.

Russell, B. (1919). *Introduction to Mathematical Philosophy*. London: George Allen and Unwin.

Shedler, J. (2010). The Efficacy of Psychodynamic Psychotherapy. *American Psychologist*, 65(2): 98–109.

Shore, A.N. (1994). *Affect Regulation and the Origin of the Self: The Neurobiology of Emotional Development*. Hillsdale, NJ: Lawrence Erlbaum.

Solms, M. & Turnbull, O. (2002). *The Brain and the Inner World: An Introduction to the Neuroscience of Subjective Experience*. New York: Other Press.

Stenger, V. (2007). *God: The Failed Hypothesis*. Amherst, New York: Prometheus Books.

Stern, D.N. (1985). *The Interpersonal World of the Infant: A View from Psychoanalysis and Developmental Psychology*. Washington, DC: Basic Books.

Strawson, P.F. (1950). On Referring. *Mind*, 59: 320–334.

Strawson, P.F. (1952). *Introduction to Logical Theory*. London: Methuen.

Strawson, P.F. (1959). *Individuals*. London: Methuen.

Summers, F. (2008). Theoretical Insularity and the Crisis of Psychoanalysis. *Psychoanalytic Psychology*, 25(3): 413–424.

Verhaeghe, P. (2004). *On Being Normal and Other Disorders*. New York: Other Press.

Wallerstein, R.S. (1989) The Psychotherapy Research Project of the Menninger Foundation: An Overview. *Journal of Consulting and Clinical Psychology*, 57(2): 195–205.

Westen, D. (1998). The Scientific Legacy of Sigmund Freud: Toward a Psychodynamically Informed Psychological Science. *Psychological Bulletin*, 124: 333–371.

Westen, D. (1999). The Scientific Status of Unconscious Processes: Is Freud Really Dead? *Journal of the American Psychoanalytic Association*, 47: 1061–1106.

Whitehead, A.N. (1925). *Science and the Modern World*. New York: Free Press.

Chapter 12

Truth

We find in Plato's dialogues many passages on truth, especially in relation to the eternal— namely, fixity, purity, that which is unchanged and unaltered—"perfect clarity" (*Philebus*, 59c). When he refers to the "plain of Truth," which belongs to the "ordinance of Necessity" (*Phaedrus*, 248b–c), he places truth at the apex of metaphysical inquiry. As a property (quality) belonging to the good and the beautiful (*Philebus*, 64e–65a) that he insists is first among all things good (*Laws*, 5:730c), he christens it as the highest value (*Phaedo*, 114e). The pursuit of truth becomes a central aim of the philosopher through the "power of dialectic" (*Republic*, 7:537d), something approximated only through a laborious rational process (*Parmenides*, 136d–e) but never fully achieved, that which is akin to wisdom (*Republic*, 6:485d).

Psychoanalysis has no formal theory of truth. When analysts speak of truth, they are often referring to empirical matters, such as patients' statements or disclosures that correspond to events in the real world, historical facts, recollection from memory versus construction via fantasy, sincere first-person narratives, and how truth is revealed or concealed in the analytic encounter. A close inspection of the psychoanalytic contributions on the question and meaning of truth is almost exclusively centred on clinical phenomena, while a genuinely unique philosophical theory peculiar to psychoanalysis remains unrealized. Throughout this chapter, I am interested in ferreting out the possibility of providing a novel perspective on psychoanalytic truth. I wish to situate my argument in the tradition of the ancient notion of *aletheia*, where truth is defined as a process of disclosedness or

DOI: 10.4324/9781003305958-12

unconcealedness. I will attempt to show that truth appears as the manifestation of particularlized psychic expressions that have their source in an unconscious ontology teleologically motivated to disclose itself. Yet the manifestations of such disclosures transpire within a broader dialectical process that constitutes the totality of truth. While each act of disclosedness reveals a particular truth via its manifestations, it simultaneously involves a closing or covering over of other facets of psychic life insofar as each act of unconcealment dialectically stimulates other acts of concealment governed by unconscious agentic forces. Although truth is the appearance of multiplicity, it also participates in a supraordinate, dynamic, and complex holism mediated by mind.

As we will see, Heidegger's project of fundamental ontology is highly relevant to psychoanalysis for its emphasis on the truth of Being as disclosedness within a concurrent shroud of hiddenness. By engaging Heidegger's revisitation of the Greek notion of truth, we may observe how compatible his philosophy is with classical psychoanalytic theory emphasizing unconscious agency, wish and defense, repetition, compromise formation, and the return of the repressed. Although truth is disclosed through a multiplicity of appearances, the question of Being acquires unique ontic significance when we appreciate how psychic reality is constituted by dynamic unconscious processes. Here I wish to advance the notion that the very conditions for truth to be disclosed must be conditioned on unconscious experience. This psychological perspective adds another layer to traditional discourse on the nature of truth, which is relevant to the field of philosophy today. Rather than view consciousness or language as the ground of being, as some contemporary perspectives insist, I argue that the unconscious is the house of Being. Here psychoanalysis has something original to offer the discipline of philosophy.

The Concept of Truth and its Relevance to Psychoanalysis

What is truth? The word itself is obfuscating. Etymologically, it derives from the Old English *trēowth,* meaning loyalty, fidelity—and hence being faithful, a pledging of trust. Today it often signifies conformity to facts or accordance with what is real; but truth claims are also adjudicated by the conveyed intent of the subject's sincerity and honesty about statements in relation to a proven standard. The former definition is what we often associate with a theory of truth: whatever is stated to be true must correspond to actuality. We see this in Plato. In the *Timaeus* he states, "As being is to becoming, so is truth to belief" (29c). Here Plato is emphasizing the distinction between what is "lasting," "irrefutable," "permanent and intelligible" (29b) from what is merely a changing "copy or likeness" of the former, the dialectic between reality and thought. Just as belief approximates truth, we can never know "the eternal things in themselves" (29c). Elsewhere, in the *Gorgias,* while adopting the persona of Socrates, Plato concedes, "I do not speak with any pretense to knowledge, but am searching along with you" (506a). We may say that these passages anticipate the *correspondence theory* of truth: a true assertion corresponds to a state of affairs in reality to which it refers. Truth is what we discover, an independent and intelligible objective fact or datum that corresponds to our mental apprehension of it.

The universal statement "This is truth" is in fact a metaphysical assertion of predication, namely, that which *is,* although truth is typically classified as an epistemological category. Truth presupposes being (ὄν, *esse*) or presence. Asserted propositions must accord with reality, specifying what *is,* namely, that which is the case. This notion of correspondence between propositions and facts presupposes metaphysical realism, which is the assertion that there is a reality independent of mind that is objective, enduring, and actual. Conformity to facts or agreement with reality is the common-sense view of truth; but this definition already begins to show difficulty when epistemologically we may be begging the question. How can we know, let alone prove, that there exists an independent reality or, more specifically, a certain feature of the external world, when all experience, all knowledge, is mediated by mind? If truth is correspondence to reality, then truth must be only a relational property, because whatever is said to be true stands in relation to something external to itself (i.e., objects, facts). But how do we determine facts, when we believe them to be independent of mind, let alone explain how they correspond with mental states that derive their meaning from their mutual relation in the first place? Here truth is said to exist "out there," yet it is determined by mutual *relata*. Here is where the correspondence theory begins to founder.

Within the analytic tradition of philosophy, truth is justified belief based on logical coherence following a formal methodology that clearly sets out propositions, gives precise definitions, and avoids contradictions. Logical truths or analytic judgements may differ from empirical facts that require synthetic judgements based on formal parameters and definitions alone. We see this in Aristotle: "everything that is true must in every respect agree with itself" (*Prior Analytics,* bk I: 47a5). For Aristotle, who introduced the entire field of inductive and deductive logic to Western civilization, truth mirrors consistency and warranted justification. The *coherence theory* of truth offers several versions. Beginning with the idealists, truth is considered to be a system that progressively develops towards a fuller completion of knowledge. Truth claims are verified when they are seen to inhere in a system of beliefs that are consistent and harmonious with one another. Alternatively, logicians and philosophers of language focus on how the truth of certain propositions must cohere correctly with other propositions within a system of defined meaning. Like correspondence of propositions with facts, coherence as a standard of correctness is a relational dynamic dependent on the truth of propositions that refer to one another and together form a coherent structure of meaning. This usually entails the epistemological distinction between true and false beliefs, both weighed in terms of their appropriate justifications. But the problem here is that justified beliefs or warranted assertions that are internally coherent can nonetheless be false.

Pragmatic theories of truth focus on the usefulness of beliefs in human affairs. In the American pragmatist tradition, true assumptions or propositional attitudes are those that promote desired outcomes; there is a certain utility, then, in how beliefs govern behaviour. Here we are concerned with the psychological motives driving certain actions, where truth is assigned value based on the practical consequences of our beliefs, which are held together and validated by community opinion. Here truth becomes whatever works and brings satisfaction. But just because something is useful or brings about a good result does not mean we should tote it under the banner of truth. True or justified beliefs can readily lead to atrocious acts (e.g., war) that are deleterious to all, just as false beliefs and assertions can lead (perhaps by luck, randomness, or chance) to success. Here we run into the same problem posed by the criterion of coherence. That a belief is useful or brings about gratification does not necessarily mean it is true. Here a major criticism is that truth devolves into subjective satisfaction—hardly an adequate criterion of truth. Yet pragmatic approaches can be appealing in a variety of ways. They are often aligned with social norms and customs that govern cultural beliefs, carry moral or practical applications, and conform to the phenomenology or *Lebenswelt* of individuals or groups identified with certain values or subjective experiences that fly in the face of others.

Within psychoanalysis, pragmatic theories have value and have been adopted by perspectivalists (Orange, 1995) and constructivists (Hoffman, 1998; Stern, 1985) who emphasize context and contingency (Stolorow & Atwood, 1992). However, there is always the danger that pragmatic approaches might collapse into relativism or radical subjectivism that defies an objectivist epistemology. Moreover, the postmodern linguistic turn in contemporary psychoanalysis runs a further risk, for truth is always linguistically determined, and hence is defined by grammatical relativism, semantics, social construction, and environmental determinism belonging to the "discourse of the Other" (Lacan, 1960, p. 312). Here objective investigation, empirical science, naturalism, and rational inquiry into the nature of the external world becomes bankrupt: if everything is relative or rests on a negotiated social consensus, there is no such thing as truth in itself.

While all the theories of truth presented so far pose philosophical problems that continue to be debated and are irresolute, these conundrums do not concern us here. There is no need to resolve these age-old philosophical disputes to show that truth is a pivotal construct for psychoanalysis. In fact, the philosopher and psychoanalyst Charles Hanly (1992) considers the concept of truth the "cornerstone" of every method of theoretical, clinical, and applied psychoanalysis (p. 1). But if this is so, why does truth elude definition, let alone consensus? Hanly wants to reinstate the importance of the modern project of truth for psychoanalysis, but he does not offer his own theory. He does, however, point to the value and pursuit of "self-honesty" in the clinical encounter, in both analysand and analyst; through adherence to this value, he believes, the truth about a patient's life will eventually be "uncovered" (p. 216).

Psychoanalysis does not ask, What is the *is*ness of truth, namely, its essence? It does not query its essential conditions or properties. It merely adopts a conventional lexicon. We see this in Freud, who, as Hanly (1992) aptly points out, espoused both correspondence and coherence theories of truth in relation to clinical data and theoretical postulates. Freud (1937) was also concerned with the question of constructions in analysis in relation to historical truth, which has led many analysts to disavow the archaeological method (or metaphor) of recovery of the past as the clinical task of psychoanalysis. Instead, there has recently been an emphasis on co-construction, mutuality, intersubjectivity, relationality, and hermeneutical co-creation, ideas allowing for many faces of truth (Spiegel, 1985). Conversely, some contemporary analysts have adopted the postmodern abnegation of truth and universals altogether (for a critique, see Mills, 2012), a stance whereby the very notion of truth becomes an illusion (Bell, 2009). Yet all along the implicit assumption in psychoanalysis has remained, as in the sciences, that our *object* of inquiry (for us, psychic reality) is "the object whose truth we want to discover" (Loewald, 1970, p. 297). Indeed, many analysts contend that there is an immediacy to unconscious truth (Blass, 2011) that presents itself in the here-and-now moments of the consulting room.

Most of the discourse on truth in the psychoanalytic literature centres on the clinical encounter. Here we find the classical preoccupation with the accuracy of patients' memories and disclosures, the correctness and meaningfulness of interpretations (Laufer, 1994), the conviction of truth induced by the analyst in the patient (Freud, 1937), and the "ideological persuasion" unconsciously foisted on patients by analysts who would have them adopt their own convictions of truth (Avenburg & Guiter, 1976). Spence (1982) focuses on the process of narrative versus the question of theoretical and historical truth, a focus that may be said to have dovetailed with the linguistic turn and dyadic systems or field-matrix approaches introduced by the American middle group. Rosenberg and Medini (1978) argue that the psychoanalytic method can get at only partial truths, because truth is always a process of emergence entangled with interpersonal problems of agreement and disagreement. Even Hanly (1992), who provides the most comprehensive exploration of the topic in the psychoanalytic literature, does not provide an answer.

The real dilemma lies, I suggest, in the bifurcation between the universal and the particular, or the one and the many. On the one hand, the search for first principles (especially the quest for universals) has been the preoccupation of metaphysics since antiquity. As Aristotle reminds us, "the principles of eternal things must be always most true" (*Metaphysics,* bk II (a), 993b25). Does truth exist in itself (as in Platonic forms or systems of propositional logic), or is it created via human relations? Ontologists will likely tell you that if you cannot support a universalist notion of truth, then your theory of truth is a meaningless construct, for it degenerates into relativism or semantics. But perhaps the bifurcation itself is misguided, for here I have emphasized the dichotomy rather than the unity of its poles; nonetheless, this binary tension within philosophy has never been resolved.

As Davidson (2004) argues, truth is a concept, not an object. Truth claims are determinations mediated by human agency through the parameters of language. "Does truth exist in itself?" is a meaningless question to linguistic philosophers because it presupposes value existing outside of human consciousness. If truth is viewed as a matter of correctness or warranted assertability, then any such determination would always be made in relation to human language and agreement, despite the fact that false beliefs may be misconstrued as truth. But if truth is "coolly distant from human concerns," then it will always be independent of human belief and "independent of our existence" (Davidson 2004, p. 1229). So the most we can say is that our knowledge is fallible regarding what we posit to be independent of mind, a norm or criterion of which we will never know. Following this line of reasoning, I would say that truth is not a fact, nor an artifact, of the external world; objects are simply assigned value and qualitative properties mediated through mind and language. This distinction dislocates the question of truth from correspondence with reality to internally and interpersonally mediated transactions. Facts merely *are,* while truth is a mental property attributed to objects or events.

Towards a Metatheory of Truth

> The investigation of the truth is in one way hard, in another easy.
> An indication of this is found in the fact that no one is able to
> attain the truth adequately, while, on the other hand, no one fails
> entirely, but every one says something true about the nature of
> things, and while individually they contribute little or nothing to
> the truth, by the union of all a considerable amount is amassed.
> Therefore, since the truth seems to be like the proverbial door,
> which no one can fail to hit, in this way it is easy, but the fact that
> we can have a truth and not the particular part we aim at shows
> the difficulty of it [Aristotle, *Metaphysics,* bk II(a), 993b1–5].

Here Aristotle highlights the double nature of truth as a community
of particulars, which everyone experiences in some way and in some
fashion, although by themselves they are incomplete, because they
fail to be properly integrated within the larger fabric of a collective
body of knowledge. In the *Metaphysics* Aristotle was attempting to
examine the first principles of causation and our knowledge of such
"in respect of truth" (bk II: 993b30). He intimates that wisdom
broaches a supraordinate assembly of knowledge—what used to be
attributed to philosophy as a whole before disciplines became sharply
divided and compartmentalized into separate academic fields and
research institutions. But we can realize elements of truth only as
individuals wed to context and contingency, despite an overarching
process in the making. Here I am reminded of Edward O. Wilson's
consilient plea (1998) for a fundamental unity of all knowledge that
would assimilate, verify, corroborate, and validate disparate fields
into an integrated metascience. While this dream may seem lofty, if
not grandiose and full of countless difficulties, the pursuit of a unified
body of knowledge was exactly the ambition of philosophy.

The meaning of truth is encumbered by its history. There has been
a preponderant focus on the binary between realism and idealism, or
on the essential and mind-independent qualities of truth as objective
fact versus our conceptualization and experience of what we perceive
and conceive to be, as well as on the definitional parameters of truth,
which has traditionally referred to a static property of a logical
proposition. It may not be possible to transcend this burden,

however. It is misleading to think of truth as one thing, which is a category mistake; rather, we should conceive of truth as being divided into different *kinds* or particulars, each of which may belong to a certain *class*. In other words, particulars may participate in certain *forms* or categories of truth.

Let me distinguish three categories of truth: (1) the *ontology* of truth, which has to do with being and essence; (2) the *epistemology* of truth, which has to do with criteria of knowledge, interpretation, belief, and justification; and (3) the *phenomenology* of truth, which has to do with how truth appears or manifests. These are distinct discourses, although they overlap and coexist on parallel process levels with various degrees of interdependence operative at any given moment. What is important for the purposes of psychoanalytic observation and applied theory is to define and elucidate the kinds of truth that inhere in a particular category or form. Although the three categories are not exhaustive, and hence stand in need of further reflection and development, they may guide us in offering a descriptive analysis of truth as a metatheory rather than as prescriptive or definitive.

Whether psychoanalysis is concerned with describing an ontological state of affairs (correspondence), determining the logical relations between statements that fit properly within a system of interpretation and knowledge (coherence), or allowing the patient's unique lived experience to unfold in the (pragmatic) treatment encounter, the analytic task becomes defined by its context and purpose in relation to the various ways truth may appear. For example, the goals of theoretical and applied psychoanalysis may be entirely different from those of clinical theory, methodology, pedagogy, and praxis. As shifting contexts and aims present themselves, so too do questions regarding psychoanalytic truth. Within the context of treatment, the question of truth speaks to a certain psychological revelation and impact it has on the subject, whose unique subjectivity is affected on the most archaic levels regulating unconscious organizing principles. This applies as well to the analyst's subjectivity and its felt reverberation on the therapeutic dyad. Here practical matters are most important, for truth is ultimately about personal, lived experience *(Erlebnis)* as self-realization and self-honesty within an intersubjective space that promotes and facilitates this burgeoning process. Here truth may be said to transpire within the broader domains of authenticity, creativity, and valuation that permeate the analytic encounter. In this context, truth may be adjudicated based on its *genuineness,* openness, frank candor, or brute manifestation in the actual moment (Latin *genuinus,* natural < Greek *geneia,* born). Here we should view truth not as an absolute category that discloses itself in its entirety, but rather as a contextual process that reveals itself a bit at a time and from many different perspectives. This is what we witness in the consulting room.

Because there are so many versions of truth that emphasize constructivist, linguistic, semantic, and performative features of speech acts, where assent, consensus, and endorsement of statements determine the strictures of truth, as well as theories we have not even touched upon (e.g., deflationary, minimalist, prosentential, and redundancy perspectives in reference to truth predicates), it would on the face of things appear prudent to endorse a pluralistic theory of truth wherein more than one property can, depending on context, make a proposition true. Here truth is delineated as a functional property that is multiply instantiated (Lynch, 2009). By and large, psychoanalysts are not as concerned with these scholarly controversies as they are with practical matters germane to their craft (*phronēsis*). From this standpoint, a metatheory of truth tailored to particular questions, purposes, and contexts may be the most sensible option on the table. But whatever approach we adopt (itself conditioned on warranted assertability susceptible to fallibility), we must concede that it is always open to flux and dynamic change based on the fact that there will never be a final end of inquiry at which data, ideas, and knowledge are complete, perfectly sufficient, and immune from further revision. This means that truth will always be a relative or contingent matter depending on our definition of adequacy and completeness, which ultimately stands in relation to our penumbral goals, purposes, methodologies, and modes of discourse.

How does a metatheory of truth apply to psychoanalytic theory and clinical process? Can truth coalesce in a conceptual scheme, and/or be signified and revealed through such a scheme? Can the theoretical models of drive, ego, object, self, and intersubjectivity all radiate elements of truth simultaneously despite the varying emphasis analysts place on different facets of psychic reality and clinical praxis?

Can we not see gradations of truth in all psychoanalytic discourses? When classical theory postulates an unconscious dominion, or Jungian theory an archetypal objective psyche, or Lacanian theory the Real (the ineffable domain of desire), these truth claims are *ontological* propositions, just as how we come to *know* the unconscious, the archetypal, and the real is mediated by various *epistemological* criteria (empirical, inferential, semiotic, rational) that are revealed as *phenomena* to both patient and analyst. Each subfield of psychoanalysis has its preferred way of conceptualizing the human condition and the analytic encounter, and some of these conceptions are at odds with one another. Can all of them be correct? Notice here that I have deliberately invoked the traditional correspondence-coherence view of truth when posing this question, the legitimacy of which is in question. Perhaps a better way to frame the issue is to ask, Are they equally germane? The answer to which is yes, each within its own frame of discourse. But what happens when the discourse of one psychoanalytic school clashes with that of another? Does this automatically make one right and the other wrong, or is this an example of how truth presents multiple appearances? It all depends what we are looking for. Those seeking one irrefutable Truth will not find it, as this expectation overlooks the multiplicity of manifestation as emergence. I will attempt to make these points more explicit when I present a clinical example.

Lacan once said that when a patient speaks, he speaks the truth, but never the whole truth.[1] We can never enunciate the whole truth, for it appears only in partial expressions. Here we may say that truth is harbored unconsciously, or as Aristotle puts it, that "the soul possesses truth" (*Nicomachean Ethics,* bk VI, 1139b15). The psychoanalyst's pursuit of truth is that of the soul-searcher, the "psyche-analyst" whose mission is to observe and interpret unconscious phenomenology. And, may I add, to heal suffering whenever possible. I suggest that the quest for truth is most useful as a phenomenological-hermeneutic project, that is, determining how truth *appears* and how appearance as such is to be *interpreted*. Truth manifestations are imbued with meaning, value, and explanatory power. But this is an idiosyncratic enterprise, for as Aristotle notes, "the truth is not that what appears exists, but that what appears exists *for him to whom* it appears, and *when,* and *in the sense in which,* and *in the way in which* it appears" (*Metaphysics,* bk IV, 1011a20). Here truth involves *metacontextual* interpretation. Whatever appears must be accompanied by a hermeneutic referent if it is to lend any significance or meaning to appearance; thus, appearance and inter- pretation are coextensive yet conjoined as a phenomenohermeneutic unit. The *quest*-ion facing psychoanalytic truth becomes, How do we interpret appearance?

Truth as Unconcealment

Heidegger's elaboration of the ground and presencing of Being as it is portrayed philosophically can be understood in a very Freudian manner, depending on what aspect of his project you engage. His dual presentation of truth as both revealing and concealing applies to how the analyst understands unconscious communication, resistance, and repression, which is highly congenial with the classical, Kleinian, and ego psychological traditions. Further, the analyst's task of bringing into the open and uncovering hiddenness from its disguised lair goes to the very heart of psychoanalytic technique.

In Section 44 of *Being and Time,* Heidegger (1927) discusses the relation between Dasein, disclosedness, and truth. This was the be- ginning of his later preoccupation with the pre-Socratic notion of ἀλήθεια, which he translates as *Unverborgenheit* or "unconcealed- ness." Truth as *aletheia* is a form of disclosure, unconcealment, or uncoveredness that reveals itself through that which appears. Heidegger argues that Plato's and Aristotle's interpretation of truth as "correctness" distorted its original meaning, and hence his cardinal concern was a proper return to the "first inception" of understanding the iteration of Being.

Lethe is the river of forgetfulness in Greek mythology. *A-letheia* is its reversal, an unforgetting of what previously was hidden. In psy- choanalysis the paradigmatic example of this phenomenon is the return of the repressed. Heidegger was fastidious in investigating how the truth of being is disclosed or uncovered from its hiddenness. This discourse fits nicely in a psychoanalytic paradigm because we are interested primarily in (1) the *act* of "uncovering" the unconscious elements of a patient's subjectivity, and (2) the *specific* "uncoverings" of what is disclosed, namely, the contents and details of mental objects, memories, fantasies, linkages to past representations, and so on. The notion of truth as unhiddenness also points to a process of how unconscious phenomena unfold and divulge themselves to patient and analyst. Truth can exist only if it is revealed, but for Heidegger what is disclosed or shines forth is something that was already present but hidden. Here we have a fine discourse on unconscious phenomenology.

In Heidegger's treatment of Phenomenon (§7, A), he is concerned with highlighting the distinct nuances of disclosure that cannot be reduced to a simple uniformity. The English word "truth" is therefore an imposition, as it forces a single categorization on appearance when truth eludes such categorization in its distinct moments. When we refer here to "appearance," we do not mean "semblance" (Heidegger equates the two meanings), or that which looks like what it is not; rather, we mean *"that which shows itself in itself,* the manifest" (*BT*, p. 51). When Heidegger begins unpacking the meaning of *phaino-menon* (φαινόμενον) as the manifest, or that which shows itself, we immediately begin to see how convoluted the concept of truth becomes. Heidegger speaks of the double entendre of appearance as something that announces itself, and in this sense is showing itself, but this showing is merely semblance—hence not a true showing itself, which makes it nonmanifest. Therefore, what is taken as the manifest could be merely a veil. What is behind the veil is the task of psychoanalytic inquiry. But in order not to further muddle our conventional discourse, phenomenon and appearance should, for our purposes here, be viewed as equivalent constructs.

Heidegger's reintroduction of the ancient concept of truth has many nuances bearing directly on the suppleness of psychoanalytic observation and interpretive technique. For example, to "disclose" is to open or reverse a closure; to "reveal" is to remove the veil; and to "discover" is to undo the act of covering. These subtle processes expose the fine distinctions in how mental functioning operates on the way ego processes allow certain material to enter consciousness while other material is barred (an operation to be differentiated from the speech utterances of free association and the enunciation of that material, which may or may not be met with censorship or resistance), and on the defensive and transferential processes operative intrapsychically and within the analytic dyad. But we may ask, What does it mean for something to show itself? A slip, an unintentional act or utterance, forgetfulness, a bungled action—are these not disclosures or revelations of a peculiar kind? Spontaneous gestures reveal a truth. Psychoanalysis generally presupposes that there are meaningful communications (as disclosures) transmitted through these events. The *event itself* is the manifest. How we come to interpret its signification is another matter.

When Heidegger discusses the concept of *logos* (λόγος) and truth (ἀλήθεια) (see §7, B), he tells us that "discourse" as *logos* "lets something be seen" by making it manifest and accessible to another party.[2] The character of speaking authentically, in particular, reveals a certain truth to be made manifest, and hence "seen *as* something," which is taken out of its "hiddenness" (*BT*, p. 56). The "Being-true" of *logos* is therefore made manifest or seen as the unhidden (ἀληθές), which must be discovered or uncovered (*entdeckt*). That which is seen is that which is unconcealed; however, it may need to be looked for because it can escape notice, as our perceptions are not always sufficiently attuned to what is disclosed. This is in contrast to "Being-false," which is an act of deceiving or of covering up (*verdecken*) something so it cannot be seen, as by deliberate obstruction (placing one thing in front of another so it cannot be seen: a defense), or of concealment.

We can readily see how the ancient conception of truth can apply to the consulting room. The notion of truth as discovery (contra construction) is the immediate presentation of a something, what Hegel (1807) refers to as "sense certainty," of a showing itself—that which is unveiled—the naked truth. Here truth is a presencing of particularized being, a self-revealing of itself. Picture the process of free association as the analysand speaks whatever comes to mind: each utterance, or its omission, signifies an unconscious communication as well as a meaning. So does silence. The trick (elusive and difficult as it may be) is in understanding the nuances and discrepancies within the contextual moment in which truth may be released, partly breached, or foreclosed altogether. Of course in practice free association is fraught with internal resistances, denial, refutations, censorship, interpersonal reservations, and countertransference enactments that stymie or occlude the pure self-revealing of intrapsychic phenomena. This intricate dynamic typifies the overdetermined defensive nature of mental processes, which reflects an inherent split in agency that is divided in its purposes and revelatory confessions, hence falling under the rubric of compromise formation and felt intrusions (fantasized or real) from the analyst/other. Yet the mere mobilization of resistive and reactive internal pressures from the analysand points to the presence of agentic forces designed to guard against the disclosure of certain truths it finds threatening, while securing a clearing for others to manifest as unconcealment.

Although analysts all work differently, in our therapeutic work we often listen to the manifest content, the themes, the derivatives, and emotional valences, thus waiting patiently for latent material and past patterns to resurface, when, spontaneously, we sense the incongruity, feel the discontinuity, observe the slip, hear the broken utterance, the pause, the silence, the confusion, the patient's self-conscious hesitancy, lack of clarity, and so on. Faulty achievements (*Fehlleistungen*) are the revelation of unconscious phenomena, the conveyance of buried truths. The slip that breaches the gap into consciousness reveals its unconscious essence: that which appears is freed from its concealment, even if unintentionally or by accident. For Freud, the ontology of unconscious truth is epitomized by the occurrence of dreams, parapraxes, and symptoms: like the dream's navel, *der Nabel des Traums* (Freud, 1900, p. 525)—a convoluted mass of condensation and displacement—truth remains at once exposed yet interred. Unconscious truth is partially disclosed in these moments, and it is not merely a matter of constructing their significance or interpreting a resistance. Of course metatruths are operative here, as the analyst engages in a parallel process of one's own in relation to the intersubjective system itself. Contra the notion of construction and reconstruction in analysis, here truth does not consist in making something out of that which appears, such as the co-creation of meaning in the therapeutic dyad (though that could later become a locus of *logos,* a hermeneutic framing by revisiting that which previously manifested). The point I wish to emphasize here is that truth *prereflexively* presents itself *as itself:* it is not assigned or co-constructed; rather, it is disclosed *as* self-disclosure, the self-showing of phenomena. Here the interpretation of meaning becomes a second-order structuring or emergent property of its original manifestation.

Heidegger's apophantical (predicate) discourse, which is derived from Husserl,[3] is concerned primarily with a secondary form of disclosing—namely, *talk*—but he wants to trace its original union to the "letting-show-self" of phenomena, or "to-the-things themselves." How would this look to the psychoanalyst? Despite the fact that Heidegger rejected the psychoanalytic concept of the unconscious,[4] his preoccupation with discovering truth within the recalcitrant realm of that which lies hidden speaks to an unconscious ontology of being in which its purpose (*telos*) is to show itself.[5] There are several distinct moves or activities in which this can occur: (1) the act of opening, or making-to-open, whereby we may investigate a state of openedness (*Erschlossenheit*)—ultimately for Heidegger this is Dasein,[6] the extant human being in the world; (2) opening up into openness (*Offenheit*), which prepares a spacing or establishes a clearing for a disclosure, one that may appear or have the potential to appear; and, finally, (3) disclosedness itself, that which shines forth as self-showing. At this stage, there is a *determinate quality* to what manifests. That which has become open is the object of our investigation, and that which is disclosed is the product of its self-manifestation. This implies some form of agency at work. Here it may not be inappropriate to make a comparison between the unconscious agentic act of preparing a psychic space for openness (as we do in treatment, or while free associating, or during the course of recollection or working through, etc.), where a clearing or region for openness is pruned away and becomes host to a sea of potential objects to be made manifest, objects specifically made determinate (e.g., memories, images, desires, affects): hence, that which is concretely disclosed.

Being in the open is where revealedness (*Offenbarkeit*) occurs. This may metaphorically signify the consulting room, or psychic reality, or the analytic discourse. And what is the condition or agent of therapeutic action? It is the creation of a psychological atmosphere in which the clearing can occur. To me it seems essential that nurturing the ground—as well as tending to the garden—for a clearing to take place determines *when* and *what* will reveal itself. This could be the genuine article, or a covering over of that article with a facade, itself a form of disclosedness, yet one that keeps the original artifact hidden.

From this standpoint, *whatever* manifests is a disclosure. One may quibble over the authenticity of the disclosure, saying it is "not really truth" because the repressed object remains hidden, or the censor barrier has prevented a further revealing, or the defense overshadows the original wish, or the conscious ego has dismissed the disclosure or resisted the interpretation, and so on, but this does not negate the fact that psychic phenomena are potentially infinite. If we look at truth only from the vantage point of a correspondent state of affairs, or consensual assent to propositions or facts, or warranted assertability as justified belief, then we miss the point (and hence the manifestation) because we are reverting to a discourse on "correctness." Is there any such thing as a "correct" defense, or are they merely revelations (revealings) as unconscious articulation?

The unconscious speaks the truth, but not the whole truth at once. What remains hidden can be revealed, only then to be covered over by another articulation, or covered up entirely as a reburial, a return to the grave of repression. One enactment may serve to promote a false truth, which is a disguise or persona, in order to cover over or reconceal an earlier appearance; but there is an unconscious intention in this act of negation, the intention to present another appearance that promotes a false presence, yet one that is nevertheless revealed. Here the lie is present although it may remain hidden, perhaps even concealed from itself as self-deception. We are not aware of our self-deception because one who is in possession of the truth or genuine knowledge is aware that one is lying by concealing a certain truism, as Sartre (1943) famously pointed out. An unconscious manifestation, to the contrary, is the revelation of a lie to oneself that has been *opened*.

And what is the role of the analyst? On the one hand, the analyst is an *opener*, for the analytic encounter sets the stage for preparing a proper clearing for psychic exploration. But I would suggest that this role is privileged primarily by the subject who discloses, because it is the agent behind the role that *allows* an opening, not just the material that is disclosed; yet the process of opening is mutually implicative in the analytic relationship. On the other hand, the analyst is a *discoverer*, as the work of uncovering is facilitated by the carefully fostered and organic ambience of the therapeutic relationship. Perhaps the analyst is the first to witness the manifest as it surfaces, especially as the patient acquires education in introspection and self-observation through the analytic method. In fact, Heidegger (1927) specifically refers to the *logos* transpiring in the speech act between interlocutors as the space where signification is acquired "in its relation to something in its 'relatedness'" (*BT*, p. 58). Here "interpretation" unfolds within a "relationship" in which potential multiple meanings surface from a clearing based on a certain setting forth, exhibiting, laying out, recounting, and so forth, that transparently applies to the clinical encounter.

Clinical Illustration

There are countless examples from clinical experience that any analyst can draw on to illustrate the power of unconscious disclosedness as the revelation of hidden truth. Here I present a fragment of a session from a patient who was about one year into his six-year analytic treatment. Rather than focus on the historical dynamics of his case and his developmental traumas, I will for concision present the following interchange as the patient associated from the couch. A central theme in the patient's life at this time was his inability to see women as loving, nurturing subjects, as well as sexual beings, roles he tended to compartmentalize and keep unintegrated rather than form a holistic metarepresentation. Before entering analysis, he had made a suicide attempt following a breakup with a "sexually aggressive" woman he both desired and was repulsed by. That had led him to reactively seek meeker, "safer" women who were nonthreatening but "boring" and "plain." He had just begun dating a new girlfriend at the time of the session to be reported, and just immediately before this exchange we were discussing the "lines" between love and sex that he felt were "blurred" in his mind:

Patient: We were lying in bed and I wanted to tell her about what we had talked about, about my mom and dad, even my brother, that I always felt like I had to chase their love ... and she tried to comfort me. I was teary-eyed when we started to talk; she was lying there with me, then she [in an affective voice] started to touch my crotch—and I yelled out "What are you doing?!" I just started bawling ... she

Analyst: apologized and held me. I couldn't stop. She kept stroking my hair ... it felt so good. [silence] Earlier that night I put my face on her belly. I remember when I was a little boy, around seven, I went to my parent's room'cuz I had an earache; Mom lifted her nightgown and said put my ear on her belly'cuz it was warm. I remember it seemed kind of odd, but it was so comforting. She never gave affection much, or hugs. [silence] I notice I like to touch people when I talk ... like women's hair. She wouldn't let me touch her face when I was little, she'd get all pissed off. [long silence]

Analyst: What is it about touch?

Patient: I don't know ... confusing.

Analyst: What comes to mind?

Patient: I can't seem to separate between these lines.

Analyst: Lines you just don't cross. [silence]

Patient: I remember now. I was up at my aunt's cottage in New Brunswick, sitting on a picnic table with my mom and my aunt and me, and Mom and her were talking about sex or something, and Mom said, "Are you small?" No, "Are you big or what?" and she poked me right in the crotch—and I said [in an exaggerated voice] "Mom!" And she said [in a mocking manner] "Mom!" back, like she was making fun of me. [silence] This is the first time I've thought of this since then. [starts crying] I couldn't believe she would touch my penis. She wasn't supposed to do that. [sobs profusely with hands in face]

Whether you interpret this clinical phenomenon from the standpoint of repression and Oedipalization, dissociation and relational trauma, and forgotten sexual abuse or as a mixture of symptom formation, fantasy, and retrieved memory, what is important to emphasize is the spontaneous process of resurfacing of a truth that had remained consciously absent yet unconsciously present until now. In fact, there are myriad truths that can be unpacked from this narrative, the most dominant of which spoke for the subject. It may further be suggested that the analytic milieu facilitated a psychic clearing that allowed a certain opening in the patient's mind, one that enabled a specific discovering (unveiling) to naturally ensue whereby the particularized truth was revealed as mnemonic linkages were recovered.

Unconscious productions that expose themselves through psychic appearances take on innumerable forms, many of them prereflectively instituted—that is, unintentionally disclosed. In this clinical example, truth instituted itself, which obliged further truths to be explored and analysed, as others were re-veiled. But a certain problematic arises when we view the truth of phenomena as merely prereflexive or, in other words, as tautologically self-instantiating. I am reminded here of Fichte's (1794) absolute self that posits or asserts (hence thinks) itself into existence. This is untenable without taking into account a material (embodied) foundation or corporeality within which mind emerges. We must account for an original ground for any phenomenon to appear. If phenomena are a pure self-showing, then an endless universe of truths exist as that which spontaneously self-manifests. But why should we grant the status of truth to that which manifests? Quite plainly, because *whatever exists is true*. Yet we have already determined that predication necessarily makes truth contingent on the relativity of perspective and the relationality of signification based on *apophansis*. Here we need to reflect on the circumstances that make such determinations possible. The propositional acts of relativity and relationality must emanate from an essential ontology, that which conditions all phenomena. In other words, we cannot speak of the manifest until we address the ground that makes the manifest possible. In order for there to be appearance at all, it must derive from an original, a priori ground.

That which manifests is actual; whatever exists is true. But what happens when truth presents as truth when it is merely semblance, or recedes into the underworld of its original hiddenness once it has revealed itself? Once again, this implies an agentic factor at play. And here Heidegger could not elude the spectre of the dialectic. In "On the Essence of Truth" Heidegger (1930) continued his analysis of revealed being as transpiring within a clearing that opens a space for unconcealment. As each space reveals the potential for truth to appear as phenomena, there is conversely a closing, in that truth may be revealed only in the wake of concealment. This movement of uncovering in the presence of covering underlies the dialectical organization of truth.[7]

The Dialectics of Truth

As Heidegger elucidates, discourse, or talk (ἀπόφαυσις), is the fulcrum allowing the *logos* of truth to be disclosed. Truth "proceeds out from" the very thing we are talking about, for truth is a self-showing articulation. Here we are interested in the phenomenology of truth, and hence its process and means of appearance, not necessarily *how* we know. Yet the two issues are inseparable because the determination of truth is always a hermeneutic enterprise, for truth is conditioned by discourse. This process is not unlike the analytic method, for phenomena show themselves through monologue during free association, as well as through dialogical exchange. Truth ensues from talk; in effect, *it* speaks for itself.[8] Here I am reminded of patients who, after a lengthy flow of speaking out loud their internal chain of thoughts, discover something known but forgotten, something previously hidden but now exposed. We should not be surprised when our patients say "I knew that all along!" for the unconscious speaks a dialectical language. Whether truth is disclosed as revealed repression or as formulated *dis*-sociative experience, other psychic processes are at the same time dialectically operative, such as ancillary reactions of covering over the bare phenomenon, or the subsequent barring of further material from entering consciousness, it thereby remaining cloaked, as uncovering leads to re-covering. Here the dialectics of truth tell a saga of the concealed unforgotten.

When Freud instituted the fundamental rule as a pledge to honesty, he observed truth as the inverse of honesty, as the radical (albeit genuine) rejection of the imposition itself. Conventional discourse bids us not to be fully honest, not to say whatever we think without censoring it: these defenses are socially conditioned from childhood. Thus, to betray the self-preservative element of defense is not natural. That is why it is only by accident, by the unintentional slip or faulty achievement (*Fehlleistung*), that truth is revealed. The ethic of honesty during free association is met with an innate tendency towards self-censorship (i.e., resisting awareness of the surfacing material, negating the significance of certain verbalizations or the analyst's queries or interpretations, and so forth); or with a covering over (such as disavowal, undoing, minimization, reversal) in the winnowing of unconcealedness. For every surfacing there is a countermeasure, and for every burying-over there is a later resurfacing. And what is buried over may remain undiscovered, or it can be re-excavated. What arises may return. This is what Heidegger meant when he referred to the binary of covering up in the shadow of uncovering. Yet, as I have described it so far, this is a simple dialectical repetition of the reiteration of oppositions.

For Heidegger (1927), the uncoveredness of truth is Dasein "there" in its existential constituency as its elemental state of Being. We are born into a world already constituted yet always in a process of becoming. In Heidegger's words, "Dasein's *disclosedness* is the *most primordial* phenomenon of truth attained" (§44, (b), *BT*, p. 263). And like unconscious order, this is not transparent. We exist *in* a world and *alongside* other entities in the world, and within our *own* internal world and *for* our own relatedness to self and others equiprimordially *with* and *through* the world that is always temporally transmuting, and hence shifting the field and figure-ground of our perspectives. This is why Heidegger insists that the structure of our disclosedness lies hidden. But what he fails to say or accept is that our primordial structure is unconsciously constituted. Our most basic constitution of Being-there as phenomena is the essence of truth because Dasein *is* its disclosure and is "in the truth."[9] This is an ontological claim, not merely an epistemological determination, as some proponents of truth wish to have it. In other words, truth is *real* but elusive: disclosedness is "factical" yet abstruse.

What is not specifically addressed by Heidegger, but implicit all along in his treatment of Dasein, is the unconscious manifestations of disclosedness. We are *thrown* into existence: this is part of our historicity and is an objective empirical fact. Those who wish to dismiss salient realism are misguided, for the pre-phenomenological presence of the past is an ontological principle already constitutive of the human being. Elsewhere I have referred to this as archaic primacy (Mills, 2010), for the past metaphysically conditions the present and the future despite the fact that it may not determine the developmental path or vicissitudes of the experiential subject. Our thrownness presupposes an unconscious ontology because it is the original ground of Being, a ground without a ground (*Ungrund*) that conditions the potential for disclosure, openness, and that which is opened, as well as what is concealed, covered over, and returned to the antediluvian origins of its unconscious abyss (Mills, 2002).

Heidegger elevates the disclosive property of "projection" as the human subject's Being-toward its potentiality and future possibilities. Here Dasein is a bid for freedom and expression of its "ownmost Being-for-Self." And this is what differentiates truth as the subject's pursuit of authenticity versus its existential tendency to fall into inauthenticity or falseness. This is where Heidegger institutes the dialectical necessity of the polarity of *movement* that Dasein is destined to enact. All human beings vacillate between authentic and inauthentic modes of being, which are ontologically given as a formal condition of the truth of Dasein's disclosedness. In actuality (not merely abstraction), it is Dasein in its authentic modes of comporting, relating, and disclosing that differentiates its transcendental moments from its ordinary, corrupt, and pathological ways of being in the world as a falsehood (Mills, 1997). What is pivotal in any substantive discussion of Dasein's falseness is the presence and ubiquity of our *pathos* (πάθος), a necessary (though insufficient) unconscious condition of what it means to be human. Heidegger refers to this condition as our *fallenness,* our proclivity to lapse into lassitude, to close off and cover up, to hide and disguise, to listen to "the they" and accept gossip, idle curiosity, ambiguity, and fiction as truth. To be human is to suffer, and this indisputable truism is part of the dialectical manifestations of Dasein's process of unconcealment in the act of concealment. The dialectical structure of being human is to be both *in truth within untruth,* its double face.[10]

Truth always resurfaces; the unconscious always reveals itself, usually in cryptic and circuitous ways. Analyses of these resurfacings point towards *aletheia,* or in Heidegger's (1966) words, "the opening of presence" (p. 390), the light of Being. This is what I take to be the project of psychoanalysis, to be continuously open to the light of what is presented from the shadowed netherworld. Despite the fact that in 1927 Heidegger reintroduced philosophy to the question of truth by revisiting the ancients, which with his enunciation of the truth of Being became a lifelong preoccupation, he failed to appreciate that unconcealment as the manifest is the instantiation of unconscious self-revelation. What this means is that unconscious agency is an a priori organization that reveals itself through the manifestations of consciousness. In other words, *the unconscious is the house of Being.*

The dialectics of truth (as the simultaneous process of disclosedness and hiddenness) dovetails nicely with a psychoanalytic framework of unconscious motivation and defense. A fundamental tenet of psychoanalysis is that mental agencies are interactive, expressive, and communicative, and transpire in tandem with one another governed by an unconscious nucleus under the influence of psychic determinism. These forces in the mind are born of compromise and are mutually implicative, all clamoring for release of the life within. There are fundamental divisions, splittings, and oppositions that characterize the interpsychic fabrics and interpersonal relations that transpire within and between separate subjects, just as transference and countertransference are mutually operative at any given moment in the analytic environment, let alone our general orientation to the world at large.

The dialectics of consciousness and unconsciousness, wish and defense, the pleasure principle versus reality, desire and prohibition, primary versus secondary process thinking, awareness and repression, and the inter-constellations of drive, ego, object, self, and intersubjectivity all speak to the dialectics of truth from their own standpoint. Whether we evoke the trinity of It, I, and superego, imaginary, symbolic, and real, or embodiment, affect, and cognition; the dynamics of projective identification, where splitting, projection, and introjection form a reciprocal dialectical pattern; the perpetual compromise functions, formations, and substitutions fashioned through internal conflict; or the relationship between inner and outer, self and other, the selfobject milieu, and the interpersonal system itself—all are conditioned on unconscious motivations and their ensuing consequences. From drive to dissociation, wish and relationality, the intrapsychic to the intersubjective, all modes of psychic activity are dependent on the contingencies of unconscious process, the central activities of which form the ground of psychic reality. Thus, the dialectics of disclosedness and concealment become the edifice of psychoanalytic theory.

Coda

The concept of truth is relevant to every intellectual discipline in the history of ideas, yet it remains elusive and enigmatic. In some discourses we are accustomed to think of truth as the semiotic signification of universality and finality, a category of the ultimate. In others, truth is foreclosed, subjective, or purported not to exist. The very word imports an act of hubris—a proclamation of grandiosity, a definitive statement about the real. Yet this final, absolute signification stamped in the meaning of the word has acquired sundry meanings and interpretations peculiar to various schools of philosophy, not to mention the common man. The notion of truth has many potential meanings all at once, from the universal to the particular, the private to the social. We may historically observe theories of truth centring on correspondence to reality or factual events; logical coherence; epistemological sincerity and justified belief; empirical verifiability; linguistic determinism; social constructivism; pragmatic utility; relativism; and an unfolding supraordinate process or complex holism. Truth has also been elevated to the ontological status of virtue—the striving of pure reason and science, the noble good, the ideal or sublime object of knowledge, and hence the property of the enlightened mind.

In revisiting the ancient notion of *aletheia* as disclosedness or unconcealment, we have discovered a psychoanalytic contribution to truth conditioned on an unconscious ontology responsible for the simultaneous acts of revealing and concealing. The dialectics of truth allow for distinct categories and instantiations to emerge as meta-contextual appearance, which may be said to constitute a general metatheory of truth. The question of truth may be seen as most useful if conceived as a phenomenohermeneutic project, yet one that participates in an overall process of being-in-becoming, which conditions the fount of appearances that spring from its essential ontological structure. As the house of Being, the dynamic unconscious provides a logical model for the ground and explication of psychic appearances as such.

Truth lies in the endless manifestation of appearances that in themselves shine forth as authentic phenomena (insofar as they simply *happen*), but by themselves they are only micro-units of a greater totality or unfolding process of becoming that reveals itself as momentary intercessions. Here truth becomes an encompassing principle, which can be revealed only as a plethora of appearances, for its holistic structure cannot all appear at once. Therefore truth is a logical category of unity and inclusion, but its distinct appearances never disclose its wholeness. This will ensure that any appearance of truth will always remain half-hidden, behind the back of truth, so to speak. Perhaps this partial hiddenness metaphorically represents the privileges of the abyss, for the concealed and undisclosed forms of being that are imperceptible yet always present may be said to properly belong to an unconscious agency, yet one that allows for multiple appearances within the broader ontological configurations that comprise psychic reality. The unconscious is continually self-concealing as it is revealing, traversing the openings it generates for itself as it retreats into its closings within its underworld. And here we have a genuine psychoanalytic theory of truth.

Notes

1 The exact reference eludes me, but the remark may have been made on one of Lacan's televised lectures designed for the French public.

2 *Logos* is a convoluted concept that has acquired many different meanings throughout the history of philosophy. Λόγος is customarily translated as "reason," "meaning," "judgement," "intelligence," "concept," "word," "definition," "assertion," "ground," or "relationship," which means it always succumbs to interpretation. Heidegger argues that its original, basic signification is "discourse."

3 *Apophansis* was introduced in traditional phenomenology by Husserl in his *Logical Investigations*. Recall that Heidegger was Husserl's pupil and he dedicated *Sein und Zeit* to his mentor. When I visited the Husserl-Archives at the Institute of Philosophy, Leuven University, Belgium, I was allowed to examine the autographed copy Heidegger gave to Husserl upon its publication. Close inspection of the book revealed copious hand-written question marks ("?") inserted by Husserl in the margins throughout the book.

4 William Richardson (1993) alerts us to Heidegger's criticism and dismissal of Freud's metapsychology (p. 54). In fact it was the Swiss psychiatrist and psychoanalyst Medard Boss who introduced Heidegger to Freud's work. According to Boss, Heidegger "couldn't believe that such an intelligent man could write such stupid things, such fantastical things, about men and women" (Craig, 1988, p. 34). Keep in mind that Heidegger was institutionalized at the Haus Baden Sanatorium (where Boss worked) for a mental breakdown and alleged suicide attempt following his interrogation by the denazification commission shortly

after the end of World War II for his involvement with the National Socialist Party. There he underwent therapeutic treatment by a trained psychoanalyst, Dr. Viktor von Gebsattel (see Askay and Farquhar, 2011). Later, once Boss and Heidegger had established a firm friendship, the latter's Zollikon Seminars were delivered to psychiatrists and various medical professionals at Boss' home over a ten-year period (1959–1969). This was the impetus for Boss (along with Ludwig Binswanger) to initiate the Daseinsanalytic method of psychotherapy.

5 Here I am speaking of a formal, purposeful unconscious agency driving all mental acts. For a more elaborate account of unconscious agency and teleology, refer to *Origins: On the Genesis of Psychic Reality* (Mills, 2010, pp. 134–136).

6 Dasein is Heidegger's term for the human being, literally translated as "Being-there." We find ourselves born into a world already pre-given and constituted, where we exist alongside others within established social structures, and thereby come to developmentally cultivate various existential capacities for relating to our world, others, and ourselves as psychological creatures. Dasein's disclosedness as Being-in-the-world is Heidegger's project for a fundamental ontology outlined in *Being and Time*.

7 Compare to the dialectical binary tension he creates between Being and truth in his lecture series of 1941, which has been translated as *Basic Concepts* (Heidegger, 1981), especially in three sections of Part I, Second Division: §10. Being is the most intelligible and at the same time concealment; §13. Being is the most said and at the same time a keeping silent; §14. Being is the most forgotten and at the same time remembrance. In these sections he highlights the hidden, repressive, and silent voice of unconscious being.

8 Recall that the It *(Es)* is Freud's final theoretical designation for dynamic unconscious processes.

9 Heidegger makes the claim that truth reveals itself as freedom, which is its very essence (*Essenz*). For Heidegger, what truth is really about is essence—not things, but rather about what makes something what it is. Here he returns to his ancient roots. For Aristotle, essence is that which makes a thing what it is, without which it would not and could not exist. What we customarily translate as "essence" (ουσία) is "the what it is to be"' (*to ti ein einai*). In his earlier work, Aristotle was referring to universals when he spoke of essence, which he viewed as primary substances. If they "did not exist, it would be impossible for any of the other things to exist" (*Categories*, 5: 2b5). Later he emphasized the definitional properties that signify a thing's essence, or the characteristics it has to have to make it what it is (see *Topics*, I: 5, 101b37). This requires us to think about the ground of truth, what is truly fundamental, that which makes truth possible. Heidegger's conclusion (1930) is that "the essence of truth is the truth of essence" (*Das Wesen der Wahrheit ist die Wahrheit des Wesens*) (p. 140). This is not a simple tautology. Essence is what makes things what they really are, and thinking about the nature of essence should be the locus of our critical inquiry. And for Hegel (1830), essence *must appear* in order for anything to be made actual (*EL* §131). In other words, truth exists.

10 Heidegger does not profess to have a grand synthesis of everything, unlike Hegel's philosophy of Spirit (*Geist*). His project of fundamental ontology outlined in *Sein und Zeit* ends abruptly, offering no closure or finality. The truth of Being remains unfinished. In this sense, there is no proper conclusion, just a sober open-endedness. Perhaps this is fitting given that truth and falsehood are disclosed as an endless multiplicity within the compound structures of worldhood shrouded in a hidden underworld where there is no ultimate sublation (*Aufhebung*) or Absolute overarching process driving the nature of disclosedness itself. It merely *is*.

References

Aristotle (1984). *The Complete Works of Aristotle: The Revised Oxford Translation*, ed. J. Barnes. 2 vols. Princeton: Princeton University Press.

Askay, R., & Farquhar, J. (2011). *Of Philosophers and Madmen*. Amsterdam: Rodopi.

Avenburg, R., & Guiter, M. (1976). The concept of truth in psychoanalysis. *International Journal of Psycho-Analysis*, 57:11–18.

Bell, D. (2009). Is truth an illusion? Psychoanalysis and postmodernism. *International Journal of Psychoanalysis*, 90:331–345.

Blass, R.B. (2011). On the immediacy of unconscious truth: Understanding Betty Joseph's 'here and now' through comparison with alternative views of it outside of and within Kleinian thinking. *International Journal of Psychoanalysis*, 92:1137–1157.

Craig, E. (1988). An encounter with Medard Boss. *The Humanistic Psychologist*, 16:34–47.

Davidson, D. (2004). Truth. *International Journal of Psychoanalysis*, 85:1225–1230.

Fichte, J.G. (1794). *The Science of Knowledge*. transl. P. Heath & J. Lachs. Cambridge: Cambridge University Press, 1993.

Freud, S. (1900). The interpretation of dreams. *Standard Edition*, 4/5.

Freud, S. (1937). Constructions in analysis. *Standard Edition*, 23:255–269.

Hanly, C. (1992). *The Problem of Applied Truth in Psychoanalysis*. New York: Guilford Press.

Hegel, G.W.F. (1807). *Phenomenology of Spirit*, transl. A.V. Miller. Oxford: Oxford University Press, 1977.

Hegel, G.W.F. (1817/1827/1830). *The Encyclopaedia Logic*. Vol. 1 of *Encyclopaedia of the Philosophical Sciences*, transl. T.F. Geraets, W.A. Suchting, & H.S. Harris. Indianapolis: Hackett, 1991.

Heidegger, M. (1927). *Being and Time*, eds. J. Macquarrie & E. Robinson. New York: Harper & Row, 1962.

Heidegger, M. (1930). On the essence of truth. In D.F. Krell (ed.), *Basic writings*. New York: Harper & Row, 1977, pp. 113–142.

Heidegger, M. (1966). The end of philosophy and the task of thinking. In D.F. Krell (ed.), *Basic Writings*. New York: Harper & Row, 1977, pp. 369–392.

Heidegger, M. (1981). *Basic Concepts*, transl. G.E. Aylesworth. Bloomington: Indiana University Press, 1993.

Hoffman, I.Z. (1998). *Ritual and Spontaneity in the Psychoanalytic Process*. Hillsdale, NJ: Analytic Press.

Lacan, J. (1960). The subversion of the subject and the dialectic of desire in the Freudian unconscious. In *Écrits: A Selection*, transl. A. Sheridan. New York: Norton, 1977, pp. 292–325.

Laufer, M.E. (1994). Formulation of interpretation: From truth to experience. *International Journal of Psychoanalysis*, 75:1093–1105.

Loewald, H.W. (1970). Psychoanalytic theory and the psychoanalytic process. In *The Essential Loewald: Collected Papers and Monographs*. Hagerstown, MD: University Publishing Group, 2000, pp. 277–301.

Lynch, M. (2009). *Truth as One and Many*. Oxford: Oxford University Press.

Mills, J. (1997). The false Dasein: From Heidegger to Sartre and psychoanalysis. *Journal of Phenomenological Psychology*, 28:42–65.

Mills, J. (2002). *The Unconscious Abyss: Hegel's Anticipation of Psychoanalysis*. Albany: SUNY Press.

Mills, J. (2010). *Origins: On the Genesis of Psychic Reality*. Montreal: McGill-Queens University Press.

Mills, J. (2012). *Conundrums: A Critique of Contemporary Psychoanalysis*. New York: Routledge.

Orange, D. (1995). *Emotional Understanding*. New York: Guildford Press.

Plato (1961). *The Collected Dialogues of Plato*, eds. E. Hamilton & H. Cairns. Princeton: Princeton University Press.

Richardson, W. (1993). Heidegger among the doctors. In J. Sallis (ed.), *Reading Heidegger: Commemorations*. Bloomington: Indiana University Press, pp. 49–63.

Rosenberg, E.H., & Medini, G. (1978). Truth: A concept in emergence. *Contemporary Psychoanalysis*, 14:424–432.

Sartre, J.-P. (1943). *Being and Nothingness*, transl. H.E. Barnes. New York: Washington Square Press, 1956.

Spence, D.P. (1982). Narrative truth and theoretical truth. *Psychoanalytic Quarterly*, 51:43–69.

Spiegel, R. (1985). Faces of truth in the psychoanalytic experience. *Contemporary Psychoanalysis*, 21:254–265.

Stern, D.B. (1985). Psychoanalysis and truth: Current issues (a symposium): Introduction: Some controversies regarding constructivism and psycho-analysis. *Contemporary Psychoanalysis*, 21:201–207.

Stolorow, R.D., & Atwood, G.E. (1992). *Contexts of Being.* Hillsdale, NJ: Analytic Press.

Wilson, E.O. (1998). *Consilience: The Unity of Knowledge.* New York: Knopf.

Chapter 13

Freedom and Determinism

In his *Five Lectures*, given during his historic trip to Clark University, Freud (1910/1957a) tells us that "mental processes are determined" (*SE*, p. 29). He continues to proclaim that "psycho-analysts are marked by a particularly strict belief in the determination of mental life" (p. 38). What exactly does Freud mean by this? Does he mean that all aspects of mental life are caused? If so, by what? Are mental processes the product of antecedent events or activities that follow fixed universal laws governing the course of future affairs and actions following a particular trajectory of causation informed by the necessity of nature? Is such a trajectory permeable or unalterable, predetermined towards a teleological end or subject to plasticity? To what degree is determinism subject to purposeful choice, intentionality, volition, agency, and transmogrification versus the rigid requirements of fixed necessity? Is determinism compatible with freedom, even if they dialectically operate on mutual yet disparate levels of parallel processing? How does the role of motivation answer to the freedom versus determinism debate?

Brenner (1955) declares that a fundamental hypothesis underlying the theoretical edifice of psychoanalysis is the principle of "psychic determinism, or causality" (p. 2), which is the doctrine that nothing in the mind happens randomly or by chance. Therefore, there exists a "causal connection" between every mental production and psychical events that precede it in some form of deterministic manner whereby there is no metaphysical possibility of indetermination, accidental occurrence, arbitrariness, or meaningless phenomena to transpire.

DOI: 10.4324/9781003305958-13

Psychoanalysis is premised on the notion that there must be an original cause (or causes) for every psychic event, and following the principle of sufficient reason, there must be an adequate answer to this proposition based on a rational, hence meaningful, explanation. Psychoanalysis speculates that this so-called cause is motivated by an unconscious wish or intentional state of affairs that is not transparent to consciousness. Such psychic causality is responsible for all productions of conscious life, from dream states, fantasies, and parapraxes or faulty function (*Fehlleistung*), to clinical symptoms found normatively throughout the human race. Therefore, psychic determinism becomes an indispensable pillar of psychoanalytic thought.

Hartmann (1939) is content in dismissing the philosophical problem of freedom "because it is so equivocal in meaning" (p. 10), instead adopting a pragmatic approach that focuses on freedom from symptoms, and freedom to act (also see Waelder, 1936b). For Hartmann, freedom is the exercise of control by the ego, while for Kohut (1977), it emanates from the "center of initiative" within the self (p. 245). Menninger (1955), on the other hand, defines freedom as something of a "shibboleth" that "tends to disappear when one attempts to define it" (p. 803). Freud (1901/1960) observed that we have an attitude towards the insistence of personal freedom as a compulsory feeling or conviction, despite the fact that we are not entirely in control of all our conscious thoughts, affects, and motor actions when under the influence of everyday psychopathology, thus drawing into question the legitimacy of free will. If freedom takes its conscious form as a feeling of conviction or compulsion guiding one's actions, then is there any real difference between drive and psychic determinism? If one extends this line of argument further, namely, that freedom is inner compulsion, then it would not be entirely incorrect to assume that the ultimate form of freedom is suicide, thus observing Nietzsche's (1886/1989) thesis: "The thought of suicide is a powerful comfort: it helps one through many a dreadful night" (p. 91). Perhaps this is one reason why Lacan (1947/2006) says that "madness is freedom's most faithful companion" (p. 144).

Throughout this chapter, I will endeavour to foray into an admittedly indelible topic, one that may surprisingly take us into unsuspected territory. Psychoanalysis may offer us a potential solution to the longstanding philosophical conundrum of reconciling freedom with determinism by showing that what we call "psychic determinism" (*psychischen Determinismus*), and hence tend to equate with a lack of freedom in our experiential lives, is actually the expression of an underlying freedom, the freedom of unconscious expression. What I further wish to argue is that freedom and determinism are dialectically informed modes of unconscious intentionality orchestrated by unconscious agency. More specifically, freedom and determinism are bifurcations of the same ontological process that is executed by the unconscious ego in all mental productions. In other words, psychic determinism is the expression of its own freedom, and freedom is the instantiation of its determinate powers. This is not a tautology: each activity has inverse relations despite being dialectically constituted. The end result, I suggest, is that both freedom and determinism are modes of causation. Freud is interested in describing and explaining phenomena that derive from previous states of psychic motivation that give rise to psychical events or mental processes. What I intend to show is that these derivatives emanate from a psychic state of unconscious freedom, and are themselves the expression of such freedom, a free causality.

The Freedom versus Determinism Binary

Philosophy has historically been preoccupied with the freedom-determinism binary, and in the rise of modernity, from Leibniz and Spinoza to Kant, Schelling, and Hegel, it was almost exclusively concerned with the problem of evil, moral agency, and theodicy. For the medieval, modern, and idealist philosophers, freedom is ultimately conditioned by God, whom is the ground for the condition of freedom itself. It is neither necessary nor desirable for us to import that kind of fantasy into our discussion. What is germane, however, is to explore how freedom and determinism are grounded, hence constituted, *within* psychical processes that do not presuppose the ontological necessity of a Creator, Absolute Ground, or Principle of the Ultimate. Because we are experiential embodied beings that inhabit spacetime, we must offer a naturalized account that is subject to objective verification, logical coherence, and phenomenal lived experience. Because we are often introduced to the freedom-determinism binary in an antithetical fashion, where there is no immediate discernable sense of synthesis, hence already setting the tone for a discursive discourse on incompatible opposites, we are less accustomed to entertaining the notion that freedom and determinism are dialectically informed constructs that are necessarily manifested in any form of definition, demarcated scope of inquiry, psychological dynamic, or philosophical category that attempts to investigate their meanings.

The traditional philosophical doctrine of determinism subscribes to a natural science worldview where it is assumed that all present states of affairs are necessarily predicated on antecedent events that brought those occasions or experiences into being in the first place, and that they are propelled from universal causal laws that operate within nature itself independent of consciousness. It may be argued that the scientific revolution fortified such a binary in its insistence that every occurrence, including all possible future events, could be explained from a reductive (parsimonious) paradigm that implicitly eradicates the principle of freedom. In other words, determinism is the view that everything has an original cause, is absolutely dependent upon such causes, is governed (mastered) by preexistent ontological forces, and operates in accordance with necessary (non-accidental), predefined (established), or fixed (non-negotiable) natural laws that impel the coming into being of all things or proceedings. There are hard and soft determinists, from the extreme (fatalism) to the liberal (voluntarism), whereby free will is either negated *in toto* or allowed under certain circumstances, just as there are sundry forms of determinism that owe their allegiance to the forebear of history, one's environment, genetics or heredity, language and the symbolic order, cultural forces, scientific, mathematical, or logical explananda, or at the other extreme, theological providence.

Within the history of science, logical positivism, and Anglo-American analytic philosophy, it may be argued that the relationship between cause and effect assumes a linear notion of time followed by rigid parameters. The effect is always preceded in time by its cause, which follows a regularity of succession. To say that A causes B, is to say that whenever A happens it is followed by B, or that an instance of A is always followed by an instance of B. Following formal rules of inference, these logical propositions are presented in the form of modus ponens:

$$p \supset q$$
$$\underline{p}$$
$$q$$

From this standpoint, cause and effect cannot occur simultaneously nor have a variable sequence. In other words, a cause cannot follow its effect. Nor can an effect be the cause of a future effect. In my opinion, these definitional properties have palpable limitations. Why would we assume that a cause cannot generate other causes in the effects it produces? This implies that an effect is a terminal end point or finality it itself, when it could be a springboard for a new beginning or generative process that amplifies on its developmental or epigenetic constitution. A series of original causes as archaic events could readily be interpreted as the primordial forces behind the process of becoming that are gathered and assimilated within a self-organizing organism that is self-activating and self-governed. The notion that cause and effect is a temporal, invariable sequence is to beg the question of determinism.

Freud (1906/1959) was clearly a determinist, and in the context of explaining faulty achievements (*Fehlleistungen*), he specifically tells us so: "I demonstrated that a whole number of actions which were held to be unmotivated are on the contrary strictly determined" (*SE*, pp. 104–105). In fact, Freud (1916–1917/1963) views the whole scientific *Weltanschauung* as pledging a worldview that takes "the determination of natural events" (*SE*, p. 28) as a requisite part of its platform. The reason why Freud believed in strict determinism is that he could not buy into the notion of indeterminism, that is, the possibility that volition could occur independent of psychophysical antecedents. And or good reason: How could thought transpire without a brainstem? He furthermore could not entertain the idea that anything could be indeterminate or subjected to crass unpredictability or acausality. For Freud, certain natural and logical laws govern internal (psychical) events and their transactions, and under the right circumstances, they are ascertainable. He insisted that every mental event has an antecedent motive or *function* that brings about or impels a psychic process to express itself; and he thought that it is indeed possible to trace such events back to their earliest primordial determinants (Freud, 1900/1953), despite conceding that we may hit an impasse in fully understanding the motive or its meaning.[1]

Jones (1924) subscribes to a deadlock view of freedom and determinism and makes the general presumption that the two constructs are logically incompatible, when this supposition begs the question in the first place. Jones' "incompatibility thesis" assumes that freedom and determinism are irreconcilable, when, in my opinion, he commits a false dichotomy by failing to see how they are dialectically related, and hence are mutually implicative categories.

Let us first begin with the notion of determinism. Determinism can be viewed as a natural thrust or process, that is, as belonging to nature, or that which is *given*. We are thrown into a body as part of our facticity, as well as a family and social context, and the broader cultural environs that geographically, linguistically, economically, and politically influence our experience of self and world. These ontological antecedents exist a priori and unequivocally condition our being in the world. We are restricted by various natural laws the field of physics is adept in explaining; and just as we cannot defy gravity, we can hardly deny the objective presence of the past and the historical contingencies that have shaped our experience of contemporary societies. These ontological features are part and parcel of our collective historicity and comprise empirical facts that inform our epistemological foundations of biology and culture.

But not only is our throwness given, so too is our unique individual and autonomous ways of encountering, perceiving, assimilating, and organizing lived reality as a meaningful creative function or act, what we may call the *phenomenology of freedom* that is inherent in the very structure of experience itself. Psychoanalysis has typically focused upon the structural and behavioural parameters of freedom defined as *freedom from* versus *freedom to*, such as freedom from disabling symptoms or neurotic misery, and the ability to live and act in functional and adaptive ways derived from "conflict free" spheres of experiencing the world. In the humanities, especially within the context of *freedom for* liberty, or *freedom of* rights, the emphasis has been on freedom from bondage, constraint, and intimidation or duress caused by others versus freedom to think, perform, act, dream, and imagine. These capacities to do things are enabled by degrees of contextual variance, malleable parameters, and multitudinous objects of choice within a penumbra of possibilities available to the human subject. This is generally referred to as the distinction between positive and negative freedom, whereas one is self-determining or in control over their life versus the degree to which one is free from interference from others. While the former emphasizes autonomous rule and self-regulation, the latter focuses on the condition of not being prevented from doing something, hence giving rise to Bentham's term "negative liberty," which is the absence of coercion. Whether we view freedom as a conditional state of relational affairs oriented towards a libertarian notion of free will, where there are degrees of freedom both from within and without, we must still concede that freedom has real limits.

Psychoanalysts are used to interpreting the notion of freedom to the analysand through the language of defense, such as a need to escape from emotional pain, or to be set free from oppressive childhood complexes, and this is why the philosophical attraction of freedom is important to an individual. Certainly the historic signification of emancipation and liberty is attractive to collective democracies for tangible reasons; however, for our purposes, the real issue becomes explaining freedom as an agentic function within deterministic confines: namely, the fact that we are born into a specific body, culture, and language without any consultation in the matter whatsoever. We have no more control over the empirical fact that we are the product of our biological parents' procreation or union, and were born into a particular family in a particular time and geographic space, than we have over the scientific discovery that the earth revolves around the sun. However, within those confines, we still enjoy degrees of freedom to experience, think, and act within the found givens of our embodied cultural existence. Therefore, it is philosophically compatible and justifiable to say that we are thrown into determinate circumstances which we interpret to be indeterminate in terms of its potentiality and possible meanings. From this perspective, there is no need to retain the rigid bifurcation between freedom and determinism because both are equally plausible, complementary, and dialectically co-constituted, experiential realities.

What I wish to displace is the assumption that a so-called free act is caused from inner mental states *devoid* of other conditions, such as our mind-brain dependence or external stimuli. No psychical act (e.g., will) is independent from our embodied constituencies, such as antecedent neurophysiological processes or environmental situations. This antiquated polarization reinforces the untenable notion that free will is the product of *uncaused events*, when causation may be viewed as the dialectical union of freedom and determinism. This is why Aristotle (1984) used the term *cause* (αιτία) to mean the reason for something happening.

The contrived binary between freedom and determinism has been historically successful because it signifies a psychological artifact and wish that the human species needs to promulgate in order to have a convenient meaning at its disposal for answering the painfully fraught subjective reality that we *all* at times feel both determined and free. How do we reconcile such a contradiction in our lived experiences? How do we answer to the psychological paradox this antipode generates within the human subject? If determinism is the foreclosure or erasure of possibility, while freedom is being-toward-possibility, then are we able to provide an adequate solution to this conundrum?

Freud on Free Will

It is rather ironic that Freud had theoretically secured the radicalization of freedom within the human psyche but had not realized that he had done so. If he had, he would have never dismissed the notion of free will, because, according to his thesis, our will is determined by unconscious forces that give rise to its conscious counterpart; and therefore, consciousness would be the derivative and materialization of unconscious process. In other words, consciousness is the ontological extension and expression of unconscious structure (Mills, 2002). Here it is more appropriate to refer to *freed will* as the product of determinate unconscious agency, that is, the conscious instantiation of unconscious intent.

Because Freud himself bought into the freedom-determinism binary and did not conceive of a dialectical relation between the two polarities that form a reciprocal (categorical) unit, he was further seduced by the hard determinism of his day. Freud (1916–1917/1963) believed that human beings "nourish a deeply rooted faith in undetermined psychical events and in free will, [however,] this is quite unscientific and must yield to the demand of a determinism whose rule extends over mental life" (*SE*, p. 106). Notice that Freud uses the word "faith" (*Glauben*), as in a need or wish to believe. Earlier he tells us that:

> Many people, as is well known, contest the assumption of complete psychical determinism by appealing to a special feeling of conviction that there is a free will. This feeling of conviction exists; and it does not give way before a belief in determinism. Like every normal feeling it must have something to warrant it. But as so far as I can observe, it does not manifest itself in the great and important decisions of the will: on these occasions the feeling that we have is rather one of psychical compulsion, and we are glad to invoke it on our behalf ... According to our analyses it is not necessary to dispute the right to the feeling of conviction of having a free will. If the distinction between conscious and unconscious motivation is taken into account, our feeling of conviction informs us that conscious motivation does not extend to our motor decisions. (1901/1960, *SE*, pp. 253–254)

Here Freud nicely draws attention to our "feeling of conviction" of personal freedom, the experiential quality of which "exists" and is a normal human emotion. He takes objection to the notion that this feeling and the will are one and the same, and in effect disputes that it plays a vital role in volitional processes of great importance. Here I would argue just the opposite. This disposition, what Freud equates with a compulsion, is manifest in the will, and, I argue, is the motive, intent, or causal thrust behind the compulsory nature of the will. It is only on the condition that one feels so passionate or driven about "great and important decisions" that the will feels its "right to the feeling of conviction." To re-appropriate William James, not only do we have the will to believe, we have the right to believe. Here freedom is actualized through the will, but originally motivated by unconscious determinants that are also the instantiation of its freedom. Despite the hypothesis that conscious free will is informed by unconscious determinants, such determinism is the agentic expression of its freed will, or more appropriately, its intentionality, that secures an avenue for free expression in consciousness. Hence we have faulty achievements; paradigmatically, the slip. It is only on the basis of a contingency—an accident—that you can intend to say one thing but reveal what you really think, the meaning and motive of which is masked in the slip. The unconscious intention is revealed only on the condition that it was an unintentional or faulty occurrence. Here you have the free reign of unconscious intentionality unconstrained by the boundaries or parameters of conscious restraint or culture.

The tendency we are conditioned to commit without realizing it, I suggest, is that the term 'free will' (*freien Willens*), which is customary parlance, is assumed to signify a conscious act; therefore, the implication is that we are not justified in superimposing that intentional act and linguistic usage on unconscious processes. I challenge this assumption. We could conservatively relegate the term 'will' to consciousness, however, this would not resolve the question of how the will is ultimately conditioned, motivated, or informed by antecedent forces. Here we must appeal to original ground, or the unconscious conditions that make conscious will possible. In a nutshell, this is the psychoanalytic contribution to this debate. For Freud, the desiring subject is split or divided into competing agencies that have different unconscious wishes, conflicts, and defenses that stand in embattled relation to one other, each exercising their degree of intentionality and counter-intentionality that often leads to compromise formations. Incompatible and reactionary unconscious desires skirmish over their bid for unique and differentiated expressions, which make their way into modified forms of consciousness and behaviour. Although the end product of a compromise may be argued to typify a lack of freedom on the part of the conscious subject, on a more primordial level, it is the triumph of unconscious metamorphosis negotiated through agentic mediation. To me, this constitutes an act of freedom, but not necessarily free will. This is why Schopenhauer (1818/1958) uses the expression *liberum arbitrium indifferentiae* to connote a will that is free in the metaphysical sense before it takes its form as conscious phenomena.

In certain places in his writings, Freud pessimistically concludes that free will is an illusion, which seems to be the consensus of many analysts, past and present (see Jones, 1924; Menninger, 1955; Modell, 2011). Freud (1919/1955a) soberly casts observation on the fact that the ego is disillusioned by clinging to fantasies of all its possible future states of fulfillment it cannot achieve, and those that have been "crushed" by "external circumstances," hence a reminder that the reality principle is laboriously at work in eradicating "our suppressed acts of volition which nourish in us the illusion of Free Will" (*SE*, p. 236). Here I would argue that Freud confuses the internal thrust of the spirit of conviction with the assumption that external reality always vanquishes those so-called fantasies, when both are operative within any given moment and give rise to a dialectical tension. But Freud (1930/1964) also speaks of a "desire for freedom" (*SE*, p. 96), which usually manifests in response to some form of injustice; and this desire itself serves to further the development of civilization. Here freedom evolves through the context of a moral discourse that serves a pragmatic good, and also exposes the motivation of freedom inherent in desire itself. To desire is to experience an internal valuation that is free in-itself, that is, as the ground of its own independent self-experience. Here Freud lends privilege to the autonomy of the individual over that of society. "The urge for freedom, therefore, is directed against particular forms and demands of civilization," for man "will always defend his claim to individual liberty against the will of the group" (*SE*, p. 96). In other words, our will to freedom is aroused when we feel oppressed by others.

These statements show both an ambivalence and commitment to the phenomenology of freedom, whereby a libertarian notion of personal free will is contrasted against the imposition of collective constraints. Freud's reference to the desire, urge, or wish for freedom (*Freiheitsdrang*), which is often associated with a drive or compulsion, is once again interpreted as having both causal, hence deterministic, versus unconstrained—viz. free—characteristics that impel desire itself. We should not assume that desire is merely a product of consciousness or will, but rather, that it fuels the drives (*Triebe*) or instinctual activity that must secure an object choice for satisfaction. In other words, desire and drive inform urges or pressures that are felt within conscious affect states Freud (1915/1957b) describes as a "feeling of compulsion," or in Vergote's (1997) words, "pulsional desire" (*Désir pulsionnel*). Here freedom is allowing a feeling to take hold in us that compels our desire to think and act, and this must be mediated by an agent (originally governed by unconscious agency) in its choices and possible range of actions it has at its disposal. Because drives have an aim (*Ziel*) or purpose, which are only satiated or frustrated by objects selected or repudiated by the (unconscious) ego, there are, by definition, elements of freedom ontologically inscribed in the very constitution of the drives. Therefore, even if we were in agreement with Freud's renunciation of free will, it would not negate the notion that degrees of freedom enacted through unconscious determination condition the will based on a prior form of teleology. To this point I will elaborate on shortly. But before I do so, it is important that we address what is perhaps Freud's most famous reference to freedom in the psychoanalytic lexicon, namely, the fundamental rule or free association (*freien Assoziation*).

In his comments on the evolution of the free associative method, Freud (1923/1955c) observed that everything that occurred to a patient's mind from a certain starting-point also stood in relation and internal connection to that starting-point guided by a "strict determination of mental events" (*SE*, p. 238). Freud once again focuses on parapraxes as the prime example, which are "strictly determined" (*streng determiniert*) yet "revealed" as an "expression" (*Äußerung*) of "suppressed intentions" (*unterdrückten Absichten*) or a "clash between two intentions," at least one of which was unconscious (*SE*, p. 240). Notice that Freud uses the language of intentionality. When he speaks of strict determinism, he is evoking the notion that events are determined from within by intentional unconscious processes. So even when he states in *Beyond the Pleasure Principle* (1920/1955b) that neurotic symptoms are "determined by early infantile influences," their "fate" (*Schicksals*) is largely "arranged by themselves" (*SE*, p. 21). The ambivalent tension in Freud's use of deterministic language must be interpreted within the context of an unconscious agency determining the directionality or trajectory of these conscious productions.

On the one hand, Freud (1916–1917/1963) wants to champion a determinism over free will when it comes to psychic events; yet on the other hand, he extends a notion of agency to unconscious choice that freely selects objects for instinctual gratification. An argument can be made that he distinguishes free will (a conscious construct, which he wants to subordinate in causal efficacy) from freedom, which in principle does not strictly adhere to conscious determinism. In fact, he wants to emphasize the "higher degree of freedom of association" (*SE*, pp. 106–107). But this freedom of association is *influenced* by unconscious determinants. Because psychoanalysis has long established that mental events are *overdetermined*, that is, influenced by a multiplicity of forces and sources of motivation operative within the mind all at once, what Waelder (1936a) calls the principle of multiple function or co-determination, the notion of "strict" determinism becomes tenuous when we analyse the minutia of these distinctive causal processes. Therefore, the term 'influence' seems to better capture the inherent (albeit at times intangible) power, malleability, and multifarious nature of determinism.

Freud never tires in emphasizing the notion that nothing is arbitrary, indeterminable, or unconnected in psychic associations or correlations that hook up certain verbal disclosures or behavioural enactments with their prior shapes or antecedents that are "always strictly determined by important internal attitudes of mind" (1916–1917/1963, *SE*, p. 107). In this context, what is free is not unbounded, but rather connected or linked to particular mental elements that form a signifying relation in the psyche based on prior unconscious organizations. Here determination is *linkage*, hence a relational dynamic.[2] It is not a predetermined cause or state of affairs that bring about a fated or preordained end, but rather an intricate connection or combinatory of signifiers that have semiotic associative functions derived from such intrapsychic "attitudes." So the freedom inherent in association is the *recovery* of the linkage or set of relations to previous internal mental elements, contents, and processes that were not previously known or consciously articulated; hence they are unconscious derivatives, yet they form the psychic background that produce such associations to begin with.

If these "internal attitudes" ultimately produce the ground of association, then they themselves are either strictly determined, or they are subject to determination from other forces. Yet this strict determination, I argue, is being issued or directed by an unconscious agency. How is it that we can trace back the link to a previous state of events, but we cannot trace back the point of origin, that is, to the issuing agency itself? It is because the issuing agency is ultimately free and grounds its own ground through the expression of psychic material that makes its way into consciousness, which is the horizon of its own becoming. Although we may trace back the content, if conditions are favourable, to points of origination, we cannot directly uncover the ground of grounds, because our conscious agency or free will is already participating in a process that cannot peel open its own agency without becoming self-reflectively aware of its freedom in doing so. The conscious content of free association is *derived* from our own internal mental life, a derivative of our own agentic organization and free expression. Whether intended or not, Freud's thesis on free association radicalizes the ontology of unconscious freedom.

Psychic Determinism as Teleology

In Chapter 12 of *The Psychopathology of Everyday Life*, Freud sets out his clearest views on psychic determinism, what he equates with "purposive ideas" (*Zielvorstellungen*) and "motivations" that inform our conscious thoughts and actions (1901/1960, *SE*, p. 240). He reiterates that nothing in the mind is accidental, undetermined, or arbitrary, for conscious choice and action are attributed to "determinants from the unconscious" (*SE*, p. 243). In offering a number of clinical facts from case studies and examples from his own self-analysis, he traces back the associative network of connections that emanate from an unconscious determinism where "the existence of highly composite thought-processes which are quite unknown to consciousness" (*SE*, p. 247) become disclosed through dreams, slips of the tongue and pen, forgetting, errors, misreadings, mislaying objects, failures in memory, bungled actions, superstitions, and chance phenomena. Freud believed that chance is the residue of design. In other words, pure chance occurrences do not exist in the psyche, rather they are influenced by unconscious causal-motivational factors that are teleologically constituted.

Freud's (1901/1960) use of "purposive" language is no coincidence. In fact, such psychic determinants have a "hidden motivation" (*SE*, p. 271), hence a *telos*, aim, or end goal, that may be revealed through parapraxes or unveiled through an analysis of associations and their relational linkages to earlier, even archaic, origins. As discussed before, these associations are free (*freien*) insofar as they reveal "in every case a disturbing ideational content—a complex;" in other words, intrapsychic conflict "determined by an ideational content that is operative" in the mind (1906/1959, *SE*, p. 105). Freud (1906/1959) further tells us that such spontaneous thoughts or actions, such as fiddling with things, humming a tune, or playing with objects belies the hidden motivation "that is not arbitrarily chosen but will be determined by their relation to his secret—to his 'complex'—and may, as it were, be regarded as derivatives of that complex" (*SE*, p. 109). Therefore, Freud attributes purposeful ideation to psychic determinism that may reveal clandestine motives through conscious derivatives. Here, not only is psychic determinism an unconscious operative process, it operates *a fortiori* as teleological intent. For how could an intention be revealed unless it was already purposefully conceived in the first place?

Because unconscious ideas are purposive and motivational, not only is the notion of psychic determinism compatible with teleology, it is presupposed (Flew, 1970). The principle of psychic determinism presupposes unconscious intent, the cardinal characteristics of which include a motive, purpose, aim, and final end. But contra Aristotle, unconscious motivation oriented towards a finality or end-state is not predetermined in its path or outcome. The unconscious ego must secure an avenue and object choice in thought, affect, fantasy, and action that satisfies the aims of drives. Recall that Freud (1915/1957b) delineates the components of a drive (*Trieb*) as constituted by a source, force, object, and aim. Because drives are in-themselves incapable of being known directly, an unconscious *Ding an sich*, so to speak, they may only be known through their phenomenal appearances. Yet Freud enlists the help of consciousness in procuring satisfaction for the drives by selecting objects of desire, and here we may compare psychic determinism to Aristotlean causality, which emphasizes overdetermination.

Just as a drive has a source derived from its biological embodiment (material cause), it also has a force or pressure (efficient cause) that propels it to act, a complexity in its organization (formal cause), and a motivational object it purposefully chooses to secure gratification (final causality). Here there is a continuity and interdependence among all causal phenomena. If every psychic act has a sense or purpose, causality and teleology are inseparable ontic processes. This is why multiple motivations exist in the mind and can be expressed or revealed in a single act, which arise from concurrent forces that exert their influence on the "mutually opposing action—of two different intentions" (1916–1917/1963, *SE*, p. 44). Furthermore, several motives may inhere in a "*single* psychical cause," which Freud (1910/1957a) insists "always have a meaning" (*SE*, p. 38). Here he joins company with the great philosophical rationalists who believed the universe is intelligible and governed by natural laws that have a purposeful and meaningful structure based on rational necessity. But with one exception: teleological structure is self-organizing, hence not predetermined or fixed in its end result or constitution. The unconscious mind executes freedom of choice in its aims, objects, and paths towards achieving fulfillment, which it can inhibit, delay, negate, or seize upon through dynamic determinants. And if dynamism is the touchstone, then freedom and determinism are not mutually exclusive processes.

A possible answer to the freedom-determinism binary rests on our understanding of overdetermination, where there is purported to be a confluence of forces operative upon the mind all at once, each one of which could potentially influence and bring about a whole host of psychical effects; and therefore our psychic register requires a more sophisticated form of information processing than a mere economic principle of mental functioning. There exists a supervenience of various psychophysical pressures whereby each force depends upon the efficacy of the others and their inherent mutual relations. They may each have a disproportionate amount of organization, zest, and intensity, which may exert various degrees of impetus and order within the psyche, or congeal all at once to bring about an effect(s) where there are multiple valences, each having their own causal efficacy. This level of complexity introduces the necessity for agency to answer to these problematics and overdetermined demands placed on the psyche to mediate the multitude of dynamic determinants that inform our dispositions and affects, desires and defenses, and cognitive metarepresentations that impel us to think, feel, and act.

Unconscious thoughts have a certain degree of order, force, intensity, directionality, and loci that are teleologically organized and expressed through circuitous routes that find their way into conscious productions, whether that be through impulses, emotions, fantasy, behaviour, or the speech act. In this way we may explain such productions as being directed by agentic currents guided by *unconscious intentionality*. Here I do not wish to subscribe to the same train of thought as the phenomenologists who insist that intentionality is a psychical activity and property of consciousness. Contrarily, I maintain that psychic acts derived from unconscious determinants have telic aims that are intentional (*intentus*) and *about* objects, hence purposeful and goal oriented, and that they are internally aimed towards or directed at mental objects. They are furthermore directed by an unconscious agency.

Just as dreams and fantasies are subjected to the organizing principles of condensation, displacement, compromise formations (contaminations), and distortion, so too do symptoms have a manifest "sense," purpose, or "intention" (1916–1917/1963, *SE*, p. 269) that symbolically represent internal conflicts or wishes, the origin of which are varied and complex, issuing from the differentiation and transmogrification of competing unconscious motives, such as repressed or dissociated impulses. And here psychic determinism is essentially identical to the doctrine of freedom: from dream content to parapraxes, neurotic symptoms, and psychopathology, "unconscious thoughts find expression as modifications of other thoughts" (1901/1960, *SE*, p. 278). In the context of the psychopathology of everyday life as normativity, these unconscious modifications that inform conscious enactments operate "with a *freer use* of the means at hand" (*SE*, p. 278, italics added). In other words, unconscious thoughts are transposed—that is, set free—by modifying themselves through the slip, faulty achievement, or "incorrect function" they signify.

Earlier we observed how Freud (1901/1960) confirmed that our conviction of having free will, which informs our conscious motivations, does not annul our belief that such conviction is also informed by unconscious motivations that work in tandem with conscious intentions and volition (see *SE*, p. 254). Here we may situate the locus of freedom in the unconscious "*capacity for expressing itself*" (*SE*, p. 279, italics in original). Notice that Freud emphasizes a capacity or faculty of potentiality. In this context, causation is the capacity to move from inherent potentiality to determinate actuality. In other words, causation is a developmental process that derives from original conditions and progressively unfolds through a series of mediations and modifications to achieve a completed state. Not only is freedom compatible with determinism, it becomes the ground for determinate expression. But in order to have freedom, we must have agency.

Unconscious Agency

Is unconscious experience caused? Or is it causal? This hegemony is of course a false dichotomy, yet one reflective of our typical discourse in conceiving causation. If our analysis of freedom and determinism, so far, has borne any fruit, we have concluded that the two constructs are dialectically constituted and mutually implicative. Therefore, you cannot have one without the other. However, are we going about this question the wrong way? Is it possible to conceive of freedom and determinism as identical processes rather than emphasizing the dichotomous perspective highlighted at any given moment? Put another way, is there an inverse relation to each pole that collapses into an indistinguishable synthesis? In other words, this polarity only makes sense if we fail to articulate the supraordinate holistic process that binds this dichotomy into a formal unity.

As we have intimated, for there to be psychic determination or causation, there must be a *determiner* or source of activity that executes this formal act of bringing about mental functioning to begin with, what we may equate with unconscious agency. Freud was never able to adequately answer to the question of a unifying agency because he divided the mind up into competing "agencies," "systems" (1900/1953, *SE*, p. 537), or "entities" (1923/1961a, *SE*, pp. 23–26) culminating in his mature, tripartite structural theory of 1923. Although Freud did offer an adumbrated attempt to explain how the I (*Ich*) epigenetically developed out of the It (*Es*) as a differentiated and modified agency derived from its initial natural embodiment (see 1923/1961a, *SE*, p. 25; 1926/1961b, *SE*, p. 97), he was not able to explain this developmental process with any precision.

In *Origins: On the Genesis of Psychic Reality*, I offer a systematic psychoanalytic metaphysics articulating the birth of psychic agency (Mills, 2010). Here I argue that structures of subjectivity are themselves conditioned a priori by an unconscious agency that is responsible for all forms of mental life to materialize and thrive, including consciousness. My reasoning relies upon the principle of sufficient reason, namely, that there must be an original ground for every mental event that stands in relation to every mental object. In many respects, the principle of sufficient reason is no different than the doctrine of psychic determinism: all activity of mind must precede from a prior state of organizational processes. Psychic activity does not pop up *ex nihilio*; it must surface from an unconscious organizing principle I have metaphorically called the *abyss*. This unconscious abyss is itself a crude form of agency that performs executive functions and initiates determinate choices and actions through intentional manoeuvres we are accustomed to refer to as drive derivatives, wishes, fantasies, defenses, compromise formations, self-states, dissociative enactments, or otherwise anything we may label as belonging to unconscious experience. The locus of this abyss rests within an agentic function that may be properly attributed to an unconscious ego that possesses formal capacities to execute intentional choice aimed towards purposeful ends, what we have already described as unconscious teleology.

How am I to convince the reader that we all possess unconscious agency? Let me begin by asking how could memory, representation, and semiotics be possible? Without an internal executor or agency that performs formal functions of perceptual processing, categorization, retention, synthesis, unification, semiotic linkage, and information exchange, how could human experience be encoded, organized, transmuted, and transmitted via speech and behaviour? Where would such activity come from? How could it be carried out if it was not initiated from an inner sense of functional form?[3] In other words, consciousness is neither a necessary nor a sufficient condition for explaining these psychic processes that by definition transpire outside of consciousness. Unconscious productions have a certain force and presence enacted by a formal (impersonal) agentic ego that lies at the heart of all teleological activity. How else could we explain mental events that are operative within psychic regions or territories unknown to immediate consciousness when they appear unannounced? Appealing to neuroscience, biology, or brain discourse gets us nowhere. Cognitive science cannot answer the question of agency because it makes consciousness an epiphenomenon, hence properties of the brain that possess no causal powers of their own. And if we are content in boiling down mind to brain states, then what becomes of freedom and agency?

The coming into being of psychic reality may be understood from the standpoint of a developmental monistic ontology whereby there is a progressive unfolding of desire into an organizing and unifying process system we equate with the unconscious ego as an impersonal executive-synthetic agency. This agency is merely formal, hence it is not a personal agent or subject in any proper sense, which is commonly ascribed to human consciousness or selfhood. The abyss is initially immersed in its own corporeal sentient embodiment and awakens as appetitive motivational longing, its initial Being-in-relation-to-lack. The abyss erupts from its self-enclosed original unity as pulsional desire. Such desirous rupture is in response to feeling its need, urge, or craving to experience and satiate the lack, which takes various initial forms that eventually breach into consciousness as ego proper. Originally, desire takes itself as its initial object through a form of pre-reflective self-consciousness I refer to as *unconscious apperception*, the pure experiential self-sense belonging to pre-cognitive unconscious thought. The development of unconscious subjectivity ultimately follows an organic process based on a series of dialectical mediations beginning as unconscious apperception and culminating in self-conscious reflection, the sublated domain of conscious human experience. Yet this initial rudimentary process of desirous rupture and apperception constitutes the birth of the human psyche, for mind is an epigenetic, architectonic self-organizing achievement expressed as a dynamic, self-articulated complex to-tality or psychic holism.

Unconscious mind is a *series of spacings* that first instantiate themselves as a multitude of *schemata*, which are the building blocks of psychic reality. A schema is a desirous-apperceptive-ideational unit of self-experience that is teleologically oriented and dialectically constituted. Schemata may be viewed as microagents with semi-autonomous powers of telic expression that operate as self-states as they create spacings within the unconscious abyss. Schemata may take various forms, from the archaic to the refined, and instantiate themselves as somatic, sensuous, affective, perceptual, and conceptual (symbolic) orders within the psyche, each having their own intrinsic pressures, valences, intensities, intentional and defensive strategies, and unconscious qualia.

The microdynamics of schematic expression can be highly individualistic in their bid for freedom, creativity, complexity, and agentic intent, and are tantamount to the instinctual and defensive processes we are accustomed to attribute to unconscious mentation in general. The difference here is that schemata are inherently both free and determined, or perhaps more appropriately, freely determined, that is, they are self-constituted and determinate within the natural parameters in which they find themselves and operate. This means that schematic expression is highly contextual and contingent; yet schemata exist in a multiplicity of process systems that commune, interact, and participate in a community of events that mutually influence the unique constitution of each schematic structure within the sea of the mind. This overdetermination of psychic processes ensures that unconscious agency ultimately underlies the constitution of all mental functioning.

The multitudinous complex microsystems or communities of schemata evolve from an interceptive source we may properly attribute to an unconscious ego or processor as the locus and executor of subjective agency. While schemata persist and sustain their existence within the abyss of psychic reality, the unconscious ego is the synthetic unifying agency of mind. Furthermore, it is the unconscious ego that assigns agency to schemata, which allow for their autonomous actions. In this way, agency allows for both unconscious freedom and unconscious determinism, for schemata are autonomous self-organizations that teleologically define and execute their own course of actions. Here emanations from the abyss conform to a sort of *free determinism*, where psychic life arises from and is animated by its own generative forms of self-organization and self-expression—at once given, forged, and constructed. In this way, with qualifications, *freedom and determinism are modes of self-causation.*[4] In other words, mind is generated by unconscious process that fashions its own being.

The unequivocal centrality of agency in the constitution of mind becomes a pivotal and indispensible concept for understanding psychic complexity and justifying the existence of determinate freedom. Unconscious agency is ultimately responsible for all aspects of psychic functioning, from the most elemental and primitive to the most sophisticated, because, following the principle of sufficient reason, psychic reality must stand in relation to its original form. From unformulated and inarticulate unconscious experience to reflective self-conscious reason inherent in the formation of self-identity, all psychic activity derives from its original ontological foundations.

The Essence of Human Freedom

In *Philosophical Investigations into the Essence of Human Freedom*, F.W.J. Schelling (1809/2006) concludes that "free is what acts only in accord with the laws of its own being and is determined by nothing else either in or outside itself" (p. 50). This is the hallmark of German idealism. The will (*Willkür*) defines and grounds its own ground, and is the positing and assertion of itself without imposition, a common theme from Fichte to Hegel and Schopenhauer. Perhaps it was Plato who first canonized the priority of choice within will as a defining element of the soul (see *Phaedo*, 99b; *Laws* X, 904c), later finding a foothold in Whitehead's impersonal account of the cosmos as a valuing, emotive process system in its bid for freedom, further leading Sartre to advance his thesis on radical freedom, which became the creed and rally cry of the existentialist movement.

Freedom itself is a contradiction—the word contradicts itself [ME *fre* < OE *frēo*, to love]. To be free is to have no origins, no home, no attachments, hence no determination or conditions, yet it is dependent on contingency, which defines its conditions. Free will, in particular, is a contradiction, for if will were truly without constraint or conviction, it would not will, hence determine, anything. Perhaps we can conclude that freedom is a tautology: it appeals to itself by conditioning its own conditions, a redundant repetition. In this way freedom, as it was for the idealists, is a return to a self-constituted form of self-posit.

If something is caused, then how can it be free? Can something be causally free, that is, free to cause despite being free of causation? And if we are either caused or causally free, are we still free to cause through the act of determination? If psychic determinism is a form of mental causation, and freedom is something that is absolutely undetermined, then how can this dichotomy be reconciled? If freedom and determinism are viewed as complementary modes of self-causation, then perhaps this dialectic may begin to close the conceptual divide and offer a plausible solution to this conundrum. From this standpoint, freedom and determinism are self-activating forms of causation organized as the dialectical instantiation of potentiality and actuality.

I believe it is fair to presume that definitions of freedom and determinism are subject to grammatical relativism and mean different things in different linguistic contexts. If 'free' means without constraint or conditions, then it does not exist. For how can anything be devoid of causality? Pure freedom would have no foundation or ground of being, hence no organizational structure, place of agency, or mechanism for initiating action.

Although the term 'determinism' usually signifies the philosophical doctrine that all events or decisions are preceded by antecedents that conform to natural laws independent of human will, to 'determine' is to decide conclusively and with authority, to regulate or give direction to (especially after deliberation), or to cause or bring about a conclusion, hence to limit, terminate, or end [Lat. *determinare*, to limit: *de-*, off + *terminus*, boundary]. Determinism has freedom engraved within its very definition, as evinced in the words 'determined,' namely, what was decided or resolved; 'determinate,' firm in purpose or resolute; and 'determiner,' the agent that chooses.

If freedom is defined as inherent autonomy guiding the parameters of choice and action, then it is teleologically constituted rather than strictly determined by a biological urge (*Trieb*) based on an economic principle of self-regulation or teleonomy oriented towards a pre-determined finality. This is one reason why Sartre was so opposed to psychoanalysis, because he interpreted, wrongfully I might add, that Freud's model of the mind collapsed into material reduction. Sartre (1946/1957) is notorious for his romanticized view of human freedom, to the point that he denies determinism because we *are* freedom: we are not free not to be free. Yet he adds this important stipulation: while freedom is absolute, our power over situations is constrained. This crucial distinction allows Sartre to conclude that, despite our thrownness or the environmental dilemmas we face, we are always able to choose because we cannot do otherwise, even if our choices are severely truncated or unsavoury. Because the range of human choice and action is (in principle) infinite, and therefore ultimately unpredictable, freedom virtually has no bounds. But this conclusion is, in the end, a theoretical abstraction that belies pragmatic reality. Unbounded possibility is a fantasy guiding conscious choice fueled by unconscious identifications. In this sense, Sartre's absolute libertarianism is tantamount to determinism—we are condemned to freedom. Like psychoanalysis, Sartre views the human condition as being both inherently free to choose, yet within confines that are themselves a form of bondage. However, what differentiates existentialism from psychoanalysis, is that, for Sartre (1943/1956), choice is restricted to conscious deliberations of judgement, although he does allow for a form of unconscious self-deception, what he calls bad faith (*mauvaise foi*); namely, negation or the denial to choose authentically. Psychoanalysis, on the other hand, shows how choice is predicated on unconscious determinants that bring particular choices into concrete existence through thought, affect, and action. For Sartre, the end of freedom comes with death. But for both Freud and Sartre, death conditions freedom.

If it is at all possible to garner some consensus on the nature of this topic throughout the history of Western philosophy, perhaps it is this: the essence of human freedom lies in the *capacity to choose*—to make decisions that motivate our direct, concrete personal actions—with a variety of overdetermined sources—sources that are multifarious and not simply mechanical, linear, or preordained by a fixed tropism with no other options or available avenues for alternative responses. The capacity for choice always ensures that under the same circumstances, 'I could have done otherwise,' that there are alternative courses of action at any given moment, and that the future is not predestined or fated. This means that the concept of freedom is intimately tied to the *capacity to act* performed by an experiential subject who decides to summon or seize upon such capacities to begin with. This definition naturally extends to unconscious processes, for the capacity to choose is enacted upon by unconscious intentional dynamics. Such capacities are also indispensably tied to the ontology of agency, which is the driving force behind motivation, choice, and action. In this context, freedom and determinism are identical.

To determine is to bring about through intentional or volitional action a state of events whereby one is free to choose the grounds for the sake of which to desire, imagine, contemplate, and behave. This equally applies to an unconscious will, for any psychic activity must derive from an agentic organization informed by the abyss of desire. The capacity to choose the grounds, that is, the contextual or contingent conditions upon which we think and act, lies within the powers and imagination of the human mind. In this way, causation qua freedom is our form of inner sense. If determinism is causation, and freedom is the actualization of possibility via agentic choice, then causation is an ontological determinate power responsible for the actualization of freedom. Freedom and determinism are the same.

Notes

1 One such example is when we encounter "the dream's navel" (*der Nabel des Traums*), which leaves an "obscure" (*Dunkel*), convoluted, and indiscernible mass (Freud, 1900/1953, *SE*, p. 525), thus occluding any clarity of meaning.

2 Recall that it was Hume (1748/1975) who refuted the notion that there was a "necessary connexion" between cause and effect. Instead, he argued that the regularity of succession between antecedent causes and resultant effects exhibits a temporal precedence which is *conjoined*, not that a prior occurrence necessarily creates an effect. Hume rejects the claim that temporal precedence necessarily causes events because necessity cannot be observed to exist. All that is observed is the conjunction of cause and effect that follows a regular succession. There is no necessary connection between the two series in time, only that one follows the other; and hence the human mind attributes strict determinism to temporal events rather than simply viewing them as successions that are conjoined. In other words, there is no necessity, only relational linkage. One does not necessarily bring the other into being, only that they are interpreted to be joined together or united.

3 In *The Facts of Causation*, D. H. Mellor (1995) ends his book by concluding that "the form of inner sense is causation" (p. 243).

4 The reader should not assume I am suggesting that agency is a self-caused cause, such as God in religious terms. What I am attempting to convey is that the experiential subject fashions its own self-organization and self-expression through its own determinate powers of self-definition and self-articulation. This is, in part, the essence of freedom.

References

Aristotle. (1984). *The complete works of Aristotle* (The Revised Oxford Translation, 2 vols., J. Barnes, Ed.). Princeton: Princeton University Press.

Brenner, C. (1955). *An elementary textbook of psychoanalysis*. Garden City, NY: Anchor Books.

Flew, A. (1970). Psychoanalysis and the philosophical problems of free will. In C. Hanly & M. Lazerowitz (Eds.), *Psychoanalysis and philosophy*. New York: International Universities Press, pp. 126–154.

Freud, S. (1953). The interpretation of dreams. In J. Strachey (Ed. & Trans.), *Standard edition of the complete psychological works of Sigmund Freud* (Vols. 4–5, pp. 1–630). London: Hogarth Press. (Original work published 1900)

Freud, S. (1955a). The 'uncanny.' In J. Strachey (Ed. & Trans.), *Standard edition of the complete psychological works of Sigmund Freud* (Vol. 17, pp. 217–252). London: Hogarth Press. (Original work published 1919)

Freud, S. (1955b). Beyond the pleasure principle. In J. Strachey (Ed. & Trans.), *Standard edition of the complete psychological works of Sigmund

Freud (Vol. 18, pp. 1–64). London: Hogarth Press. (Original work published 1920)

Freud, S. (1955c). Psycho-analysis. In J. Strachey (Ed. & Trans.), *Standard edition of the complete psychological works of Sigmund Freud* (Vol. 18, pp. 235–254). London: Hogarth Press. (Original work published 1923)

Freud, S. (1957a). Five lectures on psycho-analysis. In J. Strachey (Ed. & Trans.), *Standard edition of the complete psychological works of Sigmund Freud* (Vol. 11, pp. 1–55). London: Hogarth Press. (Original work published 1910)

Freud, S. (1957b). Instincts and their vicissitudes. In J. Strachey (Ed. & Trans.), *Standard edition of the complete psychological works of Sigmund Freud* (Vol. 14, pp. 109–140). London: Hogarth Press. (Original work published 1915)

Freud, S. (1959). Psycho-analysis and the establishment of the facts in legal proceedings. In J. Strachey (Ed. & Trans.), *Standard edition of the complete psychological works of Sigmund Freud* (Vol. 9, pp. 103–114). London: Hogarth Press. (Original work published 1906)

Freud, S. (1960). The psychopathology of everyday life. In J. Strachey (Ed. & Trans.), *Standard edition of the complete psychological works of Sigmund Freud* (Vol. 6, pp. 1–310). London: Hogarth Press. (Original work published 1901)

Freud, S. (1961a). The ego and the id. In J. Strachey (Ed. & Trans.), *Standard edition of the complete psychological works of Sigmund Freud* (Vol. 19, pp. 3–66). London: Hogarth Press. (Original work published 1923)

Freud, S. (1961b). Inhibitions, symptoms and anxiety. In J. Strachey (Ed. & Trans.), *Standard edition of the complete psychological works of Sigmund Freud* (Vol. 20, pp. 75–174). London: Hogarth Press. (Original work published 1926)

Freud, S. (1963). Introductory lectures on psycho-analysis. In J. Strachey (Ed. & Trans.), *Standard edition of the complete psychological works of Sigmund Freud* (Vols. 15–16, pp. 1–463). London: Hogarth Press. (Original work published 1916–1917)

Freud, S. (1964). Civilization and its discontents. In J. Strachey (Ed. & Trans.), *Standard edition of the complete psychological works of Sigmund Freud* (Vol. 21, pp. 59–145). London: Hogarth Press. (Original work published 1930)

Freud, S. (1968). *Gesammelte werke, Chronologisch geordnet* (18 vols., A. Freud, E. Bibring, W. Hoffer, E. Kris, & O. Isakower, in colloboration with M. Bonaparte, Eds.). London/Frankfurt am Main: Imago Publishing Co. Ltd. (Original work published 1940–52)

Hartmann, H. (1939). Psychoanalysis and the concept of health. In *Essays on ego psychology*. New York: International Universities Press, Vol. 1964, pp. 1–18.

Hume, D. (1975). *An enquiry concerning human understanding* (3rd ed., L.A. Selby-Bigge, (Ed.). Oxford: Oxford University Press. (Original work published 1748)

Jones, E. (1924). Free will and determinism. *Essays in Applied Psychoanalysis*, Vol. 2, pp. 178–189.

Kohut, H. (1977). *The restoration of the self.* New York: International Universities Press.

Lacan, J. (2006). Presentation on psychical causality. *Écrits* (B. Fink, Trans.). New York: Norton, pp. 123–158. (Original work published 1947)

Mellor, D.H. (1995). *The facts of causation.* London: Routledge.

Menninger, K. (1955). Freedom. In B.H. Hall (Ed.), *A psychiatrist's world.* New York: Viking Press, Vol. 1959, pp. 803–808.

Mills, J. (2002). *The unconscious abyss: Hegel's anticipation of psycho-analysis.* Albany, NY: SUNY Press.

Mills, J. (2010). *Origins: On the genesis of psychic reality.* Montreal: McGill-Queens University Press.

Modell, A. (2011). Commentary. Discussant for panel: "Neuropsychology and the future of psychoanalysis: A debate." Div. 39, Psychoanalysis, annual spring meeting of the *American Psychological Association*, New York, NY, April 14.

Nietzsche, F. (1989). *Beyond good and evil* (W. Kaufmann, Trans.) New York: Vintage Books. (Original work published 1886)

Plato. (1961a). *Phaedo.* In E. Hamilton & H. Cairns (Eds.), *The collected dialogues of Plato.* Princeton: Princeton University Press, pp. 40–98.

Plato. (1961b). *Laws.* In E. Hamilton & H. Cairns (Eds.), *The collected dialogues of Plato.* Princeton: Princeton University Press, pp. 1225–1516.

Sartre, J.P. (1956). *Being and nothingness.* (H.E. Barnes, Trans.). New York: Washington Square Press. (Original work published 1943)

Sartre, J.P. (1957). *Existentialism and humanism.* P. Mairet (Trans.). London: Methuen, (Original work published 1946)

Schelling, F.W.J. (2006). *Philosophical investigations into the essence of human freedom.* (J. Love & J. Schmidt, Trans.). Albany, NY: SUNY Press. (Original work published 1809)

Schopenhauer, A. (1958). *The world as will and representation* (2 vols., E.F. Payne, Trans.). New York: Dover. (Original work published 1818)

Vergote, A. (1997). *La psychanalyse à l'épreuve de la sublimation.* Paris: Cerf.

Waelder, R. (1936a). The principle of multiple function: Observations on over-determination. *Psychoanalytic Quarterly*, Vol. 5, pp. 45–62.

Waelder, R. (1936b). The problem of freedom in psycho-analysis and the problem of reality -testing. *International Journal of Psycho-Analysis*, Vol. 17, pp. 89–108.

Chapter 14

Civilization and its Fate

When Einstein (1932) approached Freud on behalf of the League of Nations and asked the question: "Is there any way of delivering mankind from the curse of war?" (*SE*, p. 199), Freud (1932) responded with reservation, suggesting that perhaps it may only be mitigated. This is the general tenor of his anthropological treatment of humanity: until base instinct (*Trieb*) is sufficiently harnessed and transformed in the service of reason, our world communities will continue to be plagued by the dark marauders of our own insidious nature. Why war?—because hate and violence are "a piece of unconquerable nature ... a piece of our own psychical constitution" (Freud, 1930, *SE*, p. 86). With this dismal portrait of human relations, we may never come to throw our hatred down.

People are slaughtering one another all over the world in the name of religion, ethnic purity, and nationalism under the guise of freedom, justice, ethical duty, and social reform. Within the past few decades alone, contemporary ethnopolitical warfare has raged throughout the strife-torn territories of the Middle East, Africa, Eastern Europe, South and East Asia, Central America, Russia, and the Ukraine where civilian populations are the primary targets of terror—marked by sadism and butchery, while women and children comprise a large percentage of the incurred human rights atrocities. Those close to the front lines of ethnic and religious conflicts are oppressed by political violence, whether they are refugees who have lost their families in ethnic cleansing campaigns, to civilians who must dodge sniper fire everyday to run to the market to fetch a loaf of bread. When the

DOI: 10.4324/9781003305958-14

constancy of violence, terror, and war continue to saturate our daily consciousness, we can only anticipate where it will emerge next.

To what degree will our disparate cultures be able to rise above this mode of existence, where violence becomes the right of a community, either chosen or impugned? This is further compounded by the historical fact that brutality was the driving force behind the emergence of law, which still requires the use of violence to be enforced. Can actual force be replaced by the force of ideas, or are we condemned to the perversions of *pathos*? Given Freud's (1932) ontological treatise on the structure of the psyche, "there is no use in trying to get rid of men's aggressive inclinations" (*SE*, p. 211), they are as natural as breathing; for we can never escape from the fact that our minds are primitive. *Homo homini lupus est*—"Man is a wolf to man."[1]

The history of the human race is forged on traumatization, resentment, and the need for revenge, which preoccupies collective human consciousness and fuels pathological enactments. Aggression and violence directed towards others is part of human nature, an insidious derivative of our *pathos*. For the Greeks, to be human is to suffer, to be susceptible to pain (*pathētos*), to endure illness, in short, our accruing pathology. Our *pathos* may even become fused with desire, as in "antipathy," a passion (*patheia*) against (*anti*) another. Mental illness stems from this basic constituency of mind. This is why Freud (1916–1917) observed that we are all "neurotic" (*SE*, p. 358), that is, ill, whereby the human aspect is saturated with anxiety, suffering, and despair—it's just a matter degree. We are all deeply affected by our *pathos* to the point that what truly differentiates individuals and societies from one another is our level of functionality and adaptation to psychic pain. In other words, human pathology is normative throughout all cultures and all times. Being "normal" is merely another word for *pathos*.[2]

Psychopathology (πάθος) is the essence of man,[3] and it is from this standpoint that all else shall be measured. Desire precedes and supersedes reason, for primitive forces govern the psyche, which are arguably responsible as well for the exalted achievements of reason itself. Irrationality—*pathos*—is our primordial being, and it is from this ontological ground that all else materializes and makes itself known through various forms of human enactments. Reason always remains a tool, if not a slave, of desire.

Throughout this chapter, I will endeavour to provide a speculative account of the future of humanity based on a discernible pattern of violence and exploitation of the Other that characterizes human motivation and deed. I must confess that I can hardly do justice to this topic in the limited scope of this project, which would take volumes to address. At best I hope to frame the issue and the inherent problematics it poses, and certainly not pretend to offer any viable solutions, for I am unable to resolve the dilemma. Instead, I shall be concerned with a narrow scope of questions that investigate whether our pathological propensities as a human race will likely bring about our extinction, or whether we can transmogrify our destructive impulses through the relational negotiation of collective valuation practices that transcend our more primal constitutions. I hope the reader will forgive me for raising more conundrums rather than furnishing practical answers. Will the fate of civilization succumb to sordid desire inspiring our demise, or will human accord triumph in the end? The real issue involves: To what degree will the will towards violence be sublimated into the higher tiers of self-conscious ethical reflection that reason can afford?[4] We are a world divided by race, religion, ethnicity, economics, politics, and culture, where strong emotional bonds fuel and sustain separation and difference among our communities. I do not wish to express platitudes, illusory ideals, or provide false hope—the evidence, the brute facticity of impoverishment, suffering, cruelty, and murder—points to the most archaic configurations of psychic development that permeate our valuation practices.

Within today's multicultural and geopolitical world community, differences and prejudices continue to divide and polarize human relations into firm oppositions that become fortified within rigid group identifications that inform collectively shared value systems. What I mean by "prejudice" is that human beings are inclined towards the preferential self-expression of valuation based on self-interest and self-valuation. Ethnic, religious, cultural, and national identities are forged through prejudicial valuation practices that in some cases even legitimate heinous forms of injustice such as genocide, terrorism, human enslavement, and child trafficking. When collective identity is so firmly established in bipolar relation to the Other, is it possible for such valuation practices to abate under the rubric of peace? Prejudice, hate, and violence are no more likely to disappear than the reality of the external world, therefore the question becomes one of amelioration.

The Positive Significance of the Negative

As Hegel completed the final installments of the *Phenomenology of Spirit*, Napoleon was outside the city walls of Jena ushering in a new age—history was being transformed once again by the revolutionary currents of the dialectic. The battle of Jena may be said to parallel the very negative character of the dialectic itself, as conflict and violence pave the path towards progression. The self-generative process of the dialectic may provide us with a logical model for addressing the problem of *pathos*; but unlike Einstein's bane of war, the dialectic may also be the boon for its solution, one that nevertheless retains its destructive features as it wages combat against itself.

Both Hegel and Freud offer a view of the human condition that is characterized by destruction, negation, and conflict; yet it is paradoxical that such negativity also becomes an animating force behind the elevation of ethical self-consciousness. Like Spirit or Mind (*Geist*), which is the sublation (*Aufhebung*) of its previous historical moments, psychic maturation is the sublimation (*Sublimierung*) of primitive mental processes. Although Hegel's language may seem odd to modern sensibility, he is really attempting to describe what psychoanalysis refers to as the individual and collective psyche. Hegel and Freud would likely concede that through reason lies the hope that communities and cultures torn apart by discordant value practices can be united through collective ethical commitments. If humanity is to vanquish the pathology of base desire for the optimistic voluntarism enlightened by reason, it becomes important to understand how reason itself is the knight of desire designed to transform our pathologies.

We do not have to embrace Hegel's entire philosophical system, which is neither necessary nor pragmatic, in order to appreciate how his logic of the dialectic has utility for psychoanalytic thought.[5] Through his *Logic*, Hegel may be instructive in examining the evolutionary development of history achieved through negation and conquest in which further predictive possibilities for the future of humanity may be inferred. Hegel's (1807) *Phenomenology* personifies the drama of world Spirit (or what we may contemporarily refer to as humanity) as the coming to presence of pure self-consciousness through the process of self-estrangement, identification, and self-recognition through the mediation of the other. World hero eventually achieves Truth, satiates the lack, and arrives at full self-actualization only after traversing the arduous and protracted terrain of alienation through the vicissitudes of desire. Spirit—civilization—is therefore a constant activity, pure unrest. "It is just this unrest that is the self" (*PS*, p. 12). Hegel refers here to the unrest of *Aufhebung*, as dialectical process continuously annulled, preserved, and transcended. To recall, Hegel's logic of the dialectic involves a threefold process by which the lower relation becomes subsumed within the higher relation, at once being canceled, surpassed, but retained.[6] This pure activity of the dialectic is constantly evolving and redefining itself through such simultaneous movements, hence becoming the architecture—the ground—of *Geist*, our shared common humanity. And the driving force behind world history, behind the very process of the dialectic, is death and destruction.

Readers unfamiliar with Hegel will likely find his degree of abstraction overly abstruse and tedious, and his grand synthesis of everything has a grandiose tenor in ambition and level of generalization.[7] This is partly based on the metaphysics of his day where the most celebrated Modern philosophers and German Idealists were preoccupied with the relationship and unity of mind, nature, science, religion, ethics, and aesthetics. In the words of Derrida (1982), "Hegelianism represents the fulfillment of metaphysics, its end and accomplishment" (p. 73). It may be helpful to view Hegel's project as an attempt to describe the fundamental processes of human thought and activity as the progressive development of cognition and culture. As the human race evolved, so did our capacity for domestic socialization, civil obedience, ethical reflection, and rational thought. However, Hegel is primarily concerned with expatiating the universal while subordinating the particular; therefore, he is first and foremost interested in offering a philosophical system that applies to all people within all historical contingencies.

Hegel's notion of mind, and that of all of history, encompasses a process in which a subject is opposed to an object and comes to find itself in the object. This entails the mediation of it becoming other to itself, with the reflection out of otherness back to itself. The process of the development of the self and that of civilization is therefore a process of differentiation and integration. For Hegel, Being is characterized by an undifferentiated matrix which undergoes differentiation in the dialectical process of Becoming that in turn integrates into its being that which was differentiated through its projection, reclaiming it and making it part of its internal structure. The outcome of the integration is once again differentiated then reintegrated; unification is always reunification. Therefore, spirit comes to be what it already is, the process of its own becoming.

Spirit as the striving for pure self-consciousness ascends towards an absolute understanding of itself and comes to a unity constituted by the bifurcation and rigid opposition that it generates from within itself. It is precisely through such opposition that consciousness brings itself into reunification. Thus spirit, in its evolution, undergoes a violence at its own hands. By entering into opposition with itself, it raises this opposition to a higher unity and thus sublates it in a new structure. As each shape or content is confronted with radical opposition, each shape is made to collapse when its non-absolute form is exposed. Indeed, it is always driving the movement on from one shape to the next. Thus, the character of the dialectic is that of negativity and conflict; it is tempestuous, feral, and dynamic. Spirit as such is the source of its own negativity as inversion and destruction pave the way for its progression forward.

There is a necessity to the dialectic that informs the internal structures of the psyche; namely, there is a certain determinism to negation. The operation of such determinate negativity comes about through the collapse of each shape. As negation of a certain content takes place, it derives a certain content from the negation. Therefore, it links shapes into a necessary progression as each form turns into a new one. However, as each form is surpassed, the experience of its alteration is that of death, its end. But for Hegel, death always leads to rebirth. The dialectic is therefore the oscillation between life and death, never separate from one another. For Hegel (1807), spirit is always "tarrying with the negative"— confronting Death, for

to hold fast what is dead requires the greatest strength; ... the life
of spirit is not the life that shrinks from death and keeps itself
untouched by devastation, but rather the life that endures it and
maintains itself in it. It wins its truth only when, in utter
dismemberment, it finds itself. (*PS*, p. 19)

As determinate negativity, spirit vanquishes itself as it destroys itself.
It kills itself as it gives itself life. This is the "tremendous power of the
negative" (*PS*, p. 19), staring death straight in the face, converting
it into the positive. It is precisely through such negativity that there
is progression, destroying itself in the service of raising itself—the
positive significance of the negative.

If the dialectic becomes a logical model in its application towards
a global amelioration of psychopathology, then we must be able to
logically demonstrate whether it has the potential to bear any fruit.
We may appeal to historical facticities that trace the epigenesis of
humankind and perhaps even come to the conclusion that, despite all
the carnage and social decay, we have evolved into more a civil and
enlightened species, even though human aggressivity and immorality
captures the locus of our attentions everyday as a TV screams. But a
historical account alone carries less predictive value, for we have
no means of being able to predict with much accuracy the future
contingencies that will affect the teleological progression of human
psychodynamics, hence contingencies that always inform the mediatory interventions mind assumes in each immediate shape it encounters. We may do better to stay on ontological ground, a ground
that informs our collective anthropology; and we must be able to
demonstrate the internal consistency and systematic coherency of the
dialectic that Hegel's Logic affords.

The self, as well as the collective psyche, or what we may call the
universal soul (*anima mundi*)—psychic processes that belong to us
all, is an epigenetic construct, thus a teleological movement that is a
procreative self-articulated complex holism.[8] As a self-generative
telic will, cognition is free in its encounters with the contingencies of
its reality, taking into account the exigencies of its environment and the
novelties of immediate experience. Therefore, spirit is not pre-designed
or predetermined towards a presupposed end, but rather its end is
a transformed achievement—"the logical and ontological Alpha of the

cosmos, but only after it has emerged as its logical and ontological Omega" (Findlay, 1971, p. 93). It emerges through the process of mediation and negotiation with the existential realities it confronts.

Our faith in the transcending power of mind over the combative regimens of world discord is acceptable only to the extent at which we believe in a progressive trend towards increased solidarity through collective self-conscious rationality. The level of psychic development Hegel points towards is hardly achieved by intellectuals let alone the masses, for reason is often eclipsed by the primal lure of desire. If the facts of history and human nature do indeed lean towards a steady progressive self-conscious liberation of rational freedom, then to what degree is this the result of our aptitude to bridle and sublimate our primitive proclivities for the ideals of conscience and the rational demands of a civil society? The promise of increased unity in the face of disharmony augers well for a collectively shared and constructive value system; however, the ostensive prevalence of global division and chaos saturated by prejudicial and physical conflicts may leave us with a less optimistic interpretation of the fate of humanity.

The problem of destructiveness becomes the central task of our investigation, for if Hegel is correct, it becomes the stallion of unification as it gallops towards the horizon of reason. But if our aggressive trends continue to go unchecked, Freud's admonition of the possible extinction of the human race carries foreboding merit. Our analysis of the positive significance of the negative will lead us to conclude whether a philosophically informed psychoanalysis may genuinely offer a contribution to peace.

Psychoanalytic Anthropology

The primary significance of destruction is never so forceful as in Freud's (1920) postulation of the death drive (*Todestrieb*), the foundation that governs psychic development to which "*the aim of all life is death*" (*SE*, p. 38). Negativity is always the base agitation of any organism—the destruction that constructs life—the purpose of which is to return to the original lost unity of its symbiotic state. The notion of original unity is instructive for our understanding of a principle of world harmony devoid of the more pathological instantiations of human aggression because, for both Freud and Hegel, consciousness emerges from an unconscious undifferentiated unity with its primordial nature. Just as Freud (1920) speculates on how the organic arises from the inorganic (see *SE*, pp. 36–39), as the general object of anthropology, Hegel (1830) traces the dialectical emergence of the feeling soul from the abyss of its indeterminations; at first unseparated from its immediate universal simplicity, it then divides and rouses itself from its mere inward implicitness to explicit determinate being-for-self.[9]

For Hegel, spirit begins, like ego development for Freud,[10] as an original undifferentiated unity that emerges from its immediate self-enclosed universality to its mediated determinate singularity. This is initiated through a dialectical process of internal division, self-externalization, and introjection as the reincorporation of its projected qualities back into its interior. Through the complexities of mediation and sublation, mind achieves higher levels of unification until it arrives at a full integration of itself as a complex whole, uniting earlier finite shapes within its mature universality. The need for social order, unification, and harmony are motivational factors that inform the ideal of global tranquility which human violence, hate, evil, and terrorism threaten to deteriorate, an ideal imbued with the residue of early symbiotic conditions.

The ego ensnared in the stage of primary narcissism (Freud, 1914, *SE*, p. 100), like spirit asleep in the undifferentiated abyss of its self-absorption (Hegel, 1830, § 408, *Zusätze*, 2), constitutes the psychological and ontological precursors for differentiation and development. To what degree do these conditions play in our wish for higher degrees of unity, concord, and moral self-realization? Are we to understand world spirit as "the universal brotherhood of man" (Harris, 1983, p. 411) that seeks absolute unity, or is this merely a wish to return to the "oceanic feeling"[11] of symbiosis like a fetus in the peaceful sea of its mother's womb? To what degree is this an illusion that preoccupies so many minds, like the parallel wish for union with God, the exalted father who shall make our home safe and free from our helplessness and pain (see Freud, 1927; 1930)? But whether these are fantasies or not, they represent moral ideals: "Thou shalt not take the name of the Lord thy God in vain!"—don't you dare assault my desire!

One would be hard pressed to find someone who would not value the ideal of peace, with communal harmony, accord, and co-operation marshaled in the service of social progression. But the very nature of the need for progressive unification is also dialectically opposed to destructive and regressive inclinations that derive from earlier primitive shapes of our psychic constitution we seek to act out or recover during conflict precipitated by opposition. If the desire for unification is a derivative of our original psychical ontology, then both progressive and regressive desires may be said to emanate from the same mental (symbiotic) configurations which may further possibly serve the same aim. Both seek unity or peace of a different kind and in a different form: one through the attainment of higher integrated complexities, the other a wish to return to the warm blanket of its initial undifferentiated beginning— unity is nevertheless their goal. Here *unity* should be understood within the symbolic context of psychological integration, where strong affective bonds for concord, union, and amalgamation are achieved and internally experienced as a transcendental ideal. Following Hegel, this would require some integrative function that would attempt to bind or resolve opposition, or for Freud, serve the pleasure principle through sublimation. But if the drive towards destruction is responsible for both progress and regress, growth and decay, then how are we to determine which one will advance and which one will succumb to the tyranny of the other? This brings into question how the nature of negativity and destruction influence the self-preservative drives in their quest for unification and mastery.

Freud (1923) tells us of two competing forces in human nature: the will towards life and the will towards death manifested as Eros or libido, the sexual force responsible for erotic life, and its antithetical companion conceived under the drive towards destruction. This dual class of innate drives comprises those, which seek to preserve and unite, and those which seek to kill and destroy, both giving rise to what may be characterized as our caring and aggressive propensities. "Neither of these drives are any less essential than the other; the phenomena of life arise from the concurrent or mutually opposing action of both" (Freud, 1932, *SE*, p. 209). Furthermore, they scarcely operate in isolation, both borrowing from the resources of the other as an accompanied or alloyed counterpart, drawing a certain quota from the other side, which in turn modifies its aim or is even used to achieve its aim.

This union between life and death is the ontological fabric of the human mind to which all other dialectical polarities arise including the universality of Love and Hate. Self-preservation is clearly an erotic impulse but it must have aggression at its disposal in order to accomplish its task; just as in love, the aggressive drive is utilized in order to gain mastery and possession over an object in which the attachment to it brings about. Although the self-preservative drives stand in stark opposition to destructive ones, the two are dialectical complementarities that reflect their confluence. Here we have a similar structural dynamic of the Hegelian dialectic with negativity begetting progression in the service of achieving higher aims. Just as Being is in opposition to Nothing, so is life and death, two sides of a symmetrical relation, their necessary unity.

Collective identity is based on the strength and intensity of emotional ties among its members and the mutual identification with shared valuation practices, thus giving rise to diversity, opposition, and prejudicial division between individuals, cohorts, cultures, societies, and nations.[12] The greater discrepancies such as race, religion, ethnicity, nationality, and political affiliation that bring about more pronounced forms of prejudice and contempt are not surprising. The increased enthusiasm in nationalism, religious identity, and separatism among our diverse peoples point towards the need to define ourselves in opposition to difference, rallying greater collective fellowship among its identified members, and thereby strengthening the cultural narcissism that hold societies together—all in the service of the self-preservative drives that align with similarity and cultural identification.[13] In *Group Psychology and the Analysis of the Ego*, Freud (1921) underscores the universality of prejudice:

> Every time two families become connected by marriage, each of them thinks itself superior to or of better birth than the other. Of two neighboring towns each is the other's most jealous rival; every little canton looks down upon the others with contempt. Closely related races keep one another at arm's length; the South German cannot endure the North German, the Englishman casts

every kind of aspersion upon the Scot, the Spaniard despises the Portuguese. We are no longer astonished that greater differences should lead to an almost insuperable repugnance, such as the Gallic people for the German, the Aryan for the Semite, and the white races for the coloured. (*SE*, p. 101)

This is a profound observation that equally applies today: regardless of our era of diversity, multiculturalism, tolerance for difference, interethnic, interfaith, interracial, and social pluralism, there is always a suprasignifier of judgement unconsciously operative based on the identification of similarity and difference that infiltrates every form of prejudice and ideology. There is such a narcissism of even minor differences between individuals and cultures that the very sound of rap music blaring from an open car window could lead one so judgementally inclined to conclude that the true meaning of "culture" is to be found growing in the bottom of a test tube. We are further informed by scientists that we now have the empirical means by which to measure the degree and intensity of our disgust for minor differences by observing the pupil size of an individual. It is a universal biological fact that regardless of light differences, our pupils dilate when we like something and become pinpricks when we perceive something to be a repellent (see Morris, 1998). It is comforting to know that when uncertain about whether or not someone is friend or foe, all you have to do is look at the centre of his or her iris to determine if it is the size of a pinhead.

The nature of identification has its origins in early ego development whereby the child takes its parents as ideal objects who, along with their value systems, become internalized within personality formation and effect the germination of moral conscience as well as the capacities for love and hate. Whether personal or collective, identity is defined in opposition to difference and identification with similarity. But we also realize that identification is overdetermined, multiply instantiated, and based on a plurality of forces and ambivalent attitudes that inform how the objects, content, form, valence, qualia, and intensity of identifications are constituted. This structural dynamic alone may be said to account for the need for division, uniqueness, and prejudicial self-preferences as opposed to others who stand in marked difference; but it also potentially explains the dialectical complementarities at play on other unconscious levels. Nevertheless, the confluence of destructive and self-preservative forces compounds the nature of identifications and social relations where desire justifies murder and reason is manipulated to assuage primal instinctual urges in the service of narcissistic pursuits.

There are such countless examples of the polarization of values and ideals that stand in opposition to others that you could spend the rest of your life trying to catalogue them all. In many cases of group prejudice, valuation practices assume a form of collective identification based on a simple rigid economy. Intolerance to difference that precipitates extreme forms of violence may be said to represent a regression to our most primitive constitutions when bad (self)objects are regurgitated from the mouth as poisonous projections of evil and hatred that must be annihilated, what Klein (1946) would refer to as the paranoid-schizoid position. In many cases, extreme prejudice is the product of pathological narcissism. Patriarchal value placed on male children over female children has historically led to infanticide that is still practiced today in parts of China, India, Africa, and the Middle East. Since the Taliban took power of the government of Afghanistan, women have had to wear burqas; and have been beaten and stoned to death in public for not having the proper attire, even if this simply means not having their mesh cover the front of their eyes. After James Byrd Jr. was dragged from his feet down a rural road by a chain secured to the back of a pickup truck until his right arm and head were literally torn from his torso just because he was black, the devastated town of Jaspers Texas was greeted three weeks later by a Ku Klux Klan rally. Genocide continues to rip through our world claiming innocent lives, from the Hutu's massacre of the Tutsis in Rwanda, to the Serbs mass extermination of Bosnian Muslims, to the systematic slaughter in Kosovo, not to mention the recent plethora of killings initiated by the Arab Spring, which are still reigning in psychopathic Islamdom. While these are extreme cases, one need not look further than one's own country to confirm the ethnic and patriotic narcissism that envelopes us all.

Both Hegel and Freud stress the importance that civilization is a process. But these aforementioned events hardly resemble the mores of a civilized culture as irrational fanaticism justifies barbarity broaching the brink of insanity. The primitive economy of rigid identification that justifies these extreme forms of savagery has at its disposal all the unbridled resources of the death drive turned outwards. The drive towards death is transformed into the destructive drive when it becomes projected onto external objects. In this way, self-preservation is maintained by destroying extraneous threats as objects of hate are rendered impotent. "Hate, as a relation to objects, is older than love. It derives from the narcissistic ego's primordial repudiation of the external world with its outpouring of stimuli. As an expression of the reaction of unpleasure evoked by objects, it always remains in an intimate relation with the self-preservative drives" (Freud, 1915, *SE*, p. 139). Yet self-preservation versus pleasure induced in killing are two different inflections of narcissism. Sadism, the derivative of hate, is nowhere so evident as with the deranged techniques conceived and used to torture, maim, and murder millions of victims in the Holocaust, and in the killing fields under the Khmer Rouge government, as well as in the death camps manufactured by Bosnian Serbs in the name of ethnic cleansing.

The Bosnian concentration camps were one of the most horrific human slaughterhouses, because the means of extermination were laborious and perverted, the aim of which was to produce the most excruciating amount of pain, mental anguish, and suffering possible (see Danner, 1997, pp. 55–56). Although it is illegitimate to make comparisons, the killing at Auschwitz was largely mechanized and bureaucratic, while the genocide at Omarska was emotional and personal, mainly depending upon the simple and intimate act of beating. These techniques were inefficient, time-consuming, and physically exhausting, yet they were habitually and systematically employed to intentionally demoralize and demolish, bringing warped pleasure to the guards and paramilitary units who, through their innovative means at devising methods of torture, could greatly bolster their prestige. The use of rape warfare on women—especially adolescents and children—is another such example of the chilling psychological and sociological rationale for the deliberate and systematic means of deteriorating the opposition from within their own support systems by depleting their morale, ego defenses, and will (see Allen, 1996). Here we can see how reason is distorted under the dictatorship of psychopathic narcissism. It is in moments like these that one can hear the voice of Luther—*die Hure Vernunft*—"reason is the whore of humanity."[14] We can rationalize away anything, even our morality.

Is the death drive so intent on persecuting humankind that it will eventually bring us to ruin? The bleak forecast of the continual historical reign of terror by sick minds in positions of power and privilege may lead us to rightfully conclude that "men are not gentle creatures who want to be loved" (Freud, 1930, *SE*, p. 111), rather they want to exploit, con, use, conquer, humiliate, torture, and kill. In *Civilization and its Discontents*, Freud (1930) writes:

> The fateful question for the human species seems to me to be whether and to what extent their cultural development will succeed in mastering the disturbance of their communal life by the human drive of aggression and self-destruction .... Men have gained control over the forces of nature to such an extent that with their help they would have no difficulty in exterminating one another to the last man. They know this, and hence comes a large part of their current unrest, their unhappiness and their mood of anxiety. (*SE*, p. 145)

It may be argued that religion and ethnicity—including race and language—are the main reasons for divided group identifications, and this is inseparable from certain belief systems and valuation practices that inform culture. Together, ethnicity and religion form the social value structures that become the macrocosm of any culture, which furthermore acquire personal and collective meaning that validates nations and keeps them together. Ethnic and religious identification is so strong that even between closely related ethnic and religious groups, rigid group identifications keep societies from embracing shared qualities simply because of minute differences that threaten cultural narcissism. When dispute over land continues to flare throughout Eastern Europe, the Middle East, and Africa, ethnicity, religion, and nationalism become more demarcated with group identifications more virulently opposed.

The stronger the intensity of emotional bonds between people, the stronger identifications become. Group identity fosters unity and progression, but it may also lead to discord and regression—

the dynamic that fuels both peace and war. In my opinion, group identifications are responsible for the process and advance of civilization as collective value systems govern the ideals of a community. As a general rule, any movement that encourages greater emotional attachment to others strongly militates against the loom of destruction, for love is the engendered ideal and the heart of conscience. When people are governed by empathy and conscience, reason is marshaled in service of justice and the pursuit of the ethical. This too requires an inversion of aggression that becomes the internal judge of conscience, where guilt and shame equally inform our moral choices, as does reason.

Take for example, two different cultural responses to involvement in World War II. Germany experiences a great deal of universal shame for their infamous role in history that fractured world order, yet they still acknowledge and remember their history, teach it in the classroom, and maintain public museums, camps, and monuments, while the Japanese still live in collective denial of their involvement in the war. The official government policy does not recognize its historical atrocities or past war crimes, which are omitted from textbooks and prohibited from being taught in public schools. Here we have two responses to collective shame: acknowledgment with the educational concern that history should not repeat itself, and denial in the name of "saving face." We shall not deviate far in saying that one is a healthy response of remorse to guilt and shame, while the other is an infantile attempt to maintain a cultural narcissism where the superiority of the Japanese race is inculcated in schoolchildren every day and institutionally solidified by national identity.

I use these previous examples arbitrarily as merely illustrative of particular instantiations of collective identification, yet they occur everywhere. Regardless of what examples we focus on, which always runs the danger of introducing ancillary distractions, whether they be distantly historical or more contemporary in world attention, the phenomena of collective identification equally apply to any culture or society throughout time. Although particularity is culturally relative and contingent upon the interaction between group relations and the social environs that inform collective identity, it also transpires within a greater universal process governing object relations. Here it is important to stay focused on the universal rather than the particular, for the more crucial locus of our inquiry concerns human nature itself, namely, that which is common to us all.

The End of the World

In this age of terrorism post 9/11, world anxiety becomes our number one preoccupation. When deranged minds are willing to sacrifice their own lives during the suicidal terrorist acts of committing murder, no one or nation is immune from threat. In the wake of such persistent anxiety, "unhappy and paranoid" becomes the epithet we shall apply to characterize collective humanity. And just as Freud's seminal work, *Das Unbehagen in der Kultur*, described the unease, trepidation, and unhappiness within the culture of his day during the early rise of Hitler, we may justifiably conclude that the scale and ferocity of cross-cultural/interfaith/interethnic aggression has intensified and gotten much worse since his time. The fantasy that men are inherently gentle creatures who are born good, free of dispositional sin, and untainted by primitive intent can no longer be sustained by critical reason. It is an empirical fact that by all historiographical accounts of cultural anthropology, human civilization has been forged on human conflict, attachment deficits in parent-child rearing practices, emotional, physical, and sexual abuse, traumatization, dehumanization, and war. Given the historical progression of civilization, what reasonable trajectory do we posit for the future of humanity?

The astrophysicist and cosmologist Brandon Carter (1983) has provided a mathematical formulation that predicts the probability of human extinction. Given that there are nearly 8 billion people alive on this planet today, and that we are amongst the most people who have ever lived in the history of the human race, from a predictive statistical standpoint, it is speculated that there is an approximate 5% chance that we will expire within a couple hundred years and a 95% chance that complete human extinction will occur in approximately 7000 years, with a possible degree of freedom extending this figure to just over 9000 years. This is known as the "Doomsday Argument." In other words, if all the humans alive today are in a random place in the human history timeline, then we are nearer to extinction than not.

While there are different versions of this scenario that vary in scope and formulation, including critiques, refutations, and rebuttals, philosopher John Lesley (1996) has championed this argument in his chilling speculations on the end of the world. One cannot entertain the actual risks of complete human annihilation based on such brute evidence without sinking into worrisome pessimism. Lesley draws alarming attention to the underestimated existential dangers that threaten human extinction, including the notion that we could become extinct fairly soon. Despite the recognized risks of natural disaster, including volcanic eruptions, the earth colliding with asteroids or comets, astronomical explosions like supernovae, galactic centre outbursts, and solar flares, or a complex breakdown of the earth's biosphere, we are well aware that most of the immediate threats to the survival of the human race come from man. We damage our own ozone layer, dump toxins into our air, lands, and seas via mass industrial pollution, increase greenhouse effects that ruin our ecosystems, and introduce fatal viral diseases and new varieties of plague that infiltrate our continents. Soon the world could become uninhabitable. From nuclear war to germ warfare, radiation poisoning, biological and chemical warfare, terrorism, criminality, technological manipulations such as genetic engineering disasters, food infections (i.e., salmonella bacteria), computer-initiated network malfunctions, internet viruses, or techno-war that jeopardize human survival, and scientific hubris—like biohacking, nanotechnology, or careless physics experimentations "at immensely high energies, [that] will upset a space-filling 'scalar field' and destroy the world" (Lesley, 1996, p. 1)—these are but a few very serious reasons not to dismiss the ubiquitous threat of world annihilation.

We are facing a planetary ecological crisis due to global warming, despoliation of our natural resources, mass scale industrial pollution, desertification, deforestation, widespread collapse of ecosystems, and extreme climate change. World overpopulation is nearing a record tipping-point, where food and water scarcity will bring about more famine, drought, pestilence, and death. Global catastrophic hazards have escalated due to the environmental crisis, encroachment by man, destabilized markets, hegemonic politics, the ubiquitous dread of nuclear war, terrorism, infectious diseases, techno nihilism, and psychological self-interest driving everything from vain desire to the local economy and international relations, not to mention the anathema of evil, abuse, trauma, greed, and the psychopathology of everyday life. Our recalcitrant dependency on fossil fuel is gradually suffocating the planet. Greenhouse warming, climate catastrophes, and aberrant weather phenomena occur every day throughout the globe and yet we do very little to mitigate it, let alone reverse its course. Moreover, we have caused the Anthropocene. Despite the fact that we see the ruin with our own eyes and do practically nothing to mitigate the ecological crisis, world masses have adopted a global bystander effect (Mills, 2020), where denial and abnegation of social responsibility lie at its very core. Regardless of the degree of gravity we assign to these calculated risks imperiling our existence, we cannot ignore the ominous threat of planetary extinction unless humanity unites in moral preventative action.

In our contemporary era of geopolitical and religious violence that legitimizes the morality of war with the support of military science, our conflict of cultures begets and bears witness to increased human tragedy and traumatization. There are pernicious threats associated with the subversive activities of fundamentalist religious groups that embrace ethical relativism and prescriptivism based on collective ideology just as there are repercussions from foolish decisions made by narcissistically grandiose politicians who hype up a country's citizenry based upon an appeal to emotion in the pursuit of national self-interest. If we don't kill each other by destroying our environment through chemical, biological, and nuclear war, leading to loss of biodiversity, disease, disastrous climate change, greenhouse calamity, desertification, and pollution of our planet, then overpopulation will surely erode our environment and tax our natural resources to satisfy basic human needs, which will likely lead to mass panic, mayhem, and global warfare. When people have no grain to eat, the moral principle of human rights becomes a vacuous concept.

Prejudice and Valuation

The polarity of human desire, the nature of personal and collective identifications, and the combative forces of social and cultural oppositions all operate within anthropological and ontological structures that give rise to civilization and the historical manifestations of pathology. Civilization, even more so than nature itself, is responsible for most of our malaise; but it is also responsible for our remarkable advances in education, technology, science, medicine, human rights, aesthetics, and moral conscientiousness that enhance the quality of human life, most of which having occurred in our lifetime. But along with these advances have also come the technology to extinguish the entire human race. This is especially disturbing when fanatical and paranoid minds have means and access to weapons of mass destruction. This places us in the precarious position of attempting to anticipate the possible fate of humanity, for the predictive validity of the progression of civilization hinges on whether aggression will be restricted, displaced, inverted, and/or sublimated for higher rational, ethical, and aesthetic pursuits.

With regard to the question of the possibility of global amelioration of pathological enactments, the issue becomes one of degree. Since prehistory, culture has undergone an evolutionary process of becoming, which is responsible for what we have come to call civilization, our evolved contemporary valuation practices. However, like Freud (1932) observed, "uncultivated races (sic) and backward strata of the population are already multiplying more rapidly than highly cultivated ones" (*SE*, p. 214). While there are many socioeconomic, political, and psychological reasons for this, they nevertheless obstruct the optimal transformation of our *pathos*.

Prejudice forms a basic constituency in our psychic constitutions, for we all pass judgements on others based on our preferential appraisal of what we value and are accustomed to find familiar and/or pleasing. The double edge of the dialectic (as negativity resulting in higher unity) exposes us to a dilemma, for the dialectic is the ontological dynamic underlying prejudice itself. Part of the problem facing us is that prejudice is ontologically constituted in the most rudimentary aspects of human consciousness. Like the nature of the dialectic, prejudice has both negative and positive valences. While violence and destruction are the instruments of prejudice, so too are caring and love. Prejudice is not merely a negative construct; prejudice defines our valuation practices, which are the Mecca of individual and communal life. Rather than conceive of prejudice as simply a pathological anomaly, prejudice is also responsible for our most revered ideals. As I have said elsewhere (Mills & Polanowski,

1997, pp. 11–13), prejudice in its essence is the preferential self-expression of valuation. All prejudicial disclosures express value preferences. Preferences are prejudicial because they signify discriminatory value judgements that are self-referential. Preference presupposes prejudice for preference typifies the priority of determinate valuation. To prefer is to value and to value is to judge: judgements by nature are valuative. All judgements are imbued with value, which presuppose self-valuation and self-interest, because valuation is a particular form of subjective self-expression. Thus, valuation is prejudicial, for it involves a relation between difference and similarity that is necessarily self-referential. Every human being by nature is prejudiced; it is simply a matter of degree, and towards what particular object one's prejudice is directed.

Prejudice is a neutral psychological predisposition that informs the ontology of human subjectivity. Prejudice is an elementary aspect of conscious and unconscious life that gives rise to the self, the nature of personal identification, individual and collective identity, culture, and shared value practices. Prejudice as valuation is therefore responsible for our shared ideals as well as the deviations of abnormality and perversion. In its ideal condition, prejudicial valuation informs our social mores and ethical practices. In its larger scope, ethics is the harvest of subjective universality. As such, selfhood and culture give rise to morality that is individualistic and interpersonally bound within a psychosocial matrix of negotiation and intersubjective validation. Value determinations, I suggest, are the result of interpersonal mediations and identifications with collective ideals and are therefore intersubjectively constructed and validated through the dialectical process of our social and cultural prejudices. Applying Hegel, the succession towards greater unity, cooperation, and peace among nations is progressively forged by the movement of the dialectic as prejudice constantly gives rise to new and higher order forms of novelty and creative complexity. These existential complexities ontologically stand over and above individual practices, for they are mediated in the face of social and cultural interpersonal forces that negotiate and intersubjectively affirm collectively shared value systems and practices over others. As with the epigenesis of the self, the process of this negotiation rests on the nature of identification.

Ideals do not exist in a moral vacuum: they are created by the larger sociocultural milieu that becomes individually and idiosyncratically internalized throughout development; yet they are always open to change and transmutation. These early internalized ideals become the formative basis of a cohesive self and social structure, which remain in flux and unrest due to the dialectical unfolding of the nature of subjectivity and social relations. The parallel process of valuation in individual and collective development is constituted a priori within the larger ontological structures that make worldhood possible. Such pre-established ontological conditions (as thrownness) provide the ideal objects of identification that are necessary for selfhood and for the emergence of values—yet they are always up for renegotiation. This emerging process of valuation gives rise to greater *aporias* in selfhood, communal forces, socio-political drift, and international relations. However, the dialectical nature of prejudice that gives rise to civilization leads to an internal ambivalence, a dilemma it fights within itself. In this sense, values can never be fixed truths or universal essences. Instead, they necessarily materialize out of prejudice, negation, and conflict. Acquiring new life in the wake of destruction, the death of particular values is preserved in the ashes of history, nostalgia, and desire. As humanity elevates itself to higher degrees of complexity, so do its ideals.

From this account we may say that valuation inherently yearns for greater levels of unification and complexity. This would seem to suggest that the structurally constituted dynamic progression of the dialectic ensures that civilization will remain ontologically predisposed to seek and maintain order, accord, and social progression while allowing for a vast variance of novelty, freedom, and complexity to emerge. But with complexity and freedom come the inherent risk of individual and collective psychopathy and social regression that threatens the progressive unification and self-preservative acclivity towards holism. To what degree will progression win out over regression in the face of our contemporary ecological emergency, projected world overpopulation, food, water, and land scarcity, environmental peacekeeping, ethnic, and religious conflicts, terror, and war? In order to provide a more systematic and rigorously justified account of the constructive forces of civilization within the destructive shapes of worldhood, we need to closely examine Hegel's logic of the dialectic and determine if the positive significance of the negative will in the end vitiate the primitive propensities that compel human relations towards destructive acts.

The Logic of the Dialectic

One of the more interesting aspects of Hegel's (1812) dialectic is the way in which a mediated dynamic forms a new immediate. This process not only informs the basic structure of his *Logic*, which may further be attributed to the general principle of *Aufhebung*, but this process also provides the logical basis to account for the role of negativity within a progressive unitary drive. The process by which mediation collapses into a new immediate provides us with the logical model for the improvement of civilization. And it is precisely this logical model that provides the internal consistency to its specific application to the amelioration of pathology. As an architectonic process, spirit invigorates itself and breaths its own life as a self-determining generative activity that builds upon its successive shapes and layers that inform its appearances; therefore, collective mind constructs its own monolith. It is this internal consistency that provides us with a coherent account of the circular motion of the progressive drive towards higher manifestations of psychical, social, and cultural development.

Hegel's use of mediation within the movements of thought is properly advanced in the *Science of Logic* as well as the *Encyclopaedia Logic*, which prefaces Hegel's anthropological and psychological treatment of Spirit. In the *Logic* (1812), Being moves into Nothing which then develops into Becoming, first as the "passing over" into nothing, second as the "vanishing" into being, and third as the "ceasing-to-be" or passing away of being and nothing into the "coming-to-be" of becoming. Becoming constitutes the mediated unity of "the unseparatedness of being and nothing" (*SL* § C, 2, p. 105). Hegel shows how each mediation leads to a series of new immediates, which pass over and cease to be, as that which has passed over in its coming to be, until these mediations collapse into the determinate being of *Dasein*—its new immediate. Being is a simple concept while Becoming is a highly dynamic and complex process. Similarly, *Dasein* or determinate being is a simple immediacy to begin with, which gets increasingly more complicated as it transitions into Essence and conceptual understanding. It is in this early shift from becoming to determinate being that you have a genuine sublation, albeit as a new immediate, spirit has a new beginning.

In Hegel's treatment of consciousness as pure thought represented by the *Logic*, as well as his treatment of world history in the *Phenomenology*, and the Anthropology and Psychology sections in the *Encyclopaedia*, spirit continues on this circular albeit progressive path conquering each new opposition it encounters, hence elevating itself in the process. Each mediation leads to a new beginning, and spirit constantly finds itself confronting opposition and overcoming conflict as it is perennially engaged in the process of its own becoming. In the *Logic*, the whole process is what is important as reason is eventually able to understand its operations as pure self-consciousness; however, in its moments, each mediation begets a new starting point that continually re-institutes new obstacles and dialectical problems that need to be mediated, hence eliminated.

But thought always devolves or collapses back into the immediate. This dynamic is a fundamental structural constituent that offers systematic coherency to Hegel's overall philosophy of spirit as well as its specific relevance to the problem at hand. Culture mediates opposition and conflict it generates from within its own evolutionary process and attempts to resolve earlier problems unto which new immediacy emerges. Mediation is therefore an activity performed from within society and cultural forces that in turn make new experience possible. When disparate cultures and societies are taken together as a conglomerate with endless processes within over-determined processes, the whole movement of civilization itself becomes an ever-increasing logical synthesis.

Hegel envisions this general structural dynamic throughout all contexts of spirit, giving the movement of spirit its logical substance. Each immediacy has a new kind of claim that tests spirit's past shapes, which in turn must be put into practice in the novel experiences it confronts. Spirit is faced with the tussle of having to take each new immediate and integrate it within its preexisting internal structure, thus incorporating each novelty within its subsisting mediatory faculties. This structural dynamic takes into account the ubiquitous nature of contingency, for spirit is simply not just extending a part of itself as mediation that is already there; it has to incessantly vanquish each new experience it encounters in all of its freshly discovered and potentially unacquainted future environments. The ongoing process of confrontation is the burden of spirit's odyssey, with each encounter signaling a spewing forth from the unconscious well of what it has already incorporated from its past, thus defining the emerging context for each new stage it confronts as unexpected reality.

The Infinite Progress of the Infinite Regress

Through the interaction of mediated immediacy, teleology becomes defined in each moment, with each immediacy being only a moment in the process of civilization. As spirit passes into new stages, it educates itself as it transforms itself, taking on new forms, expanding and incorporating larger aspects of its experience into its inner being. Preparing itself for its next confrontation, it guarantees there will always be a new stage. Because civilization is the self-sublation—what might not be inappropriately called sublimation—of its earlier primitive activity, the logic of the dialectic provides us with a prototype for understanding the underlying functions and power of the negative that propels civilization to overcome its increased oppositions, which it generates from within itself. Because civilization generates division and opposition within itself, each new mediated immediacy allows for contingencies and complexities to operate within existing dynamic structures. This is the freedom of the power of the negative, for it may seek to operate within a destructive and regressive fashion rather than align with the upward current of human growth, social consciousness, tolerance, acceptance, and ethical progress. This further ensures that there will always be pathological forms of human activity: the thought that we could ever stop thinking in terms of difference such as ethnicity, religion, language, or race is simply an illusion.

Human beings will always seek separate unique identities (whether as individuals or as groups) in opposition to others based on the values they choose to identify with. This tendency further guarantees that nationalism, ethnic and religious identity, political factions, and separatist movements energized by rigid group identifications will never perish, for identity is what keeps people together; we may only hope that their pathological instantiations will abate and become marginalized to minor aberrations that fail to identify with greater collective global visions. But in all likelihood, we will only see spheres in the amelioration of *pathos* determined by contingent world events.

If we may offer a prediction of the future of civilization based on Hegel's logical model, then perhaps we will see many infinite progresses of many infinite regresses insofar as civilization climbs up the rungs of the ladder, it will also experience slippage, regression, and withdrawal back to earlier manifestations of its being. In this century, this explanation may be said to account, in part, for Hitler and the Holocaust, Stalin's gulags and reign of butchery, Pol Pot's killing fields, Saddam Hussein's gassing of his own people, the genocide in Bosnia and Rwanda, Milosevic's relentless crusade of ethnic cleansing, the grisly "choppings" in Sierra Leone, and more recently, the terrorist attacks on the US Pentagon and World Trade Center. But as evinced by Hegel's *Logic*, as well as our empirical social advancements, given the synthetic and upwardly mobile acclivity of the dialectic, as a rule, increased ascendance and social unification overreaches the regressive instantiation of annihilating forces.

Yet with each destruction comes a new construction of mediated immediacies that give rise to new values and social ideals. Freud's contribution is invaluable to Hegel's position because, as they both maintain, negativity is the core constituent of life: death and destruction will not only be a universality in all possible future worlds, it is a necessary ontological dynamic that assures the upward progression of change, prosperity, and maturation—the very essence of the striving for our ideal possibility-for-Being.

With most of the world's continents engaged in some form of military conflict, it may be argued (at least theoretically) that the United Nations becomes an ethical paragon for global peace and unity; and with the fight for freedom, democracy, and human rights, social consciousness has made an advance forward. But it has done so at the cost of condemning and displacing other cultural valuation practices that imperil international security, where *might* becomes the *right* of a community in the service of the collective whole. But collective identification has its limits even among nations with focused mutual goals, which further leads to resistance and stifling efforts at negotiation and diplomacy. Because each nation has loyalty to its own self-interests, an ethical diaspora is inevitable: cultural narcissism is highly recalcitrant to outside interference pressuring political reform. This may be observed by the fact that despite indubitable knowledge of the slaughter and concentration camps in Bosnia, former President George Bush Sr. and his administration was not about to send US troops to intercede fearing the ghost of Vietnam, a repetition the Clinton administration faced dogged by a country absorbed by its own concerns. It may be further said that the international community's failure to appropriately intervene in the Rwanda massacre as well as the question of ground troops surrounding the crisis in the former Yugoslavia reflects a collective preoccupation not to uncritically jeopardize the lives of its own citizens.

In these situations, collective identifications that sustain national identities ultimately serve self-preservative functions, for we are bound to identify more with our own kind than a stranger in a foreign land. The brute fact is that we value our own over others: the general principle of human life becomes an abstraction when compared to the concrete social realities each country faces. This is particularly relevant when internal division and upheaval fractures the cohesion of a country's infrastructures, such as the separatism movement in French Quebec Canada and the omnipresence of discrimination and racism that torments the United States. When industrialized countries, such as the ones in North America, are unable to shelter and provide food and clothing for their own homeless populations who die every night on the streets, they find themselves in the conundrum of determining the most optimal means of disseminating their social resources. Value is ultimately prioritized under the rubric of a particular society's self-interests, but this often encompasses wasteful concessions to popular prejudice. It is truly sad when the American public is more concerned about where the President's penis has been rather than helping the needy through humanitarian aid.[15] This is a fine example of Heidegger's (1927) *das Man*, where the herd is lost in the corrupt fallenness of idle talk and curiosity of "the *they*."

The process of civilization vacillates between dialectical moments of progress versus regress as the process itself secures and mobilizes an infinite progression with infinite points of regression. Following the logical coherency of the upward ascendance of the dialectic, we may further estimate that progress will surpass the regressive and destructive forces that tyrannize world accord. What is truly infinite about the evolution of humanity is the process itself. What we see is an infinite (universal) pattern, each side being contrary moments as each merge into the other. This pattern is genuinely infinite for it is a self-maintaining process; each alteration collapses into a new moment, which is its being-for-self in its mediacy. By standing back and seeing the recurrent pattern within a new context, world spirit is enabled to affect the transition to a new immediacy that is truly sublated. Civilization, like Spirit, is always faced with the relative novelty of each new shape. Yet it approaches each new opposition not as a static antinomy doomed to stalemate, but rather as a self-contained pattern; the infinite generates new finites as a fundamental repetition of itself—a self-maintaining process that generates its own process as a dynamically self-articulated complex holism.

Hegel's odyssey of spirit may be applicable to our understanding of the trek of culture and its march over the ever-increasing proliferation of human aggression. As our world confederations gain greater amity, consensus, and cohesion, the intersubjective negotiation of valuation gives rise to new novelties, complexities, and increased unity. But the more convoluted social realities become, destructive forces continue to grow in abundance. We may surmise that the insidiousness of human pathology will recede in certain pockets of communal affiliation but flow in others as the valences of power and prejudice undergo the vicissitudes of transformation. No longer is the standard of culture measured by whether or not one uses a bar of soap, but rather by the values we espouse in relation to others, especially the promise to keep our aggressions in check. Now our degree of civility is to be equated by the mutual agreement, despite outliers, not to point our missiles at one another—quite an accomplishment for decades of fear and cold war! Yet this existential reality underscores the fact that aggression will always play a part in our value practices and the ontological relations that comprise worldhood.

Whether in politics or business, advances in culture are due to the process of negotiation and mutual recognition, which leads to the mutual desire to understand, communicate value preferences, and support each other cooperatively despite vast differences that define our identities. The need for mutual recognition, validation, and affirmation of cultural values and worth leads to understanding; and in turn, understanding leads to empathy and care. Despite the continuing tumultuous Mid-East peace negotiations where rigid ethnic and religious identifications insure irreconcilable division, the process signals the human willingness to seek some viable solutions in the name of co-existence, which is itself a productive dialectical movement. Whether they advance in peaceful resolution through mutual negotiation remains a possibility only the future can command. But given the current state of military conflict in the Middle East, where social chaos, lawlessness, mass trauma, civilian revolt, and religious fundamentalism including messianic fanaticism fueled by systemic hatred for the Other, where The End of Days is preceded by a prophetic apocalypse, it becomes a logical prediction that World War III is just around the corner.

When social and psychic conflict remains irresolute, the human species has the compulsion to repeat its traumas in the effort to resolve them. Not unlike Nietzsche's eternal recurrence, the compulsion towards control and mastery may be generally attributed to the *Aufhebung* of cultures as civilization becomes more integrative, refined, and balanced. But as Freud points out, the repetition of destruction is a retrograde character of our species that must be harnessed and channeled into appropriate directions if we are to survive as a human race. It is in the austere face of violence and havoc that continue to pollute our globe where we may observe the pessimistic resonance of Freud's dismal conclusion that offers us "no consolation."

As long as people are deprived of the most basic needs that comprise human necessity, there will always be atypical suffering, seething envy, hate, and murder. And in the uncultivated masses that bleed world tranquility, destruction and violence will be the primary instruments of human deed with each act of aggression begetting new aggression in order to combat it. With the perseverance of peace, perhaps this cycle will culminate in a more docile set of human relations. Through mutual dialogue and the open exchange of value preferences, new ideals, conventions, and policies will emerge, even though this may in all likelihood require the aggressive encroachment on societies and cultures that fail to develop shared global identifications.

Living in the End Times

Hegel (1900) once said that human history is the "slaughterbench" (*RH* § 27) of happiness—a progressive yet poignant achievement. But happy or not, happiness is nevertheless what we covet, what Aristotle (1962) called "the highest good attainable by action," that is, "living well" and "doing well" (see Bk. 1, § 4, 15). Some of us live well and some of us do well; but for most of the world population, happiness is a foreign reality. Ephemeral moments of pleasure are not happiness: they are not the *eudaimonia* Aristotle envisioned. Even the satisfaction of life's simplest pleasures is often minimized, postponed, or held in abeyance for other desires that have not yet been actualized. Desire is such a complicated creature that it is responsible for generating our most detestable beastly attributes as well as our most cherished and exalted ideals. As being-in-relation-to-lack, desire seeks to assuage its anxiety, to go beyond its finite appearances and fill the hole, the lacunae in its being—simply the wish for wholeness we call peace (Mills, 2010). The nature of value inquiry is a lived existential ordeal that must endure the gauntlet of anxiety and dread that pave the successive path towards the fulfillment of human e*thos*. It is this positive significance to the power of the negative that becomes the engine behind our moral prosperity even when the dark shadow of our aggressivity and destructive inclinations loom over the sky like a black plague.

"*Fundamental insight.* — There is no pre-established harmony between the furtherance of truth and the well-being of mankind" says Nietzsche (1878), p. 198. Harmony is made by humankind through the call of conscience and the puissance of reason—a rational passion. And as Freud (1933) tells us, the "intellect ... is among the powers which we may most expect to exercise a unifying influence on men—on men who are held together with such difficulty and whom it is therefore scarcely possible to rule ... . Our best hope for the future is that intellect—the scientific spirit, reason—may in process of time establish a dictatorship in the mental life of man" (*SE*, p. 171). Is it such a utopian expectation to think that we can subordinate our pathological natures to the monarch of reason? Perhaps this is the true meaning of faith. For even if there are no emotional ties that exist between people, cultures, or nations, the bonds of reason conjoin us in mutual appreciation for the *ought* that dictate even our most irrational moments.

Having offered this optimistic gesture, we are still left with uncertainty, tenuousness, and platitudes. We have recently experienced a crisis of liberal capitalism in North America and the UK, which has led to economic exploitation of the masses engineered by those who want to make obscene amounts of money quickly and unabashedly at others' expense. And the rest of the world has its own financial crises, most recently as the United States and members of the European Union are in chaos over fiscal mismanagement with the added irritant of various central banks and China calling for economic reform. This has only been compounded by the fuel crisis destabilizing markets all over the world. When there is the US deregulation of financial institutions, with a conglomerate of powerful lawyers, politicians, economists, accountants, and lobbyists manipulating laws around the exchange of commerce, taxation, and corporate profits, then citizens will naturally be enticed, taken advantage of, and swindled—partly because some people are gullible and/or unreflective—acting on unbridled wish-fulfillment and whim—and partly because they are simply overburdened by so many demands and responsibilities within our stressful contemporary societies that the pleasure principle is sure to ring its bell. "We want relief! And be quick about it."

As Slavoj Žižek points out, like many reformed or neoMarxists before him, such greed is generated by the seductive system of capitalism itself, which beckons only desire and personal self-indulgence. In Freudian terms, we only think about our own gratifications. The vulgar popular expression is: "Fuck everyone else! The only thing that matters is me." This is a common sentiment. I further suggest this is a failure of value inquiry, a painful revelation about our collective moral psychology. We are destroying our planet, sullying and stealing natural commodities from impoverished countries that are sold off by corrupt government officials, hence causing new poverty and hunger where people turn to rioting, looting, and killing because they have no rice or wheat, thereby generating social calamities that potentially have world-wide effects. When people are deprived of the basic necessities for human survival, it is illogical to reproach the outrage fueling such desperate acts of aggression and social discord. "Would you want to be treated like an object that does not matter to the rest of the world?" That is rational conscience speaking. The object here is actually a unity of subjects—a collection of people who are exploited because the Law says they can be. Remember that the Law is what the people in political power determine to be the case. It can change at any time, contingent upon the instrumental functions that bring that about. When collective social systems facilitate ecological risk and allow world erosion to happen, we must critically target the ultimate sources of responsibility. In industrial countries, the populace clearly experiences such trickle-down effects when spikes in gas prices immediately affect the cost of transportation and availability of food and produce. And when people in non-industrial or developing countries have no credit cards to rely on to offset their lack of capital or debt, it becomes a matter of life or death.

As our planet faces increasing desertification due to climate change, environmental pollution, and human spoilage, water wars are generating global concern and economic exploitation.[16] The shortage of drinking water compounded by corporate pollution is resulting in the poisoning of our water supplies. Industrial pollution is credited for producing biologically contaminated water due to the mass dumping of chemicals, pesticides, rocket fuel, and pharmaceuticals discarded by large animal factories and sewage treatment plants. Furthermore, the capitalist privatization of water leads to large-scale neglect of water systems by introducing contaminants that are directly hazardous to citizens, particularly those in disenfranchised nations. Exacerbated by a lack of proper sanitation, millions of people die each year due to water-borne diseases, primarily small children up to the age of 5, and as many as 1 out of 10 in India. Industry is always thinking about the "bottom line"— the cheapest way is the desired norm if you are a businessman. As long as capitalists control water supplies, they can exploit the rest of the world. It is understandable that, under these circumstances, how large groups of peoples would succumb to squalid instinct where "Everyman for himself!" is the bottom line. Living is squalor, without dignity or a dime, leads to perpetual insecurity, sorrow, bitterness, and the need for revenge. If this continues without global intervention, we can predictably foresee the eruption of mass social psychopathy, where disenfranchised countries become a breeding ground for death, depravity, and terrorism.

Žižek (2010) alerts us that the two principal dangers confronting our world today is unbridled capitalism and fundamentalist religious extremism (p. 131), which he believes is leading to an "apocalyptic zero-point." But the real culprit he focuses on is the global capitalist system itself.

> [The] 'four riders of the apocalypse' are comprised of by the ecological crisis, the consequences of the biogenetic revolution, imbalances within the system itself (problems with intellectual property; forthcoming struggles over raw materials, food and water), and the explosive growth of social divisions and exclusions. (p. x)

From "invisible" migrant workers deprived of all privileges and used as slave labor in order for us to have dollar stores and cheap blue jeans, to "crazies" who announce their "irrational" intent on using a nuclear device or potent biological and chemical weapons—to a large degree the question of money is always looming in the background. Money motivates everything. We are erecting walls to keep our bordering countries out, and constructing walls within our own nations like "gated communities" designed to protect us from "the criminal other." "Love thy neighbor" is replaced with mistrust and fear, whereby the Other becomes a threat, source of envy, or persecutory object. Ignoring all warning signs, we are living in collective denial and omnipotent disavowal of our impending peril under the illusory fantasies of grandiose hubris sustained by hegemonic ideologies. "When will the next natural disaster occur? When will the next bomb go off, or plane fly into a building?" As Žižek (2010) puts it: "we know very well that this will happen at some point, but nevertheless cannot bring ourselves to really believe that it will" (pp. x–xi).

Despite the fact that reason tells us to stop the exploitation, corruption, indulgences in excess, and the destruction of our natural resources, we still want. Here wanting becomes a perennial quandary. And human desire wants immediate satisfaction. Its popular motto is: "Fill the Lack! Chop, Chop!" As a society, we often live in the moment. We want, and want more. This inner mantra becomes an incessant insatiable whine. Restraint, compromise, and self-restriction become an unwelcome trespass. The reality principle is conveniently forgotten when urge, impulse, and caprice are beguiled by immediate objects of tantalizing pleasure. And conscience becomes compartmentalized because the complexities of social order and world discord pose overwhelming impasses to pragmatic resolutions. Here the collective psyche, insofar as it personifies the universal psychological dispositions inherent to humanity, remains in an ambivalent state of inner worry and unmediated conflict.

If we entertain the possibility of the doomsday argument, and that we may very well be living in the end times, then we are approaching a cataclysm that may no longer be preventable. Unlike Freud who had an ambiguous air of skeptical guardedness, yet one with a pessimistic undercurrent, Hegel was more optimistic. I am not so sure we can readily amalgamate the two poles. Each represents a dialectical position and creates an almost insurmountable tension, what Žižek (2006) calls a "parallax gap," namely a point of irreconcilable contradiction or antinomy where there is no discernible synthesis.[17] Žižek (2010) points towards, in his words, a "pathetic case for communism" (p. 5) as a possible reference point for rectifying our world crises, but this suggestion violates human nature.[18] As long as a macrosystem supports capitalist self-interest, human need and greed will gravitate towards self-pursuit over that of shared equality or the uniform distribution of material wealth through financial egalitarianism. Such a condition, namely global communism, would have to be superimposed on us by a supreme force, hence state intervention, even if it was for our own good. It is more plausible that we will increasingly seek modifications and amendments in neocapitalism reflective of controlled or regulated democratic systems that institute structural improvements through refined checks and balances safeguarding shared collective interests valuing socialistic commitments. Short of a global centralized currency that is regulated, policed, and affects everyone, perhaps some transnational system of socialistic democracy will emerge in the future as a logical synthesis informing the sublation of humanity through natural compromise.

A more pessimistic outcome is that the dialectic would reach an implosive climax or irresolvable breaking point where we have a deadlock of oppositions that lead to snowballed eruptions within multiple social climates that contaminate the world scene with war, famine, and ecological disaster. Even if one pole eventually vanquishes the other, it would be at everyone's expense. If we accept Žižek's premise that unbridled liberal capitalism is a world nemesis bringing the end of days, then it would likely take a series of catastrophic global events before we are forced to curb its enthusiasm. This would necessitate a mass mobilization of geopolitical, diplomatic, and economic reform. But as long as there are political hegemonies that drive world relations based on capitalist principles that on one hand clamor, "We are all equal!" but on the other hand admonish, "You have to earn it. There are no free handouts!," then I am afraid we will have to accept the premise of natural law theory—namely, what is natural to do is what is right to do (e.g., "It is not natural to give away your resources, for this is contrary to self-preservation and self-interest," or "Others will have to work for it just like me," or "We can't take care of the whole world!" and so on).[19] We can equally imagine the inverse (another dialectic) if we were on the receiving end of exploitation and abuse—"It is *natural* to kill those who cause us suffering!" And here we return to the question of *pathos*. Some of us *by necessity* have to suffer more than others.

In order to envision salient global solutions, we need more than mere awareness or collective self-consciousness; we must be willing to give up what we are comfortable with in our immediate lives for the sake of the symbolic Other and *act* for a higher principle of valuation, even if this realization is simultaneously motivated by enlightened self-interest and/or self-preservation. I can't see that happening anytime soon. Perhaps the message itself is important enough to reiterate. But if I were a betting man, I would say we are on the brink of extinction.

Notes

1 Derived from Plautus, *Asinaria* II, iv, 88; See Freud (1930), *SE*, p. 111.

2 I realize that the antipode between normativity and pathology poses numerous
definitional and epistemological problems, as does my attempt to obviate the
issue by collapsing their differences into a universal category that would apply to
all human beings. This is equally difficult when offering speculations on a collective psychopathology because we lack a clear referent or criteria on what
exactly constitutes health and illness to begin with, which is likely to shift based
on different cultural norms and social practices. I do not wish to engage this
complex issue here, which deserves serious attention in another forum. I only ask
the reader to entertain the notion that, although we may not agree about the
hermeneutics, scope, and breadth of the phenomenology of pathology inherent
in individual and collective social life, let alone the issue of the type or form and
the degree of their instantiation, I wish to stay focused on the psychoanalytic
premise that internal conflict is intrinsic to the human psyche and social relations, which manifests itself in both individuals and groups. A return to the
ancient notion of *pathos* helps us locate a common shared, lived experience where
anxiety, despair, and emotional anguish are acknowledged as a universal ontological dimension to the development of civilization and humanity. It is within
the confines of this context that I wish to situate my arguments. Here the
question does not become whether there is a core of health in our subjective or
collective strivings that stand in relation to our pathologies, only that any discussion of such pockets of health or flourishment is to be situated within the
psychological predicament of our thrownness as being in relation to *pathos*.

3 Within this context, I specifically use the masculine gender to emphasize the
notion that men are usually deemed to be the chief instruments of power, aggression, and violence, whom have historically and primarily inflicted suffering
on others over that of women. Here I do not wish to assign principal responsibility for collective prejudice and aggression to only one sex, only to highlight the
particularly identified phenomena of male dominance. However, an equally
plausible case can be made for how women, the first and original love objects for
both sexes (see Freud, 1940, *SE*, p. 188), and usually the crucial attachment
figure that dominates the early childrearing scene, can easily foist their personalities and will on their children, sometimes quite insidiously, to the degree that
either gendered child is equally and potentially exposed to such power differentials. The cycle of relatedness from parents of both gender further fortified
within various familial and cultural practices, ensures that pathological accom-
modations and manifestations, which arise within each individual, have overdetermined sources. Just as females who are born within an oppressive
patriarchy inevitably suffer in various ways, whether directly or indirectly, so do
males who receive an austere maternal factor during their upbringing due to
cyclical patterns of real or perceived modes of relatedness from parental authority. These patterns may, of course, become entrenched within personality
structure and form the basis for a transgenerational transmission of developmental trauma that have cultural specificity leading to further repetitions and
pathological enactments. What is essential, hence necessary and non-accidental,

is that the human species has an intimate relation to *pathos* that inevitably saturates our being.

4 Here I am in agreement with Hegel's (1807) architectonic dialectical trajectory that reason is a developmental achievement borne of conflict and negation, the poignant striving for self-consciousness. Ethical reflection becomes a necessary part of the sublation (*Aufhebung*) of reason despite the fact that it resonates within the feeling soul (*Seele*) and comprises our most basal desires and strivings, which Hegel (1830) nicely enumerates in the Anthropology section of his *Philosophie des Geistes*, which is Part 3 of the *Encyclopaedia of the Philosophical Sciences*. In other words, we do not have a clean bifurcation between desire, reason, and ethical self-consciousness, for they are unified within the synthetic strands of the dialectic as a complex holism.

5 I have attempted to show how Hegel's logic and philosophical psychology are instrumental for advancing psychoanalytic thought. See *The Unconscious Abyss: Hegel's Anticipation of Psychoanalysis* (Mills, 2002), where I discuss Hegel's dialectical logic in the context of his unconscious ontology.

6 Hegel's dialectic has historically been misinterpreted and grossly misrepresented by psychoanalysts and philosophers of science, most notably Karl Popper, to be a threefold relation of thesis-antithesis-synthesis. This dialectic was advanced by Fichte (1794) in his *Wissenschaftslehre*, which referred to the process of thought and judgement; thus, it is an imprecise and over-simplification of Hegel's dialectic.

7 I would argue this claim could equally apply to the celebrated theoretical physicist, Stephen Hawking, whose entire life project had been preoccupied with understanding every aspect of the universe propounded in his grand "theory of everything."

8 See Sean Kelly (1993) who provides a comprehensive account of Hegel's theory of complex holism.

9 See Hegel (1830), §§ 388–403. This process is also the logical model Hegel (1812) follows from his *Logic* in his anthropological description of the soul, where a universal determines itself into particulars, showing how each mediation forms a new immediate, which is the general thrust of the dialectic.

10 For both Hegel and Freud, the inchoate ego is originally encased in a unity and is therefore modally undifferentiated from external forces—the inner and outer are fused in a symbiotic organization. Freud (1930) informs us "originally the ego includes everything, later it separates off an external world from itself. Our present ego-feeling is, therefore, only a shrunken residue of a much more inclusive—indeed, an all embracing—feeling which corresponded to a more intimate bond between the ego and the world about it" (*SE*, p. 68). For Hegel, the natural soul moves from an undifferentiated unity to a differentiated determinate being; so too for Freud, ego boundaries gradually become more contrasted, constructed, and consolidated throughout its burgeoning activity. Freud notes that originally an infant is unable to distinguish between its own ego and the external world as the source of stimulation and sensation. But eventually the

organism comes to discern its own internal sources of excitation, such as its bodily organs or somatic processes, from external sources of sensation, (e.g., mother's touch, breast, etc.), that become set apart and integrated within ego organization. It is not until this stage in ego formation that an object is set over against the ego as an existent entity that is outside of itself. Once the ego moves from primary to secondary narcissism, attachment to external cathected (love) objects form the initial dynamics of object-relations and character development.

11 See Freud (1930) on the "oceanic feeling" in relation to religious sentiment and early ego development, *SE*, pp. 64–68.

12 It may be argued that identity is largely the result of the identification process itself, which is influenced by myriad causal and overdetermined factors that are encountered throughout our life experiences and internalized within personality formation. Along with drives and their transformations, the nature of identification accounts for much of the intrapsychic motivations, intentions, desires, and conflicts that comprise psychical and social reality. Identity, whether personal or collective, is ultimately in the service of narcissism or self-interest, thereby affecting the ideals we espouse and the valuation practices we choose to identify with over others. Despite the overdetermination of identification, the values and mores individuals and societies adopt are fundamentally the result of the complexities of narcissistic object choice, the psychosocial functions they serve, and the evolutionary demands of the self-preservative drives.

13 This is not intended to be an ontologically reductive claim, only that consciousness and the complexifications of identity and culture are predicated on embodied biological forces that condition or influence the way in which identity, personality formation, and collective thought and behaviour are expressed.

14 This quotation is attributed to Martin Luther by E. M. Cioran (1998) in *The Temptation to Exist*. Also see "The Last Sermon in Wittenberg, 1546" (Luther, 1546): "And what I say about the sin of lust, which everybody understands, applies also to reason; for the reason mocks and affronts God in spiritual things and has in it more hideous harlotry than any harlot. Here we have an idolater running after an idol, as the prophets say, under every green tree [cf. Jer. 2:20; I Kings 14:23], as a whorechaser runs after a harlot. That's why the Scriptures call idolatry whoredom, while reason calls it wisdom and holiness … . Such wisdom of reason the prophets call whoredom." (p. 374–375).

15 Here I am referring to the Clinton-Lewinsky affair.

16 F*or a disturbing account of this phenomenon, s*ee the recent film documentaries, *Blue Gold: World Water Wars*, by Sam Bozzo (2008)*, and Flow: For Love of Water, by Irena* Salina (2008).

17 Žižek (2006) makes the proper locus of his philosophy the parallax gap, where there is a fundamental displacement of difference that poses an "irreducible obstacle to dialectics" based on a pure shift of perspective that can lead to no higher synthesis (p. 4).

18 Freud criticizes communism for its naïve philosophy of human nature based on a fantasy principle that ignores the instinctual basis of human aggression. In

Civilization and its Discontent, he argues that even if private property was not allowed by the state and material wealth was distributed generously among peoples, it would do nothing to eradicate our aggressive proclivities. He elaborates the fantasy that: "If private property were abolished, all wealth held in common, and everyone allowed to share in the enjoyment of it, ill-will and hostility would disappear among men. Since everyone's needs would be satisfied, no one would have any reason to regard another as his enemy; all would willingly undertake the work that was necessary ... [T]he psychological premises on which the system is based are an untenable illusion ... . Aggression was not created by property. It reigned almost without limit in primitive times, when property was still very scanty, and it already shows itself in the nursery" (*SE*, p. 118).

19 I would argue that it is "logical" to have government exercise some control, regulation, or oversight over capitalism based on utilitarian and socialistic commitments that improve the financial stability, social security, and quality of life of the populace, including those controlling the wealth, but it is not necessarily "instinctual." What is instinctual or natural is to be concerned first and foremost with one's own affairs, including securing resources for one's immediate familial and communal priorities out of pragmatic necessity. We primarily make decisions based upon emotional unconscious factors—both innocent and prejudicial—that resonates within the deeply felt interior of our beings. These unconscious agentic processes, I argue, have an affective exuberance that is somatically absorbed within our embodied sentience that simultaneously, emotively and semiotically interjects an overarching valuative tone. This naturally includes an amalgamation of the most innately intuitive, feeling, moral, and spiritual sentiments that coalesce within the personality, but also the most primitive, conflictual, agonizing, and phantasmatic. And I would argue much more so than cognition (see Mills, 2010). Even if we accept the evolutionary argument that memes—the cultural equivalent of genes—drive complex social systems through a replicatory process of mimesis, they would not likely extend past one's immediate social milieu unless other contingencies or environs would ingress upon the motivation systems comprising such social organizations. In other words, we prefer to stay close to home. And sometimes, perhaps more than others, what is natural is not always good. Therefore, natural law or desire governing human nature and interpersonal relations must be subjected to developmental and educational forces that introduce critical analysis, ethical self-reflection, domestic gentrification, and collective valuation practices for the good of all.

References

Allen, B. (1996). *Rape Warfare: The Hidden Genocide in Bosnia-Herzegovina and Croatia*. Minneapolis: University of Minnesota Press.

Aristotle. (1962). *Nicomachean Ethics*. Trans. M. Ostwald. Englewood Cliffs, NJ: Prentice Hall.

Bozzo, S. (2008). *Blue Gold: World Water Wars*. Documentary film. Vancouver International Film Festival.

Carter, B. (1983). The anthropic principle and its implication for biological evolution. *Philosophical Transactions of the Royal Society of London*, A 31, pp. 346–363.

Cioran, E.M. (1998). *The Temptation to Exist*. Trans. R. Howard. 2nd Ed. Chicago: University of Chicago Press.

Danner, M. (1997). America and the Bosnia Genocide. *The New York Review of Books*, XLIV, 19, 55–56.

Derrida, J. (1982). *Margins of Philosophy*. Trans. A. Bass. Chicago: University of Chicago Press.

Einstein, A. (1932). Letter to Freud, July 30, 1932, "Why War?" [Einstein – Freud Correspondence], *Standard Edition of the Complete Psychological Works of Sigmund Freud*, Vol. 22. Trans. & Gen. Ed. J. Strachey, in collaboration with A, Freud, assisted by A. Strachey & A. Tyson. London: Hogarth Press.

Fichte, J.G. (1794/1982). *The Science of Knowledge*. Trans. & Eds., P. Health & J. Lachs. Cambridge: Cambridge University Press.

Findlay, J.N. (1971). Hegel's Use of Teleology. In W.E. Steinkraus (Ed.), *New Studies in Hegel's Philosophy*. New York: Holt, Rinehart and Winston.

Freud, S. (1914). On Narcissism: An Introduction. *Standard Edition of the Complete Psychological Works of Sigmund Freud*, Vol. 14, pp. 67–104. Trans. & Gen. Ed. J. Strachey, in collaboration with A. Freud, assisted by A. Strachey and A. Tyson. London: Hogarth Press.

Freud, S. (1915). Instincts and Their Vicissitudes. *Standard Edition*, Vol. 14, pp. 109–140. London: Hogarth Press.

Freud, S. (1916-1917). *Introductory Lectures on Psycho-Analysis. Standard Edition*, Vol. 16. London: Hogarth Press.

Freud, S. (1920). *Beyond the Pleasure Principle. Standard Edition*, Vol.18. London: Hogarth Press.

Freud, S. (1921). *Group Psychology and the Analysis of the Ego. Standard Edition*, Vol.18. London: Hogarth Press.

Freud, S. (1923). *The Ego and the Id. Standard Edition*, Vol.19, pp. 3–66. London: Hogarth Press.

Freud, S. (1927). *Future of an Illusion. Standard Edition*, Vol. 21, pp. 3–56. London: Hogarth Press.

Freud, S. (1930). *Civilization of its Discontents. Standard Edition*, Vol. 21. London: Hogarth Press.

Freud, S. (1932). Reply to Einstein. "Why War?" [Einstein – Freud Correspondence]. *Standard Edition*, Vol. 22, pp. 197–218. London: Hogarth Press.

Freud, S. (1933 [1932]). *New Introductory Lectures on Psycho-Analysis. Standard Edition*, Vol. 22. London: Hogarth Press.

Freud, S. (1940). *An Outline of Psycho-Analysis. Standard Edition*, Vol. 23. London: Hogarth Press.

Harris, H.S. (1983). *Hegel's Development: Night Thoughts*. Oxford: Clarendon.

Hegel, G.W.F. (1807/1977). *Phenomenology of Spirit*. Trans. A.V. Miller. Oxford: Oxford University Press.

Hegel, G.W.F. (1812/1969). *Science of Logic*. Trans. A.V. Miller. Atlantic Highlands, NJ: Humanities Press.

Hegel, G.W.F. (1817/1991). *The Encyclopaedia Logic*. Vol. 1 of *Encyclopaedia of the Philosophical Sciences*. Trans. T.F. Geraets, W.A. Suchting, & H.S. Harris. Indianapolis: Hackett Publishing Company, Inc.

Hegel, G.W.F. (1830/1978). *Philosophy of Spirit*. In *Hegel's Philosophy of Subjective Spirit*. Vol. 2: *Anthropology*. Trans. & Ed. M.J. Petry. Dordrecht, Holland: D. Reidel Publishing Company.

Hegel, G.W.F. (1900). *Reason in History*. Introduction to the *Lectures on the Philosophy of History*. Trans. J. Sibree. New York: Willey Book Co.

Heidegger, M. (1927/1962). *Being and Time*. Trans. J. Macquarrie & E. Robinson. San Francisco: Harper Collins.

Kelly, S. (1993). *Individuation and the Absolute: Hegel, Jung, and the Path Toward Wholeness*. New York: Paulist Press.

Klein, M. (1946). Notes on some Schizoid Mechanisms. *International Journal of Psycho-analysis*, 27, 99–110.

Lesley, J. (1996). *The End of the World: The Science and Ethics of Human Extinction*. London: Routledge.

Luther, M. (1546). The Last Sermon in Wittenberg, 1546. *Luther's Works*, 54 Vols. Philadelphia: Muhlenberg Press.

Mills, J. (2002). *The Unconscious Abyss: Hegel's Anticipation of Psychoanalysis*. Albany: State University of New York Press.

Mills, J. (2010). *Origins: On the Genesis of Psychic Reality*. Montreal: McGill-Queens University Press.

Mills, J. (2020). The Global Bystander Effect: Moral Responsibility in our Age of Ecological Crisis. *Journal of Futures Studies*, 25(2), 61–76.

Mills, J., & Polanowski, J.A. (1997). *The Ontology of Prejudice*. Amsterdam/Atlanta: Rodopi.

Morris, D. (1998). *The Human Species*. Aired July 12 on The Learning Channel (TLC).

Nietzsche, F.W. (1878/1977). *Human, All Too Human*. In *A Nietzsche Reader*. Trans. R.J. Hollingdale. London: Penguin.

Salina, I. (2008). *Flow: For Love of Water*. Documentary film. Sundance Film Festival.

Žižek, S. (2006). *The Parallax View*. Cambridge, MA: MIT Press.

Žižek, S. (2010). *Living in the End Times*. New York: Verso.

Acknowledgements

Throughout this work, I have produced, with permission, revised portions, emendations, and expansions of various peer-reviewed articles that have appeared in previous modified forms: "Deciphering the 'Genesis Problem': On the Dialectical Origins of Psychic Reality." *The Psychoanalytic Review*, (2002) 89 (6): 763–809; "Psyche as Inner Contradiction." *Continental Thought & Theory*, (2019) Vol. 2, Issue 4: 71–82; "Existentialism and Psychoanalysis: From Antiquity to Postmodernism." *The Psychoanalytic Review*, (2003) 90(3): 269–279; "The False Dasein: From Heidegger to Sartre and Psychoanalysis." *Journal of Phenomenological Psychology*, (1997) 28(1): 42–65; "Lacan on Paranoiac Knowledge." *Psychoanalytic Psychology*, (2003) 20(1): 30–51; "The Essence of Evil." In R.C. Naso & J. Mills (Eds.) (2016), *Humanizing Evil: Psychoanalytic, Philosophical, & Clinical Perspectives*. London: Routledge; "Recognition and *Pathos*." *International Journal of Jungian Studies*, (2019) 11(1): 1–22; "God: The Invention of an Idea." *Essays in the Philosophy of Humanism*, (2011) 19(2): 61–79; "Toward a Theory of Myth." *Journal for the Theory of Social Behaviour*, (2020) 50(4): 410–424; "Deconstructing Hermes: A Critique of the Hermeneutic Turn in Psychoanalysis." *The American Journal of Psychoanalysis*, (2011) 71 (3): 238–245; "Psychoanalysis and the Ideologies of Science." *Psychoanalytic Inquiry*, (2015) 35: 24–44; "Truth." *Journal of the American Psychoanalytic Association*, (2014) 62(2): 267–293; "Freedom and Determinism." *The Humanistic Psychologist*, (2013) 41(2), 101–118; and "Civilization and its Fate." *Studia Philosophica Wratislaviensia*. Supplementary Volume: English Edition, (2013):195–222. I wish to thank the publishers for their courtesy.

About the Author

Jon Mills, PsyD, PhD, ABPP is a philosopher, psychoanalyst, and retired clinical psychologist. He is Honorary Professor, Department of Psychosocial and Psychoanalytic Studies, University of Essex, Colchester, UK; Faculty member in the Postgraduate Programs in Psychoanalysis & Psychotherapy, Gordon F. Derner School of Psychology, Adelphi University, NY, and New School for Existential Psychoanalysis, CA; and is Emeritus Professor of Psychology & Psychoanalysis, Adler Graduate Professional School, Toronto, Canada. Recipient of numerous awards for his scholarship, he is the author and/or editor of over 30 books in psychoanalysis, philosophy, psychology, and cultural studies including *Debating Relational Psychoanalysis: Jon Mills and his Critics* (Routledge, 2020); *Inventing God: Psychology of Belief and the Rise of Secular Spirituality* (Routledge, 2017); *Underworlds: Philosophies of the Unconscious from Psychoanalysis to Metaphysics* (Routledge, 2014); *Conundrums: A Critique of Contemporary Psychoanalysis* (Routledge, 2012); *Origins: On the Genesis of Psychic Reality* (McGill-Queens University Press, 2010); *Treating Attachment Pathology* (Rowman & Littlefield, 2005); *The Unconscious Abyss: Hegel's Anticipation of Psychoanalysis* (State University of New York Press, 2002); and *The Ontology of Prejudice* (Rodopi, 1997). In 2015, he was given the Otto Weininger Memorial Award for Lifetime Achievement by the Canadian Psychological Association.

Index

a metatheory of truth 305–309; truth of myth and myth of truth 242–244; as unconcealment 309–315
Truth and Reconciliation Commissions 175

Ukraine 154
unconcealment 200; truth as 309–315
unconscious agency 344–348
unconscious ego 34–36
unconscious politics 177–180
universality 140–141

violence 143–144

war on terror (Bush administration) 154
Weber, Max 238
Whitehead, A.N. 15
Winch, Peter 236
Windelband, Wilhelm 235
Winnicott, D.W. 75–80, 82
World Soul 209
world without recognition 183–186

Zollikon Seminars (Heidegger) 62

9781032306254